HEINEMANN

CHILDREN & YOUNG PEOPLE'S WORKFORCE

Brenda Baker

Kate Beith

Elisabeth Byers

Maureen Daly

Sharina Forbes

Sue Griffin

Hayley Marshall

Editor: **Wendy Taylor**

ALWAYS LEARNING

PEARSON

Published by Pearson Education Limited, Edinburgh Gate, Harlow, Essex, CM20 2JE.

www.pearsonschoolsandfecolleges.co.uk

Heinemann is a registered trademark of Pearson Education Limited

Text © Brenda Baker, Kate Beith, Elisabeth Byers, Maureen Daly, Sharina Forbes, Sue Griffin, Hayley Marshall 2012
Designed by Tony Richardson (Wooden Ark Ltd)
Typeset by Wooden Ark Ltd
Original illustrations © Pearson Education Limited 2012
Illustrated by Tony Richardson and Mark Ruffle
Cover design by Sam Charrington
Picture research by Kath Kollberg
Cover photo © www.imagesource.com

The rights of Brenda Baker, Kate Beith, Elisabeth Byers, Maureen Daly, Sharina Forbes, Sue Griffin and Hayley Marshall to be identified as authors of this work have been asserted by them in accordance with the Copyright, Designs and Patents Act 1988.

First published 2012

ARP impress 98

British Library Cataloguing in Publication Data

A catalogue record for this book is available from the British Library

ISBN 978 0 435 07549 1

Copyright notice

Printed and bound by Ashford Colour Press Ltd., Gosport

Acknowledgements
The authors and publisher would also like to thank the following individuals and organisations for permission to reproduce text, diagrams or summaries of ideas:

18: Figure 1.2 adapted from A Theory of Human Motivation, *Psychological Review* 50, 4 (A.H. Maslow 1943), 50(4) (1943):370-96. **28**: Figure 1.3 adapted from Open University Press *Role and Status of Play in Early Childhood Education*, 1989, Open University Press (Moyles, J. 1989). **44**: Figure 1.4 adapted from *Learning by doing: A guide to teaching and learning methods*, 1988, Oxford Polytechnic. (Gibbs, G. 1988). **85**: Figure 3.4 from NHS/Change4Life Campaign. **91**: Table 3.2 adapted from http://www.meningitis.org/symptoms, information courtesy of Meningitis Research Foundation. **93**: Table 3.3 adapted from Department of Heath Routine Childhood immunisations from November 2010, © Crown Copyright. **100**: Table 4.1 adapted from Skills for Care (2008) *Leadership and management strategy update*, Leeds: Skills for Care. **190**: Information about Choice theory model courtesy of the William Glasser Association International. **212**: Common Assessment Framework (CAF) © Local Government Association, available from the Children's Improvement Board. **278**: Kirkpatrick Model from Kirkpatrick Partners, LLC. www.kirkpatrickpartners.com. **279**: Information about Fleming's VARK model © Copyright Version 7.1 (2011) held by Neil D. Fleming, Christchurch, New Zealand. **354**: list adapted from National Quality Improvement Network (2008) *Quality Improvement Principles: A Framework for Local Authorities and National Organisations to Improve Quality Outcomes for Children and Young People*, London: National Children's Bureau National Quality Improvement Network (2008), © Crown copyright. **349**: Table 17.3 adapted from Early Years Quality Support Improvement Programme (EYQIP) 2008), © Crown copyright. **363**: quote courtesy of the National Childminding Association (NCMA).

Every effort has been made to contact copyright holders of material reproduced in this book. Any omissions will be rectified in subsequent printings if notice is given to the publishers.

Websites
Relevant websites are suggested in this book. To ensure that links to the websites are up to date and work we have made them available on our website. To access the links go to www.pearsonhotlinks.co.uk and search for the title of this book 'CACHE Level 3 Extended Diploma for the Children & Young People's Workforce Student Book' or the ISBN '9780435075491'.

Contents

About the editor and authors   4

Introduction   5

About this book   6

CP1	Extending understanding of theories of children and/or young person's care or development	Kate Beith	10
CP2	Understand the role of policies in children and/or young people's settings	Kate Beith	48
CP3	Maintaining the health of children and/or young people	Brenda Baker	74
CP4	An introduction to leadership and management	Maureen Daly	98
CP5	Supporting the development of study skills	Hayley Marshall	124
CP6	Working with families of children and/or young people	Sue Griffin	146
CP7	Working as part of more than one team	Sue Griffin	170
CP8	Supportive approaches to behaviour management	Hayley Marshall	186
CP9	Formal recording for use within the real work environment	Hayley Marshall	208
CP10	Research to support practice when working with children and/or young people	Elisabeth Byers	224
CP11	Support children and/or young people's development of art, drama and music	Sharina Forbes	248
CP13	Learning about planning for given frameworks or curricula	Hayley Marshall	270
CP14	Supporting numeracy and literacy development in children and/or young people	Sharina Forbes	292
CP15	Observing children and/or young people's play to inform future support	Hayley Marshall	316
CP17	Managing quality standards when working with children and/or young people	Kate Beith	338

Glossary   367

Index   371

About the editor and authors

Wendy Taylor (editor) trained as an early years teacher at the University of East Anglia. Over the past 35 years she has enjoyed a diverse career working with children and adults while teaching, childminding, managing a pre-school and lecturing in further education. Until 2010, Wendy was CACHE Chief Examiner for Children's Services developing qualifications and assessments and overseeing marking and standardisation. She is currently working at The Alban Way Children's Centres where she supports families with children under five.

Brenda Baker has worked in early years settings and as a primary teacher. She then moved to an FE college to teach childcare and education and, for a number of years, managed the Health and Social Care Department. After leaving the college she continued to teach, delivering training to family support workers and teaching assistants. In recent years she has worked with awarding bodies, including CACHE, to develop qualifications and to produce support and assessment materials for learners and teachers. She is a member of the CACHE Expert Panel.

Kate Beith has a wide experience in early years; as a teacher, head teacher, trainer, adviser, author, principal of a large international training college and currently in an exciting role as assistant director for schools of an international organisation following the EYFS framework and National Curriculum. In her current role, Kate is responsible for quality assurance in early years, professional development and training. She has managed, delivered and written CACHE qualifications and has been involved in campaigns to raise standards in early years care and education.

Elisabeth Byers worked in a nursery, reception and year 1 class prior to teaching early years students in the FE sector. She has taught on a range of CACHE early years programmes including NVQ, the Foundation Award, Level 2 and 3 childcare programmes. Elisabeth has also been programme coordinator for the Level 2 and 3 teaching assistant courses. She is currently teaching higher education students and is programme director for the Foundation Degree in Early Years.

Maureen Daly has worked in early years settings for many years. She has also been an FE lecturer, teaching programmes from entry level to foundation degree, and is currently Head of School at West Herts College. Maureen has been an external examiner for foundation degree programmes and has been involved in the writing of a foundation degree and BA with a route in Hospital Play Specialism. She has also authored books and resource materials.

Sharina Forbes has worked in the early years sector for 22 years, starting her career in a maternity unit. She has also been a live-in nanny, managed a day nursery, worked in Europe and been an outstanding childminder! For the last 12 years Sharina has been heavily involved in the training and development of adult learners and now manages her own training company which offers CYPW qualifications through CACHE.

Sue Griffin has worked in a variety of roles in the field of early years training for over 30 years, mostly with playgroups and childminders. When she was at the National Childminding Association, she worked with CACHE staff to develop qualifications for childminders, and was a member of the CACHE Curriculum Committee. She has written a range of distance learning materials for the National Extension College, and is now a freelance writer and author.

Hayley Marshall worked as an early years educator before becoming a lecturer in early years and childcare. She has taught a wide range of CACHE courses from entry level to level 3 in colleges of further education and at a secondary school in Milton Keynes, where she was head of the childcare department. She has previously written tutor resources for CACHE courses and continues to lecture part time while also working as an early years specialist.

Introduction

Welcome to this new book from Pearson for the *CACHE Level 3 Extended Diploma for the Children & Young People's Workforce*. As a learner you can use this book to help you to complete the CACHE Extended Mandatory units CP1 to CP10 and your choice of Extended Optional units from CP11, CP13, CP14, CP15 and CP17 so that you can make up the credits needed to gain the full Extended Diploma.

The book has been written by authors who specialise in the knowledge you need to acquire to be an excellent practitioner. They all began where you are now and have gone on to have fulfilling, challenging and stimulating careers. Use this book to tap into their expertise and develop the skills to equip you for a similarly worthwhile career, perhaps working in a children's centre, school or nursery. You can also use this qualification as a stepping stone to higher education if you wish to study further.

Whichever route you choose, there are many exciting opportunities for you to explore in the current children's and young people's workforce and I wish you all the best as you embark on your career.

Wendy Taylor

About your course and assessment

The CACHE Level 3 Extended Diploma for the Children & Young People's Workforce consists of 3 parts. To gain the full Extended Diploma you will have to complete all three parts.

1 The CACHE Level 3 Diploma for the Children & Young People's Workforce (QCF), known as the 'CYPW units' which are made up of:
   - Shared Core units (SHC 31–SHC 34)
   - Core units (CYP 3.1–CYP 3.7)
   - Early Years Mandatory Pathway units (EYMP Units 1–5)
   - A selection of Optional units (CYPOP)
     To make a total of 65 credits

2 Additional CACHE Extended units
   - Extended Mandatory units (65 credits)
   - Extended Optional units (20 credits)
     To make a total of 85 credits

3 Three extended assessments
   - Based on knowledge that you have gained during the whole learning programme

Assessment

The CYPW units are **internally assessed** by an assessor or tutor at your centre or workplace, using a range of methods which could include: a portfolio of evidence, written assignments, direct observation or an optional Assessment Task set by CACHE.

The additional CACHE Extended Mandatory and Optional units will be **internally assessed** using Assessment Tasks set by CACHE.

The three Extended Assessments will be **externally assessed** by CACHE using themes and criteria set by CACHE.

Preparing for assessment

The Assessment Tasks and Extended Assessments are designed to stretch you and to be challenging. You will need to set aside time to complete extra reading and to discuss plans with other learners and your tutors.

Read the task and assessment criteria carefully. Make a realistic plan to use the time you have available. If you find the criteria difficult to understand, book a meeting with your tutor and ask questions.

There are a number of key terms used in the assessment criteria, for example: *consider, explain, describe, discuss, analyse, evaluate, reflect.* Make sure you understand the difference between these terms and write your answer accordingly. The examiner will be looking to see whether you have met each specific criterion.

Don't be put off by the terms *analyse, evaluate, reflect* and worry that you can't achieve these higher level skills. We all use these skills in our day-to-day lives. For exmple, remember the last time you bought a mobile phone? You definitely used all three of these skills before making your purchase.

About this book

This book will support you through your CACHE qualification. You will find all the Extended Mandatory units in this book and a good choice of Extended Optional ones.

All the chapters closely match the CACHE specification for each unit and are structured so that they are easy for you to follow. The main headings match the learning outcomes in the specification, while the smaller headings meet the various assessment criteria.

You will also find a wealth of features to support you in your study and useful information to guide you towards completing some of your assessment tasks.

Key features of the book

The book is full of useful features to help you gain your Extended Diploma.

In practice

A short feature at the start of the chapter that puts the learning into context.

Case study

Scenarios you might come across in your work, with questions that will make you think hard about what you might do in the same situation.

Key terms

Definitions for some of the more complex terminology used.

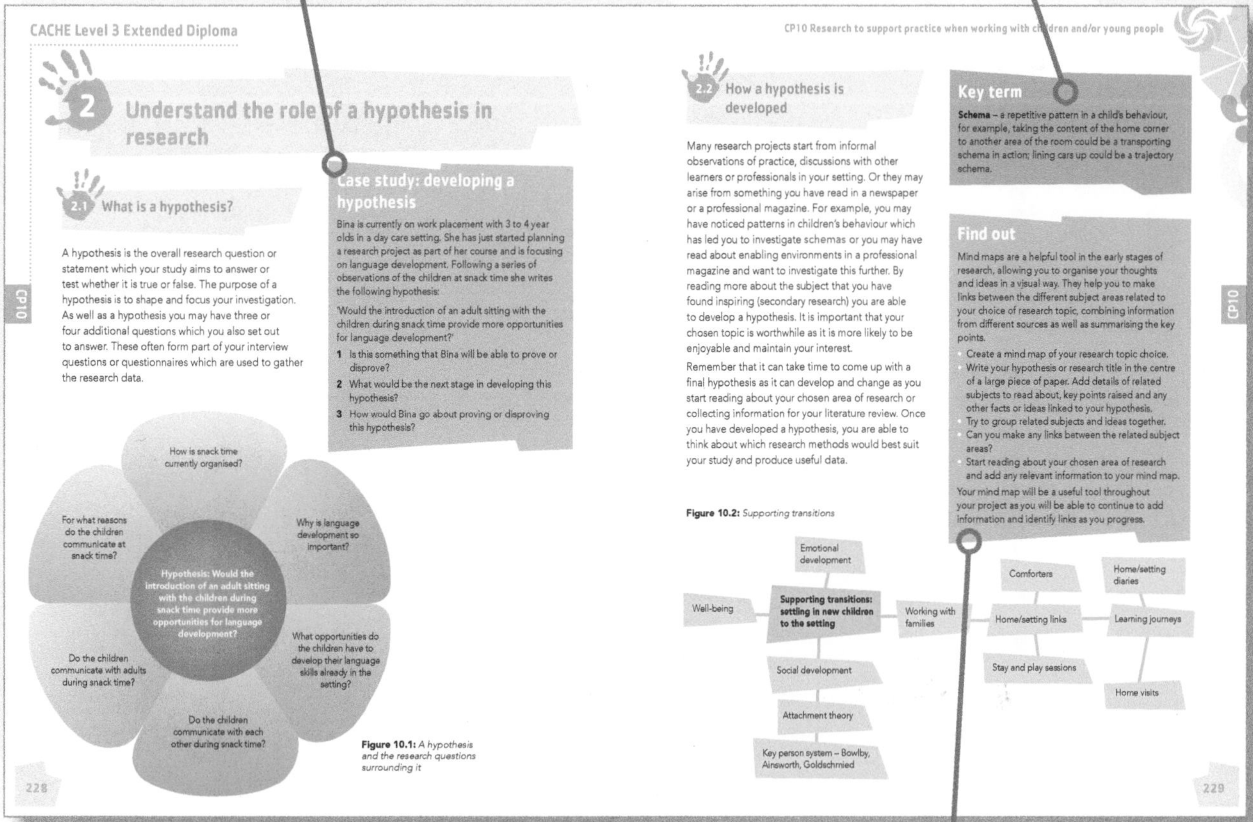

Sample textbook page (pages 228–229):

2 Understand the role of a hypothesis in research

2.1 What is a hypothesis?

A hypothesis is the overall research question or statement which your study aims to answer or test whether it is true or false. The purpose of a hypothesis is to shape and focus your investigation. As well as a hypothesis you may have three or four additional questions which you also set out to answer. These often form part of your interview questions or questionnaires which are used to gather the research data.

Case study: developing a hypothesis

Bina is currently on work placement with 3 to 4 year olds in a day care setting. She has just started planning a research project as part of her course and is focusing on language development. Following a series of observations of the children at snack time she writes the following hypothesis:

'Would the introduction of an adult sitting with the children during snack time provide more opportunities for language development?'

1 Is this something that Bina will be able to prove or disprove?
2 What would be the next stage in developing this hypothesis?
3 How would Bina go about proving or disproving this hypothesis?

Figure 10.1: A hypothesis and the research questions surrounding it

2.2 How a hypothesis is developed

Many research projects start from informal observations of practice, discussions with other learners or professionals in your setting. Or they may arise from something you have read in a newspaper or a professional magazine. For example, you may have noticed patterns in children's behaviour which has led you to investigate schemas or you may have read about enabling environments in a professional magazine and want to investigate this further. By reading more about the subject that you have found inspiring (secondary research) you are able to develop a hypothesis. It is important that your chosen topic is worthwhile as it is more likely to be enjoyable and maintain your interest.

Remember that it can take time to come up with a final hypothesis as it can develop and change as you start reading about your chosen area of research or collecting information for your literature review. Once you have developed a hypothesis, you are able to think about which research methods would best suit your study and produce useful data.

Figure 10.2: Supporting transitions

Key term

Schema – a repetitive pattern in a child's behaviour, for example, taking the content of the home corner to another area of the room could be a transporting schema in action; lining cars up could be a trajectory schema.

Find out

Mind maps are a helpful tool in the early stages of research, allowing you to organise your thoughts and ideas in a visual way. They help you to make links between the different subject areas related to your choice of research topic, combining information from different sources as well as summarising the key points.

- Create a mind map of your research topic choice.
- Write your hypothesis or research title in the centre of a large piece of paper. Add details of related subjects to read about, key points raised and any other facts or ideas linked to your hypothesis.
- Try to group related subjects and ideas together.
- Can you make any links between the related subject areas?
- Start reading about your chosen area of research and add any relevant information to your mind map.

Your mind map will be a useful tool throughout your project as you will be able to continue to add information and identify links as you progress.

Find out

Opportunities to find out more about key topics or items of interest.

So what does this mean?

Practical ideas for ways you can use your knowledge and apply it in a work setting.

Reflect

Questions that will encourage you to think more deeply about your own or other people's practice in work with children.

So what does this mean?

The timeframe is a major factor in any action planning. The time given to an action should be specified and negotiated. The range of factors that could be considered when setting a timeframe for a focused action may include:

- the level of detail of the area for action
- the activities involved, e.g. a questionnaire may need time to be written, collected and collated
- the time allocation for individual people involved in developing areas as identified
- the ordering time and purchasing of resources
- any financial planning that may have to be sought for or planned for in another financial period.

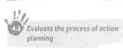

4.3 Evaluate the process of action planning

The aim of the process should be to create the best possible outcomes for the children concerned. In the process effective implementation will be more likely if practitioners are encouraged to:

- ask themselves challenging questions
- observe themselves in their work
- consult effectively with children and families on their views.

Effective support by the setting should include training and guidance to support practitioners to develop these skills. Practitioners can also be supported to develop ways of conducting peer observations of colleagues through training or by mentors. If an action plan has a focus outcome, and process-related standards and indicators, then practitioners observe and evaluate their practice as it really is.

If it is recognised that making self-assessment judgements is complex and needs evidence, then debate can be encouraged. Practitioners can then decide on, and implement, improvements.

An effective leader of any effective action planning process which results in improved practice will:

- plan training, guidance and resources to support reflective practice
- consult with children and families
- develop peer observation
- promote reflective practice through case studies, diaries, multimedia recordings, discussion with adults and children, and action learning

Reflect

Consider the celebration of the best outcome of any activity that you might have been involved in, in any area of your life.

- How was it celebrated?
- How did it make you, and everyone else involved, feel?
- Why do you think you remember this?
- What impact do you think it had on other areas of your life?

This might help you to remember that celebrating positive commitment or action is vital to the morale of colleagues, parents, children and yourself. It can also act as a reminder that there are many areas to celebrate when addressing any areas of concern in a children's setting.

- develop support networks with settings undertaking quality improvement
- create a culture of sharing issues and learning from each other
- join external networks where providers can share good practice and discuss practice issues.

Assessment activity 4.1, 4.2, 4.3

You are part of a team which has undergone an external audit of your workplace setting. With a learning partner:

- discuss ways in which your team can implement any changes that may be required as part of the audit
- analyse some potential factors which may influence your team's implementation of any actions
- carefully evaluate the action planning process in relation to how the plan can be implemented effectively by your team.

Record your discussion.

CP17 Managing quality standards when working with children and/or young people

5 Understand how own role in staff appraisals and continual professional development support maintaining a quality provision for children and/or young people

Your role in supporting and maintaining quality provision for children is crucial for your development and that of each child. This will encourage you to become a reflective practitioner (as described in Unit CP1), which is essential to your understanding of best practice.

A reflective practitioner can enable children to enjoy and benefit from their learning.

5.1 The role of self-evaluation and appraisals in maintaining quality provision

Self-evaluation is at the heart of being a reflective practitioner and is a skill that you will develop through practice. This process will:

- allow you to set clear standards for all aspects of your provision from staffing, health and safety and the learning environment through to relationships with children, parents, other professionals and the local community
- help you to develop good-quality management and administration systems
- give a clear and shared aim, developing core strengths and focusing on any areas of development within your team, thus enhancing team spirit

360

361

Assessment activity

Activities which relate to the CACHE tasks you will be given to support you in preparation for assessment.

In the real world

A taste of the real-world experiences of other early years practitioners, which will give you a feeling for the type of job you might want to apply for.

CACHE Extended Assessment

General guidance for tackling Extended assessment tasks. These describe one way in which the CACHE assessment themes might relate to subjects covered in the chapter and how you might tackle one of the assessment criteria.

CACHE Level 3 Extended Diploma

CP8

In the real world

I always found Shanika's behaviour very difficult. She would kick and bite other children at the holiday play scheme. After a while I started to really dislike her. I noticed that the other children didn't seem to like her much either as she often played alone.

Although I didn't mean to, if ever there was a disagreement I would automatically shout out Shanika's name because I thought she was involved. The other children started to call her 'naughty Shanika' and her behaviour just got worse and worse.

Then a new practitioner started at the holiday play scheme. His name was Richard and Shanika instantly liked him. Her behaviour really started to improve.

Richard told me about different models of behaviour management. I realised that I had been contributing to Shanika's behaviour. With Richard's help I started to notice all the good things that Shanika did and made sure that I praised her and made her feel part of the group. She is so much happier now and so am I. I have stopped shouting all the time and started to think about my impact upon all of the children.

Check your knowledge

1 Which behaviour management model discusses the helicopter, drill sergeant and consultant style of adult?
2 What is the term used to describe the process in which children learn not to do something by discovering the outcome themselves?
3 What did Glasser's (1998) choice theory model say were children's five basic needs?
4 Outline the behaviour shown by adults who have 'lost control' according to Ginott's (1971) model.
5 Identify the role of the child or young person in Kounin's (1970) model.
6 Suggest three ways that an adult can help to build children and young people's self-esteem.
7 How might children and young people feel when involved in conflict?
8 Describe how children and young people might demonstrate boredom at each stage of their life.
9 Being hungry affects children's and young people's ability to concentrate. What else is essential to help children concentrate?
10 Describe one factor that might make children feel unsafe in their environment.

206

CP8 Supportive approaches to behaviour management

CP8

CACHE Extended Assessment

Theme: Children and young people's development

Grading criterion

B1 Discuss the relevance of a recognised theory or philosophical approach in contributing to the chosen theme.

When looking at your extended project, you might begin by examining the way that the models of supportive behaviour management differ from each other. You might like then to explore contrasting ideas and explain how they differ from each other.

Remember to think about how each model views the child.

When thinking about the approaches of each model, you could explain how they affect children and young people's development by introducing the concept of the effects of low self-esteem. You could examine how differing models support the development of children's self-esteem. Ginott stressed how important it is for adults to not lose control. He explains loss of control as overreacting, being cruel and threatening. At this point you could draw in to the discussion Cline and Fay's drill sergeant.

You could complete your discussion by explaining how important it is to nurture children and young people's self-esteem and how this supports their overall development, play and learning. You could then give examples of models that you believe would support children and young people to develop high self-esteem and the reasons why.

This is an example of how you might approach one criterion of your Extended Assessment. You must successfully complete all the criteria at each grade to achieve that grade. You will achieve the highest grade for which you have successfully completed all the criteria. For example, to achieve a B grade you will need to meet the requirements of the B1, B2 and B3 criterion, as well as C1, C2, C3 and D1 and D2.

When trying to understand the requirements for your Extended Assessment, it is always a good idea to talk to your tutors. Fellow learners and workplace colleagues are also useful sources of information.

Further references

The following are sources of useful information on the topic of supportive approaches to behaviour management.

Books and articles

Canter, L .and Canter, M. (1992) *Assertive Discipline*, Bristol: Behaviour Management Ltd

Cline, F. W. and Fay, J. (2006) *Parenting with Love and Logic: Teaching Children Responsibility*, 2nd edition, Colorado Springs: NavPress Publishing

Dreikurs, R. (1968) *Psychology in the Classroom: A Manual for Teachers*, 2nd edition, New York: Harper and Row

Ginott, H. (1971) *Teacher and Child*, New York: Macmillan

Glasser, W. (1998) *Choice Theory*, New York: Harper and Row

Jones, F. (1987) *Positive Classroom Discipline*, New York: McGraw-Hill

Kounin, J. S. (1970) *Discipline and Group Management in Classrooms*, New York: Holt, Rinehart and Winston

Osler, A. (2001) *Children's Rights, Responsibilities and Understandings of School Discipline*, Research Papers in Education 15 (1) pp. 49–67, London: Routledge

Useful websites

To obtain a secure link to the websites below, visit www.pearsonhotlinks.co.uk and search for this book by using its title or ISBN. Click on the section for CP8.

Love and Logic – includes information about behaviour management strategies for parents and teachers.

Behaviour Management – information about supportive behaviour management techniques which includes an explanation of emotional intelligence approach.

The Burrhus F. Skinner Foundation – information about his work which includes information about behaviourist theory.

Information about the ABC programme to support boys' development.

207

Further references

Carefully selected sources of useful information that will help you to take your study further.

Check your knowledge

A quick-fire round of questions to check how much you have remembered from the chapter.

Extending understanding of theories of children and/or young person's care or development

CP1

This unit will help you to understand that theories are not just something that have to be learned while you are studying, but are a set of carefully planned and tested principles that you can apply to your work with children. This will help to ensure that the outcomes for their development are the best they can be.

A deeper understanding of these theories will develop your role as a reflective practitioner in whatever area of work with children and young people you choose to enter.

Learning outcomes

By the end of this unit you will:

1 Know the role of theories in informing practice when working with children and/or young people

2 Be able to apply theories to workplace practice

3 Understand the relevance of identified theories in relation to own workplace practice and personal development.

In practice

Chun Hei, a 2-year-old child in Red Key Children's Centre, spent long periods of time wrapping everything up, from bricks in tea towels and dolls in blankets to crayons in paper. Sheila was on a student placement and regularly observed Chun Hei wrapping up many items in many ways during her play. By sharing her observations with the team at the end of the day, Sheila learned that it was important to provide a variety of resources for Chun Hei to continue to wrap in many areas of the nursery.

By the end of this unit you will have an understanding of a range of theories underpinning your practice, which will help you to understand behaviour like Chun Hei's. You will be able to support the development of a very young child trying to make sense of their world through a pattern of behaviour such as wrapping objects!

1 Know the role of theories in informing practice when working with children and/or young people

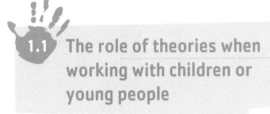

1.1 The role of theories when working with children or young people

The main role of theoretical research in supporting children's development is to ensure a deep understanding of how development takes place and how it can be supported.

Becoming a reflective practitioner

When you are working in any aspect of care and education you need to become a **reflective practitioner**. To really appreciate how to support the children you work with, you need to have a deep understanding of how they develop. A knowledge of the theories of child development will help you to understand why a child does something and then to reflect upon how you can best support this. Theories are constantly being researched and developed, and knowing about such research can help you to provide relevant learning experiences and high-quality learning opportunities.

Key term

Reflective practitioner – someone who is prepared to evaluate their work with children, always considering and using their understanding of the theories of child development in practice.

The theories that are vital to your work as a practitioner will ensure you understand children's:

- development
- behaviour
- reactions
- styles of learning
- attachment and transition needs.

Reflect

There is much debate about nature versus nurture among the theorists who have endeavoured to underpin our work with children and young people. This debate is about whether a child or young person's innate qualities (those they are born with) influence their physical and behavioural traits or whether the environment you create can make a difference.

In your study group or with a learning partner, consider whether there may be some behavioural management strategies that could support a 6-year-old child who is finding it difficult to form relationships with his peers. Consider whether this is something that is part of his personality and may not be able to be supported. You might want to share your discussion with your tutor or workplace supervisor!

Look at **Figure 1.1** below and think about how you can use the knowledge you will gain about the theories that underpin your work with children and young people.

- ensure each child's optimal development
- understand how each child develops as an individual
- use new theories and developments to update practice
- develop key relationships

Theories underpin your work with children and young people to...

- understand individual learning styles
- develop strategies to support children's learning
- support children's behaviour

Figure 1.1: *Knowledge of theories underpins work with children and young people.*

Common theories of development that influence working practice

There are common theories of children's development that will influence your practice. These theories will help you to support the learning framework you may be working within, understand how to communicate with children, explore children's relationships, consider how children feel and support their play. The common approaches to theories of development are:

- constructivist
- behaviourist
- social learning
- attachment
- psychoanalytical
- humanist.

Review **Table 1.1** to find out more about these theories and the people who researched and developed them. You will find many of them referred to in this unit, but others are discussed elsewhere in this book.

Table 1.1: *Common theories that influence our practice when working with children*

Theoretical approach	Brief description	Original theorists	Impact of theory on work with children and young people
Theories of cognitive development			
Constructivist	Considers the ways in which children and young people make sense of their environment and learn actively as a result	Jean Piaget (Stage of development)	Importance of developmentally appropriate activities
		Lev Vygotsky (Zone of proximal development)	Enabling practitioners to support a child's learning and extend their thinking
		Jerome Bruner (Scaffolding)	Importance of an adult understanding when to support a child's learning
Behaviourist	Considers how children and young people respond to stimuli	John B. Watson (Classical conditioning) Ivan Pavlov (Classical conditioning/ experiment with dogs)	Classical conditioning helps us to understand children's phobias or anxieties
		B.F. Skinner (Operant conditioning)	Enables adults to consider positive reinforcement to manage behaviour
Social learning	How children can learn through imitation and observing suitable models	Albert Bandura (Bobo doll experiment)	Ensure that the adult is a positive role model for children and that they have a range of opportunities to engage in imitative play
Theories of social and emotional development			
Attachment	Babies need to form strong attachment with their main carers	John Bowlby (Separation anxiety/ monotropism)	Has ensured we are aware of transitions and the importance of key relationships for very young children
Psychoanalytical	Children's personalities and actions are determined by their subconscious mind	Sigmund Freud (The id/the ego/the superego)	Has emphasised the need to consider the emotional aspects of a child or young person's development
Humanist	Children and young people's basic needs are met by considering personality and motivation	Abraham Maslow (Hierarchy of needs)	A positive environment and positive relationships are an important part of supporting every child or young person's needs

CP1

These theories are suggested approaches to development and have been used as a basis for past and current research by respected practitioners. Research frequently develops the theories created and sometimes disproves aspects which enable us to review our practice (an important element of reflective practice). An example is the research of Chris Athey, supported by Tina Bruce, who built on Piaget's theory that young children have schemas; this work is at the centre of current practice of working with children under the age of 3.

You will learn more about schemas in Units 10, 13 and 15 but, in brief, a schema is a pattern of linked behaviour that a child demonstrates in their play through actions and language. A pattern such as 'posting' may link to seemingly disassociated activities. Children use schemas to make sense of their world and they are a normal reaction to events and the world they live in.

By reading articles and books and researching recommended websites, you can access a great deal of knowledge about ways of developing children's learning – theories are constantly being updated, revised and applied to current practice.

Find out

Chris Athey has developed Piaget's theory that young children have schemas in their learning. Tina Bruce worked with her as a research assistant at Froebel College. Find out how Athey developed Piaget's theory and how schemas can be used to identify a young child's interests. You could use the Internet or some of the books listed at the end of this unit including *Early Child Education* by Tina Bruce and *Extending Thought in Young Children* by Chris Athey.

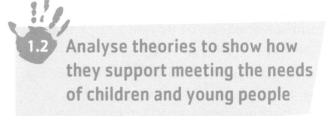

1.2 Analyse theories to show how they support meeting the needs of children and young people

It is important to understand that many original theories relating to children are developed and challenged as research and experience provides more knowledge. Theories are sometimes disproved through extended practical research but are often enriched and developed. Because learning is holistic, you should consider the fact that theories relating to children's social needs are also linked to how they learn.

In this section we will examine how theories meet the needs of the children you are working with, in each of the following areas:

- gender difference
- emotional needs
- social needs.

Key terms

Transitions – important times in a child or young person's life when they move from one key phase to another. Most children will experience these transitions, for example, from home to school. There are also some transitions that are experienced on an individual basis, for example, moving to another area or even to other carers.

Schema – a repetitive pattern in a child's behaviour, for example, taking the contents of the home corner to another area of the room could be a transporting schema in action; lining cars up could be a trajectory schema.

Holistic – an approach that takes the whole person into account, not just one or a few aspects of their health and well-being.

Gender difference – refers to the differences between boys and girls. There are obvious biological differences but there is some belief that personality and other differences are genetic.

Gender difference

There is a range of research that offers different opinions about the contrasting achievements of boys and girls. It is an area where practitioners can sometimes have some strong personal views and therefore it is not always easy to analyse the research that is available. The debate regarding nature versus nurture is very much at the core of current theories about gender differences.

Reflect

Do you have any views about gender differences that you think could influence the way you support boys and girls in your practice?

Nature

There are theories, such as those by Steven Pinker, an evolutionary psychologist, which view the differences between the genders as being part of the way we have evolved; therefore they are natural.

Some of the points Pinker made are listed below.

1 Girls have more effective links between the two parts of their brain than boys.

2 Girls have an earlier development of their cerebral cortex.

3 Boys have a greater blood flow in their brains which is connected to physical action.

Key terms

Evolutionary psychologist – considers the way humans adapt to their changing physical and social environment taking into account changes to brain structure and cognitive behaviour.

Cerebral cortex – the part of the brain that is responsible for thinking, perceiving, producing and understanding language. It is divided into areas called lobes which have special functions. They influence intelligence, personality, motor function, organisation and touch.

Nurture

Social constructivist theories include those by Barbara Rogoff. She inferred that the environment in which children are nurtured can foster gender differences, that girls are often given more responsibility and so become more responsible. She gives a clear example of this when she writes about the Luo people in Kenya, a society where boys sometimes looked after younger siblings in the absence of an older daughter in the family. The boys studied were proved to be more caring than their peers who did not have the same opportunity.

Penny Holland has carried out much research into gender differences and feels that boys may have aggressive tendencies. In her work, Penny Holland highlights research by people such as the neuroscientist Susan Greenfield: her research suggests that testosterone levels in boys may not be the cause of aggression, but that aggression is more likely to be a result of pursuing an activity that is aggressive.

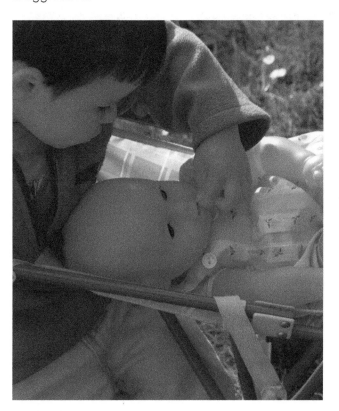

Playing with dolls or in the home corner can encourage boys to be caring.

CP1

Case study: discouraging aggressive play

Kate was leading a reception class in Bingfield School and observed that many of her boys were engaged in aggressive play such as fighting in the role-play area. One or two children also brought toy guns to school that were given to them by their parents. They also liked to dress up as 'army' when they had the opportunity. Kate had attended a course about how she could turn this play into something more positive. She decided to follow the children's interest and led a topic where they all created their own superheroes, designing and making costumes. These superheroes had extra powers that were not related to guns or aggressive forms of play. Kate took pictures of the children and placed them on the wall with captions. She also involved the parents in helping the children to make their costumes and to write a brief booklet about the topic.

1 Which theoretical perspective supports Kate's approach to superheroes?

2 What would you have included in the brief booklet to parents to encourage less aggressive play through the superhero theme?

Many theorists' views on gender have been challenged.

- **Sigmund Freud** has been criticised for his Oedipus and Electra complex theories. These refer to a mother's close relationship with her son and that of a father with his daughter. It is now becoming accepted that an empathetic and caring father is valuable to a child's development – so you have to consider carefully if this disproves the Oedipus complex. There is now much evidence that a father makes an effective main carer, and that his involvement in the upbringing of his children can have very positive effects.

- **Kohlberg**, in his theory of the stages of moral development, has been challenged because he gave more importance to the opinions of males rather than females in his research. Practitioners working with children and young people do not feel that this is a valid theory because of the positive enforcement that is now used to ensure

that all children's opinions are valued.

- **Piaget** was criticised for offering a very male view of child development.

- **Bowlby** was questioned about his views on attachment which only related to mothers being needed by their children in their early years. However, there is evidence that children can experience separation anxiety if they leave the main carer – and this may be a man. As a result he adapted this theory.

So what does this mean?

In your practice, it is useful to consider some gender difference theories that might be reflected in a positive environment.

- Ensure that a similar range of experiences are offered to boys and girls – that includes risk taking for all.
- Consider turning aggressive play into something positive as Kate did in the superhero play.
- Make sure that boys have opportunities to read and talk (their literacy levels are often less developed than those of girls).
- Follow the child to support their individual needs (whatever their gender).
- Encourage independence and responsibility.
- Ensure that all children are part of a warm, caring environment.
- Give opportunities for physical activities and freedom to move in large spaces.

Emotional needs

The emotional needs of children can be supported by understanding how they manage their feelings, their levels of self-esteem, their interactions with others and their emotional intelligence. These are theories that form the basis of the way we work to support children's development.

Key term

Emotional intelligence – a child or adult's ability to manage a variety of social situations. They can exercise self-control over their impulses and emotions, and show an awareness of other's feelings and emotions.

Research into brain development has influenced our practice in relation to links between the emotions and learning. You will already be aware that children in your care may be affected in a learning situation if they are unhappy or sad for some reason. Therefore it is important that a child is supported to be emotionally stable, while meeting their needs, so that they can be receptive to learning.

Sigmund Freud (1856–1939)

Sigmund Freud's work was criticised in later years. However, his theory of **psychoanalysis** is important because he encouraged society to change the way that emotional development is viewed and to make us aware that we have **unconscious** minds. He also influenced the development of counselling and therapy, which are often part of the way that some children's emotional needs are supported in many settings today.

In his **structure of personality** Freud stated that our unconscious mind is divided into three parts. He believed that children gradually develop all three parts and can then make moral decisions themselves.

- The **id** is an instinctive part of our personality and is something we are born with. It responds to the basic needs of our bodies without taking into account how this impacts on others. An example is the baby who cries to be fed in the middle of the night without any feeling for their exhausted parent! When such needs are met, it is called gratification.
- The **ego** is the next stage to develop in the first few months of a child's life. It helps a child to work out that there are some effective ways to have needs met, for example, to smile or scream if they need a drink. The development of the ego can mean that a child knows that they may have to wait for needs to be met, so some common sense begins to develop.
- The **superego** part of the personality develops later in childhood and is what we know as conscience. This is when guilt will develop because of negative behaviour, or pride and confidence will grow as a result of positive behaviour.

Despite criticisms of the lack of scientific evidence in Freud's work his theory does help us to understand and meet children's emotional needs. In turn this helps a child to achieve emotional well-being in adulthood. As a practitioner you can provide the right play opportunities for children who are experiencing emotional issues, by means of praise and support from you or from multi-agency professionals such as counsellors or therapists.

Key terms

Psychoanalysis – developed by Freud, this is a complex theory about personality and what motivates people to act as they do. It explores unconscious thought process as a way to treat mental illness.

Unconscious – the thoughts processed that we are not aware of relating to suppressed feelings, personal habits, intuition, complicated phobias and desires.

Structure of personality – Freud believed that humans develop their personality in stages and that the areas of personality that develop in each stage play an important part in how children, young people and adults interact with the world.

Find out

After reading this unit, find out more about these two important theories in meeting the emotional needs of children and young people. You could use the Internet or read books such as *Understanding Early Years Theory in Practice* (see the Further references section at the end of the unit).

CP1

Erik Erikson (1902–94)

Erik Erikson, a student of Freud, also developed a psychoanalytical theory that the way an adult relates and responds to a child can have a direct impact on the way they see themselves. If a child receives negative messages from an adult, this can have a long-term effect into adulthood, on relationships or academic performance. Erikson divided this theory of our personality development into eight stages called psychosocial development. His theory emphasises that children and young people need confidence to make the transition between each stage. Five of the stages are outlined in **Table 1.2**.

Table 1.2: *Erikson's stages of psychosocial development*

Age	Stage	Outcome
Birth to 1 Basic trust versus mistrust	Babies decide if the environment is friendly and warm or unsettling in some way.	If their basic needs are not met they may have issues forming relationships.
Children aged 2 to 3 years Autonomous versus shame and guilt	As children explore their environment they begin to have some control over physical movements. They develop independence.	Children who are not given opportunities to explore or who are criticised for having an accident may feel doubt or could be less independent.
4 to 5 years Initiative versus guilt	Children are beginning to initiate activities and to learn about their gender differences.	Children need set boundaries but with the ability to be independent. If children have no boundaries they may feel no guilt.
6 to 12 years Industry versus inferiority	Children can compare themselves to their peers.	Children can experience failure in comparison to peers and feel inferior to them. Children who are very competent can lack empathy.
13 to 18 years Identity versus confusion	Young people are exploring their identity and future. They may explore their sexuality.	At the end of this stage young people may have a focus of what they would like to do or may still be uncertain.

So what does this mean?

To ensure that you give the children in your care the confidence and independence they need to develop as indicated by Erikson, you should consider:

- ensuring they have time to complete a task
- ensuring they have enough activities that they initiate from a young age
- praising them appropriately
- enabling them to make choices in an environment where they can make mistakes!
- that behaviour is guided consciously and unconsciously
- that personality is formed in childhood
- that there are stages that children and young people go through
- that personality is shaped by experiences of these stages.

Abraham Maslow (1908–70)

Abraham Maslow belongs to the humanist category of theorists. His theory of hierarchical needs stated that all the basic needs had to be met before any learning could take place. He called this self-actualisation.

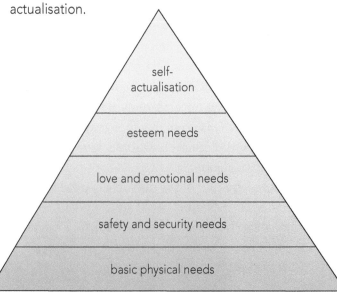

Figure 1.2: *Maslow's hierarchy of needs*

As a practitioner your priority is to create an environment which ensures that children and young people are comfortable and in which they can form positive relationships with both adults and children. According to Maslow they will then be more likely to become effective learners.

A positive sense of self-identity for children and young people is an important part of their emotional development. It is believed that the way they view themselves can have a direct impact on their learning.

John Bowlby (1907–90)

John Bowlby believed that relationships are key to meeting the emotional needs of young children. He developed an attachment theory which suggested that babies need a strong and stable relationship with their main carers to be emotionally confident in adulthood. He produced a report called 'Childcare and the Growth of Love' (1953) which was based upon his research, mainly in hospitals. This has since prompted more research and still influences childcare practice today. He later developed his theory by considering that the main carer did not have to be the person with whom a child formed an attachment.

Mary Ainsworth (1913–99)

Mary Ainsworth developed Bowlby's theory of attachment by carrying out research to show that the way a mother responds to her baby will influence the quality of attachment.

She placed mothers into three groups.

1 **Insecure/avoidant** – a mother is insecure in her role and avoids time with her child.

2 **Secure** – a mother is confident in her parenting and communication, and spends as much time as possible with her child.

3 **Insecure/resistant** – a mother is unhappy in her role and sometimes enjoys the relationship, but does not always respond to the child's needs.

The criticism of Ainsworth's theory is that there could be other factors which influence these relationships and that the views and issues of the parents may need to be considered. However, it does highlight the importance of you, as a practitioner, supporting parents in their parenting. There is much research to show that young children will be severely affected if they do not have warm, stimulating and caring relationships with a carer. Kate Cairns, a social worker and trainer in attachment, trauma and resilience, has explored the importance of attachment: 'As human beings we are all vulnerable; but we are also all resilient. And when we work together to build knowledgeable and supportive communities we increase the resilience of us all.' To find out more about Kate Cairns, see the Useful websites section on page 47.

Elinor Goldschmied (1910–2009)

Elinor Goldschmied carried out research in 1994 which highlighted the needs of children from birth to 3 years. Children need:

- acceptance from their main carers
- an opportunity to experience independent relationships
- to have a positive self-identity
- loving and responsive care.

She influenced the recommendations for best practice in early years that children should have key people in a setting to care for their basic needs and act as the main communication link between home and family.

Key terms

Attachment theory – attachment means an emotional bond between people. The basis of the attachment theory is the way in which caregivers create a secure base for each child to develop.

Key person – the practitioner assigned to each child in a setting to ensure that each child's needs are accurately identified and consistently met. Each key person has special responsibilities for working with a small number of children.

Find out

Find out from your setting if there is a key person system.

Find out what the guidance is for key people and how this system is considered to support the child. Ask if you can observe a key person communicating with a child's carers at the beginning or end of a session.

Consider the advantages of the key person system for the setting.

Key terms

Cognitive development – refers to the development from childhood to adulthood of the thought processes including memory, decision making and problem solving.

Zone of proximal development (ZPD) – the difference between what a child or young person can do without support and with support followed by a period of independent learning using the skills and knowledge acquired through working with the adult.

Social needs

Although it is sometimes difficult to separate children and young people's social and emotional needs, there is some research that clearly supports you in meeting the social needs of the children you are supporting.

Lev Vygotsky (1886–1934)

Lev Vygotsky was a Russian theorist whose research showed that children's social needs related to their **cognitive development**. Relationships with adults have to be positive and supportive in order to encourage children to be problem solvers and thinkers and to develop their language. This interaction with adults is described in his devised **zone of proximal development (ZPD)**. The ZPD indicates the point where an adult needs to interact with a child when they see the potential for them to extend their learning.

Many schools and settings working with children or young people reflect Vygotsky's theory that adults and peers play an important part in a child's learning. They do this by focusing on the role of the adult who encourages children to play together, extending their learning as appropriate. An example would be where a practitioner refers to the role of the adult when planning activities and devises more structured activities, such as shared reading.

Adults can extend children's thinking when sharing a book.

Reflect

- Has there been a time when you have seen an older child and a younger child learning from each other? How do you think this helped to support the social needs of the younger child?
- Can you think of any opportunities for this to be developed in a setting you have been in?

Jean Piaget (1896–1980)

An important part of a child's development is to understand the difference between right and wrong. Jean Piaget developed a theory of moral reasoning. He watched children at play and the rules they developed while playing. He observed that moral reasoning developed according to a child's stage of cognitive development.

Find out

Carry out some research into Kohlberg's theory of moral development outlined on page 16 of this unit. How do you think Piaget's theory of moral reasoning differed from Kohlberg's ideas? You could discuss this in a study group or with a learning partner, finding examples of children you have observed.

Jerome Bruner (b. 1915)

Jerome Bruner is an influential psychologist whose theory of cognitive growth emphasises how social and cultural factors can impact on children's learning. He considers that children are active learners who need the adult to intervene in their play at appropriate times to help them problem solve. This is referred to as scaffolding. Like Vygotsky, Bruner emphasises the importance of the relationship between the adult and the child for effective learning. He also recommends that adults should encourage children to revisit their learning and learn from what they experience.

Key term

Scaffolding – the process where adults or other more competent peers build on children's existing knowledge and skills.

Find out

Janet Moyles developed the idea of scaffolding in her spiral of play in which an adult initiates play and then supports and extends at various stages in the spiral until the children are playing and learning independently, using their extended learning. Research her well-used method of supporting children's play. You could refer to her book *Just Playing?: Role and Status of Play in Early Childhood Education* (see the Further references section at the end of this unit).

Albert Bandura (b. 1925)

Social learning theories (a type of behaviourist approach) are dealt with by researchers such as Albert Bandura. He believes that much of our social behaviour is a result of conditioning and watching those around us, referred to as observational learning.

Bandura carried out a famous experiment on Bobo dolls to show that children do learn from others. He showed three different groups of children observing an adult hitting an inflatable doll. The film he made had three different endings.

- Group A children observed the hitting and afterwards imitated the aggressive behaviour seen.
- Group B children observed the adult being praised and rewarded for hitting the doll. Afterwards the group imitated the aggressive behaviour they had seen.
- Group C children observed the adult being punished after hitting the doll and showed less aggressive behaviour.

This research highlighted that observational learning can take place without any reinforcement. Since this experiment, further research has considered why some children copy some behaviours and ignore others. This could be to do with the ability to notice the related activity and to have an accurate recall. As a result Bandura now refers to his theory as a **social cognitive theory** rather than as social learning theory.

This social cognitive theory can be used partly to promote positive behaviour by acting as a positive role model for the children in our care.

Professor Judy Dunn (b. 1939)

Professor Judy Dunn is a contemporary theorist who has led and carried out extensive research into children's friendships, highlighting the differences between the relationships of siblings and friends. The highs and lows of friendships are very important in children's lives. She highlights the fact that young children experience the same emotions as adults in their relationships such as:

- loyalty
- jealousy
- rejection
- closeness
- caring
- empathy.

She indicates that children can have friendships from as young as 2 years and choose who they want to play with, often sharing in imaginary play to help them develop mutual skills in:

- communication
- support
- trust
- mutual understanding.

Consider the statements below to find out how Judy Dunn viewed the importance of childhood relationships.

- Each child is unique.
- Children have the ability to care for each other.
- Relationships between childhood friends can be different from those between siblings.
- Children can sometimes experience a range of intense emotions in their friendships.
- Children's friendships can have a positive impact on their development.
- Friendships can give children transferable skills to support peers and communicate effectively.
- Children can develop a moral understanding of what is right and wrong.

By understanding the importance of relationships, as researched by Judy Dunn, children can be supported by observations that reflect an understanding of

friendships, independent play, groupings for activities and the way the setting encourages friendships in age-appropriate play such as role play and imaginary play.

Find out

It is important to find out more about contemporary research. You can find out more about Judy Dunn's important theories on the importance of young children's friendships in her book *Children's Friendships: the Beginnings of Intimacy*, (see the Further references section at the end of the unit).

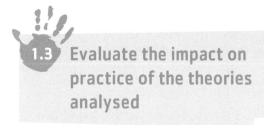

1.3 Evaluate the impact on practice of the theories analysed

An effective way to find out if your theoretical knowledge is having a positive effect on the children you are working with is to reflect on your practice in relation to the theories analysed.

Consider implementing observations and assessment of practice relating to the analysed theories. By implementing and sharing your observations with colleagues, you can reflect on:

- the effect of the environment upon the child
- how relationships are developed and transition is supported
- how children's behavioural needs are supported
- how learning is supported.

By observing children you can begin to consider how your theoretical knowledge can have a positive impact on your practice.

There are different ways of observing children and young people to ensure effective evaluation. By doing this you can collect information, then evaluate it and conclude if the theory you are analysing is effective.

So what does this mean?

When carrying out observations it is important to remember the following.

- Ask permission from your supervisor.
- Maintain confidentiality.
- Choose a relevant method of observation.
- Ensure that you have all you need.
- If it is a non-participant observation, have somewhere to observe.
- Ensure the date and time are recorded on your notes.
- Try to write what you record as soon as possible to ensure that you reflect what you have seen accurately.
- Link observations to the appropriate developmental stages and needs.

You will then have the evidence needed to analyse any relevant theory.

Although you may be aware of the different methods of observation, it is worth taking time to review them and then to apply suitable methods to your analysis, as a method of formative assessment.

- **Brief notes** – an observation does not need to be long. An instant observation of practice that is shared at the end of the day, and that affects how planning or individual needs are met, is widely used. It is an effective way of contributing to the assessment of children.
- **Free description** – a narrative recording of what you see over a brief period can be effective for looking at holistic development.
- **Time sample** – undertake a time sample to look at an activity over a period of time. This can be used to see how a child interacts or is involved in the environment.
- **Event sample** – allows you to record when things happen over a period of time, often relating to behaviour.
- **Target child** – when a specific child is observed using codes for certain words. It enables the observer to record all the information. This can also give a view of several areas of development.

- **Standardised test** – these are administered to give specific outcomes in a prescribed way such as SATs (Special Attainment Tests) used in schools at the end of Key Stage 2 and above.
- **Media recording** – using photos, video clips or sound recordings can be part of another method of observation, but can highlight areas missed in written recording.
- **Parental observations** – contributions by parents to evidence such as learning journals about something a child has achieved at home.

It is important that you reference theorists in any analysis of an observation that you submit as a form of assessment for your studies. Less formal, but still valuable, analysis might occur when you are sharing results of observations with your colleagues.

The environment

In his hierarchy of needs Maslow recommended that basic physical and psychological needs must be met in order for children to develop into confident adults. In your observations you need to consider the environment that has been created and if it is working for the children. It is essential to understand that the environment refers not only to the physical space but also to the relationships that take place.

Evaluating this might be as simple as creating a checklist to record the temperature at various times of the day; or you may observe snack and mealtimes, or carry out an event sample to evaluate the quality and amount of time children spend with key people.

An observation relating to the environment demonstrates the impact of Elinor Goldschmied's concept of key people. This concept also relates to Bowlby's theory of attachment, and reminds us that relationships with key carers are important for young children. Consider the two examples below.

1 Bianca, an early years student, is working in a day care setting. She has recorded an observation of a parent, Kim, talking to Sue, her child's key person, about the difficulty she was experiencing in putting her child to bed on time and giving her quality time after her working day. Bianca gained permission to observe.

In her evaluation, Bianca referred to a sentence from *People Under Three, Young Children in Day Care* by Goldschmied, Jackson and Forbes:

> I noticed that Sue really listened to Kim, a parent, who was concerned about the time she is able to spend with her 3 year old after nursery. Sue sat down with Kim in a quiet area and acknowledged and reflected her concerns, responding as appropriate. This highlights the importance of key relationships with the main carer as outlined by Bowlby in his theory of attachment. It also shows that the key worker system that we implement, as developed by Elinor Goldschmied and a statutory part of the EYFS, is working. It is important for childcare staff to work closely with parents and to be sensitive to the pressures they might be facing. Kim seemed upset at first but left looking happier which shows how important relationships are in our setting.

2 A common thread running through theoretical research is the need to promote independent learning. This is something Ed and his team evaluated in relation to the construction area in their reception class:

> Ed was working with a group of 4- and 5-year-old children in a reception class. He had noticed that the shelves which the construction blocks were on were very high and the children had to ask for what they wanted. Ed and his team redesigned the area to include lower, clearly labelled shelves and boxes. When working with the children after the area had been redesigned, Ed noticed that the environment encouraged more cooperative, constructive play and that the children were able to choose their materials more independently.

> By redesigning the construction area and enabling more independent play, Ed demonstrated Maslow's belief that a level of basic needs must be met before learning (which he called self-actualisation) can take place. The children may then be able to extend their learning and meet their potential in a range of areas of their development.

Reflect

In many settings you will notice that there is a great emphasis on providing a range of challenging activities for both boys and girls, although the gender differences are acknowledged. Reflect on the planning for your setting and analyse the following areas. While you do so, consider the importance of research by both Barbara Rogoff and Penny Holland.

- Range of opportunities that encourages boys and girls to play together
- The opportunity for physical activities both indoors and outdoors
- The chance for girls to join in challenging activities that may involve taking risks and problem solving
- The opportunities for boys to be empathetic in role-play areas or in other areas of play

Relationships and transitions

Much of the research into children's and young people's care and development forms the basis of current early years practice. You can find out through observations how effective these influences are. The importance of attachment has already been discussed, and the effective use of the key person system to ensure that children experience a positive transition. Many settings will have settling-in plans that acknowledge the importance of the issues that children can experience when separating from their main carer.

Reflect

Consider the approach to settling in young children in your setting or a similar situation that you have experienced in another setting.

- Do you think that Bowlby's theory of attachment has had a positive influence on the communication between the main carers of the child and the key people in your setting?
- Can you identify and observe areas of practice that are effective as a result of the importance that Bowlby placed on these relationships in his attachment theory?
- If your setting uses settling-in plans for young children, then it might be useful to analyse these in relation to Bowlby's attachment theory.

In many settings the emphasis of transition from different stages is now seen as very important. Listed below is a range of positive practices that reflect this theoretical understanding.

Transition is often supported by:
- home visits
- settling-in plans
- finding out as much about children as possible before they come to a setting
- encouraging young children to bring familiar objects from home
- opportunities for parents to accompany children into class and settle them in perhaps by self-registering together or sharing a favourite activity
- visits by children to new settings
- more links between key phases such as from reception in the Early Years Foundation Stage (EYFS) to Key Stage 1 of the English National Curriculum
- sharing of information between practitioners
- transition of information between settings as agreed by parents
- support of multi-agency working
- grouping children with regard to their friendships
- working in partnership with parents and acknowledging them as the main carers.

In her work Judy Dunn focused on the importance of recognising that relationships among children are a very important part of their development. Besides making them feel valued, they can help children to develop social skills. You could carry out observations in order to find out more about the friendships of the children in your setting. You might undertake a time sample where you note who children are playing with at different times of the day or a flow chart to track specific children around the room to see who they play with and in which area. Such observations could help you to analyse the importance of friendship. You could consider and observe:
- information you have been given about a particular child and their friendships
- positive aspects of friendships such as a more reserved child playing more confidently with children in a home corner

- changes to the environment you could make to encourage more positive relationships such as opportunities to share books or play imaginatively outside.

Case study: using observation to support a child

Jerome was aware that Arvind, one of the 6 year olds, was finding it difficult to settle into an after-school club he had just joined. In consultation with his supervisor Jerome decided to observe Arvind during a session. He used an event sample in which he noted down key times when Arvind was with other children and the quality of the interaction. He was aware of Judy Dunn's research and the emphasis that she placed on friendships among children.

When analysing his observation he noticed that Arvind was more comfortable in situations when he could play with just one or two children. However, he became withdrawn in large group situations such as playing football or eating together. This enabled Jerome and his team to encourage Arvind to develop friendships through activities such as games between small groups or adult-led activities such as gardening, where the adult could encourage children to carry out tasks together and get to know Arvind.

1 Which aspect of Judy Dunn's theory was Jerome considering when supporting Arvind?

2 How do you think that Dunn's theory that friendships are important has had an impact on the way Jerome and his team supported Arvind as a result of the observation?

Supporting children's behavioural needs

Operant conditioning

Operant conditioning, as developed by Burrhus Skinner, recognises that children and young people respond to **positive reinforcement** as a way of developing positive behaviour. Most practitioners working with children use operant conditioning in their practice. This positive reinforcement can be seen working effectively through:
- reflecting positive behaviour, for example, by saying, 'I like the fact that you have just shared your apple with Naomi, Chris'

- offering rewards such as certificates or stickers for positive behaviour
- showing children that their behaviour enables you to trust them – for example, by allowing two 13 year olds to go to the shops together because they have shown they can be responsible by keeping in touch with you
- letting other adults, such as parents, know a child has behaved positively.

Key term

Positive reinforcement – a way of motivating a child to behave in a positive way and to help them to make the right decisions about how they behave. Language used is positive and focuses on positive aspects of behaviour rather than negative.

Reflect

Take the opportunity to observe in your setting how children or young people are positively reinforced for behaviour that is wanted.

- How soon are they praised after their behaviour?
- Does this link to your understanding of the importance of timing in operant conditioning?

Classic conditioning

Ivan Pavlov (1849–1936) was a Russian physiologist who conducted experiments with dogs. He discovered that they could be conditioned to react in a certain way. This is known as classic conditioning. Pavlov inferred that children can also be conditioned to react in a certain way. While this is not the basis of any practice, it can help practitioners to understand children's phobias or fears. Consider the following examples.

- Fred became very upset when a friend used a play syringe in the home corner. This kept happening and his key person discovered from his mum that he had developed a fear of needles after going to the doctor.
- John kept having accidents in his pants because he did not like using strange toilets.
- Whenever Ted sang Incy Wincy Spider one of the children did not want to join in because she was frightened of spiders.

As practitioners, if we understand how classic conditioning can affect a child, we can then find ways to support them.

Find out

As a practitioner, if you are able to understand how classic conditioning can affect a child, you can find out how you can support them effectively. Learn more about Pavlov and his experiments with dogs by visiting the Simply Psychology website. For more information see Useful websites on page 47.

How learning is supported

As shown, the way we support children and young people's learning is firmly rooted in a range of theories that we can analyse. These learning theories have encouraged the development of many aspects of the way we support children at different stages. Learning is holistic and it is difficult to refer to one area of a child's needs or development without considering another.

It was Piaget who developed the stages of learning based upon children's cognitive development. He indicated that these stages are natural and that a child cannot pass one stage until another is met. He divided development into the four stages shown in **Table 1.3**.

Table 1.3: *Piaget's four stages of development*

Stage of development	Description
Sensory motor stage Birth to 2 years	Children's knowledge and understanding is based upon sight, sound, taste, touch and smell. He felt that children remain egocentric but are developing object permanence when items exist even when they cannot be seen.
Preoperational stage 2 to 6 years	Children begin to have control over their environment and see that words represent objects which enables them to make decisions in their play. This developing knowledge may mean that their logic is not always correct, such as elephants flying!
Concrete operational stage 7 to 11 years	Children begin to classify and categorise by similarity or difference. Logic is applied to concrete things that can be seen.
Formal operational stage 12 to adulthood	This is reflected in thinking and the mastery of thought. Abstract ideas can be manipulated or adapted, the implications of thinking can be considered and that of others. Hypotheses ('what if') can be constructed.

While some of Piaget's methods of research have been challenged, his stages of development have influenced learning frameworks, including the EYFS. The framework has distinct stages of learning that are based on some of Piaget's stages of development; it recognises what children are able to do at certain stages of their development and that each child's individual requirements must be met by following their particular interests and needs.

The impact of his theories upon current practice has meant that:

- new ideas that are presented to children should consider the level of development they have reached
- children's individual needs should be considered (this can be reflected in individual learning plans or annotated planning)
- open-ended questioning is used when supporting play
- children need to learn actively and experience real-life situations such as role play
- children need time to concentrate on their play, as enabled by free-flow play
- young children learn through schemas as defined on page 14.

Your observations of children should help you to analyse the impact of Piaget's theories of learning.

Key terms

Egocentric – a child or adult who focuses on their own interests and opinions rather than considering those of others is considered to be egocentric.

Object permanence – refers to the fact that objects exist even when they are not seen, heard or touched.

Free-flow play – takes place in an environment that encourages children to choose and revisit their play. Each child can develop at their own pace, and practise making choices and managing the consequences of choice. This type of play encourages a more flexible and open-ended approach to play.

Find out

Choose a child to observe over a period of time.

- What did you find out about their schemas?
- How has this knowledge informed your planning?
- What did you provide to extend this child's use of schemas?

So what does this mean?

Take a pad of sticky notes and a pencil when you are next in your setting. Firstly ensure that you are aware of the general stage of cognitive development that each child is at. Make brief observations of one or two children learning actively.

- What were they doing?
- What was the context? For example, Tom was in the sandpit and was adding sand to the water to ensure that his sand shapes did not fall apart.
- When you are with your team, share your observation in the context of active learning.
- Talk about what you could add to the sandpit the next day to extend Tom's interests.

While Piaget believed that learning was dependent upon the child's developmental readiness, Vygotsky believed that the child can be supported effectively by an experienced adult. He also felt that children can learn from each other and extend their knowledge with the timely support of an adult. This was extended by Janet Moyles in her spiral of learning where children are supported by an adult at intervals from the conception of an idea until they have extended the relevant learning; they are then ready to use the knowledge and transfer and use it in other areas of their learning.

So what does this mean?

Plan to observe a child you are working with while they are learning a new concept. You may have a record sheet in your setting or you could devise your own so that you can record the areas you need. You could use concepts such as:

- learning to put on shoes/do up buttons/put on a coat
- pouring a drink
- mixing some paint
- learning phonetically sounded blends in an organised sequence such as 'sh', 'sl', etc.
- estimating weights of objects.

Have a clear aim for your observation and then start by playing or working with the child. Step back and let the child work alone and then intervene, perhaps with some open-ended questioning. Continue to support their learning as required. This may not necessarily take place in one session but over a period of time.

Analyse the way that you supported the child and the effect you think that this had on their learning.

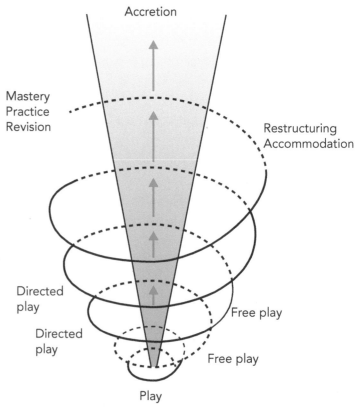

Figure 1.3: *Janet Moyles's spiral of learning (Moyles, 1989)*

Reproduced with the kind permission of Open University Press. All rights reserved.

Assessment activity
1.1, 1.2, 1.3

To develop your skills as a reflective practitioner, observe a child in your setting focusing on the age appropriate emotional and social stages of development of the child chosen. Ensure that you gain permission from your supervisor and the child's parent. You could use:

- a holistic observation
- photographic evidence
- evidence of the child's work
- evidence of talking to the child.

Analyse your observation about the child's social and emotional development in relation to theories, such as those on page 13, and consider any gender differences observed. Consider how theory supports practitioners to meet children's needs. You may want to refer to the impact of the research by Penny Holland, Barbara Rogoff or Steven Pinker in your analysis and recommendations.

Consider the next steps in the child's learning and make suggestions for:

- the role of the adult in supporting the child's emotional and social needs
- activities and approaches that would help to develop the child

Share your findings with the team and the child's parents or carers. Discuss how any suggestions you made could positively impact the learning outcomes for the child.

2 Be able to apply theories to workplace practice

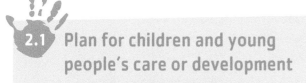

2.1 Plan for children and young people's care or development

We know that a range of theories have been developed (and sometimes challenged and adapted) that are core to the way we plan for children and young people. The theoretical knowledge enables us to plan for children's care and development in a way that will ensure each individual has the best opportunities. Take time to consider:

- **Maslow's hierarchy of needs**, which emphasises your role in providing a secure environment before any learning can take place
- **Piaget's stages of development**, which encourage us to consider how children's learning can be supported. Piaget's work also emphasises that children have to pass through one stage before another is met, so we should focus on their individual needs

- **Freud's three-stage structure of personality**, which indicates we should support children sensitively as their personality can be affected by the support and experiences we provide
- **Erikson's stages of personality development**, which indicate we should ensure children have enough activities that they can initiate from a young age. We need to praise them appropriately and enable them to make choices in an environment in which they can safely make mistakes without criticism.

The framework that you plan within will have been based on the developmental needs of the children and on theoretical research and evidence. You will therefore be expected to plan according to the stage that each child is at.

Any effective planning for children and young people will consider:

- a safe and secure environment
- the physical, linguistic, cognitive, social and emotional developmental needs of each child

- relationships and friendships
- the role of the adult
- styles of learning
- attachment and transition needs.

The planning that you may be involved in will have different stages, as outlined below.

The different stages of planning

Long-term planning

In settings with younger children where the child's patterns of play or interests are followed, any long-term planning tends to be around events in the year such as Christmas, Divali, international days, etc. For young people in school a long-term plan may be referred to as a scheme of work or a syllabus.

Medium-term planning

These are plans that are daily, weekly, monthly and sometimes termly or half-termly in schools. They will consider elements of a long-term plan. In a curriculum for young people this may refer to topics of study as part of a longer plan.

Weekly or daily plans

These are plans that refer to daily activities and for younger children should allow for flexibility and spontaneity. Any daily plan where the interests of the child are followed should consider the differentiated needs of the children involved and take into account the importance of relationships and routines.

Detailed plan

This could be an activity plan or even a lesson plan. It will consider the learning outcomes to be focused on, individual children, the role of the adult and the resources required. It could also consider a plan for routines such as snacks or dressing.

Individual plans

These could refer to plans for children's individual play, interest or learning needs, such as an individual education plan (IEP). Such plans will usually have very specific learning outcomes or targets and where possible the child and the parents will be involved.

Observation and assessment

You have already discovered in this unit, and perhaps in your practice, that observation and assessment are an important part of planning for children if you are going to follow their needs.

When observing children you are encouraged to:
- **look** – watch the children in a variety of situations and environments
- **listen** to children, colleagues and their parents
- **note** – record observations in a variety of ways.

Reflect

Erikson believed that children need to be supported in order to develop their independence.

Think of a child that you work with. How could you observe them to find out what support you might give them to become more independent?

Gathering information

When planning a curriculum you must gather as much information as possible and observations are an important way of doing this. You will:
- watch the children
- research and understand the children's stages of development
- make formal assessments
- review children's developmental records or profiles.

Settings will have different systems in place from using sticky notes to formal assessment such as Early Years Foundation Stage (EYFS) profiling.

Key term

Early Years Foundation Stage (EYFS) profile – a way of building a record of assessment outcomes throughout the reception year for 4 to 5 year olds, to support the making of final judgements.

Consider **Table 1.4** on the following page to find ways of collecting evidence from observations and assessments to inform your planning for children and young people.

Table 1.4: *Ways you can inform your planning for children and young people*

Age	Curriculum	Possible environment	Type of observation/assessment	Adults/children involved
Birth to 5 years	Early Years Foundation Stage	• Private home • Child minder's home • Day care setting • Maintained nursery school • Children's centre • Settings such as Montessori/Steiner • Reception class in a primary school	• Look, listen and note • Sticky notes • Sharing observations with child or talking about work with them • Foundation Stage profile assessment	• Practitioners • Other professionals such as speech and language specialists, community nurses • Parents • Children
6 to 11 years	• Key Stages 1 and 2 of the National Curriculum • Play-based curriculum or curriculum of country	• Schools • Breakfast and after-school clubs • Holiday camps • Specialist clubs such as football and gymnastics • Social clubs	• Curriculum attainment tests • Sharing observations as appropriate, such as photographs or assessments to target set • Varied observations, such as checklists/records of learning	• Practitioners • Other professionals such as speech and language specialists, community nurses • Parents • Children
11 to 16 years	• Key Stages 3 and 4 of the National Curriculum or curriculum of country • IB (International Baccalaureate)	• Schools • Holiday clubs • Specialist clubs • Social clubs	• GCSEs • Checklists • Formal assessment • Varied observations	• Practitioners • Other professionals such as speech and language specialists, community nurses • Parents • Children and young people

Find out

The EYFS was revised in 2012. Read it and find out more detail about the prime and specific areas of learning and development that you should use in your planning of an educational programme. They are:
• personal, social and emotional
• physical
• communication and language
• literacy
• mathematics
• understanding of the world
• expressive arts and design.

Involving children in their observation and assessment

Involving children in their own observations is a good way to put them first and to make them feel valued. It also helps them begin to take control of their learning and to be involved in their environment. Even young children can be encouraged to help you to observe and evaluate areas of their setting such as the role-play area or book corner to make it better for them. Photographs and samples of their work can stimulate discussion and add to the value of the observation. Listening to children and young people's opinions is viewed as an increasingly important way of finding out what they need. This forms an important part of any Ofsted inspection and requirements.

These observations involving children or young people can support the planning of the environment or activities. The theories that you have considered all recommend that the support we give children should be based on their individual needs. An individual learning plan (ILP) is a way of doing this as each child's needs are considered.

Children's interest and preferences in planning

It is also important that any planning considers children's preferences and interests or choices. It is therefore vital to watch what children play with and the way they play.

Children and young people also have different ways of processing information – and planning must consider these. Remember that a mixture of learning styles might be displayed, or children might move from one style to another. What you provide for the children must consider this.

A visual learner will:
- watch people speak as well as listen to them
- look for shape and form in words and numbers
- enjoy pictures in books
- enjoy visual descriptions.

An auditory learner will:
- retain and recall spoken words
- enjoy the spoken word
- enjoy different voices
- enjoy an involved explanation
- enjoy communicating with others
- speak aloud when reading.

A kinaesthetic leaner will:
- sense relative position and movement
- examine touch and feel in order to learn.

A sequential learner will:
- learn and remember things in order
- often be organised in their learning.

A holistic learner will:
- have a combination of all styles.

Differentiation in planning

Any plan is only effective if it reflects and supports each child's learning needs. Learning opportunities should maximise each child's learning, taking into account learning styles and giving children and young people the time they need to engage in their learning.

So what does this mean?

When differentiating for children in your care you should consider:
- learning and health needs
- IEPs
- the needs of children whose home language is not English
- children who may be advanced in aspects of their learning
- the actual stage of development of each child
- transient (temporary) needs such as a child whose parents have separated.

Planning the environment

As outlined by Maslow, the environment must be safe and healthy for children's learning to take place. The theoretical research that you have considered should make sure that your planning reflects:
- independence – by encouraging things such as: self-registration; appropriately labelled resources; accessible resources for the children to choose; a range of resources for the children to enjoy free choice in their play
- areas in which to socialise and make friends, such as snack areas or quiet areas in the garden.

Case study: making new friends

In Chillfield Primary School, Greta, a Year 1 teacher, noticed that there were a number of children who were isolated at play time. They were not joining in with some of the more boisterous activities such as football and climbing. Greta took time to talk to the children and found that they were having difficulty making friends at school, and being in the playground made it more difficult. Greta had seen a 'friendship stop' in another school where children could sit and chat to each other. Greta and the children designed a friendship stop using a circular bench and some scented plants. The team noticed that friendships were encouraged in this way and this had a very positive impact on the children who had been isolated. It also encouraged some of the children who normally played boisterous games all the time to stop and have a chat!

1 Review Judy Dunn's research earlier in this unit about the ways in which she indicated that friendships are important.

2 How could you encourage the importance of friendships in your planning?

Different types of planning

Planning will vary according to the setting and the needs of the children involved.

The different types of plans that could be implemented might include:

• curriculum planning for the Foundation Stage or other curriculum key stages
• care or settling-in plans for young children
• individual learning plans that focus upon the interests of the children
• individual educational plans for children or young people with specific needs
• play plans.

Planning in early years will be expected to reflect both the indoor and outdoor learning environment so that children can have a wider variety of challenges in their play. This type of environment can be planned so that the adult can support and extend children's thinking, as emphasised by Vygotsky in his zone of proximal development.

Find out

Forest Schools are an increasingly popular way to challenge children's thinking and encourage them to take risks in their learning. Bruner's theory that children's learning can be scaffolded by the adult can be effectively practised in a forest environment where children and young people are taught specific skills, and encouraged to use them independently and with increasing knowledge so that their skills develop. Try to find out more about how Forest Schools put Bruner's theory of scaffolding into practice and other theories you have read about. To find out more about Forest Schools website, see Useful websites on page 47.

Any aspects of planning should reflect the theoretical research in this unit so that children's needs can be met.

Aspects of planning

• **Flexibility and time:** changing plans, perhaps because of an unexpected occurrence such as snow. In addition, children may become so involved in an activity that it would hinder their learning if you stopped it in order to choose another activity.
• **Independent choice:** to be considered to ensure children can build relationships and confidence in their learning.
• **Open-ended activities:** activities where the children decide how to use the resources, build relationships and extend their learning through independent play and adult support.
• **Child-initiated activities:** providing plenty of resources so that the children can make choices to develop their learning through their interests and according to the developmental stage they are at. Such support can also enable them to choose to learn with other children and develop friendships as well as enjoy the challenges of working with their peers.
• **Structured/adult-led activities:** activities planned by an adult that will enable the adult to model learning and behaviour and to plan developmentally appropriate learning activities.

CP1

CP1

- **Adult-initiated:** a spontaneous or planned activity where an adult might start some play such as a game or some role play. The children might develop this on their own or in groups.
- **Involve children:** ensure that children can make choices and decisions, such as when to have a snack or wash their hands. You might even have a specific time when they discuss their ideas of what they want in their setting. This can often be a time when the adult can positively reinforce behaviour such as pouring water for a friend or contributing a good idea to a discussion.
- **Friendships and relationships:** any effective plan will reflect working with parents, colleagues and ensuring that children are encouraged to interact with each other and the adults in the setting. For younger children a softer start at the beginning of the day is good so that parents can settle their children in and liaise with a key person.

Tina Bruce's 12 features of play

Professor Tina Bruce has been mentioned already in this unit for her work with Chris Athey. She sees play as vital to a child's late development. She believes that children incorporate a variety of learning experiences into what she calls a web of learning, which may include past experiences and relationships with others. Her 12 features of play should appear in any effective planning in the Foundation Stage:

1 Using first-hand experiences
2 Making up rules
3 Making props
4 Choosing to play
5 Rehearsing the future
6 Pretending
7 Playing alone
8 Playing together
9 Having a personal agenda
10 Being deeply involved
11 Trying out recent learning
12 Coordinating ideas, feelings and relationships for free-flow play

2.2 Implement the plan for care or development of children and young people

When implementing a plan you will need to consider a variety of issues to ensure that it is effective and reflects the valued theoretical research that you have found out about. Planning will only be effective if it works!

Taking into account the theoretical research considered in this unit, the implementation of any plan for children will involve:

- preparation and setting up of environment/ activities
- supporting and facilitating (experiment/problem solve/challenge)
- intervening positively
- modelling
- engaging and interacting
- sustaining shared thinking
- extending children's learning through open questions
- planning with children
- allowing time for children to learn and develop relationships
- encouraging friendships and quality interactions
- opportunities to observe and assess.

Preparation and setting up of environment/activities

When implementing any plan, the way you prepare is essential. Any team should have systems in place which will ensure that you can set up the environment appropriately. These may be based on creating a safe and secure environment as outlined by Maslow, or one that is age appropriate which follows Piaget's theory that activities should be appropriate to a child's stage of development.

So what does this mean?

To ensure that an environment is healthy and safe for your planned activities for children, you must follow a range of legal requirements, policies and procedures such as:

- requirements for space
- requirements for heating
- requirements for ventilation
- expected ratios
- screening of all adults in the setting
- health and safety policy
- regular resource and environment checks.

Besides setting up appropriate activities that enable exploration and independent thought, the environment must also allow for space and recording of observation and assessment.

When setting up the environment there should be areas that give space to learn and work together and that clearly identify areas of learning. Each adult will have an area of responsibility at various points in the day to ensure that the environment is constantly meeting the needs of the children. Children could be part of the set-up process. The setting of activities should consider:

- space to play and learn
- areas to be reflective and for children to observe their environment
- enough variety to enable choice
- enough adult supervision to enable quality interactions
- clearly labelled resources
- activities which encourage both boys and girls to participate.

Case study: extending children's learning

In Overview Children's Centre the team for 3 to 4 year olds were developing how they set up the room before the children arrived so that they had more choice to decide how they wanted to play. One morning Shula set up a selection of six large cardboard boxes and some fabric. The children were very involved in the area all day and the boxes became a train that the children could sleep on, using the fabric as the seat, covers and curtains.

1 How do you think Shula could support this activity considering Janet Moyles's spiral of play?
2 How could Shula scaffold the children's learning in this area?

Supporting and facilitating

Through the work of people such as Skinner, Bowlby, Dunn and Holland, you have learned that the role of the adult is important in ensuring that children have good relationships and that you can support their learning. Facilitating children's learning will vary according to the age of the children involved.

- **Under 3s** need you to really understand how they want you to support them and what they can do. You can do this by closely observing their schemas and working closely with their main carers. Supporting their routines is important and routines can also be important opportunities for interaction and developing relationships.

- **3 to 5s** require you to give them time to respond to your questioning and space to enable them to choose what they want to do. Rather than support areas of development separately you should consider their learning to be holistic. Your role is to inspire and fascinate the children and support their learning. Relationships with other children and adults are still key.

- **Children and young people over 5 years** – your role is to ensure a growing independence in their learning and to support the complexity of their relationships and encourage communication with peers and adults.

Encourage children to express themselves.

Intervening positively

Your role in supporting children's learning and development is important, as outlined by Skinner in his theory of positive reinforcement. While encouraging independent learning, you need to ensure that the children engage positively in their play and extend their learning. You should not dominate the play or learning since children need to retain ownership and the ability to make independent decisions. You could ask yourself the following questions before intervening in any activity.

- Is there a danger of me disrupting the play?
- Am I welcome to be involved?
- How will I develop the learning that is taking place?
- How will I move away from the activity once I have extended the children's learning?

Reflect

Think about a time in your setting where you have observed an adult extending a child or young person's learning by intervening positively.

Did it relate to Janet Moyles's spiral of learning or Bruner's idea that the adult can scaffold the child's learning through appropriate intervention?

Modelling

A very effective way to support children's learning is to ensure that you act as a positive role model in the way you talk and do things. This relates to the social learning theories which emphasise the importance of ensuring relationships with children and young people are positive. We should raise their self-esteem using strategies such as modelling rather than criticising. Modelling is not telling them what to do but simply behaving and doing things in the right way. The examples below show ways that behaviour can be modelled:

- rolling a ball to a toddler
- making sounds to a baby
- tidying up and putting items in the right boxes for a 4 year old
- writing a word with a 5 year old
- listening to a child's opinion with a 10 year old.

Engaging and interacting

Your role as an engager of children and young people, and the way you interact, is crucial to their learning and development. This was emphasised by behaviourists such as Piaget, Vygotsky and Bruner. Initially you must find out what interests a child. You can then join in their play or conversation without dominating in any way. This is a skill that can take time to develop and can be learned through observing more experienced colleagues.

So what does this mean?

Consider trying to engage with a child in the sandpit.

- Sit alongside the child initially and observe what they are doing.
- Model an activity such as filling a bucket, using a spade and turning it out.
- See if they move towards you.
- Keep repeating the task.
- You might model some language or use some open-ended questioning such as 'What if I tap the bucket?'
- You could invite the child to pull the bucket up and see what happens.
- Once they have done it a few times you might gradually move away.

This type of modelling scaffolds the child's learning and places an importance on your interaction with the child. The way you model for them and the language you use needs to be appropriate to the child's stage of development and learning.

Sustained shared thinking

Key term

Sustained shared thinking – a means whereby the adult extends a child's thinking and understanding of concepts through language.

This is an important way of using language to encourage a child to think more deeply about what they do or say and therefore deepen their understanding. It encourages children to process information and explore different concepts. This usually happens when a child is engaged in an activity and the adult has time to extend the child's thought process.

Open-ended questioning is a great tool to extend children's thinking as it helps to develop discussion (rather than just giving instructions). However, you do need to give children time to respond to an open-ended question. Open-ended questions begin with:

- How?
- Why?
- What if?

A favourite of early years practitioners is to engage a child in a deeper level of thinking with 'I wonder if…?' or 'Tell me about…'. Try using this with a child and see if you can engage in extending their learning and the language that they use.

Reflect

Think carefully about a time when you were playing alongside a child and talking to them about what you were doing.

- Do you think that you were extending their learning to a deeper level?
- Can you think of ways in which you could have used open-ended questions more effectively?

If you think this is an area that you could develop, make a real effort to think about it when you are talking to children.

Planning with children

Including children in planning is probably one of the most beneficial things you can do. It can be an adult-initiated activity and something that you do regularly or a spontaneous conversation. By working with children to find out what they want you can take their learning in some amazing and imaginative directions. Possibilities could be a 'post it' board and a time set aside to place children's ideas on it; you can then consider these in your planning. You could also set up planned focus groups or student councils for older children or young people.

Allowing time for children to learn and develop relationships

One of your roles is to ensure that children have the time to make friendships and extend their learning. As part of a team you can encourage flexibility to allow children to complete activities at their own pace and revisit their learning or continue an activity at another time.

Encouraging friendships and quality interactions

In many of the theories that you have read about in this unit, there is a focus on the importance of friendships and quality relationships. Part of the role of the key person is to ensure that their children are involved in activities and that there is time to observe them during the day. It may also be that for younger children the key person has a small group activity with their key children or key 'families' (which refers

CP1

to a group of key children). It is also essential that the adults working with the children give time for interaction and use every opportunity during the day to do so. This could be during an adult-led activity or just while putting on a coat to go outside.

Find out

Review this unit and note what the four factors were that Judy Dunn specified as being the mutual skills that can be developed through friendships.

Opportunities to observe and assess

When you are implementing planning you will be aware that it is part of a planning cycle and that observation and assessment are also part of this. During the day you may take the opportunity to make brief notes that contribute to the planning for the next day or you might plan an observation as part of the assessment of individual children. This aspect of your plan will ensure that you are able to meet the needs of each child and ensure they experience the best possible provision.

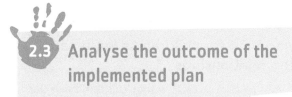

2.3 Analyse the outcome of the implemented plan

There are many ways to find out how effective your plan has been from the perspective of:

- the environment
- the activities
- the learning outcomes
- the interaction
- individual children.

These areas are all based on the theories that have been identified in this unit that relate to:

- development
- behaviour
- reactions
- styles of learning
- attachment and transition needs.

When analysing the implemented plan there will be a range of people who may contribute effectively to this and who may have some involvement in your setting. This is referred to as a **multi-agency approach** and includes:

- health workers
- social workers
- mentors
- advisers/consultants
- speech and language therapists
- inspectors
- colleagues
- educational psychologists
- parents.

Key term

Multi-agency approach – a variety of agencies working together as appropriate – for example, speech and language services, social services, etc. to improve outcomes for children and young people.

Review of daily planning

The outcomes of the planning can be analysed on a daily or weekly basis to review planning for the next day or the immediate future. Any analysis of planning should show flexibility and the ability to adapt at any moment in the process. A plan should always be changed according to your evaluations so immaculately presented planning is not always desirable. It is good practice to write comments on the planning to help you analyse the effectiveness of the plan. This is called annotated planning.

Assessment

The results of any assessment that will show the effectiveness of the curriculum and any formative and summative assessment will help to review the impact of the planning on learning.

Key terms

Formative assessment – the ongoing recording of children and young people's learning and development.

Summative assessment – the way that findings are concluded with contributions from other professionals, parents, colleagues and the child or young person.

Find out

Early Childhood Environmental Rating Scales (ECERS) are a set of standards that have been developed through research to enable settings to audit their own provision for children from birth to 6 years and feed into a cycle of self-evaluation. To find out more about ECERS, see Useful websites on page 47.

A range of evidence for assessment should include:
- samples of work
- profiles
- targets.

Auditing

Another way to analyse the outcome is to audit. This is a form of self-evaluation which fits into an inspection framework.

An audit will enable you to:
- reflect on practice and consider the resources and experiences provided for children, taking into account both indoor and outdoor experiences
- plan for improvement, identifying strengths and needs.

You can audit by:
- giving questionnaires to parents
- holding discussions
- talking with children
- making observations.

In any analysis you will:
- reflect
- identify
- agree priorities
- celebrate success
- prioritise for development
- action any identified areas
- collect evidence and celebrate what you have done.

Self-evaluation

Considering your own practice is an important part of any analysis of planning. You can reflect on this on pages 42–44.

Talking to children and young people

Part of analysing the success of planning is to review any targets set for children. You can analyse their success through assessment but also by talking to them to find out what they think they have achieved. This will place them at the heart of the process of evaluation and enable them to be masters of their own learning. You can:
- talk to each child individually
- find out what they enjoyed
- perhaps make a list of points to discuss with older children and young people
- give strategies for self-improvement, however simple
- find ways that you are going to identify progress to ensure that the child or young person is motivated.

This type of analysis will enable practitioners to review and adapt the planning to help support the children's views and needs.

2.4 Evaluate the benefit of using theories to underpin planning

By considering the theories that you have looked at, you will be able to plan very effectively as you deepen your understanding of why children behave in certain ways and how they learn. You can then carefully consider your approaches to supporting their development.

Briefly consider some of the following theories and how they validate planning and improve outcomes for children.

Piaget's theory of cognitive development

The activities planned for children are meaningful as they promote active learning and are planned around the needs of the children and their stages of development. Frameworks such as the EYFS ensure that we differentiate for each child in our planning and have an understanding of each child's stage of development to do this.

Vygotsky's zone of proximal development

Vygotsky suggests that even young children can be challenged in their thinking and the role of the adult is carefully considered. This theory also enables us to consider how important children are to each other in developing their learning and thus children are encouraged to play together independently.

Classical conditioning

This theory, researched by Pavlov and later Watson, is not used in practice, but it enables us to consider why children or young people develop phobias or fears.

Positive reinforcement

Skinner's theory of recognising positive behaviour as a way of managing unwanted behaviour creates an environment where children have positive relationships with each other and develop self-esteem. This aspect of children's development can be specifically referred to in planning and activities, such as circle time, which can help to reinforce this.

Case study: reinforcing positive behaviour

Jan was on a student placement in Bandies Primary School working with a class of 6 to 7 year olds. She had recently been studying theories based on the benefits of reinforcing positive behaviour. Jan knew that the behaviour of some of the children was challenging so she decided to share her approach of ensuring that positive behaviour was recognised and valued.

She asked the teacher if she could try something that had been discussed in one of her tutorials. If the children did something positive they placed a marble in a large, clear jar. When they had 20 marbles they were given half an hour where they could choose their own activity.

1 What sort of positive behaviour do you think Jan might recognise?
2 What effects do you think this could have on children with challenging behaviour?
3 Which theory has Jan benefited from analysing to support her practice?

Observational learning

As part of his social learning theory Albert Bandura indicated that children learn from observing others. This means that you should be a role model for children. Bandura's theory allows adults to be in a situation where they have the time to model learning in areas such as construction play for under 5s or lunchtime when the adult can model social skills such as talking to each other, serving one another, etc.

Hierarchy of needs

Maslow placed a real importance on ensuring that children have their basic needs met before they can learn. As a result we carefully consider how we can create a safe and healthy environment for children and young people where they can learn. Legislation also exists to ensure certain standards are met.

Attachment theory

Bowlby's theory of attachment has taught us that relationships must be taken into account when planning for very young children. Parents are encouraged to come into the setting to settle their children or special settling-in plans are developed to make the transition from home to another setting as smooth as possible.

The effect on children of linking planning to the theories discussed is that practitioners can:

- build on what children know and do
- ensure children feel secure and valued
- ensure that all children are included in the learning environment
- value the importance of partnerships with parents/carers

- provide a careful structure/balance of child-led and adult-supported activities
- give time for both children and adults to observe and respond
- intervene in children's learning when needed
- provide a safe and well-planned environment.

Find out

Consider what you have read about Skinner's theory of positive reinforcement. How do you think it is reflected in the planning of your setting and what are the benefits of using positive reinforcement?

Assessment activity
2.1, 2.2, 2.3, 2.4

Plan a detailed adult-led activity for a group of children in your care. Gain permission from your supervisor.

Review what you have learned about planning in this section. Choose your activity based on what you know about the children, including their interests, and gather information by talking to them, your colleagues and their parents.

Consider:

- how you will plan the environment for this activity
- selecting age-appropriate resources for the children that give them independent choices

- the role of the adult in scaffolding the children's learning
- making some focus observations of the children during the activity
- how you are going to differentiate to meet the children's needs
- how your activity is going to be flexible and challenge the children's thinking.

When you have completed the activity share it with your team and analyse the results in relation to the theories of play that underpin planning as outlined on pages 29–41.

3 Understand the relevance of identified theories in relation to own workplace practice and personal development

3.1 Draw conclusions regarding the relevance of identified theories to own work role

If you can summarise and draw conclusions about the theories identified in this unit, and how they are relevant to your role, it will help you to develop as an effective practitioner in your chosen area of work with children. It will also help you to recognise that how you support children's and young people's learning arises from extensive experimentation and research that is continually challenged, updated and built on.

Understanding the theories enables you to:

- provide an environment that facilitates independent learning
- build trusting relationships with children
- recognise the importance of valuing the child's main carer
- understand how each child develops
- ensure children have a wide range of challenging experiences
- act as a role model for behaviour and learning
- understand that children can be vulnerable and must be supported sensitively
- support their learning in appropriate ways and interact when appropriate
- value the importance of observing children and allow for flexible planning
- ensure the children can contribute to the planning and assessment of their own learning
- value the children's interests and preferences
- work as a team with other professionals for the benefit of the child.

Find out

Bowlby challenged his own theory of attachment and allowed for the possibility that the main carer in a child's life does not have to be the mother. He stressed the importance of recognising this attachment. Consider how this theory could have an impact on the practice of a day care setting that cares for children from birth to 12 months. How could the practitioners use the knowledge that they have from this theory in their daily practice?

Observing children can help you to provide the best activities to develop their learning.

So what does this mean?

Tina Bruce created the 12 features of play as outlined on page 34.

- How relevant are these to your practice or a colleague working with children in the Foundation Stage?
- Can you identify how each of these features underpins the practice of working with young children?

3.2 Reflect on own practice in relation to use of theories which underpin planning for care or development

At the beginning of this unit the reflective practitioner was referred to. If you are considering how the theories that have been discussed affect your own practice then you have started to be a reflective practitioner too!

Reflect

- When did you last think about some aspect of your practice and how you could improve it? You should do this as a matter of course when working with children and young people.
- Which theory discussed in this unit underpins the aspect of your practice that you want to develop?

An important part of the reflective process is how you review your practice. The process of reflection should be seen as positive and a way of solving problems. This can be done through:

- team meetings
- focus groups
- delegation of responsibility
- carrying out research
- reflective discussions.

To enable you to reflect on your practice and relate it to the theories discussed, you might want to:

- further your knowledge of the important aspects of the theories discussed to deepen your understanding of children and young people
- consider the activities and experiences you provide and your role within this
- undertake continuing professional development in an area of your practice such as building relationships with children.

So what does this mean?

Ask yourself the questions below so that you can evaluate your practice in relation to the theories discussed in this unit.

- What is my role in the setting in relation to building relationships with parents?
- How can I improve my knowledge of the children I work with?
- How can I ensure that the children build valuable relationships?
- How can I ensure that I provide activities that both boys and girls can access?
- How does my team view me?
- When should I share my reflections and who with?
- How can I use my reflections to influence future planning?

Peer observation is a great way to help you evaluate your practice with the children and identify any training needs you might have. It is also an opportunity to celebrate and recognise the things that you do well.

Table 1.5 suggests ways you can evaluate the key theories in relation to your role.

CP1

Table 1.5: *How you can use key theories to become an effective practitioner*

Create an independent learning environment	Have reflective discussion with mentor Attend team meetings to evaluate the use of the environment Carry out peer observation of your support of children's independent learning
Develop child-initiated activities	Develop open-ended questioning through peer observation Reflect on how to model ideas Support development by studying developmental theories Evaluate the resources available as a team Observe the children's independent play Attend training on areas such as extending children's thinking
Value children's interests and experiences	Reflect on how you listen to children Consider how you could gain more information from parents Observe the children in their learning and share your observations with colleagues Evaluate your planning for the children's individual interests as a team
Recognise the needs of a child as an individual	Explore the concept of the key worker system and consider how you could develop this role in your practice Explore your role in any settling-in plans and how they can be developed Observe the child regularly and share your observations Reflect on how many adults support the child and consider how this might be reduced Talk to parents about their children's preferences Review how your environment makes a child feel that they belong
Consider how you work with others to maximise children's care and learning experiences	Find out about your role in working with other professionals Ask a peer to observe you communicating with another professional

In 1998 Gibbs depicted reflective practice in a cycle. By following this cycle you could develop your practice in relation to the theories discussed.

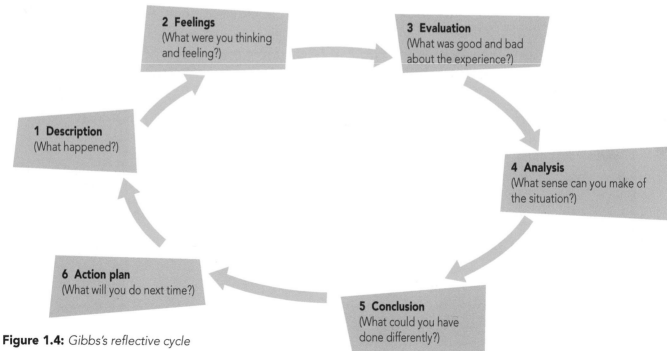

2 Feelings
(What were you thinking and feeling?)

3 Evaluation
(What was good and bad about the experience?)

1 Description
(What happened?)

4 Analysis
(What sense can you make of the situation?)

6 Action plan
(What will you do next time?)

5 Conclusion
(What could you have done differently?)

Figure 1.4: *Gibbs's reflective cycle*

Reflect

Consider how theoretical research has encouraged children to think independently.

- Can you think of a time when you could have encouraged this more with the children you work with?
- How would they have benefited from a different approach?
- Which particular theory does this situation relate to?

3.3 Develop a personal development plan

Use your knowledge of the theories of how children develop as part of your continued professional development in the form of a personal development plan. This will help you to create your own goals with your manager. It is important that any personal development plan is shared and supported by the people you work or study with.

In relation to the theories studied you may want to identify an opportunity to:

- explore the role of the key person or become a key person for a child
- develop your planning of activities to consider open-ended questioning
- explore how you could create a self-registration system to give children a sense of belonging
- consider ways to involve children in the planning in your setting, perhaps with specific times or a board where their ideas can be displayed and shared
- consider activities such as snack time which could encourage friendships in your setting.

Listed below are steps you can take to create your personal development plan.

1 Think about your skills, strengths and weaknesses. Talk to others if it helps.

2 Focus on areas you want to develop.

3 Create targets or goals and state how you want to achieve them. Be realistic.

4 Share the plan with your manager or colleague.

5 Implement the plan with regular review meetings.

6 When you have completed the plan, meet to evaluate how you have met your targets and the impact it has had on your performance.

How to benefit from feedback

- Self-reflect – think about what you have done in a thoughtful and reflective way.
- Listen to others' comments and ideas so you can consider your performance from different viewpoints.
- Consider how the children and adults involved, such as colleagues or parents, have benefited.
- Consider the impact on changes in practice by observing the children and their peers, and talking to children, colleagues and parents about changes.
- Consider your training needs.

Assessment activity 3.1, 3.2, 3.3

Create a personal development plan that relates to an area of need you have identified while reading about the theories in this unit. It could relate to:

- your role in supporting children's development
- creating the appropriate environment
- building relationships
- extending children's thinking
- following the interests of the children.

Before you create the plan, refer back to sections 3.1 and 3.2 and the identified theories that support our work with young children. Reading this will help you to understand the importance of the theories supporting your practice in your current role.

Ensure that your plan has clear targets and methods of achieving them, and state how it will inform your future practice with children or young people.

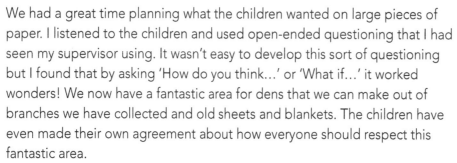

In the real world

I have been working in a class with 7 to 8 year olds in a very challenging school. My colleagues and I had been watching the children play outside over a few weeks and I was worried that the children seemed to be very destructive. Among other things, they threw some of the lovely equipment around that we had carefully chosen for them.

I work with a great team so we sat down and discussed what we could do. Eventually we decided that the children needed to be involved in choosing what they wanted in the outside area. I was asked to facilitate this.

We had a great time planning what the children wanted on large pieces of paper. I listened to the children and used open-ended questioning that I had seen my supervisor using. It wasn't easy to develop this sort of questioning but I found that by asking 'How do you think…' or 'What if…' it worked wonders! We now have a fantastic area for dens that we can make out of branches we have collected and old sheets and blankets. The children have even made their own agreement about how everyone should respect this fantastic area.

Check your knowledge

1 Briefly describe a reflective practitioner.

2 What is Vygotsky's zone of proximal development?

3 What did Judy Dunn highlight in her research in relation to friendships?

4 What sort of observation would you use to see if a child was able to access their learning independently?

5 List the four stages of development that Piaget stated children had to go through based on cognitive development.

6 Which framework recognises that children learn and develop in different ways?

7 What is an auditory learner?

8 Briefly describe sustained thinking.

9 What is positive reinforcement?

10 How could peer observation help you to reflect on your practice?

CACHE Extended Assessment

Theme: Children and young people's development

Grading criterion

B3 Analyse aspects of your learning from the chosen theme that could improve your future practice.

In preparing for your assessment, you could take time to consider the theories that support care and development and how you have incorporated them into your practice. Choose a plan from your setting that you regularly use and are going to implement. Carefully consider key aspects of the theories in relation to the objectives of a plan that you will implement. This could be a curriculum plan, a care plan or an activity plan. After you have implemented the plan, analyse if you met the objectives in relation to the theories you identified. Consider analysing the effectiveness of areas such as scaffolding, building relationships or the role of the adult in extending children's thinking.

You could analyse the effectiveness of the plan through observations, professional dialogue or a record of a team meeting. To reflect on your role in relation to the theories identified, you could create a personal development plan with clear targets and how you will achieve them, identifying the possible impact on your future practice.

This is an example of how you might approach one criterion of your Extended Assessment. You must successfully complete all the criteria at each grade to achieve that grade. You will achieve the highest grade for which you have successfully completed all the criteria. For example, to achieve a B grade you will need to meet the requirements of the B1, B2 and B3 criteria, as well as C1, C2, C3 and D1 and D2.

When trying to understand the requirements for your Extended Assessment, it is always a good idea to talk to your tutors. Fellow learners and workplace colleagues are also useful sources of information.

Further references

The following are sources of useful information on the topic of extending understanding of theories of children and young people's care or development.

Books and articles

Athey, C. (2007) *Extending Thought in Young Children: A Parent-Teacher Partnership*, London: Sage

Bruce, T. (2005) *Early Childhood Education*, 3rd edition, London: Hodder Education

Daly, M., Byers, E. and Taylor, W. (2006) *Understanding Early Years Theory in Practice*, Oxford: Heinemann

Dunn, J. (2004) *Children's Friendships: the Beginnings of Intimacy*, New Jersey: Wiley-Blackwell

Goldschmied, E., Jackson, S. and Forbes, R. (2003) *People Under Three, Young Children in Day Care*, 2nd edition, London: Routledge

Holland, P. (2003) *We Don't Play with Guns Here: War, Weapons and Superhero Play in the Early Years*, Oxford: Oxford University Press

Moyles, J. (1989) *Just Playing?: Role and Status of Play in Early Childhood Education*, Berkshire: Open University Press

Useful websites

To obtain a secure link to the websites below, visit www.pearsonhotlinks.co.uk and search for this book by using its title or ISBN. Click on the section for CP1.

The Forest Schools website aims to give you more information about this popular aspect of outdoor learning.

The Department for Education website provides information about education and services in England.

The Early Education website will give you a range of information about resources, current issues, research, thinking and practice in early years.

The ECERS UK website provides information about the use of environmental rating scales in auditing and self-evaluating your environment if you are working with Foundation Stage children.

Kate Cairns's website provides information about her work with vulnerable children and young people.

The Simply Psychology website will give you some simple explanations of the theories referred to in this unit.

Understand the role of policies in children and/or young people's settings

CP2

The aim of this unit is to understand the rationale that underpins the development of policies when working with children and young people. Policies should be owned and understood by everybody they affect, from children and young people to parents and colleagues. The way that a policy is implemented will have a positive impact on the setting and everyone involved if there is a shared understanding of the values that underpin it.

Learning outcomes

In this unit you will:

1 Understand the role of policies within a children and/or young people's setting

2 Understand the requirements which underpin a policy

3 Understand how to develop a policy for a real work environment caring for children and/or young people

4 Understand how to implement a policy in a real work environment caring for children and/or young people.

In practice

When Daphne was studying for her CACHE Extended Diploma she found that the policies and procedures of each setting she worked in were quite long and not always easy to understand. On her last placement, in Shayward School, Daphne was asked to be part of a team of teachers, early years professionals and parents who were developing a learning and teaching policy. The team shared the draft policy with the head and governors, and eventually it was shared with the whole community and placed on the school website. The policy used simple language and had visual links to the children's everyday learning to highlight the values of the policy. Daphne really enjoyed being part of this process and felt that she understood the policy and why it was so important to have a document that described the learning and teaching in the school.

After studying this unit you will find that, by involving different stakeholders in creating a policy, everyone in that community will be more likely to work towards common goals with a shared set of values.

1 Understand the role of policies within a children and/or young people's setting

A policy is a guide to how practitioners intend to work with children and young people. It is a guide to good practice so that you can ensure that each child is safe and given the best in care and education. Policies are also a way of achieving consistent standards in the workplace. There is a range of policies that may be required by legislation and available for all stakeholders to read.

In this section you will find out how to:

- differentiate between the role of policies and the role of procedures in the workplace
- explain the purpose of policies when working with children and young people.

Key term

Stakeholder – someone who has an interest or is involved in the workplace. This could refer to parents, teachers, early years practitioners, governors and multi-agency practitioners.

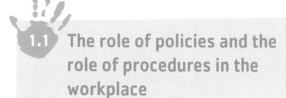

1.1 The role of policies and the role of procedures in the workplace

A policy in any setting will regulate the way you work and lay out clear aims and expectations as to how you will work. A policy will contain:

- a title
- a date of implementation and a review date
- clear aims
- an insight into what the management or organisation believes is important
- the role of the named stakeholders in implementing the policy.

It is important that any organisational policy is not changed when a new manager arrives but is part of a system of policy review.

A policy is a statement of what must happen and the procedures are the steps and sequences required to achieve the policy.

Table 2.1 outlines the differences between policies and procedures.

Table 2.1: *The differences between policies and procedures*

Policy	Procedure	Example
A policy can be open to interpretation or discretion.	A procedure is detailed and has clear steps to achieve the policy.	A policy about the late pick-up of children may not be clear until you read the steps which state how long you wait before phoning a parent who is late to pick up their child or who to contact if the parent is unavailable.
A policy is an essential part of defining the values of a setting.	A procedure is the tool to achieve these values.	A setting may have a dietary policy which shows that it values each child's needs. The procedures will show how these dietary needs are identified and ensure that the right food is given to children or young people with such needs – for example, ensuring a child who is coeliac has no gluten products.
A policy may be written by a manager and agreed by a group of people to ensure understanding and adherence by all staff members.	Procedures should be written by adults who are practising with children and young people and understand their needs.	A policy relating to outdoor play may be led by a manager and their deputy and written by members of the setting who are working outdoors on a daily basis.

Table 2.1: *The differences between policies and procedures (continued)*

A policy controls the way adults work and behave.	A procedure outlines the details as to how they will behave in the work setting.	A policy may include a professional dress code which will indicate that a certain style of dress is required. The procedures will detail what you are required to wear in the setting, for example, smart trousers or low-heeled shoes.
A policy outlines the systems of a setting.	A procedure details the ways in which the system will be met.	Any setting will have an emergency evacuation policy. The procedures will show how adults and children are expected to leave the building, for example, by using the nearest fire exit and taking two children at a time down the fire escape.

A policy is part of the strategy of any setting that you will work in. However, you will discover that the procedures are more flexible and may change more often due to:

- a change of environment
- a change of personnel
- an advancement in technology.

Case study: reviewing policies and procedures

At Bronwen Children's Centre, Fatima, who was responsible for operations, needed to lead a review on the emergency evacuation policy and procedures. This was prompted by some building work for a new under-3s facility on the original meeting point, which was displayed on a plan for all adults and children in case of an emergency. She met with the manager, Lou, and the three room leaders, Jess, Catherine and Jamie. They reviewed the policy and felt that the intentions were clear. They also agreed to install a computerised fire board which indicated where a fire might be located. A member of their team, who had been an incident controller, had left.

1 Are there any changes that will affect the Bronwen Children's Centre emergency evacuation policy statement?

2 Can you think of any changes that will be made to the procedures?

A good policy will ensure that you know what your role entails in implementing the policy and what the consequences are if you do not follow the required procedures.

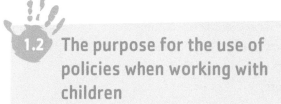

1.2 The purpose for the use of policies when working with children

Policies and procedures are in place to ensure that your setting runs in the best way to meet the needs of each child. If policies are clearly defined then they will be understood by you and all the adults who are responsible for working with the children in your setting.

Reflect

Consider the range of adults who work with children in your setting or one you have experienced.

- With which adults should a policy relating to managing children's behaviour be shared?
- How would you ensure that they had read and understood the policy?

Figure 2.1 shows how a set of clearly defined policies and procedures will benefit any workplace environment with children.

Figure 2.1: *Benefits of clearly defined policies and procedures*

The main purpose of policies and procedures is to ensure that children are safe, healthy and have the best possible learning opportunities.

Even the policies that relate to adults will ensure that the children have the best possible care and education because they impose professional expectations and guidance on those who look after them.

There will be guidelines relating to:

- children and young people and their parents
- adults working with the children and young people.

Find out

Ask if your setting has the policies and procedures that relate to your work with children in one document. Take time to look at the range of policies. Which of the policies do you think should be shared with the parents? Find out if the setting has a procedure for doing this.

Where appropriate, you should make children and young people aware of the policies that relate directly to them. You may be able to share a policy with older children and young people but it may be that you find other ways to ensure that young children are aware of some of the policies that are there for their best interests. Consider the examples below.

Behaviour policy in a reception class

The teacher and practitioners in the class could create an agreed set of rules that show the ethos of the policy, perhaps reflecting respect for each other. The children could add their marks to the agreement. It could then be laminated and placed in the classroom at the children's level. Attention could be drawn to it in different ways on a regular basis, perhaps in circle time or when managing a specific behavioural issue.

Child protection policy in an out-of-school club for young people

The young people could be made aware of the policy, perhaps via a workshop or a booklet informing them how to keep themselves safe, and that they have a right to feel safe or to tell anybody if they are worried. The people who they could talk to could also be identified and they could meet them in one of the sessions.

Outdoor learning policy in a reception class

If there are guidelines on how items should be used, such as in an exploring or design and technology area, or how many children can be in an outside area, then these can be shared with children during circle time or by displaying photographic instructions.

The policies in this setting make sure the adults can support the children's learning outdoors and know how to keep them safe.

Assessment activity 1.1, 1.2

Choose one of the policies in your setting. It could be the:

- behaviour policy
- learning and teaching policy
- safeguarding children policy.

1 Read the policy and highlight the difference between the aims of the policy and the procedures.

2 Briefly describe ways in which you could ensure that this policy underpins the relevant practice of all the adults working with the children and young people.

3 List the ways in which you think the outcomes for children and young people will improve as a result of effective implementation of this policy.

4 Describe an activity that you could carry out with a group of children to help them to understand an aspect of the policy.

2 Understand the requirements which underpin a policy

Policies are not usually written without some form of requirement by the legislative bodies which monitor the standards of care and education for children. In this section you will learn about:

- the relevance of policy development relating to a range of issues to include legislation, assisting **service users** and staff, informing practice, costs of policy implementation, resources needed to implement policies, monitoring policy implementation
- how policy implementation impacts on the service users, the staff, the community and other stakeholders.

Key terms

Service users – sometimes used to refer to those children and young people who the workplace supports in their care/learning.

Ofsted – Office for Standards in Education, Children's Services and Skills.

2.1 Relevant factors in policy development

Legislation

Any workplace will be inspected by legislative bodies such as **Ofsted** which will require a range of policies and procedures to be in place. This will form part of their inspection when inspectors visit the premises. They will find out if the policies are in place and if the procedures to implement them are effective by:

- asking to see the written policies
- seeing evidence of the procedures
- asking staff if they are aware of and understand the policies and procedures
- asking parents if they are aware of the policies and procedures relating to them
- finding evidence that the policies are shared in an accessible place such as in a handbook or on a website
- seeing evidence of a policy review schedule.

In England, Scotland, Wales and Northern Ireland there are government offices which inspect settings for children and young people to ensure that they are working within legislative requirements. If you work in one of these countries you will need to know what the legal requirements are to make sure that both you and the children have the best possible outcomes.

England

Ofsted regulates and inspects settings so that they achieve excellence in the care of children and young people, and in education and skills for learners of all ages.

Ofsted follows legislation to regulate and inspect:

- childcare and children's social care
- Children and Family Court Advisory Support Service (Cafcass)
- schools
- colleges
- initial teacher training settings
- work-based learning and skills training
- adult and community learning
- education and training in prisons and other secure establishments
- council children's services
- services for looked-after children, safeguarding and child protection.

Scotland

In Scotland most of the inspection of settings involving children and young people is carried out by HM Inspectorate for Education (HMIE). Inspection covers a range of sectors including:

- stand-alone pre-school centres
- primary schools, including those with nursery classes
- secondary schools, including community-based learning and development (CLD) as part of secondary, and aspects of transition
- special schools
- independent and all-through schools (schools for children aged 3 to 19).

Northern Ireland

The Education and Training Inspectorate for Northern Ireland (ETI) is responsible for inspecting and ensuring that the following areas of provision meet legislative requirements:

- alternative education provision
- Department of Culture, Arts and Leisure
- further education
- higher education/initial teacher education
- post-primary
- pre-school
- primary education
- special education
- work-based learning
- youth settings.

Wales

In Wales the inspectorate, Estyn, works within the School Effectiveness Framework (SEF) which is a key policy for education reform and the one to which all other education policies are aligned.

Estyn is the office of Her Majesty's Inspectorate for Education and Training in Wales. Estyn is responsible for inspecting and ensuring that the following settings in Wales work within legislative requirements:

- nursery schools and settings that are maintained by, or receive funding from, local authorities (LAs)
- primary schools
- secondary schools
- special schools
- pupil referral units
- independent schools
- further education
- adult community-based learning
- youth support services
- local authority education services
- teacher education and training
- work-based learning
- careers companies
- offender learning.

Find out

You can find out more about the inspectorates in England, Scotland, Wales and Northern Ireland by visiting their websites. You can find details of their websites in the Useful websites section at the end of this unit on page 73.

There is a range of legislation that settings must consider and which will influence the policies that are created. **Table 2.2** shows key legislation that influences the policies you will come across when working with children and young people.

Table 2.2: *Relevant legislation to policies*

Key legislation	Details
United Nations Convention on the Rights of the Child, 1989	This has been signed by many countries, including the United Kingdom, and ensures that children and young people under 18 have their own special rights. It is divided into articles. Our key policies stem from the UNCRC.
Every Child Matters, 2004	Although this is no longer compulsory, many settings still use this guidance. Every Child Matters has five outcomes: • Be healthy • Make a positive contribution • Stay safe • Achieve economic well-being • Enjoy and achieve These were to be achieved across children and young people's services. It is now referred to as 'Helping children to achieve more'.
Human Rights Act, 1998	This was not specifically designed to protect children but means that they have the same rights as adults. The rights of parents and children are respected. The government is considering reviewing this act.
Children Act, 2004	This Act is dedicated to improving the Every Child Matters outcomes for pre-school children, childcare for working parents and parental information services.
Equality Act, 2006	This Act enforces equality legislation upon age, disability, health, gender, race, religion or belief, sexual orientation and transgender status.
Race Relations Act, 2000	This Act relates to the way children and parents are supported equally whatever their race or religion.
Equality Act, 2010	This Act ensures equality in employment and education. The Equality Act replaced most of the Disability Discrimination Act (DDA). However, the Disability Equality Duty in the DDA continues to apply.
Special Educational Needs and Disability Act, 2001	This means that children and young people have a right to inclusive education and that premises need to be reasonably adjusted to accommodate a child or young person with specific needs. Changes are being made to some of the wording to this document by the government legislative team.
Protection of Children Act, 1999	This Act set up a register of names of people who are unsuitable to work with children. Anyone working with children has to be vetted by the Criminal Records Bureau (CRB).
Safeguarding Vulnerable Groups Act, 2006	All people working with adults and volunteers, children and vulnerable people are screened. Vulnerable adults include those with learning difficulties.
Childcare Act, 2006	This enforces the welfare requirements for children and the Early Years Foundation Stage (EYFS).

Acts which protect you as someone working with children and young people include the:

- Health and Safety at Work Act
- Control of Substances Hazardous to Health Regulations (COSHH)
- Manual Handling Operations Regulations
- Health and Safety (First Aid) Regulations
- Sex Discrimination Act
- Race Relations Act
- Disability Discrimination Act
- Data Protection Act
- National Minimum Wage Act.

Find out

With many countries around the world now celebrating Universal Children's Day, Ofsted explains how the United Nations Convention on the Rights of the Child is helping to ensure that some of our most vulnerable children and young people are being given a voice. Find out more about this important part of our legislative history for children by visiting the UNICEF website.

The EYFS

The revised EYFS framework sets standards for all early years settings and requires a range of policies in:

- children's learning and development
- safeguarding and welfare requirements.

The policies cover:

- special educational needs
- safeguarding children
- procedures to be followed if an allegation of child abuse is made against a member of staff
- non-collection of children
- behaviour management
- confidentiality
- working in partnership with parents and carers
- accidents and emergencies
- medication and sickness
- intrusive medication
- students
- health and safety
- equality of opportunity

- lost/missing children
- existing injury form.

How the policy assists service users and staff

By having clear policies and procedures, the staff will have clear guidelines on how to work with children and young people to achieve the best possible outcomes.

Figure 2.2 demonstrates how polices can assist children, parents and staff.

Figure 2.2: How policies can assist children, parents and staff

How the policy will inform practice

Any policy will develop your practice in the workplace. The policies you read should be clear and concise and revised regularly to make sure they reflect best practice.

The right-hand notes in **Figure 2.3** indicate how you will act as a result of one policy.

Queen's Children's Centre Medicine Policy

Our statement of intent

With regard to managing medicines and medical procedures, all children have a right of admission to our centre and to be included as long as they are able to participate in our activities.

This policy relates to children with short-term, long-term or special medical conditions which need medication or treatment. We will try to support individual medical needs, ensuring that all regulatory and health requirements for both the child and staff are met.

Procedures

1 Procedures for children with long-term medical conditions

We will draw up a care plan, in consultation with parents and health professionals where appropriate, for children with long-term medical conditions who need continuous medication, medical treatment or a special diet because of:

> *You must produce a care plan*

- allergies
- epilepsy
- asthma
- diabetes.

Each care plan contains:

- the child's name
- details of the condition
- special requirements e.g. dietary needs
- medication needs (stating possible side effects of medication)
- emergency symptoms
- what to do in an emergency
- who to contact in an emergency
- the role of staff members.

> *You must ensure that all these points are included in a care plan*

The care plan will be signed by the child's parent/carer.

> *You must always get the plan signed by the parent or carer*

Our staff will be given special training in the administration of medicines or medical treatment. Training must be given by a health professional and confirmation of competency to carry out any procedure must be signed by the health professional.

> *You cannot administer long-term medication without training*

Care plans and medical records will be securely stored as stated in the 1998 Data Protection Act. All records should be accessible to all staff caring for the child.

> *You must store medical records securely, where staff are able to access them*

2 Procedures for children with short-term medical conditions

Children well enough to attend the centre may still need medication, such as antibiotics, for a short period. A medicine form will be completed by the parent/carer.

- The parent/carer must sign the authorisation.
- The staff must sign when they have administered the medicine, noting the time given.
- The parent/carer must sign that they know that the medicine has been given.
- Prescribed medicines must be in their original container, labelled clearly with the child's name, name of the medicine and the required dosage.
- Non-prescription medicines such as Calpol may be administered when there is a health reason to do so at the discretion of the setting manager and if agreed by the parents/carer.

> *Permission from a parent or carer is needed for the setting manager to administer Calpol*

- Non-prescription medicines must be in the original container, clearly labelled with the child's name, and the dosage required.
- A medicine form must be completed as for prescribed medicines.
- A reminder such as a timer can be used to remind staff members of the time a medicine needs to be given.

> *You should always use a medicine form with prescription medicines*

3 Procedures for storage of medicines

- Medicines must be locked and stored securely out of the reach of children.
- Medicines to be kept in the fridge must be kept in a clearly labelled plastic container.
- Staff must keep any personal medication, that they have to have at work, securely and inaccessible to the children.
- For off-site activities adults may carry a child's asthma inhaler on their person and must ensure that these inhalers are kept away from other children.

> *The timing for administering medicines is important*

> *Medicines must be kept out of reach of children*

Figure 2.3: *A children's centre medicine policy and what it means for practitioners*

Policies will help you to understand what is acceptable in your practice – for example, how to administer medicine as outlined in the Queen's Children's Centre Medication Policy. You can know what your role is and how decisions are made, for example, where to store medicine. If you read the procedure of a policy you will know what to do, for example, how to ensure you give medicine at the correct time. If a policy is easy to follow and understand, and contains all the necessary information, including legal obligations to your setting, then your practice will be informed. The expectations and boundaries detailed will help you to achieve the best for all children and young people. If a procedure is discussed and practised regularly, each step will be achievable and will progress towards the expected outcome.

Reflect

Read a policy from your workplace and consider how it will help you to understand what to do to support a child or group of children.

Costs that may be involved in implementing the policy

All local authorities will give guidance on writing policies that will not incur costs. However, when implementing a policy, there could be extra costings to ensure that the policy can be carried out. The costs could be:

- equipment, for example, extra signage for emergency exits to comply with regulations
- extra staff to go on outings to ensure ratios are met
- a stipend for a special educational needs coordinator (SENCO) to implement a special educational needs policy
- payment for CRB checks to ensure that everyone coming into the setting is suitable

- training for staff in policy areas such as behaviour management
- first aid training so that every member of staff has paediatric first aid training.

Case study: finding funding

It was agreed that a behaviour policy needed to be created for JC Youth Club. With the help of an adviser, the manager, Ted, drew up a policy with members of his team.

Two of the team were worried that they found it difficult to manage behaviour without getting frustrated on occasions. Some of the young people who attended the club were challenging to say the least. The adviser identified a two-day behaviour management course which focused on positive reinforcement in managing young people's behaviour. Ted managed to get some funding from the local authority for the course and JC Youth Club funded the remainder out of their budget.

1 Discuss with a partner whether you think the cost of the course was worth it in implementing the policy.

2 Consider how settings could seek funding for any cost that might arise from implementing legally required (statutory) policies.

Resources needed to implement the policy

As discussed, a policy may need financial resources so that the best possible outcomes for the children and young people are ensured. Other resources could involve:

- time for a working party to research and create a policy
- meetings to explain and share the policy
- a change to the environment to accommodate a policy, for example, a nappy changing area that is moved from a prominent place to somewhere more discrete
- a checklist that may have to be created to ensure better health and safety procedures

- appointments of specific people such as a designated safeguarding staff member
- a new staff handbook to ensure all staff are inducted more effectively
- workplace training to develop the knowledge needed in a policy such as an assessment policy.

So what does this mean?

Listed below are the resources that could be needed to create an effective outdoor health and safety policy:

- a staff member to check the outdoors every day
- an effective checklist of equipment to use
- someone to manage any issues that might arise from a daily check
- time for a group to create a policy
- visual reminders for the children such as the numbers allowed on a slide
- appropriately staffed areas to maintain required legislative adult-to-child ratios.

Find out

Review the EYFS revised framework and find out what it advises about the safeguarding and welfare requirements.

Monitoring policy implementation

Once a policy is in place and being used, it is easy to forget about it and leave it in a handbook that is rarely used or on a beautiful website for prospective parents. Writing the policy is the first step but ensuring that it is implemented is more challenging.

It may be that the group writing the policy is responsible for ensuring it is implemented effectively through:

- regular review items on an agenda
- specific observations relating to the implementation
- continuing professional development that arises from implementation
- continually monitoring any systems such as observations, planning or assessment that relate to implementation
- surveys and feedback from service users such as parents
- inspections
- auditing of the workplace.

You can also ensure a policy is implemented by being reflective and thinking about how effectively you implement the procedures from a policy, for example, changing a nappy effectively. You might even ask your supervisor to observe you in relation to a workplace procedure you are following.

2.2 The impact of policies

Service users

Two of the main sets of people who will be affected by any policy will be:

- the children and young people
- their parents/carers.

Table 2.3 on the following page includes ways to ensure you find out the service users' views and understanding of policies and how you measure the expected outcomes of the policy.

Table 2.3: *Ensuring that policies have the best impact on outcomes for children and young people*

Policy example	Examples of impact upon children and young people	Examples of impact upon parents/carers
Safeguarding policy	• Develops more effective screening of visitors through policies • Includes children and young people in procedures by ensuring they can find ways to feel safe or report any concerns about their safety	• Gives confidence to parents that children are cared for • Ensures parents in vulnerable situations have a framework of support • Parents may have to receive checks if volunteering in school
Key person policy	• More continuity and quality of care for children and young people because of communication between home and school • Transition from home to school should be smoother for young children • Individual needs will be met • Child less likely to have long-term separation issues if key worker policy and procedures are understood and implemented	• Will be less likely to feel anxious about separation • Will feel respected if views and experiences as a parent are considered • Individual needs should be met • Will have more relevant knowledge about their child's day in the setting
Assessment policy	• Children and young people should be consulted about targets set as a result of observation as appropriate to age/stage of development • Will be encouraged to be involved in their learning through appropriate consultation during observations and assessment • Quality and level of learning should be appropriate and relevant to their needs	• Will have clear evidence of their child's stage of learning • Should be able to contribute to the assessment process by giving information about their child at home • Will have clear guidance as to how they can be involved in the expectations of any targets set
Behaviour management policy	• Consult with children and young people on ideas for behaviour expectations via activities such as student councils • Shared behavioural expectations such as classroom targets can be shared and created with children and young people • They will be clear about what is expected • They will feel respected because of positive behaviour reinforcement • They will experience a consistent approach in managing their behaviour	• Parents will have a clear understanding of the expected behaviour for their child in the setting • Parents will feel that they can seek advice from the setting about any behavioural concerns • They will be encouraged to share the same values at home so that their child experiences some consistency • Confidentiality will be maintained when the setting is managing any behavioural issues

Staff

The implementation of any policy will impact upon the staff in a setting: a policy is a set of principles that will help to define the values of the setting and it will also give very clear expectations as to how the staff should be practising.

A well-implemented policy should ensure that each member of staff is clear about their role in making the policy work effectively in a range of circumstances. If introduced carefully and with clarity, a policy should ensure that each member of staff understands:

• any legal or statutory requirements behind the policy, for example, CRB checking
• that the policy will ensure consistency in the setting, for example, wearing latex gloves when cleaning a bleeding wound
• that they are able to ask any questions they may have about the policy such as clarification of terminology

- any issues arising from poor practice when implementing the policy will be managed fairly
- that they are contributing to a professional approach in looking after children
- that they will receive any continuing professional development required as part of the policy implementation, for example, paediatric first aid training
- any requirements, for example, working with other agencies that may be advised in a SEN policy
- how a policy might replace or relate to an existing policy.

Review **Figure 2.4** to see the practical impact on your time as a member of staff involved in the implementation of a policy.

involvement in a working party to set up or review implementation

attending team meetings to consider how policy will be implemented

attending training

reading a policy

Why implementing a policy can impact a practitioner's time

researching statutory requirements such as ratio requirements in EYFS

helping to cascade to parents

changing any aspect of the environment to support policy implementation

ensuring a colleague is aware of newly implemented policy in induction

changing practice such as completing daily safety checklists

Figure 2.4: *The impact of being involved in the implementation of a policy on a practitioner's time*

Community

Any policies will affect the group of people who are directly involved in the community, such as:

- children and young people
- parents/carers

- other professionals
- governors
- practitioners
- workers such as administration staff or chefs
- the wider community which may include people living nearby.

There is much evidence to show that centres whose policies reach out to the community and support all families will improve:

- educational attainment in the long term through policies such as behaviour or inclusion policies
- children's chances by working with parents guided by partnership with parents policies.

You should also consider the fact that:

- policies on integrated services in children's centres can impact on educational attainment in primary schools
- a policy for extended schools can have a positive effect for disadvantaged children and young people
- an EYFS policy which encourages high-quality early years experiences can support better social development
- a children's centre with an effective equal opportunities policy will ensure a cohesive community offering opportunities for a diverse range of people within it.

Other stakeholders

The groups listed below may be made up of other people who are impacted by policies in children and young people's settings. In different ways such groups can help to review procedures, share practice, plan collaboratively and formulate strategies to ensure policies are effectively implemented.

Groups could include:

- health care professionals
- governors
- volunteers
- administrators.

Collaboration among stakeholders will be important when implementing policies that promote the best care, education and resources needed.

Assessment activity 2.1, 2.2

Imagine you are the manager of a children's centre in an urban setting. Prepare information for a group of governors about an outdoor learning policy that you want to develop for the children's centre. In no more than 250 words, outline:

- the reason for the policy
- the legislation that underpins the need for the policy
- who will be impacted by the policy in the community
- any cost of implementing the policy relating to staffing and resources
- how the policy will need to be monitored.

3 Understand how to develop a policy for a real work environment caring for children and/or young people

In this section you will:
- explain what needs to be considered when developing a policy
- explain a system for monitoring, evaluating and reviewing policy.

3.1 Considerations when developing a policy

Several issues must be considered when developing a policy to ensure that everyone can clearly understand it.

Language level

A policy does not have to be complicated and it is important to consider the target audience when it is being created. It must be clear, easy to follow and understand, and contain all the necessary information, including the legal obligations of your setting and practice.

Therefore the language should be:
- clear
- concise

- explained, for example, the use of abbreviations
- objective.

Consider the extracts from two policies below.

Sample 1

It is the best intention of our Halldace Children's centre to ensure a range of effective communication that will ensure a cohesive collaboration between all stakeholders working in the interest of all the children therein.

Sample 2

At Halldace Children's Centre we aim to communicate effectively with parents, carers and other key people involved in the care of the children, such as health professionals, so that we can work together to gain the best outcomes for our children.

You will notice that Sample 1 has some complicated words and phrases that may need some explanation. This could easily deter parents or carers from reading or understanding the policy any further. They could also feel that policies are not really for them to understand.

However, Sample 2 is clearer and more user-friendly. The one sentence clearly tells us that:

- the aim of Halldace Children's centre is to communicate effectively
- the centre wishes to communicate with parents, carers and other key people, giving an example of health professionals
- they want to get the best outcomes for the children in the centre by working effectively.

So using clear language in a written policy will:

- ensure continuity of information given to employees and service users
- mean less chance of misinterpretation
- set clear expectations and boundaries
- often bring greater compliance than verbal information.

It is also important to consider parents and carers whose first language may not be English. A policy may need to be written in other languages so that it can be clearly understood by everyone.

Case study: making a policy

In a primary school, in an urban setting, where many of the parents spoke Urdu, the head teacher, May Donahue, was concerned that the homework policy would not be understood by many of the parents. She contacted a local community project that offered to translate school documents and to translate at any meetings for Urdu-speaking parents. May decided to have the policy translated into Urdu and to offer to meet any parents who wanted her to explain it. She was concerned that some children were spending far too long on their homework and she wanted to encourage parents to stop them after a certain time.

1 How do you think that translating the homework policy into Urdu would impact upon the children?

2 Why do you think it was important for May to consider meeting the parents with an interpreter?

Aim and rationale

Every policy should have an aim and a rationale so that everyone involved will understand the reason for the policy and who it is for.

Key terms

Aim – the reason for doing something.

Rationale – explains why something is being done.

The aim of a policy for children should be a brief statement of 'what' the policy is intended to accomplish. This should only be one or two sentences describing the general intent with respect to the specific topic of the policy. The policy statement should be general enough to provide some flexibility in implementation and to allow periodic changes as it is reviewed.

The rationale or purpose statement explains 'why' the policy is being written.

The rationale may also contain or refer to:

- background materials
- explanatory details regarding educational, environmental, legal, regulatory or other factors that led to the development of the policy.

Consider the examples of some aims and rationales of policies below.

Foundation Stage settling-in policy

Aim

We aim to make the setting a welcoming place where children settle comfortably. We will consider the individual needs of children and their families.

Rationale

We have developed this policy because we want children to feel safe, stimulated and happy in our early years department and to feel secure and comfortable with our teachers. We also want parents to have confidence both in their children's emotional well-being and to be active partners with settling-in and developing their children's learning. This policy acknowledges the overarching principle of positive relationships as required in the EYFS revised framework 2012.

CP2

A Special Educational Needs Policy for Young People

Aim

Our aim is to ensure that every young person in our school has fair access to the curriculum, is included in mainstream learning, is supported fairly and without discrimination.

Rationale

This policy has been developed in accordance with the Special Educational Needs and Disability Act 2001. It has been created to support young people with special educational needs, and their parents, and to outline the ways we will support young people's assessment and learning in our school.

What can and cannot be done

You will have already understood that a policy should emphasise the philosophy of the setting and the legal requirements. It is also critical that as many people as possible feel ownership of the policy by being involved in creating it or being given the time to read and question the contents.

So what does this mean?

When writing a policy:

- keep it as short and clear as possible
- set out the procedures in a clear and simple way
- if necessary, support the policy with cross references to sources of additional information such as a SEN handbook or other policies
- ensure that the format is suitable
- identify any training needs to implement the policy
- consider how easy the document is to understand
- consider how will you share it.

What you should *not* do when writing a policy is to create something that you have copied from another setting. While policies will often have clear guidelines from a local authority, each setting is unique and this must be reflected in the documentation.

For example, in the guidance to creating a 'working in partnership with parents' policy, a local authority

may offer advice on how you will:

- develop good relationships with parents and carers
- share appropriate information
- ensure parents and carers feel welcome at your setting
- consult with parents and make sure that you respond positively to their requirements
- ensure that parents keep you up to date with any changes regarding their child that may have an effect on the child's well-being and guide them to the people they should communicate with in the setting. For example, this could refer to a recently developed allergy or medical need.

Time constraints

When developing a policy for children, any time constraints will have to be considered carefully. Look at **Figure 2.5** for some examples of what these constraints might be.

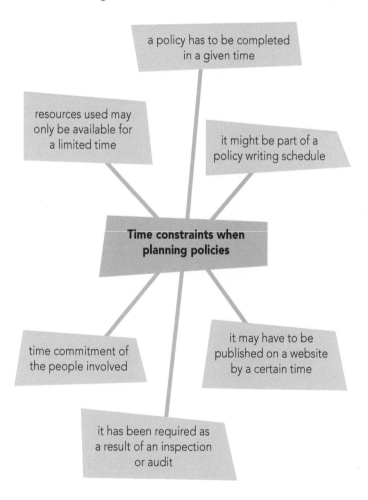

a policy has to be completed in a given time

resources used may only be available for a limited time

it might be part of a policy writing schedule

Time constraints when planning policies

time commitment of the people involved

it may have to be published on a website by a certain time

it has been required as a result of an inspection or audit

Figure 2.5: *Time constraints when planning policies*

Any exemptions to the policy

It is very important that parents sign policies to acknowledge they have read and understood the implications of a policy. Occasionally there may be a parent or practitioner who requires an exemption to a policy and is unable to sign it. This could be on the grounds of religion or belief. An example could be a parent who does not want their child to take part in a particular curriculum activity. If the policy has a statutory requirement then the parent may have to appeal to:

- the head of the setting
- a governing body
- a representative from a local authority.

Policies might also have exemption clauses.

Find out

How might the following parents want an exemption to a policy?

- A Hindu parent reading a policy on no jewellery for children
- A Jehovah's Witness parent reading a first aid policy

Might any requests result in an exemption clause being added to a policy?

Person responsible for implementation

Several people may be involved in implementing a policy, including:

- the governing body or trustees
- a head teacher, manager or leader
- a designated working party
- a specialist such as a SENCO.

The people responsible for ensuring a policy is implemented should have clear guidelines, a time frame for implementation and review, and a clear remit to share the policy with the stakeholders involved.

To ensure the policy is implemented, consideration should be given to:

- a way of launching and sharing the policy, for example, a meeting
- where it is to be available, for example, on a website or in a handbook
- how it will be shared with the children involved
- how practice is expected to reflect the policy.

Find out

A good job description should contain a reference to the employee's responsibility for implementing the policies and procedures of the setting. The role of a line manager is then to ensure that the employee understands how to follow the procedures of the policy.

Consider ways in which you would want support to implement a missing child policy in your workplace. What do you think you would need to know to implement this policy effectively? (If you are working in a setting following the EYFS you are required by Ofsted to have a missing child policy.)

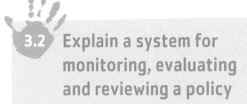

3.2 Explain a system for monitoring, evaluating and reviewing a policy

Every workplace setting must have ways of checking whether or not their policies are effective.

- To monitor a policy is to see how effectively the procedures are working in the setting.
- To review the policy is to look at the written policy and see if it needs to be changed in any way. This could be because of statutory requirements or even changes to the setting.

Consider **Table 2.4** on the following page to find out how a policy is monitored.

Table 2.4: *How a policy can be monitored in the workplace*

Stage	Who is responsible	How
Monitoring policy To ensure that the policy and procedures remain effective and that strategies meet the overall aims of the workplace	• Managers • Designated person • Governors	• Observe practice • Link to performance management targets • Send out questionnaires to staff • Send out questionnaires to parents • Talk to children • Review planning
Reviewing policy Policies should support good practice and enable all staff to implement them. They should be regularly reviewed to fit in with the needs of a workplace setting	• Managers • Designated person • Governors	• Create a programme of review • Consider the evolving needs of the setting • Be flexible as things can change such as personnel or new legislation • Review the format with regards to clarity (perhaps it needs to be more user-friendly) • Consult with parents, carrying out any other monitoring or evidence of training that has taken place
Evaluating policy Policies should be evaluated to find out if they have had an effective impact on the outcomes for children	• Managers • Designated person • Governors	• Observe children • Audit the environment • Reflect upon practice • Send out questionnaires to parents/carers • Talk to service users

When a policy has been created it is easy to place it in a handbook or on a website and think that the work has been done. However, a policy should be a live, flexible document which is shared by everyone so that it becomes a basis for the practice of the setting involved.

Assessment activity 3.1, 3.2

You have been asked to lead a small group which is writing a policy for the late collection of children at a pre-school playgroup. Write some guidance for the group as to how the policy should be written. In your guidance, explain why the following need to be considered:

• plans for developing the policy
• who the policy is for
• how to write clear aims and a rationale for the policy
• how to write clear procedures and what they should consider
• any time constraints such as a completion date or time allocation for the group
• the expectations of people responsible for, and involved in, implementing the policy
• how the policy will be shared
• how the policy will be evaluated, reviewed and monitored.

4 Understand how to implement a policy in a real work environment caring for children and/or young people

4.1 Communicating the use of policies within the real work environment

In this section you will learn about communicating new or revised policies to:

- staff
- stakeholders
- service users.

Communicating to staff

All new staff in a setting must be made aware of policies and procedures but this can be a daunting process to absorb. These procedures are usually available in a staff handbook and should be shared during an induction process.

When you are inducted into a new setting you should expect the following support to help you understand the importance of the policies and procedures.

- Policies and procedures are introduced over an induction period of three months or more.
- The essential policies are considered first such as those relating to the health and safety of each child – for example, the medicine policy to ensure that from your first day you understand how to support children who are taking medication.
- You are given time to read any policy and encouraged to ask questions about it.
- The steps in procedures and intended outcomes should be clearly explained. For example, you always have to wear disposable latex gloves when managing an accident involving blood in case of cross-infection.

- You should be given an explanation of your role in supporting the policy, for example, using positive reinforcement when managing a child's behaviour.
- You should be given the name of any specific person you should communicate with in connection with the procedures for a policy, for example, a designated staff member (DSM) for a child protection issue.
- You should receive any training that is required, for example, basic safeguarding training.

Every adult working with children and young people should have basic safeguarding training as part of the safeguarding policy requirement.

Below are some of the policies that Ofsted will expect you to be familiar with and use as a basis for your practice.

- Safeguarding children and young people
- Safe recruitment
- Suitable premises
- Storage of documents
- Complaints
- Equipment
- Hygiene and cleanliness
- Involving and consulting with children
- Missing child
- Staff deployment and development
- Working with other agencies
- Behaviour management
- Food and drink
- Illness and injuries
- Sick children
- Staff recruitment, induction and training
- Uncollected child
- Care, learning and play
- Equality of opportunities and diversity
- Health and safety
- Individual and special educational needs
- Medicines
- Outings and visits
- Smoking, drugs and alcohol
- Suitable people
- Working in partnership with parents and carers

There are times when procedures are changed and this should always be communicated to staff through training or meetings. An email is not enough and can be missed easily.

Ideally, a revised procedure, such as an emergency evacuation, should be practised regularly to ensure that each step is achievable.

The governing body of any setting has responsibility for the statutory requirements of policies. Revised policies may not always be communicated by the leader of a setting but by a group of designated staff members who have been asked to revise a policy.

Case study: embracing revised policies

At Thames Road, a small primary school, the governing body was considering the policy review schedule. The governors discussed how the school behaviour management policy could be reviewed. One of the teachers, Jerry, had expressed an interest in behaviour management. The governors decided to ask her to lead a working party to review the policy. She did this over a two-month period, consulting with colleagues, parents, governors and children. As a result the policy was rewritten and translated into Korean as the school had a large Korean-speaking community. After it had been approved, the governors asked Jerry to introduce the policy to the community via a presentation and by placing it on the school website.

1 How could Jerry present the revised policy to ensure that it became a part of the behaviour management culture of the school?

2 Can you think of any needs that might arise from the new policy regarding continuing personal development (CPD)?

It is also important to consider the needs of staff when communicating any new or revised policy. These needs could be:

- a translated policy if English is an additional language for any of the staff
- someone to read the policy with a member of staff because of needs such as dyslexia
- individual presentations to enable less confident staff to ask questions.

Communicating to stakeholders

Many of the ways that a policy is shared with staff can be used to ensure that other stakeholders such as:

- parents
- governors
- early years practitioners/administration staff
- other professionals such as speech and language therapists or social workers

understand the policy and how to follow the relevant procedures.

Consider how areas of a new safeguarding policy could be communicated to stakeholders.

- **The governing body of the workplace setting** must ensure that it agrees upon the importance of this policy and the emphasis to stakeholders that they are complying with required legislation.
- **A governor or designated staff member** must be highlighted to stakeholders as part of the policy.
- **Procedures for safeguarding** must be highlighted through staff meetings, individual meetings and parent meetings.
- **Safe recruitment and screening procedures** must be outlined with regard to recruitment procedures and checking on staff.
- **Other agencies** must be clear about how they will be communicated with in case of any concerns.
- **Sufficient resources and time** must be allocated to enable the designated person and other staff to inform stakeholders of the policy.
- **All stakeholders** should be informed that they are able to raise concerns about poor or unsafe practice with regard to children and young people.
- **Other policies** relating to this should be highlighted, for example, a whistle-blowing policy.
- **Lines of disclosure** should be highlighted, for example, cases could be reported to the Secretary of State in extreme cases.
- **Storage of documents** must be secure and confidential.

Key term

Whistle-blowing policy – highlights how issues regarding child protection can be disclosed in a work setting.

This policy could be communicated through the website, meetings, hard copies, handbooks and inductions. The new or updated policy would need to be reviewed and updated annually and must be made available to any stakeholder on request.

Communicating to service users

Children should be made aware of new policies where relevant. For young people the workplace setting might be able to share new or updated policies or aspects of them, for example:

- ensuring they challenge anybody who does not have official identification as part of a health and safety policy
- making agreed rules for a setting as part of a behaviour management policy
- understanding the requirements of a homework policy.

Reflect

Consider the following areas of best practice when making children and young people aware of a new or revised policy.

- What do you hope to achieve through sharing part of the policy with them?
- How will you inform them via circle time, student council, etc.?
- How will you talk to children who may have additional needs such as English as an additional language?
- How will you consider their views and questions?
- How will you record what you have shared with them?
- Could you involve a child's key worker in any way?
- How will you encourage quieter or younger children to talk about their understanding of a policy?
- What do you hope to achieve by sharing the policy?

4.2 Different approaches to promoting the use of policies

The way that a policy can be promoted within a setting can be instructional or collaborative.

Instructional

This is where adults, children and young people are informed of a new or revised policy via:

- a handbook
- a document
- a website
- a notice board
- a communication book
- a meeting.

The advantages of this approach are that policies can be created quickly to meet any statutory or regulatory requirements. They could be clearly owned by the management or governing body.

The disadvantages of such an approach are that the policies may not be read carefully by people, understood or become a basis to the values and principles of any workplace setting.

Collaborative

This approach to policy sharing would ensure an understanding of the policy and procedures through:

- specific meetings
- discussion forums
- circle times or student councils
- review of implementation in staff performance management
- highlighting policies on websites and inviting online questions
- showing positive photographic evidence of policies around the setting
- ensuring various stakeholders and service users are involved in consultation, implementation and review
- holding meetings to respond to questionnaires relating to policies
- inviting specialist speakers to talk about areas relating to policies.

The advantages of this approach are that children, young people and adults are more likely to respect the policy because they have been involved in the process and feel that their opinions and concerns are valued. The values of the setting are more likely to be at the centre of the practice of the setting as ownership is felt by all stakeholders and service users.

The disadvantages are that this approach needs time and the skills of listening and communication.

4.3 Evaluating the implementation of policies

You will now understand that the governing body or management of each setting generally makes decisions about policies. Some of these are statutory and settings are legally required to have them, while others are important in the overall management and ethos of the particular school and its pupils. A new member of staff should be shown where policies are located and it is their responsibility to become familiar with them.

So what does this mean?

To find out how successful a policy has been, the people involved in its implementation should ask:

- What have been our successes this year?
- What are we trying to improve?
- How are we making sure that every child's needs are met?
- How are children and young people's health and safety supported?
- What has been done to review our policies?
- How can our service users and stakeholders access information about our policies?
- Do the policies satisfy legal requirements?
- Do the policies define the approach to the setting?
- Can the policies be understood by all members of the community?
- How does the induction programme introduce policies and procedures?
- Is there a way for service users or stakeholders to clarify an understanding of policies?
- Have training needs been identified in relation to policies?
- Are there any parent- or child-friendly versions of the policies?

Inspections by regulatory bodies such as Ofsted will help to ascertain if the practice in the setting reflects the policies and procedures that are required.

Find out

Find out how your workplace setting strives to ensure that the inspection standards required by Ofsted are met through working policies and procedures. You could do this by asking your mentor or supervisor about their approach to quality assurance and reflective practice.

An inspector will want to know if policies are designed to support good practice – and they will want to see evidence of this good practice. They will want to see a flexible programme of review which accommodates a change of circumstances or an introduction of new legislation. By observing practice, reviewing policies and talking to adults and children, an inspector will want to know:

- Is the policy clear, with appropriate aims and procedures?
- Has the policy been fully implemented?
- Are the procedures followed?
- Has the policy achieved its aims and does it ensure quality provision?
- Is it compatible with other policies in the setting?
- Does everyone involved in the setting understand the policy as appropriate?

If a setting regularly audits its policies, and involves all service users and stakeholders, then a dedication to improvement will enable everyone in the setting to:

- regularly review the way in which policies are implemented
- suggest changes that will improve practice
- follow statutory requirements
- ensure that the values and principles of working with children and young people are practised.

Assessment activity
4.1, 4.2, 4.3

On your own, or with a learning partner, create a brief presentation for a group of parents in a reception class about a new behaviour management policy. In your presentation consider:

- describing the reasons for the policy
- sharing the policy
- the values and principles behind the policy
- how it will be implemented
- how parents can reinforce the policy at home
- how it will support their children
- examples of how children will be involved in implementing the policy, such as classroom agreements
- how it will be shared in the community, monitored, reviewed and evaluated.

In your presentation you should consider using examples from the policy, brief statements, clear explanations, photographic evidence or media clips.

Analyse the effectiveness of this approach in providing parents with information. Consider other approaches you could use. Discuss how you would present this information to staff and stakeholders.

In the real world

In my day care nursery we had an Ofsted inspection which was deemed satisfactory. However, there were areas of provision that we needed to develop – for example, our relationships with children under 3.

After this inspection, one of our managers, Kirsty, went on a course about how we could self-evaluate our practice through something called auditing. Some of us were worried that it was going to be another inspection! However, Kirsty came back very excited and arranged for us all to be trained to self-evaluate our own practice and the whole environment through auditing. It was really inspiring and we used the results of our audit to highlight areas of practice that needed to be improved. It was probably no coincidence that these areas of development matched the areas of the inspection and this made us review our key person policy and the training we needed to implement this.

I am now doing an under-3s foundation degree. I am really pleased with the way our review of our relationships with the under-3s led to a valuable review of our policy and procedures for our key person system. I am really looking forward to our next Ofsted inspection to see how they think this area has developed.

Check your knowledge

1 What is a stakeholder?

2 Who might be service users?

3 What does Ofsted have to do with policy development?

4 Name two key pieces of legislation that have influenced the policies of working with children or young people.

5 Define an aim of a policy.

6 Describe the procedures of a policy.

7 List who might be responsible for implementing a policy in a work setting.

8 Name four policies that are required by Ofsted in a setting for young children.

9 Briefly describe two actions that could arise from reviewing a current policy.

10 List ways in which a new or revised policy could be effectively communicated to parents.

CACHE Extended Assessment

Theme: Professional principles underpinning practice in work with children and young people

Grading criterion

B3 Analyse aspects of your learning in your chosen theme that could improve your future practice

Carefully consider and analyse the professional principle of working with parents in relation to policy development. Choose a specific policy.

With this principle in mind analyse how you would involve parents in aspects of developing, implementing and monitoring a policy in your work place setting. Analyse the challenges that you might be presented with when involving parents in policy setting. Consider the following examples:

- parents living in a rural setting
- a parent whose main language is Urdu
- a working parent.

Identify ways of analysing the outcomes for children and young people if parents are involved in aspects of setting your chosen policy. It would be useful for you to read the Ofsted requirements for policies and procedures in children and young people's settings.

This is an example of how you might approach one criterion of your Extended Assessment. You must successfully complete all the criteria at each grade to achieve that grade. You will achieve the highest grade for which you have successfully completed all the criteria. For example, to achieve a B grade you will need to meet the requirements of the B1, B2 and B3 criteria, as well as C1, C2, C3 and D1 and D2.

When trying to understand the requirements for your Extended Assessment, it is always a good idea to talk to your tutors. Fellow learners and workplace colleagues are also useful sources of information.

Further references

The following are sources of useful information on the topic of understanding the role of policies in children and young people's settings.

Books and articles

Blandford, S. and Knowles, C. (2009) *Developing Professional Practice: 0–7*, Harlow: Longman

Tassoni, P. (2010) *Penny Tassoni's Continued Success with the EYFS*, Oxford: Heinemann

Government Acts

Care Standards Act (2000)

Children Act (2004)

Education and Inspection Act (2006)

Useful websites

To obtain a secure link to the websites below, visit www.pearsonhotlinks.co.uk and search for this book by using its title or ISBN. Click on the section for CP2.

Department for Education: Information about all aspects of children's services in England

Ofsted: Information about regulation and expected standards in England

UNICEF: Information about rights of children around the world

Foundation Years: Information about the Foundation Stage

ECERS UK: Information about auditing and self-evaluation of provision in the Foundation Stage

UK legislation website: Information about the legislation behind the policies and procedures for children and young people's care and education

Home Office: Information about legislation by the government

Nursery World: Extensive information about many issues in early years care and education

Website of the England inspectorate

Website of the Northern Ireland inspectorate

Website of the Scotland inspectorate

Website of the Wales inspectorate

Maintaining the health of children and/or young people

CP3

It is essential that childcare settings have clear policies in place to deal with ill health. These must be understood and implemented consistently by all those working in the setting. This unit deals with the important role of the practitioner in recognising and responding to ill health and in supporting and promoting the health of the children and young people in their care.

Learning outcomes

By the end of this unit you will:

1 Understand the importance of workplace policies and procedures when dealing with ill health in children and/or young people

2 Understand the role of the practitioner in supporting an unwell child and/or young person

3 Understand possible factors affecting health in children
and/or young people and how to promote health

4 Be able to support children and/or young people to improve their health

5 Understand how to respond to illness in children and/or young people

6 Understand how immunisation aims to prevent harmful diseases in children and young people.

In practice

Before Claire started her work experience in the nursery she knew about some of the common illnesses that young children contract as she had two younger brothers. During her first week her supervisor provided Claire with the nursery policy for dealing with ill health. She also explained the procedures which must be followed. Shortly after, when Claire was working with a group of children, Sam, aged 3 years, appeared listless and had a rash. Claire reported her concerns immediately to the first-aider who felt that because of his symptoms he needed immediate medical attention. While waiting for an ambulance Claire reassured Sam that his mum would be at the hospital to meet him. Claire was later praised for her actions by the head of the nursery.

By the end of this unit you will be able to recognise signs of ill health and be able to respond appropriately. You will also be aware of the factors that can affect children's health and the role of the practitioner in promoting a healthy lifestyle.

1 Understand the importance of workplace policies and procedures when dealing with ill health in children and/or young people

All childcare settings are required to have **policies** and **procedures** in place which provide guidance for practitioners on how to deal with the ill health of children or young people in the setting. While policies are unique to each setting they must meet the requirements of local and national legislation and guidelines for your home country. Early years and childcare settings are monitored by inspectorates for each home country. In England this is called Ofsted. During inspection, settings need to show how their policies and procedures work in practice to provide high-quality care and meet the health needs of children and/or young people. It is important that you obtain a copy of the policies and procedures for the setting where you are carrying out your work experience. You may find that in your own setting, policies and procedures for health are incorporated in a wider health and safety policy.

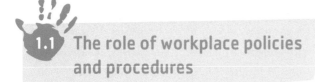

1.1 The role of workplace policies and procedures

Policies set out the principles and values held by an organisation. The policy must work to promote health and well-being, prevent the spread of infection and include procedures for practitioners to follow when children are unwell. Policies must also include a statement of how the setting will meet its goals in relation to maintaining the health of children and young people. Reviewing policies regularly ensures that they continue to be in line with current good practice. Procedures are there to guide staff on what to do in particular circumstances, providing a step-by-step approach to meeting the goals set out within

the policy. **Figure 3.1** shows a section from a nursery health policy, which explains the procedures nursery staff will follow when a child is unwell.

Procedures for children who are unwell

To protect the children in our care and our staff from infectious illnesses the following procedures are followed if a child appears unwell while at the nursery.

1 Medical consent forms must be completed for each child so that in the event of a medical emergency or accident the nursery can seek medical treatment.

2 Parents should keep children at home if they have an infection. The nursery should be informed of the nature of the illness.

3 Children must be kept at home for 48 hours after the last bout of diarrhoea or vomiting – see Health Protection Agency guidance which is available from the nursery office for exclusion of other illnesses.

4 Parents will be informed immediately their child becomes unwell. Children should be collected as soon as possible to prevent the spread of infection.

5 The nursery will administer prescribed and other medicines with consent. Medicines should be handed directly to the manager and must be clearly labelled in original bottles – see Administration of Medicines policy.

6 The nursery will work closely with parents/carers to meet the needs of children with ongoing health conditions.

Figure 3.1: *Nurseries and other settings should have a section in their health policy about procedures for dealing with sick children.*

Key terms

Policies – principles and guidelines set out by an organisation to meet agreed goals.

Procedures – step-by-step actions that must be followed to meet the agreed goals.

CP3

What is included in a health policy?

The information and procedures which should be included in a health policy are listed below. Read through the policy from your own setting and check what information is included. The list is not exhaustive, so you may find that there are additional procedures or information relevant for your own setting.

- Promoting health and well-being
- Administering medicines
- Roles and responsibilities
- Responding to signs of ill health
- Staff training
- Recording concerns
- Reporting notifiable diseases
- Reporting incidents and accidents
- Routines for reducing ill health
- Supporting children with long-term illness
- Informing parents or carers

Find out

Research key local and national legislation and guidelines relating to health in childcare settings. Consider the ways in which they influence policies and procedures which help to maintain the health of children or young people at your own setting.

1.2 The importance of implementing workplace policies and procedures

There is no point in developing policies unless they are read, understood and followed consistently by all staff. They should be written in clear language, without ambiguity. This helps to avoid any misunderstandings. For instance, stating 'children who feel ill must be isolated' may imply that they need not be supervised by an adult. Practitioners have a **duty of care** to children and young people.

If policy and procedure are not followed, the health of all children and young people is put at risk. There may also be serious consequences for practitioners themselves, including disciplinary procedures. In serious breaches of policy this could even lead to dismissal.

Key term

Duty of care – practitioners must take reasonable care so that a child or young person is not harmed either through their actions or omissions.

Children and young people

Procedures such as hand washing and cleaning of tables, toys and equipment are in place to reduce the spread of infection. Even when these procedures are followed consistently it is impossible to eliminate infection completely. From time to time children and young people will become unwell and then appropriate action should be taken to inform parents. If procedures are not followed, more serious illness could be missed. Not following procedures can also affect the health of others. Consider, for instance, a situation where it is suspected that a child has an infectious disease. If steps are not taken to isolate the child from the other children the infection may spread rapidly.

The family of the child or young person

All policies must take into consideration the family of the child or young person. Where best practice is followed families will be consulted in the process of writing policies. It is important that policies and procedures are shared with families as they must also adhere to these. For example, there will be guidelines on keeping children at home after a bout of vomiting or diarrhoea. Parents must always be contacted if a child in your care is unwell so it is essential that the setting has procedures for obtaining and storing up-to-date contact details.

Of course information about individuals must always be kept confidential, but parents have a right to know when there are concerns about ill health which may affect them or their families. Parents should be notified when infectious diseases such as measles or meningitis are in the setting. From time to time parents may ask for advice relating to their child's health. You should always direct them to their GP or health visitor. Giving health advice that you are not qualified to give may mean that a more serious illness goes unrecognised.

Staff

As a member of staff you have a duty to follow policies and procedures. It is important that you become familiar with these and ask a senior member of staff or a first-aider if you are not sure what to do in a particular situation. Ignoring policies or not following procedures could put the children and yourself at risk. All staff must also report any personal bouts of sickness, diarrhoea or infectious diseases and follow advice about when to return to work.

Case study: following procedures

Ross is a learning mentor supporting young people with behavioural difficulties in his local secondary school. One afternoon when working alongside two Year 7 pupils, Ross noticed that Aaron was not his usual chatty self and looked quite pale. When asked, Aaron said that he had pains in his head and that the lights overhead were making it worse. At break time Ross suggested that Aaron stay in the classroom to work quietly on his project. As Ross was busy in another part of the school for the rest of the day he made a mental note to catch up with Aaron the following day. The next morning Ross noticed that Aaron was not at school and asked his form teacher where he was. He was told that Aaron's parents had called to let her know that he had been taken ill the previous evening and had been rushed to hospital.

1 Describe the procedures that Ross should have followed if he had concerns about Aaron's health.

2 What might be the consequences for Aaron of not following policy and procedures?

3 What might be the consequences for Ross of not following policy and procedures?

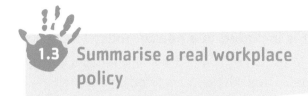

1.3 Summarise a real workplace policy

Find out the name of the person responsible for health within the organisation or setting where you work. If you do not already have a copy of the health policy they will be able to provide it. You should then read through the policy and consider how it works to maintain the health of children or young people. It would be helpful to meet with the person who has overall responsibility for health in your setting to discuss aspects of the policy or procedure and clarify anything you do not understand.

By summarising – that is, giving an outline of the main points of the policy – you will demonstrate that you understand the values and principles that your setting is working towards. You will also demonstrate that you know the action that must be taken in different situations where there may be concerns about the health of a child or young person.

Reflect

When summarising the policy it may help you to imagine that you are giving information to a new member of staff.

Assessment activity 1.1, 1.2, 1.3

Produce a booklet for new staff at your own setting to ensure that they understand the policies and procedures in relation to maintaining the health of children and young people. Your booklet must include:

- the reasons why childcare settings must have health policies and procedures in place
- the reasons why it is important for children, their family and staff that health policies and procedures are followed
- an outline of the policies and procedures from the setting, relating to health.

2 Understand the role of the practitioner in supporting an unwell child and/or young person

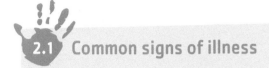

2.1 Common signs of illness

When children are unwell you may notice physical signs such as rashes or swollen glands, or behavioural signs such as not wanting to join in with play or activities.

Signs that a child is unwell

Signs could include:

- pain – abdominal or headache
- a rash
- vomiting or diarrhoea
- loss of appetite
- difficulty breathing
- a raised temperature/fever
- not sleeping, or being more sleepy than usual
- a lack of energy or interest
- irritability or seeking more attention than usual
- pallor – sometimes with dark circles around the eyes.

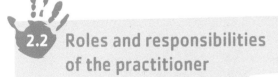

2.2 Roles and responsibilities of the practitioner

Practitioners have a duty of care for children and young people. Close observation is an essential skill because it will help you to recognise the signs that children may be unwell. Older children will often tell you how they are feeling. However, if you work in an early years setting or with children or young people with a disability or special educational need, they will be less able to communicate their symptoms.

Practitioners must be particularly vigilant when caring for babies or very young children as they can quickly become dehydrated when they are unwell. Getting to know individual children in your care will help you to notice even subtle changes in their behaviour which may indicate that they are 'under the weather'.

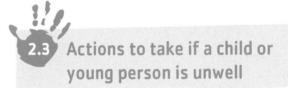

2.3 Actions to take if a child or young person is unwell

Practitioners must respond immediately when they notice signs that a child may be unwell as children can become seriously ill quite rapidly. Unless the child is known to have a minor illness, such as a cold, parents should always be informed so that they can take their child home, and if necessary to their GP. Infectious diseases such as chickenpox can spread very quickly in a nursery or school setting. When this is suspected it is important to isolate children from their peers until they are collected.

If the child or young person appears flushed and hot their temperature should be taken using a fever strip placed on their head or digital thermometer under the arm or an ear thermometer. The normal temperature for a child is around 36°C– 37°C. While children wait for parents they should be made as comfortable as possible, for instance, by giving sips of cooled water or if they have a fever, you can place a tepid cloth on their forehead.

Remember to:

- check the child's medical records for any known medical conditions
- record your observations and what the child tells you

- report concerns to the person responsible for health in the setting
- do what you can to alleviate symptoms
- reassure the child or young person
- follow the administration of medicine policy where children have medicines for known conditions.

CP3

So what does this mean?

You must be prepared if a child in your care shows signs that they are unwell.

- Read through the procedures to follow when children are unwell.
- Find out about any long-term health conditions of children or young people in your care.
- Find out who is responsible for health and names of first-aiders in the setting.
- Check out where concerns about health are recorded.
- Ask about procedures for calling for emergency help.

Assessment activity 2.1, 2.2, 2.3

You must demonstrate that you recognise the signs when children or young people in your care are unwell, the roles and responsibilities of practitioners, and the actions that should be taken.

1 Produce a poster which shows the signs that practitioners should look for which indicate that a child or young person is unwell.

2 In a pair or group of three discuss the roles and responsibilities of the practitioner if a child is unwell. Write up your discussion points and share with your class group.

3 Produce a flow chart which shows the procedures that should be followed if a child is unwell. Show all the stages, including reporting and recording procedures. Also consider all those involved with the child or young person, for example, their parents and others who may care for them.

3 Understand possible factors affecting health in children and/or young people and how to promote health

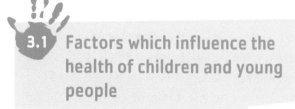

3.1 Factors which influence the health of children and young people

Food, diet and nutrition

Food provides the essential nutrients required by children and young people to keep their body healthy and to promote growth and development. It is important that children eat a range of foods.

Until around the age of 6 months a baby receives all the nutrients they need in breast or formula milk. After this age they require additional nutrients. As a practitioner, it is a good idea to keep up to date with the latest guidelines issued by the Department of Health, which do change from time to time. However, it is generally understood that developing good eating habits in the early years will reduce the likelihood of obesity which can lead to serious health problems in later life. Essential nutrients are provided by five main food groups shown in **Figure 3.2**.

Fruit and vegetables

Good source of vitamins and iron, essential for healthy tissues, bones, blood; to aid wound healing; and to protect against infection

Fats and sugars

Provide energy but should form a small part of the diet to reduce the risk of obesity

A healthy diet includes...

Meat, fish, eggs and pulses

Good source of protein, vitamins and minerals which are essential for the repair of body tissues

Bread, rice, potatoes and pasta

Good source of starch which helps give children energy and aids growth and development

Milk and dairy produce

Good source of calcium and protein essential for the maintenance and repair of tissue and healthy teeth and bones

Figure 3.2: *These food groups are required for a healthy diet, but which ones should you avoid eating too much?*

Exercise, recreation and leisure

Regular exercise must go hand in hand with a healthy diet. Obesity levels in children and young people have risen over a number of years with an increase in associated serous illnesses such as **cardiovascular** disease, Type 2 diabetes and cancers. Regular exercise, recreation and leisure activities are essential for maintaining the general fitness levels of children and young people. They are also essential for mental health because they provide an outlet for a release of energy and opportunities for building friendships.

Key term

Cardiovascular – involving the heart and blood vessels.

Physical health:

- strengthens the cardiovascular system
- increases blood flow which takes essential nutrients around the body
- develops bone and muscle structure
- improves the immune system, making it easier for the body to fight infection.

Mental health:

- improves concentration
- reduces stress
- improves sleep
- improves confidence and self-esteem.

Rest and sleep

Between periods of exercise, children and young people need time to rest and sleep. Requirements will depend on the age of the child and any additional needs. Babies will require as much as 16 to 20 hours over the course of a day. This need for sleep will gradually reduce until in the teenage years young people require around 9 hours. During the day children and young people need periods of rest or quiet activity. This is particularly important to help the body to recover and for the mind to 'unwind' after taking part in more vigorous exercise.

Rest and sleep play an important part in helping the body to heal and repair itself. Sleep also has an effect on children's brain function. You may have noticed that children who have not had sufficient sleep have more difficulty concentrating and their behaviour is more erratic. Children who are tired do not always appear sleepy because a natural response of the body is to fight the tiredness – and this causes hyperactivity.

As children become more independent they may get into a routine of staying up late and not getting enough sleep. They may choose a **lifestyle** that prevents them from getting good-quality sleep because their mind is overactive, for instance, by playing online games or watching TV before bedtime. Lack of sleep increases the risk of ill health and reduces the body's ability to fight infection.

CP3

Reflect

Consider the opportunities for rest and/or sleep in your own setting.

- Do the planned routines allow for periods of rest and/or sleep?
- Are there areas where children can be quiet and/or take part in quiet activity?

Prevention of infection

The germs that cause infection spread rapidly in childcare settings. Germs may be spread through direct contact with infected people, their blood or other bodily fluids or by indirect contact, for example, by touching dirty toys, surfaces or equipment. One of the main ways that germs are spread is via our hands. Germs can also be airborne and spread through droplets of moisture when we sneeze or cough.

Three key ways to prevent infection are personal hygiene, effective cleaning routines and immunisation.

You should also be aware of children in your care who have a higher risk of infection, for instance, those with leukaemia, other cancers, or with conditions that reduce their immunity.

Key terms

Lifestyle – the way of living and habits chosen by the child or young person or their family.

Immunisation – the act of protecting someone against infection.

Transition – a change from one stage or state to another, for instance, transferring to a new school or dealing with family break-up.

So what does this mean?

Staff in settings should take care to carry out preventative measures such as:

- effective hand washing – essential for the control of infection, particularly bacteria or viruses that cause diarrhoea and vomiting. Hands (adults and children) should be thoroughly washed using warm water and liquid soap, then dried using paper towels
- covering the mouth and nose (adults and children) when coughing and sneezing, safe disposal of tissues and hand washing
- cleaning routines – toys, equipment and surfaces should be cleaned regularly using hot soapy water
- safe disposal of bodily fluids – blood, faeces, saliva, vomit and nose discharge should be cleaned immediately using detergent and disinfectant. Bodily fluids and cleaning cloths must be disposed of safely in designated clinical waste bins
- using protective clothing (PPE) – disposable gloves and aprons must be worn when dealing with bodily fluids, soiled laundry and when handling foods or food waste
- checking the status of immunisation of children and young people and encouraging parents to have their children immunised
- ensuring that you are up to date with your own immunisations.

Emotional and social aspects

Our physical and mental health and well-being are strongly influenced by the way we feel about ourselves and our relationships with others. Emotional development is about awareness of the self and the ability to express emotions positively. Social development is about the child's ability to form friendships and develop strong positive relationships with others. Emotional and social development are strongly linked to mental health. Children and young people who have good self-esteem and wide social networks are more able to cope with transition in their lives.

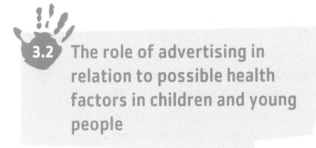

3.2 The role of advertising in relation to possible health factors in children and young people

Advertising works by persuading children or young people to buy a particular product or subscribe to a particular lifestyle. It is not possible to protect children from advertising as it invades all aspects of their lives. In this technological age it reaches children and young people via their mobile phones and computers as well as via TV or posters (see **Figure 3.3** for more information).

Figure 3.3: *Methods of advertising. Which ones were you aware of?*

Over recent years there have been concerns raised about the role of advertising and the health and lifestyles of children and young people, in particular in relation to:

- foods and drinks, including alcohol
- body image and the sexualisation of young people
- lifestyle including branding and peer culture.

Advertising is usually blamed for the increased obesity levels in children and young people. This is not surprising as the majority of foods advertised are fast foods, soft drinks, cereals, confectionery and snacks high in fat, sugar and/or salt. Although pressure from health organisations has brought about stricter rules relating to the advertising of 'junk' foods during children's programmes, concerns remain. It is the Advertising Standards Authority's responsibility to ensure that advertising aimed at children does not encourage unhealthy eating or lifestyle.

In 2010 the National Heart Forum produced a study on the marketing and promotion of food and drink to children. It was found that children as young as 2 years were aware of and responsive to marketing. Older children were also found to be influenced by marketing such as in-store promotions, packaging, competitions or branding linked to celebrities even though they were more aware of these techniques. To find out more about the National Heart Forum, see the Useful websites section on page 97.

Find out

Produce a questionnaire to help you find out:

- which advertisements are remembered by children and young people at different ages
- what parents think about the influence of advertising on the choices made by their children.

Recently there has been a lot of publicity about the ways in which advertising pressures children and young people to make unhealthy choices and the effect this has on both physical and mental health. There is particular concern about the images used in advertising, for example, very thin models or celebrities. Some photographs are even airbrushed to remove any natural body features which are viewed as imperfections. This can seriously undermine the confidence and self-esteem of children and young people who then become concerned about their own body shape and self-image. It is not only girls who are affected by advertising. Boys are also influenced by the 'well-toned' images of male models and celebrities. The result can be an unhealthy diet, and for some it may even lead to eating disorders or taking drugs.

You are probably aware of the 'brand culture' used by advertisers and the pressure this puts on children and young people to aspire to a particular lifestyle. Branding creates pressure on children and their parents to buy particular foods, electronic games or clothes to keep up with their peers. You can find out more about the role of advertising in influencing children and young people on the Media Smart website (see the Useful websites section on page 97 for more information).

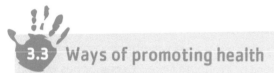

3.3 Ways of promoting health

Health promotion is not about telling children and families how they should live their lives. It is about providing information and conditions which enable them to make lifestyle choices that bring about positive change in their health. This may be initiated by government departments, private companies or third sector (voluntary) organisations. Campaigns can take many forms, with organisations using the same techniques used by advertisers as seen in the previous section. This can be as simple as a poster reminding children and young people to wash their hands or information about leisure activities on a school's website.

Campaigns which promote health may be directed towards:

- the general health of children, young people and families, e.g. diet and nutrition advice
- particular groups, e.g. to reduce the percentage of teenage girls who smoke
- particular health problems, e.g. mental health.

For health promotion to be effective it needs to be relevant and realistic. To be relevant, individuals or groups must be able to understand 'what's in it for them' by taking action or changing their lifestyle. To be realistic, health promotion messages must be supported by adequate resources. Promoting the benefits of exercise and leisure facilities will only be successful if there are suitable facilities in the setting or local area. Health promotion can involve a wide range of issues which affect the health of children and young people. Some suggestions are given in **Table 3.1** below.

Table 3.1: *Examples of health promotion*

Health issue	Possible focus	Groups or individuals who may be targeted
Food, diet and nutrition	<ul><li>Encouraging children to eat healthy snacks</li><li>Effects of alcohol</li></ul>	<ul><li>Young children</li><li>Young people</li></ul>
Exercise, or recreation and leisure	<ul><li>Benefits of leisure activities on health</li><li>Importance of exercise for babies and toddlers</li></ul>	<ul><li>Children and young people</li><li>Parents and babies/toddlers</li></ul>
Rest and sleep	<ul><li>Importance of sleep for improved school performance</li></ul>	<ul><li>Young people 11–18 years</li></ul>
Lifestyle	<ul><li>Safe sex</li><li>Positive body image</li><li>Dangers of smoking</li></ul>	<ul><li>Young people</li><li>Children and young people</li><li>Young people</li></ul>
Prevention of infection	<ul><li>Recognising the signs of meningitis</li><li>Hand-washing routines</li></ul>	<ul><li>Staff, parents and young people</li><li>Young children</li></ul>
Emotional and social aspects	<ul><li>Dealing with emotions</li><li>Building positive relationships</li></ul>	<ul><li>Children</li><li>Young people</li></ul>

Approaches to health promotion

- **Medical approach:** this works by identifying children or young people at risk with the purpose of reducing illness or mortality. For example, giving the facts and encouraging parents to have children immunised.

- **Educational approach:** this works by providing children or young people with information about particular health issues and the knowledge and skills necessary to choose a healthy lifestyle. Information may be aimed at individuals or groups. For example, advertisements on the effects on children of inhaling cigarette smoke.

- **Behaviour-change approach:** this encourages individuals to adopt a healthy lifestyle through positive communication and showing individuals alternative lifestyles and choices. There is increasing emphasis on changing the behaviour of families (including those 'hard to reach' families) towards a more healthy lifestyle. A good example of this is the recent Change4Life campaign which uses a variety of methods including online information, interactive websites, posters and programmes such as SmallSteps4Life and Play4Life.

- **Child or young person and family-centred approach:** this focuses on working closely with children and their families to identify specific needs and to support changes which will improve health. This approach works to empower children, young people and families to make any changes necessary to improve their own health.

- **Societal/social approach:** this involves making changes to the environment which bring about change in the lifestyle and choices made by children and young people. This often involves changing policy or introducing guidelines. A recent example is the campaign for healthier food in school.

Figure 3.4: *Change4Life poster. This advertising campaign targets children and their families in an attempt to change attitudes to diet and exercise.*

Assessment activity 3.1, 3.2, 3.3

Identify the factors that you consider to have the greatest effect on the health, lifestyle or emotional well-being of children and young people in your care. In relation to each factor:

1 explain the possible influence on the health, lifestyle and emotional well-being of a child or a young person

2 select two forms of advertising, e.g. from magazines, online or TV, and write about the influence each might have on children or young people

3 produce a poster which shows at least four ways of promoting health.

CP3

4 Be able to support children and/or young people to improve their health

Although health care workers such as health visitors, GPs or school nurses have specific responsibilities, all those working with children and young people have a role to play in health promotion.

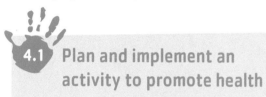

4.1 Plan and implement an activity to promote health

Before you start to plan an activity to promote the health of children or young people, it is important that you do some research into the health priorities in your own setting, in your local community or your home nation. You might then look at relevant data such as the increase in the number of children contracting measles or levels of obesity in children. This will help you to decide upon the specific focus for your own health promotion activity.

Your approach will depend upon your choice of health issue. If you work with young people who you feel lack exercise, a behaviour-change approach may be most effective. If you work in an area where a high percentage of parents are choosing not to have their children immunised, you may take a medical or educational approach.

Planning checklist

When you are planning your activity, there are a number of questions you should ask yourself.

✓ **What is your rationale?** This will be based on your research. Think about why you have chosen a particular health issue – for instance, is there an increasing number of children in the local area who are obese or overweight?

✓ **What are your aims?** Once you have decided on the general health issue for your activity you must consider what your aims are – for instance, to inform children and parents about alternative healthy options for snacks.

✓ **What are the intended outcomes?** Think about what you want to achieve – for instance, children will bring only healthy snacks to the holiday club.

✓ **Who is your target audience?** Your health promotion activity will depend upon the age of the children you work with. Your target audience may be young children, in which case encouraging hand-washing routines or getting young children to make healthier choices at mealtimes could be appropriate.

✓ **What methods do you intend to use?** You must consider the method you will use to get your message across in the most effective way. Leaflets or booklets may be appropriate for parents but for older children cartoons could help them remember the important points. You may choose to use more than one method such as a poster on healthy eating with an accompanying recipe booklet. You could consider drama, a cartoon strip, games, posters, a recorded advertisement for radio or TV and quizzes.

✓ **What resources will you need?** The resources and materials chosen must support your message and be suitable for the age group targeted. You must also ensure that any advice and information are relevant and current. Also think about visual information. It will be helpful to look at different health promotion leaflets. Often they have few words but strong graphics which make the point more effectively. You could consider the use of props or mood music.

✓ **How will you know if the activity has been successful?** At the planning stage you should also think about how you will measure the success of the activity for the child or young person and the wider family. For example, this could be through feedback from individuals you have targeted in the activity and/or by observing behaviour.

SMART targets

When planning, it is helpful to refer to SMART targets. SMART stands for:

Specific – be clear on what you are trying to achieve, whether a change in lifestyle or encouraging an action such as attending the health centre for an immunisation.

Measurable – you will need to consider how you will assess the success of the activity. Does your audience have increased knowledge or have they changed their attitudes or lifestyle?

Achievable – consider your aims and objectives carefully. Expecting young children to bring only healthy snacks to school every day would be too ambitious, so consider the improvements you could reasonably expect.

Realistic – changing lifestyle, particularly for older children and young people, can be difficult. Consider what would be realistic. Expecting a total change of diet for a family who eats junk foods may be unrealistic but encouraging the introduction of fruit and vegetables every day may seem more manageable.

Time-bound – plan a realistic timescale for your health promotion activity. Will you need to carry out the promotion over several sessions or through one activity? For example, when promoting effective hand-washing routines for children, it may take some time for them to wash regularly without needing to be reminded.

4.2 Evaluate the outcome of a health promotion activity

It is important that you do not wait until you have implemented your activity to carry out your evaluation. Recording each stage of your planning and development will help you to reflect on your own skills and the success of your activity.

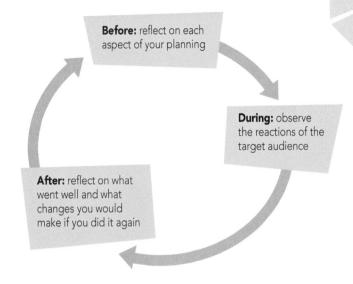

Figure 3.5: *Evaluation is required at every stage: before, during and after the activity.*

Before you begin the activity you should reflect on your aims and objectives, and consider the activity's appropriateness for your audience.

As you implement your activity you must monitor progress. Is your message being understood? What is the reaction of the individuals targeted? Also consider the involvement of the whole team at your setting. At this stage you may wish to adapt the activity or amend information to ensure that you achieve the intended outcome.

When you have completed your activity consider each stage of your planning and implementation. Firstly reflect on your rationale. Was it an appropriate choice? Was it based on research into health issues in your setting or local community? Also think about whether the methods used were appropriate and if it gave a clear message. Ask yourself questions about each aspect of your planning. For instance, were the methods chosen suitable for the age group, interests and needs of your target group? Were your resources sufficient, relevant and current? What did the children or young people learn from taking part in the activity and what was the influence on their family?

Most important is to reflect on whether your original aims and intended outcomes were met. You will need to seek feedback from your target audience,

CP3

colleagues and/or your supervisor. Depending on the age group of your audience, you could ask questions or hand out a questionnaire. This will help you to find out if they understand more about the health issue or the benefits of choosing a particular course of action. You may also need to observe the behaviour of the target audience. For example, following an activity to promote effective hand washing you could observe the behaviour of a group of children when getting ready for lunch.

4.3 Reflect on your own role within the health promotion activity

The requirement of your role is to take overall responsibility for your activity to ensure that your plans are authentic, valid and ethical. This will require you to agree plans with your supervisor at your setting and your tutor or assessor to ensure it is 'fit for purpose'. Once agreed you must then implement your activity within an agreed timescale. You have a responsibility to check that resources are available and that they and the methods used meet health and safety requirements. Consideration should be given to your own role. What was your involvement with the children and other staff during the activity?

You may have chosen to plan and implement the activity independently or as a group project. If you worked with others it is particularly important that you kept a record of your own contribution at every stage. On completion you must present evidence of your activity and your evaluation in an appropriate format for assessment.

Key terms

Authentic – meaningful activity relating to real issues.

Valid – information which is well grounded and justified.

Ethical – conduct which follows moral principles.

Fit for purpose – a suitable plan which is likely to achieve what is intended.

Assessment activity
4.1, 4.2, 4.3

1 Plan and implement an activity for a group of children which will work to promote their health.

2 Identify the outcomes from your activity and write about:
   - what the children learned by taking part in the activity
   - the effect that the activity may have on the children's families
   - the different ways that the team within the setting were involved.

3 Reflect on and write about the role that you played in the planning and the implementation of the activity.

5 Understand how to respond to illness in children and/or young people

Most children will contract an infectious illness at some stage. These can spread quite rapidly in childcare settings so it is important that you are familiar with signs and symptoms that you may come across in your day-to-day work. However, it is not the responsibility of childcare practitioners to diagnose but to respond appropriately to the symptoms. Since 1988 and the introduction of the MMR vaccine, illnesses such as measles and mumps are far less common. Not all parents have their children immunised so you need to be aware of the possibility of children and young people contracting these illnesses.

5.1 Symptoms of common infectious illnesses

Chickenpox

Chickenpox is a mild childhood illness caused by the varicella zoster virus. Most children catch the virus before the age of 10 years because it is so contagious. Early symptoms may be fever, sore throat and/or headache and generally feeling unwell. The first indication that the child has chickenpox will be red spots. Some children will have only a few spots while for others spots will cover the whole body. Spots start on the face spreading to the trunk, legs and arms. Children and young people may even have spots in their mouth and nose. These spots fill with fluid, forming **pustules**. After a few days the pustules crust over, forming scabs which eventually drop off.

Chickenpox spots can be very itchy and distressing for the child. How could you reassure them?

Measles

Measles is a particularly infectious disease caused by paramyxovirus. It is most common in children aged 0 to 4 years but older children and young people can also become infected. The first signs of measles may be cold-like symptoms, a dry cough and a temperature of 38°C or even higher. You also may notice that a child or young person's eyes are red and they complain about sensitivity to light. Before the rash appears some children have greyish-white spots, called Koplik's spots, in their mouth and throat. A few days later a brownish/red rash will appear. The spots may be separate to start with but then become joined and blotchy. The rash usually starts behind the ears, spreading to their head and neck and then to the rest of the body.

Key term

Pustules – blisters filled with fluid.

CP3

CP3

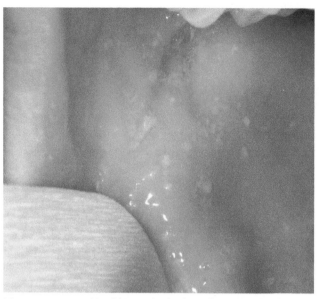

You may notice Koplik's spots before the rash appears.

Mumps

Like measles, mumps is caused by paramyxovirus. Mumps causes the swelling of the parotid glands on each side of the face. This is sometimes described as a 'hamster face' appearance. For some children only one side may be affected. Before the swelling appears children may complain of headache, pain when swallowing and/or joint or abdominal pain. They may also have a fever with their temperature rising to 38°C or more. For young children these symptoms will disappear within a week or so but boys who have reached puberty may experience swelling of the testicles.

Meningitis

The name meningitis comes from the word meninges which are the membranes surrounding the brain and spinal cord. Meningitis is an infection of the meninges. The infection can be caused by a virus (viral meningitis) or bacteria (bacterial meningitis).

Viral meningitis

Viral meningitis is the more common type and is less serious. The symptoms appear like flu: head and joint ache, high temperature and feeling generally unwell. Children may experience similar symptoms to bacterial meningitis such as neck stiffness, nausea, vomiting, diarrhoea or sensitivity to light, but children usually recover within two weeks.

Bacterial meningitis

Bacterial meningitis is extremely serious. If not recognised and treated early it could lead to brain damage or septicaemia (infection of the blood) or may even be fatal. Bacterial meningitis is more common in two distinct age groups: babies and children under 5 years and young people 15 to 18 years. The symptoms for babies and young children are different from those experienced by older children and young people. It is critical that you can recognise these different symptoms so that immediate medical help can be sought.

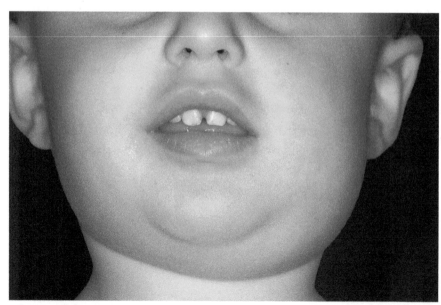

Children with mumps have a 'hamster face' appearance.

Table 3.2: *Symptoms of meningitis/septicaemia in children*

Symptom	Septicaemia	Meningitis
Fever and/or vomiting	X	X
Severe headache		X
Limb/joint/muscle pain (sometimes with pain/diarrhoea)	X	
Cold hands and feet/shivering	X	
Pale or mottled skin	X	
Breathing fast/breathless	X	
Rash (anywhere on the body)	X	X
Stiff neck (less common in young children)		X
Dislike of bright lights (less common in young children)		X
Very sleepy/vacant/difficult to wake	X	X
Confused/delirious	X	X
Seizures (fits) may also be seen		X

From the Meningitis Research Foundation. Red crosses show symptoms that are more specific to meningitis and septicaemia and less common in milder illnesses. Limb pain and cold hands and feet often appear earlier than a rash, neck stiffness, photophobia and confusion.

So what does this mean?

The tumbler test

When a tumbler is pressed against the skin of a child or young person with septicaemia the rash does not fade. This means that the child is seriously ill and you must seek emergency medical help.

If you are working with babies and young children, particular symptoms which you should look for include:

- refusing bottle/food
- being irritable but not wanting to be held or cuddled
- a stiff body or being floppy
- a swelling in the soft part of their head (fontanelle).

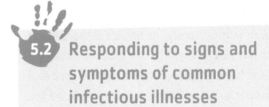

5.2 Responding to signs and symptoms of common infectious illnesses

The response must be to alleviate any symptoms as soon as they appear, as at an early stage the particular illness may not be diagnosed. For chickenpox, measles and mumps there is no cure so the response should be to alleviate any symptoms as they appear. Children may feel frightened when spots appear so it is important to reassure them that they will go away. When children feel unwell they can become dehydrated very quickly so it is important that they are given regular sips of water.

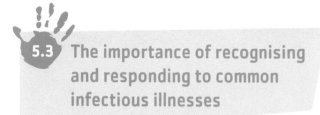

5.3 The importance of recognising and responding to common infectious illnesses

It is important to recognise and respond to common infectious illnesses for several reasons including:

- to reduce the spread of the infection
- to minimise the effects on the child or young person
- to reduce the likelihood of complications
- to protect children with immune deficiency who are higher risk
- to protect staff, young people or parents who are pregnant.

5.4 Workplace procedures

When a child show signs of illness, a manager or first-aider with responsibility for health in the setting should be informed. The parent or carer will then be contacted immediately. A record should be made of any symptoms, the time when they were noticed and who has been informed. When an infectious illness is suspected, the child or young person should be isolated from others while they wait for their parent or carer. In some settings there may be a medical room or a quiet area for this purpose. The child should remain under constant adult supervision. If the child has a fever their temperature should be checked and their head sponged with tepid water. Water should be given to relieve symptoms of a dry or sore throat or after vomiting.

It is important to:

- remain with the child
- reassure the child
- observe their symptoms closely and report any new symptoms or deterioration in the health
- keep calm
- maintain high standards of hygiene including hand washing.

When a child shows signs of meningitis, immediate medical help should be sought by calling 999.

Children and young people can return to the setting when they are recovered and do not pose a risk of infection to others. Each setting will have a policy on exclusion following guidelines set out by the Health Protection Agency. Parents or carers should be advised to take their child to their own GP as measles, mumps and meningitis must be reported to the Health Protection Agency by the doctor who confirms the diagnosis. Childcare settings must also report cases to their local Health Protection Unit. The recommended amount of time before children can return to the setting is as follows:

- chickenpox – 5 days from onset of rash
- measles – 5 days from onset of rash
- mumps – 5 days from onset of swelling
- meningitis – when fully recovered
- sickness and diarrhoea – 48 hours after the last episode of vomiting or diarrhoea.

Assessment activity 5.1, 5.2, 5.3, 5.4

For the common infections identified produce a presentation for your peers. You must include:

- symptoms of each infection
- actions that should be taken by practitioners when each of the infections is suspected
- reasons why it is important to recognise and respond appropriately
- an overview of the procedures from your own setting for dealing with infectious illness.

6 Understand how immunisation aims to prevent harmful diseases in children and young people

6.1 Immunisation schedules

Table 3.3: *Current routine immunisation programme available for children and young people from birth to 18 years in the UK*

Age	Diseases protected against	Method
2 months	Diphtheria, tetanus, pertussis (whooping cough), polio and Haemophilus influenzae type b (Hib)	1 injection (5-in-1) in thigh
	Pneumococcal disease	1 injection in thigh
3 months	Diphtheria, tetanus, pertussis, polio and Hib	1 injection in thigh
	Meningococcal group C disease (MenC)	1 injection in thigh
4 months	Diphtheria, tetanus, pertussis, polio and Hib	1 injection in thigh
	MenC	1 injection in thigh
	Pneumococcal disease	1 injection in thigh
Between 12 and 13 months	Hib/MenC	1 injection in upper arm/thigh
	Pneumococcal disease	1 injection in upper arm/thigh
	Measles, mumps and rubella (German measles)	1 injection in upper arm/thigh
3 years and 4 months or shortly after	Diphtheria, tetanus, pertussis and polio	1 injection in upper arm
	Measles, mumps and rubella	1 injection in upper arm
Girls aged 12 to 13 years	Cervical cancer caused by human papillomavirus types 16 and 18	3 injections given over 6 months – upper arm
13 to 18 years	Tetanus, diphtheria and polio	1 injection – upper arm

(from NHS Routine Childhood Immunisations from November 2010)

Although a vaccine is available for meningitis C, it does not protect children and young people from all types of meningitis. You need to remain vigilant for the symptoms even when children have been immunised.

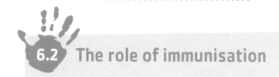

6.2 The role of immunisation

The aim of vaccines is to eliminate serious childhood illness. Vaccine for smallpox was discovered as long ago as 1796 by the British physician Edward Jenner. Further vaccines were gradually developed and by the 1920s vaccines for diphtheria, pertussis (whooping cough), tetanus and tuberculosis were in use. This resulted in a significant reduction in deaths from these illnesses. By 1955 a polio vaccine was introduced. While there is still some way to go to eliminate measles and mumps, these illnesses have been drastically reduced in the UK since the introduction of the MMR vaccine in 1988. Polio has disappeared in the UK and is extremely rare worldwide. Smallpox, which was once one of the greatest threats to children, has been completely eradicated. Vaccines continue to be developed and as recently as 2008 the cervical cancer vaccination (caused by human papillomavirus types 16 and 18) was included in the vaccination schedule for girls aged 12 to 13 in the UK.

Find out

In 1998 a paper was published by Dr Andrew Wakefield suggesting a link between the MMR vaccination and autism. His theory was never proved and his research was discredited but nevertheless resulted in many parents choosing not to have their child immunised. For a number of years following the report, immunisation levels fell and cases of measles, mumps and rubella rose. More recently the indications are that immunisation levels are beginning to rise.

Carry out research for your home country to find current data for:

- the number of reported cases of measles
- the percentage of children who have received the MMR vaccination.

Vaccine works to protect children and young people against a number of serious diseases that can cause complications or even death. When a high percentage of children are vaccinated it reduces the likelihood of the disease passing to others who are not immunised, so protecting not only the individual child but their family and wider community. This is sometimes referred to as 'herd immunity'. Immunisation levels need to be above 95 per cent to prevent these infectious diseases from circulating.

Vaccines contain a small amount of the virus or bacterium that causes the disease. Giving a vaccine triggers the child or young person's immune system to make antibodies. When the child then comes into contact with the disease, the antibodies recognise the disease and help their body to fight it. Parents should be encouraged to have their children vaccinated at the recommended time. At birth, babies will have a natural immunity but by the age of 2 months this starts to diminish. It is also important that young children receive their booster immunisation at the age of 4 years so that they are protected before they start school and during their teenage years to give long-term protection.

There are a few instances where immunisation should not be given. This includes children and young people who have had an anaphylactic reaction from a dose of vaccine. Vaccines containing live viruses such as MMR are not given to children whose immune system is suppressed because of an illness or treatment for cancer or following a transplant. An effective immunisation programme will work to protect those children and young people who cannot be immunised.

Key term

Anaphylactic reaction – a serious allergic reaction which is life-threatening.

CP3

6.3 Published information about immunisation

A wide range of advice and information about immunisation is available from the NHS website (see the Useful websites section on page 97 for more information). Public health sites for Wales and Northern Ireland will provide additional advice and statistics for these countries. You can also obtain information from a range of organisations and health settings. Check the dates of any information you use to ensure that it is current. Look for leaflets, posters and other published information in relation to immunisation from the following places:

* pharmacy
* health centre
* library
* baby clinic
* GP or practice nurse
* school nurse.

Assessment activity 6.1, 6.2, 6.3

Design a page for the website to provide information on immunisation for parents and staff. It should include information on:

* the immunisation schedule for your home country
* the importance of immunisation in promoting health
* where parents and staff can get more information on immunisation.

CP3

In the real world

My name is Maya. I have worked in the baby and toddler room in a children's centre for almost a year. I really enjoy my work. Last month the centre manager told the staff that there had been an increase in measles cases among school children in the local area.

The manager checked the immunisation records of all the children who attend the nursery. She found that one child had not been immunised. My manager asked me to meet with her parent to discuss the benefits of immunisation and to dispel any concerns. I also suggested that I should meet with the parents of babies in the nursery who are due to be immunised in the next few months. She thanked me for this suggestion and agreed that it would be a good idea.

I was pleased with the outcome of the meetings. The parent of the toddler who had not been immunised said she was not aware of the seriousness of the disease and would consider immunisation. I gave her the contact number of the health visitor so that she could discuss any further concerns. My manager told me she was happy with the way I had handled the meetings and asked if I would take on the responsibility for promoting routine immunisation. I am really pleased that she feels I am ready to take on extra responsibility.

Check your knowledge

1 Give two reasons why it is essential for practitioners to follow the health policy and procedures of the setting.
2 Identify three physical and two behavioural signs that a child is unwell.
3 What are the main benefits of rest and sleep for children and young people?
4 How are germs spread in a childcare setting?
5 What is meant by an ethical approach to health promotion?
6 Suggest three reasons why it is important to recognise the early signs of common infectious illnesses.
7 What are the symptoms of chickenpox?
8 What action should be taken if meningitis is suspected?
9 What is meant by 'herd immunity'?
10 At what ages should children receive their first and booster MMR vaccination?

CP3

CACHE Extended Assessment

Theme: Safeguarding the health, safety and well-being of children and young people

Grading criterion

B3 Analyse aspects of your learning from the chosen theme that could improve your future practice.

To achieve a higher grade you must demonstrate that you are able to undertake reflective thinking. This requires you to consider, for example, how well you dealt with an occurrence of ill health and, if it happened again, what you could do differently to improve the outcomes for the child and family. You should question all aspects of your work including your knowledge, attitudes and ways of working. This will involve seeking feedback from others: colleagues, health professionals and your teacher or assessor. Using this information you will then be able to analyse your practice by considering your strengths and weaknesses in relation to your role in supporting children or young people who are unwell.

You can then develop your evidence by making connections between your increased knowledge and skills and future practice, also showing how this will help you to become more effective in your role. If you have chosen to focus on health policy and procedures you could explore how, by developing your understanding, you would be more confident and able to deal with difficult situations.

This is an example of how you might approach one criterion of your Extended Assessment. You must successfully complete all the criteria at each grade to achieve that grade. You will achieve the highest grade for which you have successfully completed all the criteria. For example, to achieve a B grade you will need to meet the requirements of the B1, B2 and B3 criteria, as well as C1, C2, C3 and D1 and D2.

When trying to understand the requirements for your Extended Assessment, it is always a good idea to talk to your tutors. Fellow learners and workplace colleagues are also useful sources of information.

Further references

The following are sources of useful information on the topic of maintaining the health of children and young people.

Booklets/leaflets

The following are produced by the NHS and are available from GP surgeries and baby clinics, etc.

- Immunisations up to 13 months of age
- Immunisations at 12 and 13 months of age
- Pre-school immunisations: A guide to vaccinations for 3- to 5-year-olds
- Immunisations at Secondary School: Your questions answered

Useful websites

To obtain a secure link to the websites and information below, visit www.pearsonhotlinks.co.uk and search for this book by using its title or ISBN. Click on the section for CP3.

National Heart Forum

Media Smart

Information and answers to questions about immunisation from the NHS

Information and advice on MMR vaccination from the NHS

Meningitis Research Foundation: Facts about meningitis

Department of Health, Social Services and Public Safety – Northern Ireland

Public health advice – Northern Ireland

Public health advice services for Wales

Resources and information on health promotion issues from the Patient.co.uk website

Department of Health Healthy Child Programme: pregnancy and the first five years of life

Department of Health Healthy Child Programme from 5–19 years

Department of Health publications relating to immunisation

DVD

Immunisation, why our children must be protected, Department of Health (2006)

An introduction to leadership and management

CP4

Leadership and management is something we all need to know about and understand, even as new or training practitioners. We all need to use the skills of leadership and management in our everyday working practices, to manage our own workload and responsibilities. If you aspire to become a manager or the leader of a team, you should start to practise and use these skills early in your career so that, when opportunities arise, you have an awareness of your own skills and how you can make best use of them to lead and manage others.

Learning outcomes

By the end of this unit you will:

1 Understand leadership and management theories, styles and models

2 Understand the skill sets required to be an effective leader and/or manager

3 Understand how to create a sense of common purpose for team working.

In practice

Neila has been the manager and owner of a privately run day care setting for three years. She feels she does a good job managing her setting – before she became a manager she had several years' experience in various settings and had been given room and group leadership responsibilities which she had always enjoyed. Neila says that there are aspects of both leadership and management in her present role.

'I make sure that the setting runs smoothly day to day and that all the management tasks are completed – for example, organising staff shifts and making sure the setting is well resourced. I would see this as the management part of my job. But another part of my job is to look to the future and encourage and motivate the team to be involved with making ongoing improvements to our provision. I want the setting to work well within all aspects of the outcomes for children and be forward thinking and innovative – I think that is probably the leadership aspect of my role – looking forward.'

By the end of this unit you will understand more about how Neila does this, what skills she needs and how she supports and motivates her team to be innovative and forward thinking.

1 Understand leadership and management theories, styles and models

It is essential in the children and young people's sector that we have effective leaders and managers. All settings hold their leaders and managers accountable for the measured outcomes for the children in their care. Not only do leaders and managers have to work within rigid guidelines for working practices, they must also show improvements for children's care and development. They are set the task of working with their teams to ensure that the day-to-day running is effective and that practice is always reflected upon and actions are taken to improve where necessary. This is a huge responsibility and one which requires certain skills and attributes. There has been much research into the ways in which people manage and lead in institutions, both in the business world and in the area of working with children and young people. It is important to know that, while there are some similarities between business and the care sector, there are also differences and other responsibilities which make the role of leader and manager in our sector unique and distinctive.

1.1 The differences between leadership and management

Identifying the difference between leadership and management in the sector is difficult. Leaders and managers have different roles and responsibilities in each setting. In a school, for example, the head teacher is the leader of the school and a deputy may help with the managerial role. In much of the private and voluntary sector, both leading and managing may be carried out by one person. Definitions of management often focus on activities and what managers 'do', whereas definitions of leadership focus on personal attributes and an ability to inspire and motivate; however, there are skills and attributes required by both. You can see the differences and overlap between leadership and management in **Table 4.1**.

Table 4.1: *Leadership and management skills and attributes comparison (Skills for Care, 2008)*

Leadership skills and attributes	Skills and attributes for both	Management skills and attributes
• Inspiration • Transformation • Direction • Trust • Empowerment • Creativity • Innovation • Motivation	• Communication • Development • Decision making • Integrity • Role model • Negotiation • Knowledge • Professionalism • Setting standards • Flexible • Focused	• Delegation • Performance • Planning • Accountability • Finance • Team building/teamwork • Monitoring • Evaluating • Supervising • Control

CP4

What does a leader do?

You will know from your practice that there are managers, deputy managers, room leaders, team leaders, registered persons, officers in charge, heads of department, head teachers – all titles that you will have heard but which are used for different purposes.

Leaders give direction and inspire teams to work towards a vision. They are usually the sort of people that most of us follow because they make us believe in their vision – they are respected and can empower the people around them.

The Department for Eduction and Skills (DfES) has produced a booklet called *Developing Management Skills*. It tells us that leaders need a more long-term goal and a vision of the future which they are able to plan towards to bring about improvement and a 'can-do' attitude. The leader's vision has an effect on the outcomes for the children in their care and ensures good-quality practice which the whole team works towards. This model of practice tends to influence everyone within the team to become leaders in their own right and to use their initiative because they feel trusted and valued by their leader.

An effective and successful leader reflects on their practice continually and plans broadly around values, the **ethos** of the setting and the ways in which they can respond to change. Leaders should always be learning and should challenge traditional practice to make improvements which benefit the children in their care. This sort of change can be made by:

- making sure everyone is on board with the idea and believes in it
- individuals in the team feeling that this is helping them with their personal development
- creating a happy working environment where everyone feels valued, including parents and carers
- allowing individuals to use their initiative and making sure that their ideas for possible changes are listened to.

CP4

Key term

Ethos – the way in which things are run – the culture of the setting.

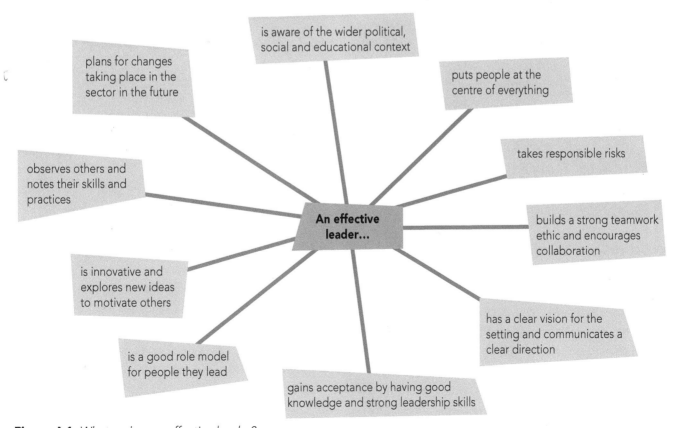

Figure 4.1: *What makes an effective leader?*

Teams which are led in this way will have greater autonomy and feel they have a voice within their setting which is listened to. Leaders make sure they can lead in this way by:

- having good knowledge and understanding of their setting and sector
- keeping a focus on external expectations and pressures
- being goal-specific and planning in a timely way
- being realistic and taking risks only when there is a strong likelihood there will be positive outcomes
- having the leadership ability to give team members this autonomy but still leading from the front – maintaining a good balance.

Find out

Taking the ideas in the list above about leading changes:

- give examples of how this could work in your setting, or
- give examples of when you have seen these changes take place.

Reflect

You may find the task above difficult because you are not yet a manager. However, as a practitioner you are required to be observant so use these skills to observe the way in which you are managed. When you first become a manager you often adopt the same management style as your manager. Do you think you would adopt your manager's style of managing? If not, why not?

What does a manager do?

A manager can be the manager of an individual setting led by the leader of a company, for example, in a chain of nurseries. The inspiration, direction and goals may come from another source and it may be the manager's role to 'manage' others to work towards these goals. On the other hand, the manager may be the sole manager and leader of the setting.

The role of the manager can be seen as organisational. We all manage our daily practice

as individuals, making sure we get to work on time, managing a particular group of key children, managing our workload for each day – these are just some of the ways in which we manage ourselves. Although some of us will be more efficient at this type of self-management than others, you may have heard colleagues say that they would have managed something 'differently' from their manager and this would have 'worked much better'. When colleagues feel like this it is often because they believe the manager did not 'organise' something well and this causes dissatisfaction among the team.

Case study: improving management

Jan is the manager of a privately owned nursery (in a chain of nurseries). She sees her management duties as procedural things which need to be done – mainly tasks such as organising staffing rotas and timesheets, providing cover, ordering resources, making sure all policies and procedures are followed, running team meetings, dealing with parents and any concerns, etc.

Jan believes she does more than these organisational tasks but she is aware that they do take up a lot of her time. She feels she should spend more time looking at possible changes and ways in which the setting can respond to those changes when they come along; she also feels guilty that she does not have a lot of time to support and develop her staff. People tell her she should delegate more but she is worried that if she does not do it herself, it will not get done properly.

1 Suggest what may be going wrong for this manager.

2 How could she make changes to ensure she gives more time to developing her team?

A manager focuses on the day-to-day operation of the setting and makes sure that everything runs smoothly. However, they will gain more respect when they have good knowledge and experience themselves and if they are flexible and responsive.

This is not to say of course that managers *only* manage organisational tasks – in most cases these managers are also leading, and doing a good and effective job of addressing both parts of the role. **Figure 4.2** shows what an effective manager needs to do.

Figure 4.2: *What makes an effective manager?*

Find out

Having looked at what a manager does, think about how the management role could be developed to widen the role. Consider the manager's role in working:

- with the children
- with the staff team
- with parents and carers
- in the community.

Think of ways in which the manager could use more leadership-type skills to improve their performance.

What are the differences?

Although it is obvious from research and practice that leading a team involves a range of tasks and skills, there seem to be some differences between what is meant by leadership and what is meant by management. To be a leader requires extra input – different ways of working in terms of looking forward and planning for the future of the setting, encouraging staff and parents to become involved in that planning and having a 'vision' for the centre. There is no doubt that a leader needs excellent communication skills but they should also work towards building relationships that bring about change and better practice in the long term.

Their knowledge of the sector should gain the respect of their team members and enable them to work collaboratively in an atmosphere of trust and openness.

However, management of the team is just as important. The tasks of organisation, making decisions, controlling and monitoring also have to be 'top of the list' so that there can be the very best outcomes for the children and the setting can be responsive to change. In some cases managers are only required to manage and the leadership comes from 'above' (for example, from the owners of the company or chain). However, you might have found that in this case the manager's job is more difficult – they have to communicate a given ethos or vision to their team, and get them on board with this ethos, when it does not come from within the team. Working in this way requires strong leadership skills.

When you consider the settings you may have worked in you might agree that most people 'in charge' of a setting use both leadership and management in their job role. Some researchers have found that the role of manager and leader is usually combined and that the management part of the role is the day-to-day running and organisation, and the leadership part of the role is providing a vision and a way forward.

CP4

So what does this mean?

A manager:

- is well organised and is a good role model for the team to follow
- manages resources and the environment
- has good sector knowledge and understanding.

A leader:

- has a vision for the way forward for the setting
- can influence others
- can respond well in a crisis
- plans for the future and keeps updating knowledge.

1.2 & 1.3 Theories, models and styles of leadership and management

Next you need to consider the various theories surrounding leadership and management. Years of research in the world of business have brought about many models, styles and theories. Some describe management and some describe leadership – both demonstrate how people might use the models to support them in their job role. In the children and young people's sector, research is continually taking place to look at the possible uniqueness of leadership in our sector and how people might be trained or use reflective practice to become better leadership practitioners.

Much of the work relating to theories of leadership and management involves:

- definitions, principles and characteristics of leadership and management (see **Table 4.2**)
- models for leadership and management (see **Table 4.3**)
- theories of leadership and management (see **Table 4.4**)
- types of leadership and management (see **Table 4.5** for more information)
- skills and attributes of leaders and managers (these will be addressed later in the unit).

The following tables provide brief summaries and comments on some of the more notable definitions, models and theories in management and leadership relevant to working with children and young people.

Table 4.2: *Definitions, principles and characteristics of leadership and management*

Name and date	Definitions, principles and characteristics of leadership and management	In practice
Walden and Shiba (2001) cited in Whalley (2011) *Leading Practice in Early Years Settings*	Walden and Shiba outline eight principles of visionary leadership. The visionary leader: 1 is observant and vigilant 2 never gives up even when there is resistance 3 changes practice by questioning the old and traditional systems 4 has a symbolic visible image and acts as a role model 5 quickly establishes new ways of working to achieve the vision 6 leads change 7 creates an innovative system for giving feedback 8 creates new approaches to improve day-to-day running.	This can be an effective way in which managers or leaders can appraise their practice – it could also assist with planning for continuing personal development (CPD) of room leaders, SENCOs, deputy managers, etc.
Whalley (2011)	Finding an absolute definition of leadership is difficult as leadership and management are used in different ways in different settings. However, for Whalley four main themes stand out: 1 to lead and influence the behaviour of others 2 where there are leaders there are followers 3 leaders come to the fore when there is a crisis or special problem – they are able to make an innovative response 4 our expectation is that leaders are people who have a clear idea of what they want to achieve and why.	Many of the leaders and managers in the sector will recognise these themes – this is useful in demonstrating that the attributes of a leader may be lying dormant in someone until they are put into a position of authority – people who lead will always have a clear goal in mind and this is comforting for those being managed by them.

Find out

What does your present manager feel is a good definition of their role in the setting?

Do they see themselves as a visionary manager?

Can they think of a way in which they have changed the practice in their setting?

Table 4.3: *Models of leadership and management*

Name and date	Models for leadership and management	In practice
ELMS Janet Moyles (2006) *Effective Leadership and Management in the Early Years*	Janet Moyles worked with a group and created the ELMS model which incorporates leadership and management together. The children and young people's management and leadership model 'fans out' like a tree to include qualities, skills, attributes, characteristics and attitudes – this metaphor also suggests that with the branches there is strength and reliability and the ability to improve and move forward (just as a tree demonstrates the ability to grow). This typology is composed of four main sections or branches: 1 leadership qualities 2 management skills 3 professional skills and attributes 4 personal characteristics and attitudes. The 'stems' will be discussed later when looking at skills and attributes.	This is an excellent tool for evaluating practice and individual skills and competencies for leadership roles – this may not necessarily be a manager's role but could be any leadership role in the setting. The typology also gives the sector a benchmark to work to so that individuals can then look at where they may have skills gaps or a need for further training and professional development.
Typology of an early childhood leader Jillian Rodd (2005) *Leadership in Early Childhood*	Another typology of an early childhood leader, which describes: • stages of professional development • personal characteristics • professional skills • roles and responsibilities. Rodd says that this 'multifaceted nature of leadership' includes all the skills above. The typology is broken down into the facets of the work: • **direct care:** novice – this is a person managing their own practice • **direct care:** advanced – working in collaborative partnerships and ongoing professional development • **indirect care:** see the need for change and be able to manage the change – to advocate for all the children, parents, carers and staff in your care.	This model is useful because it demonstrates the need for working upwards in this role – and that with experience comes wider knowledge. It can also then be used to evaluate all management facets – such as running a room.

Key terms

ELMS – effective leadership and management in the early years.

Typology – classification of a type.

CP4

Table 4.4: *Theories of leadership and management*

Name and date	Theories of leadership and management	In practice
Trait theories Stogdill (1948) Mann (1959) Bennis (1998) Gardener (1989)	Trait theory suggests that leaders have certain personality traits, for example, a leader will be someone who is exceptional and have traits such as physical strength and stamina, the capacity to motivate people, intelligence and action-orientated judgement. However, further research has found that this is not true.	It is limiting to suggest that leader-managers have certain personality traits. We also know that the leaders and managers we meet have very individual personalities. However, leaders and managers will certainly share some traits.
Behavioural theories Blake and Mouton (1964) McGregor (1970) Sadler (1997)	A further development of trait theories looks at what leaders do rather than the characteristics they have. This was the way in which leadership and management was understood in the 1960s. These different patterns of behaviour were grouped together and called 'styles' – for example, the Blake and Mouton managerial grid (1964): • **concern for task** – leader expects high levels of productivity • **concern for people** – where individuals are given high priority • **participative leadership** – shared decision making • **directive leadership** – where leaders make decisions for everyone. McGregor (1970) and later Sadler (1997) said that it was extremely difficult to categorise a style of leadership because this did not take into account the *context* of where the leadership took place.	As noted, a further development of trait theories rather than working on the idea that personality has something to do with the success of a leader or manager – concentrating on the way in which the manager or leader behaves. This can be rather judgemental as many managers will use a combination of the behaviours in this managerial grid.
Situational or contingency theories Fiedler and Garcia (1987)	This theory suggests that management and leadership is dictated not by style but by context – managers and leaders change their style to match the situation; further research showed that effective leadership depended upon interacting factors. Fiedler and Garcia (1987) maintained that three things were important: 1 the relationship between leaders and their teams 2 how the task was given to the team – was it clear and standardised? 3 the power given to the leader by a group or company increased the influence the leader had on the team.	Again it is clear that all managers will change style and tactics depending upon their setting, the job in hand and the expected outcomes. It is very important that there is a good relationship between leaders and their teams, but it is also important that the leader influences team members to develop their understanding of the more long-term goals.
Transformational theories Bass (2008)	This style of leadership is seen as a 'change agent' and moves people towards higher goals. Bass (1985) said that the transformational leader will be able to: • make us rethink the level of what we need • expand our range of wants and needs • influence people to think about higher need and not just about themselves, for the sake of the team • raise our awareness of outcomes.	This theory is more of a 'thinking theory' – it gives us an idea of how people can best be supported to become involved in a vision. This will help each individual to transform practice rather than just be pulled along with a new idea and resent being part of it.

Table 4.5: *Types of leadership and management*

Type	Characteristics	In practice
Autocratic/ authoritarian	Leader/manager communicates with a team 'top-down' All decisions are made by the manager/leader and team members are not consulted Not very common nowadays, especially in childcare and education where it is important to work towards a common goal.	This style might be adopted when a setting is part of a chain owned by a larger company. An area manager/leader making a decision for the whole company may not consult those working in individual settings. This can make those teams feel that their opinions are not valued.
Democratic	Leader/manager asks opinions and consults team members about any changes which might be made. Team members will have a say in how things are run. It does not mean that the team members get all they want all the time, but their views are considered.	In early years settings this style of management means that people are consulted. For example, if Ofsted has inspected and there is an action plan, team members are involved in making changes to meet the action plan. This means they will feel valued and included in the process, and are therefore more likely to be supportive of any changes.
Bureaucratic	May be used where accountability and transparency are very important and the risks of malpractice are critical, for example, large institutions, e.g. government. There may be lots of policies and procedures in place with the aim of reducing risk and increasing safeguarding. Bureaucratic organisations are often slower to make decisions and because policies and procedures are so important, the individual leader/manager is not always held responsible for changes made.	This might not be a common style of management in early years settings – but if it were, an example could be a manager wanting to make a change that supports better outcomes for the children but they are put off because they would need to fill in so many forms and jump through too many hoops to make it work.
Paternalistic	Tries to achieve a balance between top-down decision making and considering the welfare of the team. Paternalistic leaders/managers make decisions largely on their own, but their decision-making process takes in to account the personal needs of their workers as an important factor, and does not concentrate solely on the bottom line.	This style might apply to a manager in a chain of nurseries who works hard to ensure that the work of their team is recognised by the company and ideas from the team are passed up to senior leaders to be considered as good working practice.
Laissez-faire	Delegation is at the heart of a laissez-faire style Laissez-faire literally means 'allow to do' It is based on team members being committed and feeling responsible for projects. The team needs to be experienced and able to carry out the tasks delegated to it. As an added benefit, the laissez-faire leader/manager may have a reduced workload!	This style of management is very good when the team is working towards a common goal – for example, an inspection – as the leader/manager trusts everyone and is happy for them to be involved and make decisions to prepare for the inspection. The downfall of this, however, is that if something is not completed correctly, the leader/manager may not be aware and will be ultimately responsible.

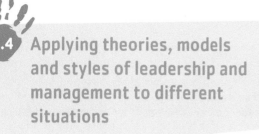

1.4 Applying theories, models and styles of leadership and management to different situations

The theories we have looked at have ranged from definitions of what makes a manager and a leader to models that can be used to improve practice across the sector and for individuals at every level. In practice, we need to be able to see where these theories are underpinning what happens in the setting.

Case studies: applying theory to practice

Behavioural theories

The manager knew that there was an issue in the baby room – the staff were not getting on very well. Lara and Mandy were taking their breaks together and leaving Sarah to do all the clearing up at lunchtime. Sarah had talked to her manager about this. The manager decided to put up a list in the baby room of jobs and times – the list separated Mandy and Lara at lunchtimes.

1 Was this:
   - concern for task
   - concern for people
   - participative leadership
   - directive leadership?

Situational or contingency theories

Feedback showed that some parents were concerned about how their children were greeted in the morning. It was all rather chaotic and disorganised, and some parents did not feel confident that their children were happy at the start of the day. The new nursery head had a team meeting and fed this back to her team – she held an open discussion and a group was formed to work on new ways of organising the welcome in the morning. During the next few months the team trialled some new ideas and the group sought feedback from parents before a final decision was made by the manager on which way the morning welcome would be organised.

2 How was the task given to the team – was it clear and standardised?

3 Did the power given to the leader by the parents' feedback increase the influence she had on the team?

Transformational theories

The play setting had been running for about six months – everyone knew that some things needed to change and improve. A new leader was appointed. He started with a meeting where he held an open forum for discussion. The subject was: Do we need to make changes?

4 Did this leader make his team rethink the level of what they needed by asking 'Do we need to make changes?'?

5 How could he influence people to think about higher need and not just about themselves, for the sake of the team?

6 How could he raise awareness of the outcomes for the setting?

Whalley (2011)

There was a crisis in the children's centre – one of the parents had become aggressive when he was asked to leave the setting and told he could not see his son because of a court order. He shouted at the key worker and demanded that he see his son.

7 How could the manager lead in this situation?

8 How should the manager respond to the parent?

9 What skills would a good manager/leader use in this situation?

A typical day in the life of a manager

Morning

Started my day speaking to a parent about fees which are outstanding. She was very upset and I needed to support her.

Answered emails and updated the rota to cover Jan while she is on training.

Went to the bank.

Discussed menus for next week with the cook. He is easily upset if I don't take up his suggestions, so I need to handle these conversations carefully.

Spoke to the room leaders about seasonal events – they have some good ideas. Jasmine can be left in charge of this and I've arranged to meet with her again at the end of the week.

Lunch

Met with new member of staff who starts next week. Time spent with him now is important so he begins with the right sort of attitude.

Afternoon

Met with Nuala who is helping me put an advert together for more staff. Nuala is experienced at wording these things and will get the task finished quickly.

Meeting with baby room staff to talk about poor practice I've observed. I'd already met the room leader so she was aware. Discussed some ideas we have for better practice and how we're going to monitor that.

Spoke to some new parents on phone to arrange visits with them for early next week.

Spent my last hour in a nursery room. I like to be around at end of day. It's important that I spend time with the children and observe practice. Besides, I miss the children when I am stuck in the office all day!

Figure 4.3: *A day at work for a nursery manager. Can you identify how this manager is leading her team and which models and theories can be applied to her work?*

So what does this mean?

A manager/leader needs to:

- take into account the setting they work in – what is required of them in their role
- consider the way in which they are going to lead/manage – which style suits them best?
- have good sector knowledge and understanding so that team members will trust their judgement
- take the lead whenever needed
- be aware that they can influence others and recognise that this is a big responsibility
- think about how they are going to respond when there is a problem.

Assessment activity
1.1, 1.2, 1.3, 1.4

Give a ten-minute presentation which:

- explains the differences between leadership and management
- summarises two of the different theories, models and styles of leadership
- summarises two of the different theories, models and styles of management.

Your presentation must include:

- a brief description of what is meant by management
- a brief description of what is meant by leadership
- a summary of the differences between management and leadership
- examples of how **two** of the theories can be applied to different situations.

You will need to provide some guidance notes on two A4 pieces of paper as handouts for your audience.

2 Understand the skill sets required to be an effective leader and/or manager

Managers and leaders require skills which they use in everyday management and in leading the setting forward and into the future while being mindful of legislative requirements and processes.

2.1 Attributes that contribute to success as a leader or manager

If you work in the children and young people's sector you will know that it is diverse and made up of many different professionals. There is also a constant demand for change and innovation to improve practice. Some people leading and managing in the sector may have been given a role because of their previous experience or because they have made it known that they want to move on and take more responsibility.

Whatever the reason, you will be aware that each person who takes on other responsibilities in leading or managing has particular attributes which are vital if they are to be successful in the role.

Key terms

Innovation – progress with new ideas.

Attributes – personal qualities.

Find out

How many people have management or leadership roles in your setting? Make a list of:
- the roles they perform
- the attributes that make them successful.

Some of the management theories you looked at earlier in the unit gave a list of attributes which are essential for effective leadership. A successful manager and leader will have the following qualities or attributes and will use them for the benefit of the children in their care and the staff they manage.

- **Good communicator:** always listening to people and their ideas as well as giving new ideas themselves. Keeping an open mind.
- **Confident:** not over-confident but having a quiet confidence in their own abilities.
- **Respectful** of others and their opinions and values, valuing their knowledge and expertise.
- **Collaborative:** able to work with others towards a common goal and not taking all the credit for a job well done.
- **Nurturing:** supportive and encouraging of staff and children.
- **Creative:** thinking of new ways to improve their own practice and that of others.
- **Inclusive:** involved in all projects and ideas, and supporting everyone to have equal access.
- **Empathetic:** understanding all sides of a situation.
- **Warm:** caring, sincere and approachable.
- **Persevering:** able to keep trying even if things are not going the way they would like.
- **Enabling:** supportive of others to be the best they can be and making things possible for them.
- **Fair:** able to treat people differently but equally as individuals.

CP4

- **Genuine:** people know they mean the things they say and can trust that they will follow through on them.
- **Reflective:** wanting to make continual improvements to their practice.
- **Responsive:** responding to need in a professional way.
- **An advocate:** supporting and speaking for someone who may not be able to do so themselves.

Therefore the successful leader and manager will always:

- set a good example to others (both children and colleagues)
- have a good understanding of the sector and what is best practice
- have respect for colleagues and know their individual skills and abilities
- be professional and professionally confident
- be sensitive and responsive to lead change effectively
- be assertive and logical in approaching what needs doing
- be supportive and an advocate for others.

If you want to improve your professional skills so that you can be considered for a role managing within your setting, you should try to develop these skills and attributes.

2.2 The importance of encouraging others to take the lead

The manager or leader must ensure that the team follows their lead and works towards a common goal. They must be sensitive when dealing with people and be consistent in their approach to team members. The effective manager will also know the strengths of their team and will encourage them to build on them and take the lead when needed. A confident manager will enjoy the prospect of encouraging others to lead as this reflects on *their*

ability as a leader.

Distributive leadership is often thought of as the way forward in children and young people's settings as it improves the service offered by the setting. This is when practitioners in the team will be encouraged to take the lead with some extra responsibilities, for example, special needs coordination, room leading, advocacy, community work, **pedagogical work** and **cultural work** to name but a few. In all of these instances the manager will need to recognise the skills of the individual and encourage them to take the lead in this area of work. It is vital that the manager and leader recognise that:

- it is always better for the individual to learn from others who already have experience of leading
- there is identification of training needed
- commitment must be acknowledged
- there is a need for ongoing support and guidance
- there needs to be an emphasis on shared responsibility, cooperation and mutual respect.

Reflect

Think about the settings you have worked in. Are there practitioners in the team who could take on extra responsibility or have expertise that is going unrecognised? If you were the manager of that setting, how would you:

- encourage them to take on those roles
- prepare them to do so?

Key terms

Distributive leadership – a cooperative way of leading.

Pedagogical work – encouraging a learning community.

Cultural work – education about celebrating differences within communities.

How does the manager and leader encourage others to take the lead?

Figure 4.4 shows one process a manager or leader could take to encourage other members of their team to take the lead.

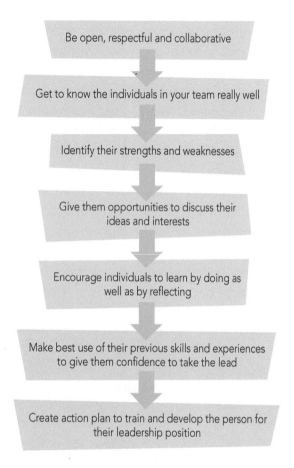

Figure 4.4: *Enabling others to take the lead*

A manager need not feel threatened by letting someone within their team take the lead in a particular area. This sharing of leadership duties will take some of the pressures and stresses from the manager, giving them more time to deal with other things. It will also have a positive effect on the team member: extra responsibility and leadership will give them the opportunity to feel valued and respected within the team. Overall the effects are positive.

- The practitioner feels valued and develops an important expertise which will improve the quality of the setting.
- The manager will feel that another facet or role in the setting is receiving attention, ensuring best practice.
- Other members of the team will see that people who work hard and continue to learn and reflect can become key members of the setting.
- Further training and development takes place and can be shared among the team.
- There is a focal point of a person who has specific expertise and who can be called upon for advice.
- The children, parents and carers who use the setting will benefit because they will see that there is an open atmosphere where people are valued and achievement is celebrated.

John Adair is acknowledged internationally as having influenced leadership and management development in many different areas of work through his action-centred leadership model. Adair's research has produced ideas, techniques and models to support managers and leaders to be more inspiring and to build an effective team while being creative and innovative. Adair also gives insight into how managers and leaders can develop their skills and become effective communicators and decision makers. He has developed models to encourage motivation among staff, and techniques for encouraging them to take the lead themselves.

Find out

Research John Adair's findings on leadership and management.

- What are Adair's eight rules for motivating people?
- What is Adair's 50:50 rule?

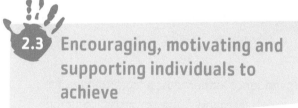

2.3 Encouraging, motivating and supporting individuals to achieve

You have looked at ways in which managers and leaders can encourage others to take the lead in the setting. However, not everyone wants to take the lead or have extra responsibility. Team members should be encouraged and motivated to do their best for the setting and the outcomes of the children in their care.

Case study: supporting achievement

Jenna has worked in the children's centre for two years; she started working there when she left college with a level 3 qualification. Jenna feels she has learned a great deal from her colleagues and the good practice which goes on around her. She loves working with the children and has recently been thinking about new ideas. Jenna approached her line manager and asked if she could work on developing outdoor play. The manager was quite enthusiastic and took Jenna's ideas to the team meeting. However, some of the other practitioners were resistant and felt that their outside play was fine as it was. After the meeting the manager told Jenna that she thought it best to leave the ideas for a while and thanked her for her contribution.

1 How do you think Jenna felt about this?
2 How could the manager have dealt with this in a more effective way?
3 How could the manager have encouraged Jenna's new ideas and supported her to introduce them to the team?

Managing a children and young people's team in any setting has many responsibilities but one of these is to encourage, motivate and support individuals within the team to achieve. The amount of encouragement and support needed will differ from one person to the next; it will range from supporting one person to carry out mundane everyday tasks to encouraging another practitioner to take on a lead role in a particular area. The manager will need to:

- encourage team members to make suggestions and voice their ideas
- consider new ideas with an open mind
- encourage and motivate team members to give of their best and achieve their best
- support and guide those who may be struggling with their particular job role
- see the strengths and weaknesses of the team as a whole and identify where gaps in expertise can be filled.

Most managers and leaders will have had no training in providing this support and encouragement. However, if the manager uses a structured approach to encouraging team members and one which is fair to everyone in the team, there will be positive outcomes. The manager will also become more experienced in dealing with this very important part of the job. This type of support needs a highly motivated manager who has:

- very good communication skills
- expertise and knowledge so that they can give appropriate feedback to the team member
- the ability to involve team members in the objectives of the setting
- the ability to make people feel valued and listened to
- the ability to monitor progress on a regular basis.

The manager may meet with individual team members on a regular basis to support them and set them actions for short-, medium- and long-term goals. The meeting gives the manager an opportunity to:

- check and monitor that the team member is doing their job well and support them to reflect on their practice
- support them to work on ways to improve practice
- motivate and encourage individuals by listening and helping them to see their own strengths and evaluate their performance
- give ideas to motivate them to achieve their goals
- support them with the tools available by providing resources or training
- recognise where something has gone well and congratulate the team member on their performance.

A practitioner who does not get this support in a structured way may lose enthusiasm and start to feel less committed and caring. They may also feel as though they are not valued by colleagues or their manager.

Through individual meetings with team members, leaders and managers can achieve a great deal and can encourage and support in a structured way. The following list gives suggestions of what individual meetings could include.

CP4

- ✓ **Job role:** discussion around individual key children and responsibilities – how things are going; any particular issues arising; ideas for improvement; solutions for challenges.
- ✓ **Particular responsibilities:** monitor short, medium- and long-term goals. Discuss resource issues and the need for any training – are they facing any challenges while managing others?
- ✓ **Training and development:** is there any ongoing training taking place? Monitor how it is going.

- ✓ **Future developments:** are there any changes on the horizon? Make more long-term plans for changes taking place – reflect on current practice.
- **Any other business:** an opportunity to discuss any personal issues or particular challenges for the team member. The time to reflect and congratulate where appropriate.
- ✓ **Agreed goals – short term:** finish the meeting productively with some short-term goals and a date for the next meeting.
- ✓ **Next meeting date can be confirmed.**

encouraging
listening to ideas; open, happy atmosphere; high expectations; valuing individuals; welcoming everyone

culture of achievement

supporting
no blame culture; celebrating skills and differences

motivating
expecting excellence; best practice as the norm; exploring new ideas and being innovative and reflective

Reflect

Have you had an opportunity to hold or take part in a one-to-one meeting with a manager? Think about:

- the possible benefits for the team member
- the possible challenges for the manager
- if this is a productive use of a manager's time.

Having looked at practical ways in which the manager can sit down with the team member and discuss how they can be supported and encouraged, you also need to consider ways in which the manager supports and encourages a 'culture of achievement' in the setting on a day-to-day basis. **Figure 4.5** shows how this can be achieved.

Figure 4.5: *Process for encouraging achievement*

Assessment activity 2.1, 2.2, 2.3

1 Demonstrate that you understand the skills required to be an effective leader and/or manager by producing an information leaflet listing the necessary attributes.

2 In a pair or group of three, discuss the importance of encouraging others to take the lead and the

ways in which you could achieve this in your settings. Write up your discussion points and share them with the whole group.

3 In a group of three, research and design your own model which tells other learners how to encourage, motivate and support individuals to achieve. Present this model to others in your group and share ideas.

3 Understand how to create a sense of common purpose for team working

Very often the leader or manager of a setting will need to communicate and lead a change or a new initiative – this can be difficult, especially if not everyone is committed to it. A decision to do something which affects everyone can only be implemented if everyone is going to take part and work towards the same goal. There needs to be a sense of common purpose.

Find out

What was the last change or initiative that took place in your setting which had an effect on everyone? Was it an Ofsted inspection or a new piece of legislation or change to policy? How did the manager in your setting lead this change?

3.1 Communicating a common goal within the work environment

In every setting there will always be a time when the team will have to work towards a new goal or objective for the good of the setting. Sometimes this goal is imposed on the setting, e.g. as a result of an Ofsted inspection or because new legislation has been introduced. At other times it may be something that the manager or leader has identified which needs to be changed in order for the setting to become more effective and successful.

Case study: promoting improvement

Emma is the manager of a nursery within a children's centre. Recently there has been an Ofsted inspection and she was disappointed with the outcome of 'Good'. The areas for improvement were to:

- ensure systematic observations and assessments of each child's achievements, interests and learning styles to plan for future learning
- match observations to developmental expectations
- develop planning to promote a challenging outdoor environment to enhance children's experiences.

Emma knows that the team worked hard before the inspection and that they are also disappointed with the outcome. Some of the team seem to be quite negative and feel that these further changes will be difficult.

1 What should Emma do?

2 How can Emma start to make the changes necessary?

3 Where would you suggest Emma should start?

4 Have you experienced this in your setting? What happened?

When something like the above happens in a setting, it is really important that the manager or leader responds in an appropriate way. Appropriate responses could include:

- acting enthusiastically and remaining committed to the work
- taking responsibility and not blaming others
- not giving up easily or feeling resentful towards the team
- letting everyone know that this is a positive thing, as they will now know how to move forward and how to improve.

The manager or leader will next need to make a clear plan and define what the objectives are. They

CP4

will also need to come up with a timescale for the improvements. This will make the team feel 'led' and will motivate them to work towards a common goal.

The purpose of leading in this situation is to let everyone know what they need to do and how the team is going to go about this. The manager will need to meet with the team as a group and explain or discuss:

- the reasons for needing to make the changes
- the strengths of the team – encourage them to see that they have all the skills needed for the job in hand
- the plan for moving forward – ask the team's opinions: Will this work? Are the timings going to be suitable?
- what can be achieved (being realistic) and how long it might take
- how everyone is on the same side and that the team can all support each other to achieve this goal
- that they need to speak to individuals about their responsibilities and individual targets.

How will working in a setting with a common goal help practitioners to improve the quality of care they provide?

The manager or leader will then need to ensure that the team continues to have a sense of common purpose and clear objectives, as well as a shared and equal commitment from all team members. They will need to make sure that effective communication and dialogue within the team continues.

3.2 & 3.3 Meeting the team's individual needs and motivating them towards a common goal

When the manager or leader has communicated the common goal or purpose, they will need to talk to individual members of the team to make sure that everyone is on task and motivated.

Initially there might be a period of time when the manager or leader needs to reflect on how the skills of the staff can be used to support the common goal. Each team member will need to feel involved in this and it may mean that the manager and senior staff take some time to observe and understand how the team works.

There might be a deputy manager or team leader who could assist with this task and then feed back to the manager. At this meeting the team leader or deputy will need to be at the centre in supporting the whole team towards the common goal.

During each meeting with individual team members, the manager or leader should explore the following areas.

Skills and experience

What skills and experience does the person have which can support working towards the common goal? Team members often have skills other people are not aware of. It is important that the manager explores their past experience and skills – this person could have an essential skill that will make all the difference to the task.

Further training

What further training is needed? This training could be given by another member of the team and may be the element which supports the team member to feel more confident with their task.

Individual attributes

What are the team member's particular strengths? A team member may be calm in a crisis or very patient; they may be able to support others or work on a particular facet of the planning. Everyone will have something they can draw upon to support the team toward their goals – no matter how small or insignificant the person might feel it is.

Communication

How does the team member communicate in the setting? Do they find it easy to talk to others and communicate their feelings or do they find it difficult to express themselves in this way?

Confidence

Do they feel confident about the changes taking place? What are their concerns and fears? How can they be supported to feel more confident? People's confidence is often built by just telling them the things they are good at and reassuring them their skills are appreciated.

Threats

What could hold them back? The manager or leader needs to find out what they think will make their task difficult.

Ownership

The manager or leader will need to look at ways in which the person can take ownership of the task in hand and therefore the common goal. Does the team member feel involved and responsible?

Support

What support do they need to complete their task? They will need to play a part in meeting the common goal but they may need to be supported by colleagues or by the belief and trust of their manager.

When all these things have been discussed and explored the individual is then:

- set a target as part of the overall objective
- given a timescale to do all of their tasks
- given an outline of how the manager/leader will support
- given a date for the next review of their target.

When the person holding the meeting has been through this whole process, the team member should feel motivated and ready to be involved in working as part of the team toward a common goal.

Reflect

Can you remember a time when you were asked to work on something with your team (such as preparation for Ofsted or making improvements suggested by Ofsted)?

- Did you feel valued as part of the team?
- Do you think your skills and attributes were made best use of?
- Did you feel involved?
- Give a best practice example of how you have felt motivated to be involved in a common goal.

3.4 Encouraging reflection by the team and individuals

Leaders and managers have a responsibility to ensure that there is a learning community where everyone – children, staff, parents and carers – is learning all the time. It can be difficult to allocate the time to ensure that this happens. However, if time is spent in discussion with team members it encourages ongoing learning, which in turn ensures practice is always good, thus making reflection an easier task.

Key terms

Learning community – a place where learning is encouraged for everyone, both staff and service users, visually and practically.

Reflection – a way in which we review what we have already done in order to improve the way things are done in future.

All team members should be encouraged to reflect on their practice. There are three possible ways in which we reflect:

1 **We do things as a matter of routine:** this might be something in our practice such as reading a story or taking children to wash their hands. It is difficult to reflect on because we do it as a matter of habit.

2 **Something goes wrong** and we reflect on why that happened and how we could prevent it going wrong next time.

3 **Think about it afterwards:** this is where we reflect later on how we could have dealt with something differently to make it more successful or go more smoothly.

Encouraging the team to reflect

All professionals are encouraged to reflect on their practice so that ongoing improvement can be made to the services which are offered. It is the manager's responsibility to ensure that all team members self-evaluate and that the team as a whole reflect on how they work.

Find out

Find out all you can about reflective practice.

- Can you say where and when reflective practice takes place in the setting you work in?
- How effective is it?
- What do you do in your setting to reflect on your practice? Do you talk about it in meetings or record it in some other way?

Reflective dialogue can be used to encourage all members of a team to look as a group at the practice in the setting. A manager or leader needs to consider the following questions to see if real reflective practice takes place. You can also ask yourself the questions shown in **Figure 4.6**.

Question	How do you know you do this?	What are you going to do next?
What opportunities do you make for reflective dialogue?	*We have team meetings monthly and this is an agenda item*	*We may come back to this at the next meeting or organise a smaller group to work on our dialogue*
Do you evaluate your own practice regularly?		
When do you reflect upon your role either as a manager/leader or as a practitioner?		

Figure 4.6: *An example of a grid to support reflective practice*

As a team you can also reflect on practice by doing some action research. If the team has concerns about a certain part of their practice, they can do some action research to explore how this practice is working. They can then decide whether any changes could be made to improve it. This can be recorded by:

- time sampling
- photographs
- a written diary or log
- observations of the children
- getting the children involved – asking their opinions.

The manager or leader needs to be up to date with all the latest news in the sector and must decide which of these changes should be fed down to the team. They should also be aware of the influences that may have an effect on the setting. They must ensure that there is always time for the team to reflect on their practice as a team or in smaller groups so that practice is continually improving. There needs to be continual discussion about pedagogy; these discussions will ensure that team members are always thinking reflectively about

their practice and the learning taking place for the children. In team meetings it is a good idea to give the opportunity to swap practice ideas.

As a team the following points need to be considered:

- opportunities for reflective dialogue
- discussions about possible action research ideas to bring about improvements
- swapping best practice ideas for learning opportunities for the children.

Key terms

Reflective dialogue – a group discussion about practice; everyone is actively encouraged to take part.

Action research – recording something in action.

Pedagogy – the principles and methods of teaching and learning.

Case study: St Bartholomew's School reception class

Natalia had been a member of the reception class team for six months. She was concerned that the children did not appear to be benefiting enough from the computer area. Sometimes there were little arguments among the children and some of them avoided this area altogether. So she started to record much time was spent in there and how many children used it at any one time – everyone took part in this by logging times and numbers on a chart hung up above the area. Natalia also wrote a diary and observed the area for ten minutes at a time, three times a day.

When Natalia looked at the results taken over a two-week period she found that it was actually the layout of the area and the access to it which were causing much of the problem. Some of the children became frustrated by the furniture layout and in turn they took this out on the children around them. Natalia and another team member looked at ways to improve this by using a different layout. They showed their idea to Jenny, a senior member of the team who had been resistant to

moving the computer area around. However, when she saw the evidence, Jenny seemed happy to consider a new layout.

Natalia and the team felt that this idea had worked well. Even though they were often very busy, and there was little time to consider and evaluate things, they decided as a team that they would do so on a regular basis from now on.

1 What challenges do you think Natalia could have met in going ahead with this action research without talking to Jenny first?

2 Do you have a way of recording information like this in your setting so that you can make improvements to practice?

3 if so, who is the person in charge of recording this information? If not, who should be in charge of this?

4 Do you have the time and the opportunity to look at practice and make changes for improvement? How would you go about this?

CP4

Encouraging the individual to reflect

If there is good reflective practice within the whole team, it usually means that individual team members are also reflective. The best way to encourage individuals is to meet with them on a one-to-one basis and include reflection in that meeting. A manager will need to demonstrate to the team member that they:

- are interested in their progress
- want to hear their ideas and possible reflections
- value their input and their skills
- congratulate them on their successes.

If a manager feels that a team member is not being reflective and is working routinely, never questioning their own practice, this meeting will provide an opportunity to:

- ask them to evidence how they make sure their practice is good
- make suggestions on how they can be more reflective
- start a discussion about their practice
- tell them they will be given the opportunity to reflect on something to see how it might improve their practice.

Reflective practice is talked about by all practitioners but an effective manager who encourages **BEST** practice will do the following.

Be aware

The manager/leader should always be aware of:

- influences of external changes to legislation and practice
- dynamics – observing the team and how they work with each other
- the children – are they happy and developing well?

Empower staff

Empower staff to feel they can take risks and improve on practice – they need to feel valued as part of the team.

Skills in staff

Recognise **all** the skills of the staff as they may be needed at some point. A manager will also need to identify when there is a need for further training.

Test and reflect

The team should always be able to tell the manager what is going on and discuss ways to make improvements. Be sure they are taking the time to reflect properly.

How could observation followed by reflection improve practice?

Assessment activity
3.1, 3.2, 3.3, 3.4

Demonstrate that you understand a manager/leader's role in creating a sense of common purpose for team working. Produce an electronic presentation which includes information on how a manager/leader should:

- communicate a common goal in the work environment
- identify individual needs and motivate others towards a common goal according to their needs
- encourage and support others to make the best of their ability to achieve common goals
- encourage reflection on achieving common goals by the team and by individuals.

You could use clips from an Internet source in your presentation.

CP4

In the real world

My name is Rosie. I am a second-year student working in a children's centre. There are lots of different things going on in the setting so I get the chance to work with little children supporting their play and with particular groups such as baby massage and the parents' support group. I am lucky because I am invited to some of the meetings that take place with the team. I don't see some of the people at the team meetings again during the week but everyone is aware of their role and happy to share ideas and talk about practice – this is really helpful.

The centre manager is very busy and is out quite a bit at meetings but she deals with the parents a lot and knows all the children's names. I have noticed my supervisor (Pam) goes for a meeting with her once a week. I had some ideas for a display in the reception area and talked to Pam, who discussed them with the centre manager. I have to go and present my ideas to her in the team meeting next week. Pam says she likes to hear ideas from students because we are in college learning all the newest ideas all the time. I am a bit nervous but I hope she is impressed and lets me do the display as I want to apply for a job here when I have finished my course. I really like it here as you always feel your ideas and views are listened to – it's a challenge but good fun!

Check your knowledge

1 Name three things a leader does.
2 Name three things a manager does.
3 What is the difference between a leader and a manager?
4 What is meant by transformational leadership?
5 What is meant by trait leadership?
6 What is meant by behavioural leadership?
7 What is ELMS typology?
8 Name five attributes of a leader.
9 Name five attributes of a manager.
10 What is meant by reflective dialogue?

Further references

The following are sources of useful information on the topic of an introduction to leadership and management.

Books and articles

Adair, J. (2008) *The Best of Adair on Leadership and Management*, edited by Neil Thomas, Abingdon: Thorogood Publications

Aubrey, C. (2011) *Leading and Managing in the Early Years*, London: Sage

Bass, B. (2008) *The Bass Handbook of Leadership: Theory, Research, and Managerial Applications*, 4th edition, New York: The Free Press

Blake, R.R., Mouton, J.H. and Allen, R. (1987) *Spectacular Teamwork: How to Develop the Leadership Skills for Team Success*, Chichester: John Wiley & Sons

Daly, M., Byers, E. and Taylor, W. (2009) *Early Years Management in Practice*, 2nd edition, Oxford: Heinemann

Department for Education and Skills (DfES) (2002b: 3) *Developing Management Skills*, DfES Publications

Donaldson-Feilder, E., Lewis, R. and Yarker, J. (2011) *Preventing Stress in Organizations: How to Develop Positive Managers*, New Jersey: Wiley-Blackwell

Jones, C. and Pound, L. (2008) *Leadership and Management in the Early Years*, Berkshire: Open University Press

Mckibbin, J. and Walton, A. (2012) *Leadership and Management in Health & Social Care and Children & Young People's Services*, 2nd edition, Harlow: Pearson Education Ltd

Moyles, J. (2006) *Effective Leadership and Management in the Early Years*, Maidenhead: Open University Press

Rickards, T. (1999) *Creativity and the Management of Change (Manchester Business and Management Series)*, New Jersey: Wiley-Blackwell

Rodd, J. (2005) *Leadership in Early Childhood*, 3rd edition, Berkshire: Open University Press

Skills for Care (2008) *Leadership and management strategy update*, Leeds: Skills for Care

Whalley, M.E. (2011) *Leading Practice in Early Years Settings*, Exeter: Learning Matters Ltd

Useful websites

To obtain a secure link to the website below, visit www.pearsonhotlinks.co.uk and search for this book by using its title or ISBN. Click on the section for CP4.

Ofsted

Supporting the development of study skills

CP5

It is important to develop good study skills to ensure you can gather and use information effectively. This unit looks at how you can do this in order to gain confidence in the formal presentation of information and data.

Learning outcomes

By the end of this unit you will:

1 Understand the role of study skills

2 Understand how to source information when planning a project or piece of writing

3 Understand how to present information

4 Be able to present information that is fit for purpose and relevant to target audience

5 Understand the need to evaluate the process involved in gathering and presenting information.

In practice

Safia is about to begin a project entitled 'Effectively managing children's behaviour'. Her chosen method of presentation is to complete a report and give a ten-minute talk to her group.

She has three weeks to complete the project and will use the learning resource centre at her college to find out more information. She has an idea of what she would like to explore, but there is so much information available that she has no idea where to start. When she types the question into a search engine on her computer, none of the returned results really matches the information she wants to find out.

Her tutor has allocated three lessons for research and Safia wants to make the most of this time, but is feeling stressed and confused by what to do next.

By the end of this unit you will know how Safia could begin to tackle the project and what she can do to make sure that she presents the data she has collected suitably.

1 Understand the role of study skills

1.1 The term 'study skills'

This learning outcome begins by exploring the techniques you can use to make sure you collect and organise data successfully.

In order to be able to learn new things and process information effectively, you will require a range of skills. These skills need to be learned and developed. In other words, you need to learn how to learn. The study skills you should apply to your chosen field of study include:

- note taking
- time management
- reading methods
- spellchecking
- using reference sources.

1.2 Methods of flexible reading

One of the most essential components of any type of study is reading more about your subject; this underpins your knowledge and understanding. There are lots of books, magazines, websites and journals relating to the issues of working with children and young people.

It is not possible to read everything about the subjects you are studying, even if they seem important and relevant to your assignment writing. So, in order to process all of this data, you need to adopt flexible reading methods.

There are four reading methods:

- scan reading
- skim reading
- speed reading
- study reading.

Scan reading

Scan reading is not a detailed or in-depth read but is useful when you are sifting through a large amount of information. You can think of it as a quick glance to look for a particular word or set of words about a specific topic. You probably use scan reading without thinking about it; for instance, you might scan read the contents page at the front of a magazine to find the section or page you are interested in.

You can apply this reading method to your studies to make a decision about whether an article or book is going to be useful. You might scan read the preface or the opening lines of the introduction in order to decide whether or not you should include it in your research.

In the same way, you can read the contents page in a book to see if any of the chapters cover your subject. For example, if you wanted to research 'measles', you could scan read the contents page which might tell you that the book has a chapter about children's health – this could be of use to you. You could then turn to the index at the back of the book and see if there were pages where measles was specifically mentioned.

Key terms

Contents page – a list of sections or chapters that you will find inside the book.

Preface – the introduction to the book. It will usually explain the subject covered by the book or the main aims it hopes to achieve.

Index – a detailed list of information about the contents of a book together with a reference to the page numbers where you can find each piece of information. It is found at the back.

Skim reading

Skim reading involves reading quickly. It allows you to 'skim' over the body of the work and pick up on the main threads or the 'gist' of what is being said within the writing.

We use skim reading every day, for example, when we receive an email or text message. You might gather the main points of the message without actually reading the finer details. You can then decide whether it is of value and worth reading in more depth.

Skim reading might be the second stage in the process of deciding whether or not you want to read something more closely because you think it will be helpful for your research.

Speed reading

This is a technique that has to be learned. Once you are proficient at it, you can absorb written information more quickly than standard reading. Unlike skim reading, speed reading should allow you to retain more information. There would be no sense in reading quickly if you did not take in or digest the information. The success of speed reading depends on a lot of practice, how interested you are in the subject, your motivation for reading the text, the amount of distractions present at the time and the type of wording that has been used. Speed reading should be used as one of a variety of reading methods as it would be very unlikely to be practical or effective on its own.

One way to increase the speed of your reading is to reduce sub vocalisation. This is reading words 'aloud' in your head. It is very difficult to stop yourself from doing this, especially if you come across new words or different terminology. We often read through things twice or even out loud when we are trying to make sense of them. If you are encountering lots of new or unfamiliar words you should take your time over them.

Key term

Sub vocalisation – saying words 'aloud' in your head when reading.

Chunking is another method which can be used to speed read. It involves reading groups of words as one whole unit and is the complete opposite of how you are taught to read. Instead of reading each word, you read whole chunks of writing at once. You focus upon the middle section of the page and allow your eyes to see the words on the outer edges of your vision. It is a skill that needs lots of practice but it can speed up reading time considerably.

Study reading

Study reading involves reading the text thoroughly for detail and is probably the method you are most familiar with. It is by using this method that you will take in the most information and digest the content, often making connections with what you have been learning. For this reason it is the most important method of reading you will use.

It is useful to plan your study reading so that you have purpose and direction.

What are the features of a good environment for reading?

It is helpful to start by writing yourself some questions you hope will be answered by reading the text. This will mean that you read purposefully and examine the text in detail.

It is sometimes called 'active reading'. It enables you to absorb and understand by linking the new information to things you already know. It can sometimes feel like a profound 'eureka' moment when you read a passage and it makes complete sense. This could be because you have had the experience yourself or you can relate it to something you are familiar with. You are also more likely to retain this information because it feels relevant.

When study reading, it can be helpful to take notes or highlight or underline useful sections. This also helps to save time if you would like to return to them.

Using a page tag or turning the corner of the page will also help you to find sections of books that have specific information you want to refer to at a later time.

Scan text
Quickly find out whether each text covers the right subject.

Skim read
Spend a little longer getting a flavour of what is said in texts on the right subject. Do they contain the information you need?

Speed read
Cast your eye over the text, taking in information, but do not spend long reading. It will help you decide if a text is worth reading in more detail.

Jot down ideas and questions
Find a focus or decide what you what to find out before you start to read in more detail.

Study read
Spend time reading in detail what you now know contains valuable information, make notes and highlight important pieces of text. You will make effective use of your study time.

Figure 5.1: *A reading process. You might want to approach your reading for study in this way. It will make sure you do not read an entire book only to find it was not relevant.*

So what does this mean?

Consider what suits you best.

- Some people like to set themselves reading targets, for example, 'Tonight I am going to read Chapter 5 and take notes.'
- Other people like to keep their book with them, reading little and often, for example, on the bus or during their lunch break.
- Create an environment that helps you to focus. Some people need complete silence in order to concentrate and absorb what they are reading. Others like to listen to music or read somewhere public such as the library.
- Keep distractions to a minimum and switch off your mobile phone, laptop and television.
- Quiet music can be helpful if you do not like complete silence. Using headphones can help to reduce other distracting noises.
- Use a page marker or bookmark so that you can quickly pick up where you left off if you are interrupted.
- Do not forget comfort breaks – you will not be able to retain the information you are reading if you are hungry, thirsty or need to go to the toilet.
- Every 20 minutes or so, get up and stretch your legs, and have a short break from reading.

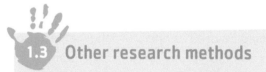

1.3 Other research methods

The various reading methods discussed above will help you to choose potential sources of information. Now you must apply different skills to make sure you make the most of this information. These include:
- using reference sources
- taking notes
- using abbreviations
- managing time
- staying motivated.

Key term

Abbreviations – words or phrases that have been shortened in a piece of writing.

Using reference sources

The reference sources you use are vital in helping you to make sense of what you are learning. Look carefully at who is providing the information and do not base all of your research upon what you have found on your computer.

- **Course textbook:** keep this with you at all times during your studies. This will mean that you can look again at any areas you are unsure of. It will address all themes of learning.
- **Dictionary:** this will help you with any unfamiliar words you come across. Misunderstanding a word could cost you considerably in your assignments. A dictionary will also help you to spell correctly when you are writing or typing up your work. Use your dictionary at the note-writing stage to make sure you do not copy errors into your final draft of work.
- **Reading list:** your school or college may provide you with a reading list. This will include books that your course tutors feel will help you to find the answers to the most important questions raised in your study. You are not expected to purchase all of these books but, by borrowing them from the library, you can assess whether or not you would like to buy them. The benefit of having your own copies is that you can make notes in them and highlight important sections of text.
- **Policy documents:** these can really help to cement your understanding of how the theories you are learning about in the classroom translate into real-world practice in the workplace.
- **Journals:** new research is published in journals. These can often be accessed online and allow the reader to see what research was undertaken and why, and what the results were. Journals can be very helpful in giving you all of the details when you hear reports in the media.

- **Newspapers:** as an example, if a newspaper reports upon findings that suggest nursery education makes children more socially aware, you can read the full research report and decide whether the newspaper has given the whole picture or not.
- **Internet:** the Internet provides a wealth of information instantly and it can be very appealing to use it for most of your research. However, take care when selecting web pages for reference, as some might not be accurate or factually correct. Some might deliberately provide misleading information in order to make you think in a certain way.

Taking notes

We all take notes in a different way. You might find it helpful to use a bound notebook, divided into units, chapters or subjects. It can be useful to keep a running set of notes relating to each stage of learning when reflecting upon what you have learned. It will also help you to be able to make comparisons and join up threads of thinking.

Sticky notes can be helpful for jotting down key pieces of information such as the names of theorists and their birth and death dates. You might like to transfer these notes onto an A4 sheet of paper under a heading so that they are in order and make sense.

Using diagrams, tables and pictures can help to cement difficult information. Tables are useful tools which reduce large amounts of information into bite-sized chunks.

Try condensing key themes onto postcards or file cards. These can be hole punched and then secured using a treasury tag. You can compile these cards into different themes such as *'current thinkers in early years'*. You can record key pieces of information such as date and place of birth, main theories and most important works. Whenever you come across a current theorist, you can create a new card and add it to your file. Eventually, you will find that you have built up your own bank of support cards. Because you have written them yourself they will be easy to understand and serve as a great 'quick glance' reminder.

Figure 5.2: *Could cards like this be helpful for you when you study?*

It is quite possible that you will use all of these methods of note taking during your studies and you might find that some are more helpful to you than others.

Using abbreviations

Using abbreviations helps to speed up the writing process. Be mindful to use abbreviations consistently – a change halfway through your notes could be confusing.

If you use 'text talk' for note taking, such as numerals for words ('4get' instead of 'forget'), remember not to use it in your final submission of work. You should also avoid using abbreviations in your final submission as they are difficult to understand.

You can also condense information by writing words briefly, for example, the Early Years Foundation Stage (2012) can be abbreviated to EYFS 12. So if the passage you have highlighted supports the A* criteria of your assignment and relates to the EYFS, you might use A*EYFS 12 to illustrate its importance.

Managing time

Studying smartly will make the process much more manageable. All the study skills we have looked at so far are designed to maximise the use of your time. Although effective study skills will reduce wasted time, it is important that you always set aside adequate time for your studies. A very good way of doing this is to produce a study timetable.

First, you need to block out the times when you are busy. And make sure that you also allocate adequate time for meals and to rest and unwind. Most people study best in short bursts of around 20 minutes. Allowing yourself a comfort break and time to physically move around will prevent you from developing aches and strains.

Timetable: Week beginning 7th October

	Mon	Tue	Wed	Thu	Fri	Sat	Sun
8 am						Work	
9 am							
10 am							
11 am			College			Work	
12 noon						Lunch	
1 pm					College		
2 pm	College	College		College			
3 pm						Work	
4 pm							
5 pm							
6 pm							
7 pm							
8 pm							
9pm							

Figure 5.3: *This learner has blocked out the time he is at college and at work. What time is left for him to plan study?*

Your timetable will act as a very good visual tool to keep your studies in perspective. Sometimes it can feel like you are dedicating your whole life to studying, especially as you near the end of your course. Give yourself rewards after a long period of study such as meeting up with friends, or watching your favourite TV programme or film.

Next, make sure that your targets are realistic and achievable. If you set yourself unrealistic targets you will soon become demoralised and feel out of your depth. Prioritise your work to meet the most important deadlines first. You might find it helpful to colour code work according to its urgency. A piece of work that must be handed in soon could be red. This must be tackled first. Something that needs to be handed in the following week is orange and should be done next. A piece of work that is not due for completion for a month could be green and left for a while.

If you find that your red pieces of works are increasing and you cannot complete them, ask for support. By being organised it will be much easier to identify where you need help and why, and for your tutor to support you.

Staying motivated

When studying over a long period of time it can be difficult to remain motivated. Working with a 'study buddy' or friend on the same course can help you to focus and remain on task. It is important that when you work alongside someone else, you still produce work that is entirely your own. Plagiarism or copying work from someone else is taken very seriously by schools, colleges and universities.

It is also important to keep focused upon the desired goal at the end of your studies. This might be going on to university, getting the job you really want or knowing that you have applied yourself and have achieved what you set out to do.

Key term

Plagiarism – this is when you take someone else's work and try to pass it off as being your own.

Getting regular feedback from your tutor will help to build your confidence, so make good use of any assignment workshops or support classes. Plan for these support sessions in advance by writing down any questions you might have. If you tick off each question, you will see the progress you are making and this will help you to see that you are meeting the objective of the task.

1.4 Your personal achievement

By developing effective study skills you will be able to make progress that is individual and appropriate to you exclusively. You will feel in control of your time and workload, and this makes it much more manageable. Good organisation will mean that you can identify any areas where you need additional support or advice. Having a well-planned study timetable will mean that you are not struggling to meet deadlines and have adequate time to work towards targets.

The methods you develop will suit the way that you learn best and enhance your likely chances of success. You can apply these study skills throughout your academic life. If you choose to go on to higher education, you will have the skills to manage your study effectively.

Assessment activity
1.1, 1.2, 1.3, 1.4

Produce a leaflet aimed at learners about to embark upon study. Your leaflet must provide:

- an explanation of the term 'study skills'
- a description of the following methods of flexible reading: study reading, speed reading, scan reading and skim reading
- a summary of the ways to take notes, using reference sources, use abbreviations, manage time and be motivated in study.

When you have completed your leaflet, discuss with a partner the importance of developing study skills in relation to personal achievement. Make notes of your discussion.

2 Understand how to source information when planning a project or piece of writing

Now you know how to approach your studies, it is important to consider where you might find appropriate sources.

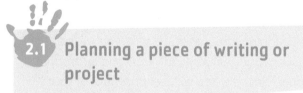

2.1 Planning a piece of writing or project

When beginning a project or piece of writing, careful planning is essential. It is the key to how successful you are in tackling the task purposefully and meeting the criteria.

When beginning a piece of work, you could approach it in stages.

1 Read the title, information or brief and decide what is required. This first stage seems obvious but it can be very easy to skim read the information and misinterpret what is being asked. Take time to read through and highlight any words you do not fully understand. You could also look for key words of what you are actually being asked to do – for example, if the word analyse is used, it is asking for something very different to the word describe.

2 Identify the areas for research. Jot down any key ideas you may have already and use these as a starting point.

3 Select the relevant information. This is where you are going to use your different reading methods (as described on pages 126–128).

4 Make notes from your research and reading. These notes will form the 'skeleton' of your writing.

5 Separate the notes into areas and themes. Check that they are suitable for what you need.

6 Make an outline plan, giving ideas about what is needed and where. If you are a kinaesthetic learner you might like to cut each section of paper out and physically move them around, looking at how they flow and making sure that each area is suitably covered.

7 Write a rough draft either by hand or typed on the computer.

8 Read through your work, checking for accuracy and making any corrections. Ask a friend to proofread for spelling and grammar.

9 Write a final draft for submission. Take your time to read through the work and fine tune if needed.

10 Keep back-up copies of your work. If a disaster happens, it is reassuring to know that with a click of a mouse you have another copy available.

Key terms

Analyse – to give a detailed examination of something by separating it into components or parts.

Describe – to give a detailed description of something.

Kinaesthetic learner – a person who learns best by doing something rather than reading about it or being told about it.

Case study: Sam's assignment

Sam has been set an assignment that requires him to write a report analysing the benefits of child-led planning. In Sam's work placement, planning follows children's interests so he knows he could gather information from there, perhaps from the staff and the children. He also remembers a lesson last term about the Reggio Emilia approach and knows this follows what children are interested in. Sam does not know much about the benefits, but he needs to make a plan to find out. Help him by answering the following questions.

1 What does 'analysing' mean Sam needs to do in his report?
2 How could he find out more about Reggio Emilia?
3 Which people could Sam talk to about planning?
4 Can Sam gather information from the children? If so, how?

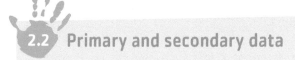

2.2 Primary and secondary data

There are two types of data you will use in your research and study: primary and secondary.

Primary data

Primary data is first-hand information you have obtained yourself, for example, through a questionnaire or interview. This type of data is valuable because it will fit the purpose it is required for. For example, if you want to find out if children like playing with sand, you could answer this question by carrying out observations and interviews with children. It would be unlikely that you would be able to find the answer to 'Do children like playing with sand?' in a book, magazine or on a website without extensive and time-consuming research. So the use of primary data can give you very specific and accurate information. It can also save time.

However, primary data can also be distorted. If, for example, you have decided that children do like playing with sand, you might then discount anything that tells you to the contrary.

It can also be very hard to obtain primary data; you might have to spend long periods of time waiting for permission to gather the data. The method you use for collecting primary data will also impact upon how successful it is; if you have not worded your questionnaire well, it might not give you the answers that you had hoped for.

Secondary data

Secondary data is collected by someone else. This is published in books, magazines, journals and online. This type of information is widely available and can strengthen your writing, especially where you are required to provide analysis. Alternatively, you might find something new that you did not already know that takes your writing in a new direction.

The disadvantage of using data that someone else has collected is that you are not fully aware of its origins. If you wanted to ask the question 'Do children like playing with sand?' a secondary source might provide the information – but it might be unreliable. The source might say that children like playing with sand because an observation was conducted of five children and all the children played with it. What the source might not tell you is that the sand was the only activity available to the children. Or the children might have been asked to play in the sand. This could mean that they did not really like playing with it – you cannot be certain that the data is reliable.

2.3 Sources of information or data

There is a huge range of potential sources for gathering information. Some will be more useful than others. You will find that the richest writing draws upon many different sources. The more varied the resources you use, the more depth and balance your writing will have.

Table 5.1 shows some of the sources that you might access.

Table 5.1: *Primary and secondary sources*

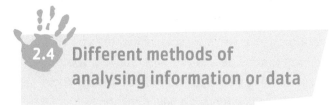

Primary	Secondary
Questionnaires	Journals
Observations	Books
Interviews	Magazines
Video recordings	Internet sites
Photographs	Newspapers
Case studies	Leaflets
	Case studies

2.4 Different methods of analysing information or data

When you have collected all of your data or information, you need to find a way of analysing it so that you can draw conclusions from it.

Figure 5.4 shows the different methods you can use to do this.

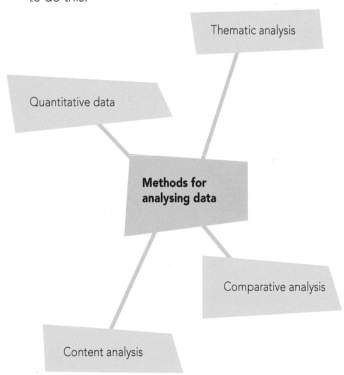

Figure 5.4: *Methods for analysing data*

Thematic analysis

Data or information can be analysed to look for trends or themes. The themes should come out of the data and information you collect – you should not look for specific themes. For example, if you were investigating good practice when working with parents, you would collect information and data about that topic. You would then analyse the information and you might discover that all your evidence suggests that some parents are harder to engage than others. This is a theme and may lead you into looking at and researching why these groups are harder to engage.

Comparative analysis

Comparative analysis is connected to thematic analysis. Using this method, you would examine all the different pieces of information you have collected and make comparisons between them. By doing this, you may find that new areas for consideration arise. For example, when you compare all the information and data you have collected, you may find that three separate books all support a statement made by your placement mentor: that some parents are harder to reach than others. Another book might suggest that parents from a particular background are often harder to engage and this could lead you to research this topic further.

Content analysis

Content analysis is carried out once all the data has been collected. This method is used for qualitative data, i.e. when you are looking for specific pieces of data in the information you have been given.

If you are reading through lots of writing on the same subject, give each piece of information a code. This allows you to measure how frequently this piece of information occurs. If in your study of engaging parents you conducted several interviews with practitioners, this would be an effective way of identifying common areas. You may be looking for practitioners who suggest there are some parents who are harder to engage, and you might also look for three or four other themes at the same time. As you go through the data, you will find that new trends emerge; these should also be coded and then searched for in all the collected data.

Quantitative data

You will need a suitable method for analysis when you are exploring quantitative data. This usually takes the form of graphs and diagrams. Presenting information in this way will give you a clear indication of trends in your data. The method you use will depend upon the type of information you have collected.

See pages 136–137 for definitions of qualitative and quantitative data.

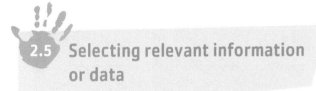

2.5 Selecting relevant information or data

In order to make sure that information or data is suitable, we need to apply criteria for its selection.

Reliable

We know that some data can be distorted or not be as clear as it is portrayed. The other consideration to be aware of is the potential for **bias**. This is when a piece of data is presented in order to lead you to think in a certain way.

Key term

Bias – an opinion or leaning that is strongly favoured for or against something.

Would we trust a manufacturer of children's play sand to answer our question 'Do children like playing with sand?' without bias? It is unlikely that the manufacturer would say children do not like sand, because they want children to play with it so that they can sell more. Therefore, it is in their interests to convince you to believe that all children like playing with sand.

It is particularly important to scrutinise web pages. Is the information part of an advertisement or written by somebody with a particular leaning or bias?

You should remain critical of what you read, and look for another source to either confirm or discount information that you feel is important. By doing this you will give your writing balance and credence.

Current

It is important that you know when the data was collected. If a study suggests there are no likely health issues as a result of smoking, it will have been compiled before we had the technology to understand the damage caused by smoking. Therefore, this data would be of no value if you were writing a report about the effects of smoking upon health. It would be misleading and inaccurate to include this source as part of your evidence.

However, not all data has to be current to be of value, and sometimes it is helpful to use examples from the past to strengthen your writing. You could use the outdated book about the effects of smoking to demonstrate that it is only in recent years that we have become more aware of the effects of smoking. In this case, the book would be essential in further proving your point.

Working with the most up-to-date textbook that supports your course will help you to think about current practice and thinking.

If there has been a significant change in law relating to a subject, such as the introduction of the Early Years Foundation Stage in 2008, it might be unwise to use books that are printed before this time. This is particularly the case if the subject relates to the changes the new legislation has brought about.

The care of children and young people tends to be subject to constant changes and to new ways of thinking. Changes in government will impact upon legislation and issues relating to service delivery – a book or article that is just a few years old can be totally outdated.

Fit for purpose

Some information you might come across during your studies will be written for a target audience, for example, professionals working in a particular field. It may be too complex to include in your research.

You will probably find that the information has been disseminated in more user-friendly terms. Often very detailed research is reported in **reputable** newspapers. Reading these articles might give you a better understanding of what is being discussed.

The information must be relevant; it may be very interesting but if it does not fit the criteria you require it is of no value to you.

Always be careful when you are using Internet sites to gather information. If the site is not from the country in which you live and study, the information might be incorrect or inaccurate.

Search engines can throw up wildly inaccurate information at times, so make sure your search criteria is very specific.

It is important that you completely understand the data you collect. If you do not, you will not be able to use it effectively.

Key term

Reputable – having a good reputation.

Level appropriate

If you are studying at level 3 it would be unhelpful to base your research on books that are designed to support a level 1 course. The writing is likely to be limited and lacking in detail to answer the questions suitably you are asking. If you select information or data that is designed for a higher level than you are studying, it may be in too much depth and detail. Without the supporting teaching that accompanies the course you may misunderstand the content or present it incorrectly in your writing.

Consider any reading list your tutor recommends, as this will include the most suitable sources for you to use.

Assessment activity
2.1, 2.2, 2.3, 2.4, 2.5

Prepare and deliver a presentation to your group about planning a project or piece of writing. This can include images, diagrams and handouts.

- Your presentation will explain the different stages involved in the planning, the difference between primary and secondary data, and how to select relevant data or information for inclusion in a project or piece of writing.
- You should discuss a range of sources which may be used to provide information or data.
- You should compare different methods of analysing data or information

3 Understand how to present information

3.1 Formal presentation of information or data

The way that you choose to present the information or data that you have collected will largely depend upon the *type* of information and data you have collected.

As stated earlier, there are two types of data.

- **Quantitative data** relates to quantity – therefore it is presented in numbers. An example of quantitative data collection would be conducting a questionnaire to discover how many people within your group own a dog. This question requires a numerical answer. The results of this questionnaire will give you numbers of how many people are dog owners, as that was what you sought to find out.

- **Qualitative data**, in contrast to quantitative data, is not about numbers and is usually about words. An example of qualitative data collection would be conducting interviews with people to find out what it is like to be a dog owner. Clearly, people would give you their opinion and so the results would be worded.

Depending upon the data you have collected, you will have a range of options when you come to present the information. **Tables 5.2** and **5.3** consider the advantages and disadvantages of a range of different presentation methods.

Table 5.2: *Quantitative data presentation*

Quantitative data presentation	Pros	Cons
Graph	Provides at-a-glance information Can be generated on a computer	Some people might not understand or might misinterpret the information Does not tell the whole story of the research
Pie chart	Makes it easier to work out percentages Visually attractive	Can be misleading Does not tell the whole story of the research
Percentages	Gives a quick account of findings	Can be taken out of context Not very helpful when dealing with small quantities of data
Table	Provides clear and concise information Summarises large amounts of data	Not as visually interesting as the graph or pie chart

Table 5.3: *Qualitative data presentation*

Qualitative data presentation	Pros	Cons
Report/assignment	Can get your point across clearly Can explain your findings in detail	Can be difficult to begin writing Not accessible for everyone to be able to read Might be limited by word count
Presentation (e.g. PowerPoint®)	Can extend and expand upon what you have found out Can include images or media to get your message across	Can be daunting to speak in front of people Time could be limited
Leaflet	Can use sections to signpost your work clearly Could include images User-friendly for the reader	Usually brief The leaflet format can be difficult to produce
Book	Information will be available for years to come Will reach a wide audience	Time-consuming to write a book Can become out of date quite quickly
Journal	Will be read by a specific audience Allows for detail and conclusions	Will only be read by people who know it exists New research might challenge your findings

3.2 Presenting your data or information

In order to present your data or information suitably you will need to make sure you understand the following terms:

- formatting
- fit for purpose
- relevant for the audience
- spellchecking
- proofreading.

These are important processes involved when presenting information and data to ensure accuracy, suitability and success in meeting criteria.

Formatting

The first thing you will need to do is format the information you have collected. When you have gathered a lot of information you need to organise it into a logical order. At this stage you will need to keep returning to what it was you wanted to find out in the first place. This will be your question, statement or assignment brief. We call this process 'formatting'.

Look at what your data is telling you. You will find that themes or trends start to emerge and you should use these themes to structure your data or information. For example, do not group all your questionnaires together (unless the results they show suggest the same thing).

Case study: gender and play

Emilie carried out some observations of children playing in her placement setting. She noticed that the boys tended to play more with dinosaurs than the girls.

She read a book about how gender can affect children's play and highlighted a section that suggested that boys like to play imaginatively with animals and dinosaurs, whereas girls play imaginatively with figures and people. She made a reference on a sticky note and attached it to the front of the book.

Emilie then spoke to three members of staff at her placement and asked each of them what the boys chose to play with. Two mentioned that the boys selected dinosaurs almost every day.

1 What theme is emerging in Emilie's research?
2 What sources of evidence support this?

Fit for purpose

Make sure that the data you gather is fit for the purpose for which you want it. It must relate to the task you are undertaking otherwise it serves no purpose.

You will need to remain focused and disregard non-related information, however fascinating, if it is not relevant to your task.

It is also important that your own research is valid, i.e. that you have used credible sources.

Reflect

Look at the gender and play case study, left.

- Would it be valid if, on the day Emilie conducted her observations, there were only dinosaurs available and no other toys?
- What if the dinosaurs were a new toy in the setting?
- What if there were only boys in attendance on the day of the observation?
- How might these factors affect or distort the results?

Relevant for the audience

Once you have collected all your data or information, think about how you are going to disseminate it and to whom. Make sure that your audience will be interested in what you want to tell them. Think carefully about making the data accessible.

If you want to present what you have studied to children, think about the words that you are using and consider any images carefully. Children might not be able to understand percentages easily, but using words such as 'most of' or 'nearly all' will help them to understand the message you want to get across. Use pictures, video clips and child-friendly images to hold their interest.

These methods of presentation would be entirely unsuitable for an adult audience and so you would need to adapt your methods to share the same information with the children's teachers or parents and carers.

Key term

Disseminate – to share information widely.

Spellchecking

It is essential that you check your spelling carefully. Misspelt words might actually change the meaning of what you are trying to say, as can missing out words.

Poor spelling also makes you appear unprofessional

and so it is especially important when you wish to share your information with a wider audience. If you are presenting information to parents and carers of children, good spelling will give them confidence in your knowledge.

You should use the automatic spellcheck programme on your computer with caution. It should never be used as a replacement for a dictionary, as it can interpret a misspelt word incorrectly and give you the correct spelling of a completely different word you did not intend to use. Make sure your spellcheck is set to the correct language, i.e. English spelling and not American.

Proofreading

Proofread your work by reading through what you have written and making any amendments. However, when you are very familiar with a piece of writing, you may not spot the mistakes because you know what you meant to say. That is why a fresh pair of eyes can be helpful.

Ask someone else to proofread your work. They do not need to know about your subject of study as they are not checking the content. They can help to identify missed words or spelling mistakes, make sure that your writing makes sense, and check for punctuation and grammar. The content of what you have written is your responsibility, so do not expect your proofreader to do your work for you.

3.3 Using academic referencing

When you read articles, books, Internet sites or any other text you might find information you want to use to support your own work. To do this, you could take a quote from the text or give an overview of the ideas in it. If you do, you must make it clear which words or ideas are from the text by referencing them.

Failing to reference work from another text is a type of plagiarism and could result in you losing marks or even being disciplined. In some institutions plagiarism is considered such a serious offence that a student can lose their place on their course if they are found to be passing off other people's work as their own.

To reference a text you need to include an in-text reference next to the quote or ideas you use and you also need to include the full details of the text in your reference list.

In-text references

The in-text reference should give the surname of the author, the year the text was written and the page number or numbers if you are using a direct quote. For example, you might use a direct quote like this:

> Riddall-Leech (2008, p.30) states that 'parents are the real experts when it comes to knowing about their child'.

Or you might want to give an overview of an author's ideas like this:

> Parents know their children better than anyone and can be great sources of information about a child (Riddall-Leech, 2008).

Reference list

When including the full details of a text in a reference list you should follow the direction of your individual institution. Each institution will have its own preferred way of recording reference lists, but the usual way to identify your sources is shown in **Figures 5.5** to **5.8**.

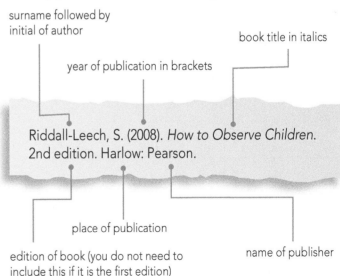

surname followed by initial of author

year of publication in brackets

book title in italics

Riddall-Leech, S. (2008). *How to Observe Children*. 2nd edition. Harlow: Pearson.

edition of book (you do not need to include this if it is the first edition)

place of publication

name of publisher

Figure 5.5: *How to reference a book in your reference list. This information will be contained within the first few pages of the book.*

CP5

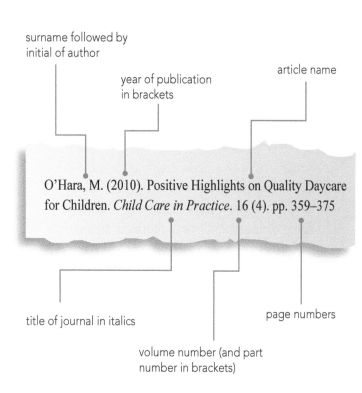

surname followed by initial of author

year of publication in brackets

article name

O'Hara, M. (2010). Positive Highlights on Quality Daycare for Children. *Child Care in Practice*. 16 (4). pp. 359–375

title of journal in italics

page numbers

volume number (and part number in brackets)

Figure 5.6: *How to reference an article in your reference list*

name of the author (this could be surname and initial)

year of publication in brackets

title of the section of website in italics with [online] after it

NHS (2010). *When to get your child vaccinated* [online]. Available from: http://www.nhs.uk/Planners/vaccinations/Pages/Whentogetvaccinated.aspx [Accessed 5 December 2011].

date accessed in brackets

weblink of the text

Figure 5.7: *How to reference an Internet site in your reference list. If you cannot find all this information, it may be that your source is not very credible and so you should be hesitant in using it.*

NHS (2010). When to get your child vaccinated [online]. Availabile from: http://www.nhs.uk/Planners/vaccinations/Pages/Whentogetvaccinated.aspx. [Accessed 5 December 2011].

O'Hara, M. (2010). Positive Highlighs on Quality Daycare for Children. Child Care in Practice. 16 (4). p. 359–375

Riddall-Leech, S. (2008). How to Observe Children. 2nd edition. Harlow: Pearson.

Figure 5.8: *Your full reference list should be ordered alphabetically, with each reference on its own line.*

Assessment activity 3.1, 3.2, 3.3

You are to write a report about at least three different format sources of information you have used in your study.

- You will compare and contrast the different formats for presenting the information or data.
- Your report should explain how you referenced the sources within your own writing and how you recorded your information sources.
- Your report should also explain the following terms: formatting, fit for purpose, relevant for the audience, spellchecking and proofreading.

4 # Be able to present information that is fit for purpose and relevant to target audience

4.1 ## Conveying information in different formats

You may be asked to present information for audiences in a range of different formats. These could take the form of written reports, diagrams or letters.

Written reports

Your written report should flow so that it is easy and enjoyable to read. Where appropriate, headings should be used to explain to the reader what they are about to read.

You might use these headings:
- Introduction
- Discussion
- Conclusion
- Reference list

This makes it clear to the reader what you are telling them and also helps you to structure your report.

Diagrammatic format

You may choose to present information in a diagrammatic format such as graphs or charts or through programs such as PowerPoint®.

When using images or diagrams you can often condense large amounts of information into easily readable and accessible chunks.

Images can have a big impact and this can make your presentation very powerful and thought-provoking. Consider images carefully and make sure they serve a purpose.

Make sure that any diagrams, pictures, charts and graphs can be easily understood by the reader.

Letter format

You may choose to present information in the form of a letter. Make sure that you are courteous and not overfamiliar in your letter writing. Use an appropriate name and only use someone's first name if you know the person and have been asked to do so. If you do not know the person you are writing to, use Sir/Madam. Sign your letter, but make sure that it also states your name clearly. An example of this is shown in **Figure 5.9**.

So what does this mean?

Here are some tips to remember when writing.
- Do not write overly long sentences and check your punctuation.
- The introduction should give a flavour of what the report says and might include findings or a brief discussion of the outcome.
- Work within the word count: too few words could mean that you have not offered enough detail, too many and you may have digressed from the main task.

Both could cost you valuable points when your work is marked.
- The conclusion should not introduce anything new; you are pulling together what you have already discussed and may be offering an opinion.

Be aware of how you present information: a typing font that is too small or detailed will make it difficult to read. Only use white paper and make sure that this is in good condition and free from bends at the corner or marks.

CP5

CP5

Jaspers Nursery
34 Windmill Street
Blaizedall
Bekingshire
BK3 44R

16th July 2012

Dear Mrs Thompson,

Many thanks for attending an interview for the position of Early Years Practitioner at Jaspers Nursery.

I am very pleased to inform you that you have been successful, and we would like to formally offer you the post. The starting salary will be as discussed, £19,334 per year. Your working hours are between 8am and 6pm Monday to Friday.

Please find enclosed your contract of employment, a copy of our policies and procedures and further information about the company.

We warmly welcome you into the staff team and hope that you will be very happy in your employment with us.

Yours sincerely,

Pamela Porter

Nursery Manager

Figure 5.9: *A letter format*

4.2 Getting ready for submission

Just before you finish your work, carry out some last checks to make sure that the final draft is ready for submission.

Your final proofread will identify any spelling errors or passages you have not fully referenced. Refer back to page 139 for guidance on how to do this.

Finally, once you are happy with your work and you have saved a copy, it is ready for submission.

Assessment activity 4.1, 4.2

While in your work placement setting, gather the following information relating to your role:
- a letter you have written to your mentor or a parent (this could relate to undertaking observations or confirming your position as a learner)
- a flow diagram of the management structure of your setting
- a reflective report on your progress within your work placement setting.

Where appropriate you should include references within your reflective report. Your work must be legible and you should use a dictionary to correct any spelling errors.

5 Understand the need to evaluate the process involved in gathering and presenting information

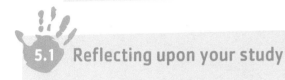

5.1 Reflecting upon your study

Once your assignment is complete, take some time to reflect upon the importance of the skills you used.

Planning

Effective planning not only saves time, it helps you to stay on top of your workload, and identify any areas where you might need support. Knowing what you need to find out before you start your research gives you focus and direction – and this makes the task simpler.

Identifying sources

Plagiarism is taken very seriously by learning institutions. Failing to identify your sources of information correctly both in the text and in your reference list could result in you being disciplined, your work not being marked or even you losing your place on the course. Referencing your work should be started in the note-taking stage, so the good practice continues into your final draft.

Gathering information

Where and how you gather information is important to your final success. It should cover a range – use more than one source. Compare and contrast the information you find, as this gives your work balance.

Presenting information

How you share the information or data you have found will depend upon your audience and the subject. Your information must always be presented well and this entails proofreading, spellchecking and correct referencing. This ensures your work is of a standard that meets the criteria and will mean that all of your careful research is demonstrated in your work.

Analysing information

Information or data serves no purpose if you do not fully analyse what it is telling you. Using different sources and methods of finding the information will give you a more rounded view of the subject you have explored. Take time to read through your information fully – it will give you a clearer picture of what it is telling you.

Assessment activity 5.1

Write a reflection upon an assignment you have previously undertaken during this course.

Consider:
- how important it was to find relevant sources of information (outline the sources you used)
- how you gathered your information
- what plans you put into place
- how you finally presented your information
- the outcomes you reached when you analysed the information you had gathered.

CP5

In the real world

I never thought that I would be nearing the end of a level 3 course. I didn't get on well at school; I found it hard to concentrate and used to behave badly because the work was too hard.

When I started college studying for my CACHE Diploma, I thought I'd taken on too much. Then I began my work placement and things just started to fall into place. I got myself organised by using a study timetable so I knew what work I had to complete and what time I had to do it.

My tutor was brilliant and explained to me that if I made good notes the assignments would begin to take shape even before I started to write them. And they did!

I used my textbook if I wanted to read further after lessons and when I needed to understand things more deeply. This really helped me to use references in my work and soon it just became second nature.

I have already been offered a job when I finish my studies at one of the settings where I did my work placement.

Check your knowledge

1 Outline the purpose of 'skim reading'.

2 Why is it important to reference the sources you use correctly?

3 What method can you use to organise yourself to make adequate time for study?

4 Describe the benefits of having a 'study buddy'.

5 Give two examples of effective note taking.

6 Why is developing study skills helpful to future study?

7 What is the first stage of planning a piece of writing?

8 Explain what is meant by quantitative data.

9 What are two considerations when selecting relevant data?

10 Explain how to use academic referencing for information sources.

Further references

The following are sources of useful information on the topic of supporting the development of study skills.

Books and articles

Buzan, T. (2010) *The Speed Reading Book: Read More, Learn More, Achieve More*, Essex: BBC Active

Moore, S. and Neville, C. (2010) *The Ultimate Study Skills Handbook*, Berkshire: Open University Press

Punch, K.F. (2005) *Introduction to Social Research, Quantitative and Qualitative Approaches*, London: Sage

Roberts-Holmes, G. (2008) *Doing Your Early Years Research Project*, London: Sage

Weyers, J. and McMillan, K. (2011) *The Study Skills Book*, 2nd edition, Harlow: Pearson

Useful websites

To obtain a secure link to the website below, visit www.pearsonhotlinks.co.uk and search for this book by using its title or ISBN. Click on the section for CP5.

BBC Student Life website to help with revision and study skills

CP5

Working with families of children and/or young people

CP6

Working with children and young people inevitably means working with their families too. Building partnership relationships with parents is essential in the interests of the children. This unit looks at understanding the significance of their family in a child's life and the demanding role of being a parent.

Learning outcomes

By the end of this unit you will:

1 Understand the role of the practitioner when working with families of children and/or young people

2 Know the differences in family structure

3 Understand the importance of working in partnership with parent(s)/carers

4 Understand factors which influence life experiences

5 Know how practitioners who work with children and/or young people can support families in times of crisis.

In practice

There may be times when you feel that parents have expectations and requirements which are difficult to meet and which occupy a lot of your working hours.

By the end of this unit you will appreciate how important it is that you develop positive relationships with parents and communicate with them in open, respectful ways.

1 Understand the role of the practitioner when working with families of children and/or young people

1.1 The processes of working with families

When we talk about having contact with parents, we mean having contact with the adults who have the main responsibility for caring for the child. This may be a child's birth parents, or someone else who has daily care of the child such as grandparents or a guardian, whether or not they are related to the child or have been legally allocated 'parental responsibility'.

When you work with children or young people, you will have contact with their parents, siblings and perhaps grandparents or aunts and uncles.

Your interactions with family members are likely to include:

- greeting and welcoming family members who bring the child to the setting
- receiving information about the child from parents such as health and developmental concerns, children's likes and dislikes, events in the child's life, and the family's preferences about food, routine care and clothing
- passing on information to parents about what the child has been experiencing and learning in the setting, and developmental progress you have observed
- enabling parents to be involved in the activities and running of the setting
- discussing and planning how to tackle a concern about their child's development or behaviour
- offering parents information and perhaps advice about an aspect of parenting

- giving parents information about agencies that may be able to offer them advice and support
- providing a listening ear and personal support in times of difficulty.

You will see that some of this is complex and sensitive, and to be able to make your interactions with families as effective as possible, you need considerable knowledge, understanding and skill, as outlined in this unit.

Reflect

During your work placement, make a note of the occasions when you are in contact with parents.

- What is the purpose of your contact with them on each occasion?
- How did their child benefit from the contact? Were there aspects of these contacts that you found challenging?
- If so, what were they?

1.2 Communication boundaries

You must always ensure that your communications with parents are carried out within professional boundaries. Your work role will determine the matters you should communicate with parents about, and you should talk to parents in appropriate ways.

CP6

Responsibility according to role

Many settings have requirements about which practitioners should engage in communication with parents for specific purposes, such as:

- payments and other contractual matters, which are handled by managers or supervisors who have set up such arrangements in the first instance
- matters of policy, which need to be communicated carefully by senior staff to avoid misunderstandings.

Learners and new members of staff should be clear about referring parents' enquiries to experienced members of the work team.

All practitioners have a role to play in greeting family members and creating an atmosphere where parents feel welcomed and at ease, but it is a child's **key person** who has the main responsibility for passing on information to parents about a child's experiences in the setting, their progress and any concerns about them. They do this in the context of having developed a close relationship with the parents, and other practitioners should not cut across this line of communication.

Responsibility for passing information concerning a family to an agency or professional outside the setting is likely to lie with senior practitioners; it would be inappropriate for a practitioner to step beyond their area of responsibility and take such action unless it has been agreed with their manager.

If a child is disabled or has special educational needs, there are likely to be several aspects of communicating about the child that must be carried out in close consultation with the setting's SENCO. The SENCO is responsible for:

- liaison with parents and other professionals concerning children with special educational needs
- advising and supporting other practitioners.

Style of communication

Practitioners should address parents in a courteous and respectful way at all times, pronouncing names correctly and addressing people in ways that they prefer.

Case study: what's in a name?

Susan was irritated by two of her colleagues at the after-school club. One kept complaining that she could not pronounce an Eastern European surname that had a lot of consonants. Another called Asian children 'Ben' and 'Sam' because she claimed she could not get her tongue around their real names. Susan pointed out to them that getting names right is important. She reminded them, 'I hate being called Sue and get annoyed when people think they can shorten my name without my permission.'

1 Why are our names so important to us?
2 How do you feel if someone pronounces or spells your name wrongly?

You are likely to encounter several **naming systems**. It is helpful to understand some of the principles that underpin these systems. For example, in some naming systems, the family name comes before the personal name. But beware of assuming that because a person belongs to a specific group, they use the system widely used in that group. You may find that a child's parents have different surnames, whether or not they are married, or parents may combine their surnames into a new family name.

Key terms

Key person – the practitioner assigned to each child in a setting to ensure that each child's needs are accurately identified and consistently met. Each key person has special responsibilities for working with a small number of children.

SENCO – Special Educational Needs Coordinator.

Naming systems – ways of constructing a person's name associated with a specific ethnic or religious group.

CP6

So what does this mean?

To help you maintain a courteous and respectful way of addressing family members:

- listen carefully to how parents pronounce the name of their child and their family name
- take particular care to check how to pronounce and spell names that are not familiar, especially if they are from a language other than your own
- practise saying names correctly
- address people using the correct naming system
- ask parents to confirm all of this for you; they will be much happier being asked rather than seeing you struggle to guess what is correct. The often quoted rule is: 'Don't assume. Ask.'

How practitioners and parents address one another varies from one type of setting to another. Childminders and pre-school/playgroup practitioners are often on first-name terms with parents who may be of a similar age to themselves and live in the same community; practitioners in nurseries, children's centres and schools may use more formal modes of address. In either case, communication should be friendly but without straying into patterns which are inappropriately familiar in a professional context.

Communication with parents should be friendly but professional.

1.3 Confidentiality

Besides thinking about *how* you communicate, you must consider *what* you communicate. In your work with families, you will gain information which you have to handle with **confidentiality**.

Key term

Confidentiality – not sharing personal information about a family without parents' permission, except where it is in the interests of the child to pass information to the appropriate professional.

The information that parents and children give you about themselves and other members of their family is given in a relationship of trust. Breaking that trust would be unprofessional and endanger your future relationship with the family. You must always give careful thought to whether it is appropriate for you to share such information with someone else, inside or outside the work setting.

Case study: confidentiality

When Padma got her first job, she felt uncertain about what information should be confidential. She asked her colleagues in the team at the nursery to share some examples of information they had found it acceptable to share within the team and information they kept confidential. They said:

'It's nearly always fine to tell others about where a family lives or are going on holiday, or where a parent works, but even that can be sensitive if there has been domestic violence in the family.'

'Any of us who has contact with a child needs to know if they have a particular dislike or fear – like men with beards – so we can step in with support if it's needed.'

1 What examples of information can you think of that it is important to keep confidential?
2 What examples can you think of that everyone in the work team should know?

Sharing information within the team

Most parents readily understand that there is certain information that must be shared within the work team. For example, if a child has an allergy to certain foods or if there is a court order forbidding a certain family member access to a child, it is important that everyone in the setting knows so the child is not put in danger. However, there might be more sensitivity about a child's HIV status which can safely be confined to the setting manager and the child's key person, since everyone in the setting should be following safe hygiene procedures.

If an event in the family's life may be affecting a child's behaviour, the key person needs to know what is causing this, but other members of the work team may not need to have access to the details.

It is always unprofessional for practitioners to discuss families in a gossipy way among themselves or with other parents, speculating on their personal affairs. A good test to use is to consider whether you would be happy for other people to talk about you and your family in such a way.

Sharing information outside the setting

If you and your colleagues become concerned about a child's developmental progress, you may want to bring in the expertise of other professionals from outside the setting. Your first step should be to discuss what you have observed with the child's parents, and seek their agreement to your sharing the information with, for example, a health visitor or speech and language therapist.

The exception to the rule of consulting parents is when a child's safety is at risk. If a practitioner detects signs and symptoms that might indicate that a child is being abused, the setting is under a duty to contact their local authority's children's services department. Since parents or other family members may be involved in perpetrating or condoning the abuse, action may need to be taken promptly without alerting the family. Any information relevant to the situation must only be shared on a 'need to know' basis.

Key term

'Need to know' basis – the professionals to whom information is passed need to have that information to take action to safeguard a child. Other people with no direct role to play in protecting the child should not have access to the information.

You might need the support of your own family and friends when you are feeling challenged by your work but you must take great care over what you say. You might tell them that you feel under pressure from supporting a family who are having a difficult time, or being concerned about a particular child. But you should never name the child or family or give any details that could lead to their identity becoming known.

Keeping written information

Written records about children must be stored securely. Settings should use lockable filing cabinets for paper records, and password protection for computer records. This will ensure that no one gets access to information unless they 'need to know'.

Assessment activity
1.1, 1.2, 1.3

1 Think about the various ways that you have observed practitioners working with parents in your work placement setting. Describe what you saw to a fellow learner and listen to what they observed during their placement. Together, draw up a list of your similar and different observations. Add to your list ways that practitioners may work with parents, besides the ways you have each observed.

2 Discuss with your colleague the professional boundaries which should apply when practitioners are communicating with parents, sharing any you have seen in practice in your work placement setting. Work together to write explanations of what the boundaries should be. Remember to consider the professional boundaries when working with external agencies.

3 Imagine you have been given the task of explaining to a new practitioner why it is important to maintain confidentiality in handling information about families. Write an outline of what you intend to tell them, and give some examples of ways of maintaining confidentiality.

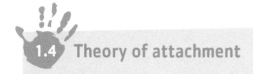

1.4 Theory of attachment

It is essential that your interactions with parents take into account the emotional relationship between children and parents. A key aspect of children's emotional well-being is attachment and bonding.

Key terms

Attachment – refers to the emotional tie which develops between a child and another person, usually an adult.

Bonding – the process of the development of these ties.

When a young child is attached to a person, they:

- try to be close to that person
- cry and become distressed when the person leaves or cannot be seen
- show relief and pleasure when they return.

The more closely the child and adult are bonded, the more secure their attachment is said to be. Secure attachments emerge when adults show themselves to be reliable and available, responding and giving attention, and become tuned in to the child's needs and wants. Research has consistently shown that if babies do not bond with an adult or if the ties of attachment are broken by separation, later in their life – as a child, adolescent and adult – they may find it difficult to enter into close, trusting relationships.

John Bowlby

The thinking and writing of John Bowlby (1907–90) have had a significant influence on policy and practice. Bowlby worked as a child psychologist, and he explored the effects on children of experiences of separation from their mothers and other family members. He referred to the psychological damage he found as 'maternal deprivation'. Two key elements of his theory were:

- **monotropy:** babies need to form one special attachment which becomes more important to them than other relationships
- **critical period:** the earliest years are crucial for the development of attachment. Babies need to have bonded, to have developed their main attachment, by the age of 1 year. Up to the age of 4, long-term separation from the main person they become attached to could cause long-term psychological damage.

Bowlby was criticised for his overemphasis on the role of the mother. However, we must see this in the social historical context of the late 1940s and early 1950s when it was predominantly mothers who cared for babies. Bowlby later acknowledged that attachments with fathers and others were possible, and later research confirmed that, especially by 7 to 8 months, babies are able to make equally strong attachments to more than one person – fathers, siblings, grandparents and others – a move from thinking in terms of monotropy to 'multiple attachments'. There is also evidence that babies with secure multiple attachments are more able to deal with unfamiliar situations and separation than those who rely on a single attachment.

Observations of babies show that from birth they seem programmed to interact and form relationships with other human beings, as long as they are responded to when they smile and babble ('innate sociability'). Adults tend intuitively to find such behaviour charming and attractive, and they are driven to respond as they develop strong emotional feelings for the baby. Attachment is reciprocal – a two-way process of love.

CP6

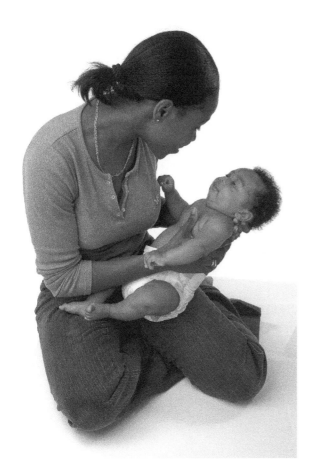

Can you see how this parent and child are bonding?

The person they seem most likely to bond with is the person who plays a major role in feeding them and providing physical care, often still the mother even in the social patterns which are now so different from 50 or 60 years ago. However, they can also attach to others who are responsive to them such as a father or other family member who contributes to these aspects of care, and spends 'quality' time with a baby, holding and playing with them. An essential element in bonding is close physical contact and getting to understand the meaning of early **non-verbal communication** in order to be able to respond to them.

Another factor which Bowlby did not pursue was the effect of the quality of the care the child received when separated from their mother. The theories of attachment and bonding have implications for practice in early years settings since good-quality care can in part compensate for the effects of separation.

The implications of attachment for practice

The main implications of attachment for practice are concerned with settling children into a setting, and the key person system. Both of these arise from normal aspects of young children's emotional development – **stranger anxiety** and **separation anxiety**.

Key terms

Non-verbal communication – ways of communicating without words, e.g. crying, body movements and facial expressions.

Stranger anxiety – a child's wariness of people they are not familiar with.

Separation anxiety – the distress a child shows if the person to whom they are attached is absent or leaves.

Most babies start to show stranger anxiety in the second half of their first year. This can range from just watching an unfamiliar person with some suspicion from the safety of their carer's arms, through to fear and distress if the unknown person tries to rush the encounter and comes too close or tries to touch them too soon. To cope with new people, babies need reassurance and support from those with whom they have made an attachment.

Separation anxiety also builds up towards the end of a baby's first year and can last well into the second, or beyond. When a child is separated from their familiar carer, they tend to progress through various stages.
- They are likely to cry, be angry and struggle to escape.
- They may then become withdrawn and sad, and resort to comfort behaviour such as thumb sucking or rocking.
- This may resolve into detachment, when the child apparently becomes calm but this can represent a loss of trust in their carers who have 'abandoned' them, and that can have long-term negative effects.

Parents may feel uncomfortable if their child appears 'clingy' but practitioners should be ready to reassure them that this is normal, healthy behaviour.

CP6

When provision for young children is of good quality, and there is consistent care from a small number of familiar adults, children are more able to adjust to separation. To help children work through their anxieties, it is good practice to have procedures for settling a child into a new setting, which progress at an unhurried pace, and also to ensure the availability of a key person.

The purpose of the key person system is that a child is able to develop a bonded attachment, extending their attachments beyond their family circle. The role of a key person includes:

- settling a child into the setting by being at hand to provide comfort and reassurance if the child becomes distressed, confused or unsettled
- providing affectionate personal physical care and contact (cuddles!) for the child, focusing on play with them, and getting to know the child well enough to be able to interpret their attempts to communicate, especially non-verbally
- being the main channel for information between setting and home, getting to know the parents and family well and gaining their trust.

Being a key person is demanding. It requires the practitioner to develop a degree of attachment to the child, in the interests of providing affectionate care, but it also requires that they are able to let go of the attachment when the child moves on to another setting, without compromising their own emotional well-being. Such professional balance develops with experience and maturity.

Assessment activity 1.4

1 Find out about how theories of attachment translate into real practice in your work placement setting. Ask for information about the key person system and settling-in procedures. Observe how these are carried out. Write down what you have found out.

2 Think about how these systems and procedures could be made more effective, and add to your description.

2 Know the differences in family structure

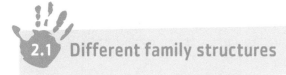

2.1 Different family structures

In our society today, families are structured in a variety of ways. A child can thrive if they have a parent or parents – and other family members – who are prepared to commit themselves to a loving relationship and mutual bonds of attachment, whatever the structure of the family they live in.

Reflect

What images come to mind when you hear the word 'family'? Does your mental picture of a family include:

- two parents or a single parent
- people of another generation besides the children and parents – grandparents, aunts and uncles
- parents of the same gender
- parents of different ethnic groups
- half-siblings and step-parents?

The picture-book image of a family as two parents of different genders and the same ethnicity, married to one another with two children (maybe of different ages) is very outdated. You will encounter a wide range of families in the course of your work, and it is important that you show your respect for each of them, however different they may be from your own family. You are likely to encounter some or all of the following.

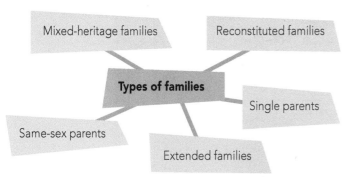

Figure 6.1: *Family structures*

- **Single parents** – a parent may be raising their children on their own because of separation or divorce, or because their partner has died, or because they have never lived in a couple with the other parent. About one in four families with dependent children in the UK are single-parent families.
- **Extended families** – some children live in families which include grandparents, aunts, uncles and cousins as part of regular daily life. This is common in some cultures which value the way family members are interdependent and supportive in caring for one another.
- **Same-sex parents** – some gay or lesbian people bring children from a previous relationship to their new partnership; some lesbians choose to conceive a baby by 'artificial' means and rear the child as a couple; homosexual couples can now legally become foster carers or adoptive parents. Now that gay and lesbian couples can enter into civil partnerships, they are able to demonstrate publicly their commitment to their relationship and to their children.
- **Mixed-heritage families** – a child's parents may be from different ethnic groups.

- **Reconstituted families** – when couples break up, parents often find new partners and form new families. This can mean that some children live with step-parents and in quite complicated networks of half-siblings and step-siblings.

Assessment activity 2.1

Write descriptions of four families, each of which has a different family structure (you could invent names and ages for each family member to help your descriptions).

2.2 Possible effects of different parenting styles

Most parents love their children and want to do their best for them, but there are many ways of going about this: there are several different parenting styles. These are shown in **Table 6.1**.

Key term

Parenting styles – various ways of interacting with children based on differing values about how children should be brought up.

There are many influences on how parents choose to rear their children, such as:
- traditions and beliefs of the cultural group the family belongs to
- expectations of the social group the family is part of
- the experiences parents had of their own childhood
- their observations of other parents
- ideas promoted by individuals who present themselves as 'experts' in the media.

There is no one 'correct' way to be a parent.

Parenting may be permissive, punitive, passive or positive in style. Each style will have effects on children's emotional and social development, such as:

* the development of their self-esteem and self-confidence
* their ability to interact with adults and other children.

Table 6.1: *Parenting styles*

Style of parenting	What parents do	Effects on children
Punitive (or authoritarian)	Parents feel that children need to be 'trained' in a disciplined way. They: • set strict limits and rules • may not explain the reasons for the rules but just say 'because I say so' • enforce the rules with tight discipline and punishment, perhaps including smacking.	Children may feel that they are constantly being told that they are unworthy or unlovable, without really understanding why what they have done is seen as wrong. They may become resentful and unhappy, have poor self-esteem and be lacking in self-confidence.
Permissive (or laissez faire)	Parents feel that children should discover the world for themselves and not be rigidly directed by adults' perceptions and rules. They: • do not set limits for their children's behaviour, but allow them to do as they wish • give the children many choices and responsibilities, expecting them to learn from their own mistakes • may find it difficult to say 'no' to their child and often give in to the demands their child makes.	Children may feel overwhelmed by the world, unable to interpret its complexities without adult guidance. They may develop unrealistic expectations about being part of a social group, seeing themselves as the centre of the world (egocentricity) and not tuned in to the needs and feelings of others. Other children may be reluctant to play with them if they always want their own way. They may behave in uncontrolled ways, failing to respond to adult instructions.
Passive	Parents may be under great stress or pressure, or lead unorganised, even chaotic, lives which leave them little time and space to focus their attention on how their children should be brought up. They: • ignore their children for lengthy periods of time, not taking an active part in interacting with them • have no consistent approach to parenting, imposing different rules at different times • are not responsive to their children's needs and wishes but react to their behaviour perhaps by shouting or smacking, but offering no explanation for their negative response.	Children are likely to be confused about how they should behave and be bewildered about dealing with the world without explanations from adults. This may have a negative effect on their self-esteem and lead to their finding it difficult to develop relationships with other adults or children, perhaps even developing antisocial behaviour.
Positive (or authoritative)	Parents feel that children should have opportunities to explore life but with adult help and guidance. They: • respond to their children's ideas, suggestions and questions • set realistic limits to behaviour, and encourage and praise behaviour which is considerate of others • intervene when behaviour falls short of expectations, explaining why it is not acceptable.	Children are likely to feel valued and loved and can understand that their behaviour can hurt other people. They feel confident in interacting with other adults and children and are welcomed by others because they think about how their behaviour affects other people.

Most parents take the positive approach to a greater or lesser extent. No parents are perfect but most manage to be 'good enough' parents. From the child's point of view, what matters most is care that is consistently loving.

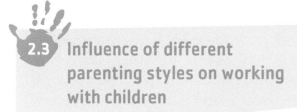

2.3 Influence of different parenting styles on working with children

The style of parenting a child experiences will affect the way they behave when they come to a setting, and their ability to understand the expectations and boundaries of the setting. Practitioners need skills in responding to children who are used to each of the different styles of parenting. You have to help the child to cope in your setting and benefit from what it has to offer, but also refrain from criticising parents' values and way of life. Never undermine parents' approach to rearing their children or suggest that parents are wrong in the way they treat their children.

Reflect

1 Henry is new to your setting and you observe that he watches everyone very warily from the sidelines. He only speaks to adults when they first address him and is tentative about joining in play activities until he is clear about what is expected of him. He says, 'I must be a good boy.' His father tells you that there are firm rules for the children at home and that disobedience is not tolerated.

How could you help Henry to build his confidence for taking part in all that goes on there?

2 Skye sometimes behaves in an uncontrolled way, does not listen to what adults say to her or follow suggestions for what to do next. She expects to have her own way and the other children do not want to play with her. Her mother says that she wants Skye to be a free spirit, unfettered by the petty rules of society.

How could you help Skye understand that there are some boundaries to behaviour in the setting, in the interests of the other people there?

3 Jaydon is destructive and physically rough with other children. His vocabulary is peppered with swear words. You observe that his mother seems depressed and apathetic; Jaydon is one of six children.

How can you help to provide some structure for Jaydon, at least during the time he is in the setting?

Assessment activity 2.2, 2.3

1 Choose a style of parenting and imagine a family where parents adopt that style. Write a description of how the parents behave towards their children. Explain some of the effects this is likely to have on their children. Give examples of how a practitioner may have to respond to a child who experiences that style of parenting.

2 Repeat this for another style of parenting.

3 Understand the importance of working in partnership with parent(s)/carers

3.1 Practitioners' responsibilities when working with parents and carers

When you work with parents, it is important that you:

- recognise parents' emotional attachment to their children
- appreciate how difficult the role of the parent is – if you are not a parent yourself, this will require some careful thought and empathy
- acknowledge parents' expert knowledge about their own children
- share information with them about their children.

Above all, you must remember that parents are central to children's lives. Practitioners who work with young children can have a great influence on those children's development and contribute significantly to their well-being, but they are likely to be spending only 30 per cent of their time in your care for a few years or even for a few months. Your presence in their life is part-time and temporary; it is children's parents who are the most significant lifelong influence. Your role in children's lives is important but limited; you complement the role of parents but take care not to see your role as that of substitute. The children are never 'yours' so you must never try to take over the parents' position.

Parents' feelings

Parents' love for their children can be very intense, even to the point of being irrational. If you are not a parent yourself, you will not have experienced such emotions, but observing parents closely will reveal the depth of their feelings.

Sometimes parents try to hide their feelings for fear of being thought of as foolish or 'fussy'; they may appear detached and uninterested. It is important to be able to see past this and acknowledge that it is

Parents and carers are the most important people in a child's life.

Case study: parents' feelings

During Pippa's first week in her first job, several children joined the nursery, and Pippa helped them to settle in. She was surprised to see a mother leaving the setting on the verge of tears, despite the fact that her daughter was already busy playing and chatting to the other children.

1 Why do you think the mother was upset?
2 What were the positive aspects of her distress?
3 How could practitioners help the mother as well as the child?

not easy for a parent to separate from their child and leave them in the care of someone else. They may have feelings of guilt that they can not be around for their child all the time. They may even become a little jealous of practitioners who spend time with their child, as they see a degree of attachment developing. Trust takes a while to build and until you have established that relationship, expect parents to be uncertain about whether you are paying sufficient attention to their child's needs.

So what does this mean?

Show that you understand and value parents' feelings for their children by:

- talking about their child as an individual and showing that you are getting to know them
- reassuring them that they are not 'being silly' in finding separation difficult and that it just demonstrates the depth of their feelings for their child.

A challenging role

Being a parent is a difficult, challenging and very responsible role; you should always show parents that you understand this. It is a 24/7 job and most parents embark on the role with little of the considerable knowledge and skills needed to be a 'good enough' parent, just learning as they go along and muddling through.

Some parents might use an approach to parenting that you feel is not helpful to their child – but always remember that the child is theirs, not yours. Your professional knowledge may suggest a particular course of action but parents may see things from a different viewpoint; you have to accept that it may be right for them and their family. Your professionalism requires you to respect parents' good intentions and the way they lead their lives and be non-judgemental in your interactions with them.

Respect for families' values and preferences

Different families want and expect different things for their children and settings must be careful not to ignore families' values and preferences. Parents are entitled to hold values and beliefs that arise from the social and cultural influences on their way of life, such as wanting their children to have a vegetarian diet. Practitioners should show respect for such values while offering children wide opportunities for learning and development.

Case study: equal opportunities

Sharon had been explaining to some parents new to the setting how opportunities were offered to children of both genders to have equal chances to participate in activities and develop their skills. One mother said, 'But we want our daughter to grow up in the culture of our religion to become a mother and homemaker like I have – not to get ideas of a career.'

1 Why should Sharon show this mother that she respects her point of view?

2 How could she present the setting's policies and attitudes to children's learning?

It may be necessary to negotiate about some aspects of children's care in order to balance parents' preferences with the well-being of the child in the setting. For example, some parents may expect and want their child to begin potty training earlier than practitioners think is realistic without putting pressure on the child.

Key term

Non-judgemental – not thinking or talking about others in ways that judge them or condemn them as wrong because they behave in ways that are based on values, opinions or beliefs that are different from your own.

CP6

Case study: finding a compromise

Jon and Claire asked Damian, Oscar's childminder, not to let 2-year-old Oscar have a nap in the afternoon as they wanted him to settle down to sleep to give them some quiet time together in the evening. But if Oscar did not have a nap, he got miserable and couldn't play. Damian offered to adjust the routine so Oscar had a slightly earlier lunch followed by a short nap to refresh him, and also suggested the idea of trying to put him to bed a little later, after a calm time of bath, bedtime story and some gentle music.

1 Why did Damian not just agree with what Jon and Claire wanted?

2 Why did he try to find a way forward that would partly comply with their request?

Value parents' knowledge about their children.

Parents' knowledge of their children

Children spend more of their lives with their parents than they do in any setting or with any practitioner. Their parents see them in different situations and with different people. This means that it is parents who know most about a child and are the most important influence on their lives. Parents are their children's first and most enduring educators; children learn patterns of behaviour, attitudes and basic skills in their earliest years which are important all their lives, and the influence of parents on this learning is immense. Professionals have lots of knowledge about children and their development in general, but it is parents who know the particular child as an individual.

Practitioners need to have accurate information about a child if they are to do their best for them and they should seek this information first of all from parents.

Sharing information

You should establish a two-way dialogue with parents; they are entitled to know that their children are kept safe in the setting and offered appropriate opportunities for development and learning. Practitioners have a responsibility to:

- feed back to parents information gained through observations of their child
- describe the progress the child is making
- explain the purpose of activities offered in the setting and how they encourage development and learning
- involve parents in formulating plans for their children's experiences to carry their development and learning forward.

So what does this mean?

To make the most of parents' specific knowledge about their children:

- ask them to tell you about their child – what they can do, what they like, what they are interested in and what upsets them
- listen carefully and show that you value what they are telling you
- make use of the information in your work with the child.

So what does this mean?

To ensure that parents are aware of what experiences their children have when they are apart from them:

- provide clear explanations about the setting's policies and procedures
- make records of observations and assessments available for parents to see, and show that you value their responses to what is recorded
- give positive information about children's achievements and praise their efforts
- encourage parents to spend time in the setting, finding out about activities and routines
- if you voice concerns about a child's progress or behaviour, be sensitive to parents' reactions of agitation or denial.

Assessment activity 3.1

Seek opportunities to learn from established practitioners (such as those in your work placement setting) about their experiences of working with parents.

1 Ask them to tell you about occasions when their work with parents has been affected by parents' strong feelings for their children and/or the effects of the challenges of being a parent. Ask them also to tell you about ways they adapt their practice to respect parents' values and preferences. It may be possible to make an audio recording of their replies and use it to help you write an account of what you have learned.

2 In your work placement setting, note how information is shared with parents, and share what you find with a fellow learner. Use your joint experiences to write a description of how practitioners should have a two-way dialogue with parents.

3.2 Ways to develop effective working with families

Your prime aim for working effectively with families should be to develop professional relationships with them, based on partnership. Partnership is about doing things *with* someone else, not about doing things *to* them. A partnership is a relationship between people who communicate well, and who see each other as equals who respect and trust one another. If one party in the relationship behaves in a way that makes the other feel inferior, that is not a true partnership.

Building a partnership of equals requires practitioners to communicate in ways which parents feel comfortable with. Be aware that when they come into a setting, parents are off their home ground, in an unfamiliar environment. They may feel at a disadvantage among people that they see as more expert and skilful in handling children than they are.

Be very careful about showing off your professional knowledge or using technical terms or jargon. This carries the risk of making parents feel de-skilled and undermining their confidence in the knowledge and skills they have.

Case study: avoiding jargon

Kim was generally acknowledged by her colleagues as being very tuned in to the children in the pre-school, but she felt that many parents were not at ease with her. She asked one of her colleagues, Pratima, to be honest with her and say why this might be. Pratima said, 'I wonder if it's to do with the way you sometimes talk about things like "fine motor skills" or "cognitive development". There's a risk that you're making parents feel that they know nothing compared with an expert like you and that's making them feel a bit silly.'

1 Why would parents feel ill at ease with Kim?

2 How could she share the meaning of these technical terms in a way that will not undermine parents' self-esteem?

We have seen already in this unit how parents are entitled to respect for:

- their deep feelings about their children and their attachment to them
- the demanding nature of their role
- their detailed knowledge of their child
- their values, preferences and way of life in their family structure
- their parenting style.

So what does this mean?

Practitioners show their respect for parents by:

- understanding the challenges of being a 'good enough' parent
- listening carefully and attentively
- taking what parents say seriously and giving them opportunities to contribute in the setting
- cooperating as far as possible with parents' requirements and wishes for their children
- not being judgemental
- making it a priority to give parents time and attention.

We have also seen that building trust takes sympathetic understanding, warm responsiveness, time and effort on both sides.

So what does this mean?

Practitioners can build trust by:

- behaving in an honest and open way
- being warm and approachable in their manner
- offering sincere welcomes with smiles and, if appropriate, a few words of greeting in a family's home language
- reaffirming the importance of parents in children's lives
- being available to parents at times when it fits in with their lives.

Assessment activity 3.2

With other learners in your group, think about the challenges that lie ahead in working with families.

1 Make a list of ways in which you can show your respect for parents, including some actions or ways of communicating that would not be respectful.

2 Identify ways in which you plan to build parents' trust in you.

3 Following your discussion, write in your own words how you hope to develop effective ways of working with families.

3.3 The benefits of partnership working with parents/carers

Working with parents requires considerable sensitivity and skill – but the benefits of doing so make the investment of time and effort worthwhile. Children's well-being, development and learning are enhanced by practitioners and parents working in partnership. Both parents and practitioners also benefit from such a relationship.

Children's well-being

Continuity of care between setting and home is essential to the healthy development and emotional well-being of children, especially young children. For example:

- parents and practitioners need to work together to ensure that a child has a balanced diet across a day and a week
- young children need the security of routines and practices in the setting that are familiar and have clear links to the way things happen at home. Babies, in particular, need to have consistent feeding and sleeping routines
- changes such as toilet training or issues arising from concerns about children's behaviour are more likely to be successful if they are approached consistently.

Children thrive better if relationships are cordial between their parents and the other important adults in their lives such as their key person. They are very sensitive to non-verbal communication and the atmosphere of a relationship between adults. They soon become aware if there is tension or misunderstanding and can become anxious or upset, even if they do not really understand all of what is said.

Children's development and learning

There is a growing body of evidence that confirms that the home environment plays a key role in children's development and learning, particularly their enthusiasm for learning. When practitioners have a good relationship with parents, they help to expand parents' understanding of how activities and experiences contribute to children's development and learning. Parents are then more able to continue some activities at home, and practitioners are more aware of experiences at home and can build on them in the setting.

If concerns arise about an aspect of a child's development or behaviour, a practitioner and parent who already have a positive relationship are able to discuss any problems promptly and constructively.

Benefits for adults

We have already seen how parents are reassured and gain confidence in a practitioner as the partnership relationship develops. From the practitioners' point of view, knowing they have parents' confidence makes them more confident in their practice, as they feel more sure that they are in tune with individual children, so their work is more satisfying.

4 Understand factors which influence life experiences

4.1 Possible effects of major life events

All families experience major events in their lives from time to time and these inevitably affect everyone in the family to some extent, including the children, whatever their age. Some events are a one-off or are resolved relatively quickly, for example:

- moving house
- a parent changing job or returning to work
- the arrival of a new baby
- starting or moving to a new school
- bereavement
- being the victim of crime
- a member of the family being in trouble with the law.

Others may be longer-lasting situations, for example:

- ill health (physical or mental) or disability of a parent or another member of the family
- relationship problems, perhaps even domestic violence

- a member of the family abusing drugs or alcohol
- a parent caring for children with little or no support from a partner or other family members
- stress from work pressures
- being the victim of abuse
- experiences of racism.

Even one-off events can have lasting influences on family members' lives. The effects on children are often indirect, resulting from the impact of the events on their parents.

Effects on parents

Such events and situations can result in pressures on parents that lead to:

- physical exhaustion (e.g. from sleepless nights and the constant work of caring for a new baby, a disabled child or an elderly relative)
- mental exhaustion (e.g. from worries about the future and feelings that they are lurching from one crisis to the next with no hope that things will improve)
- depression and feelings of helplessness or fear.

When parents reach a point of feeling that they can not cope, being at 'the end of their tether' and being short-tempered and low on patience, it becomes harder to focus on meeting their children's needs and managing their behaviour in positive ways. They may neglect their own health and well-being. In some families, the situation deteriorates to the point where social workers and even the family courts system become involved. This may bring help and support, but it can also bring another layer of distress for parents if they fear they will lose their children.

Some parents cope better than others, perhaps because they have strong inner resources of personality, and/or friends and family to turn to for practical help and moral support. But others may still be suffering from adverse influences in their own childhood or youth and be isolated in their community because they have just moved to a new area or do not speak English well.

Effects on children and young people

We have seen what a demanding role it is to be a parent, and it is clear that if additional pressures such as these arise for a family, the parents' ability to provide all the care and attention their children need is likely to be adversely affected. Children's needs may be marginalised or even neglected by parents struggling with major events.

Even events such as moving house or the birth of a new sibling can upset young children, especially if they are not carefully prepared with clear explanations. They may be upset by other events which they cannot understand such as illness or relationship breakdown; they will react to adults' distress or anger, becoming worried for the adults. Some children feel that it is their fault if their parents disagree or separate.

Older children's lives may be affected by, for example, copying the behaviour of a violent or criminal parent. Children of any age may become depressed and withdrawn or angry and aggressive as a result of what is happening within their family. Some children regress in their development, for example, wetting the bed.

Effects on the family as a whole

In families where there is a child with disability or chronic illness, there can be deep adverse effects on their siblings. They may be worried about their disabled or sick sibling, or feel that their needs and wishes are always sidelined.

Assessment activity 4.1

Read the description of the Family H.

Mother and father, Kathy and Gary, have three children – Robbie (13), Holly (10) and Zoe (5). Holly is physically disabled and has learning difficulties, and needs constant care. Six months ago the family moved to a different town when Gary started a new job; a month ago, Kathy's father died after a long illness. Kathy suspects that Gary has formed a relationship with a work colleague and they have been having bitter arguments. Yesterday, Kathy received a call from Robbie's school to say that he and some other boys had been caught stealing from a local shop and the police had been called.

With a fellow learner, think about each of the family members in turn. For each of them, write a description of some of the physical and emotional effects these events might be having on them.

4.2 Effects of socio-economic factors on families

Besides these pressures that arise within the family, many families experience difficulties as a result of their economic situation and/or their position in society.

There are many reasons that a family may have a low income, related to parents' low earning capacity, such as:

- parents' poor education attainments and qualifications and lack of opportunities
- parents' illness or disability
- a downturn in the economy resulting in redundancies
- disability or chronic illness of a family member which means a parent must provide full-time care.

Low income leads to consequences such as:

- difficulty in feeding and clothing children adequately
- living in poor housing conditions – overcrowded accommodation, a dilapidated house or bed and breakfast accommodation
- constant worry about getting into debt.

Social isolation may arise if parents have moved to an area away from the support of the extended family, or live in a community where few other people speak their home language.

Parents may feel ashamed that they cannot provide adequately for their family and they may become anxious and depressed, or angry and aggressive.

More children from lower-income groups have accidents and experience certain illnesses such as respiratory infections. There is growing evidence that children's communication and cognitive development is adversely affected by living in a low-income family.

Assessment activity 4.2

1 Carry out some research by looking at websites such as those for the Sutton Trust and the Joseph Rowntree Foundation and research on family income from the University of Oxford's Health Economic Research Centre (see the Useful websites section on page 169 for more information).

2 Write an explanation about the links between family income levels and children's development.

CP6

5

Know how practitioners who work with children and/or young people can support families in times of crisis

CP6

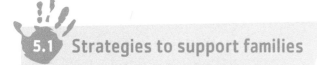

5.1 Strategies to support families

Supporting families in times of crisis or stress requires a combination of professional behaviour and sensitive compassion. The part you might play in supporting families will depend on the role you have in a setting and the form the support takes will depend on the nature of the difficulties involved.

Sometimes you can help parents with practical information, such as giving a domestic violence or addiction helpline number. Sometimes the right approach is to enable them to talk through what they need to do next. Often the most valuable form of support you can provide is to listen – much better than trying to 'take over' and 'sort things out'. Be very wary about offering advice; it is never appropriate or productive simply to tell people what to do with their lives – they have to find their own solutions.

So what does this mean?

When supporting families, use strategies such as:

- being ready to listen and to provide comfort and reassurance
- being non-judgemental
- being objective – do not impose your opinions on them
- helping parents to identify the choices and options open to them, but standing back and letting them make their own decisions, even when you think they are not making the right choices
- making sure that any information you supply is accurate and up to date
- maintaining confidentiality
- remaining calm (do not let other people's depression depress you, or get angry on their behalf)
- not letting yourself get involved in family crises and disputes
- knowing your own limits and seeking help from colleagues or other professionals for matters beyond your own expertise.

Be ready to listen to parents who need to talk about the difficulties they are facing.

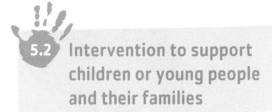

5.2 Intervention to support children or young people and their families

Generally speaking, problems are most likely to respond to intervention at the earliest possible opportunity, but trying to intervene in a family's crisis or ongoing problems uninvited is unlikely to be successful. In most circumstances, you must wait until they are ready to make profitable use of help from outside the family. The exception to this, of course, is if you think a child is at risk of harm. In this case you must follow the setting's child protection procedures. (For more information on policies, see Unit CP2.)

Sometimes parents may seek time and space to talk with you about their problems; they may share their worries with you openly, asking for your help. Others may not discuss their difficulties with you explicitly, but you may become aware of their need for support through observing their distress or anxiety. As you become an experienced practitioner, you will be able to develop your sensitivity to families' crises in a professional way, being available when your support can be accepted.

5.3 Helping families to gain access to support from professionals

As will be covered in Unit CP7, there are many agencies and professionals that can provide targeted and expert support to families in times of difficulty, and practitioners and settings can help parents by providing information about what each offers and how to make contact.

Find out

Find out what information your work placement setting provides to families about local sources of advice and support. There may be a noticeboard or information leaflets; practitioners may pass on information orally.

It is often not enough simply to provide information about agencies and services. Many parents, especially when they are feeling overwhelmed by problems, lack the confidence to seek help. You may be able to help by making initial contacts on their behalf, or putting them in touch with other parents who have used similar services and would be willing to share their experiences. Home-Start is an organisation that trains volunteers to become home visitors and provide support to parents, including helping them by coming with them to appointments and new groups. Sometimes, parents feel more at ease using the Internet to find out about sources of support since they can do so anonymously.

Assessment activity 5.1, 5.2, 5.3

Look again at the description of the Family H on page 164. Discuss the following with other learners in your group.

1 How do you think this family might be helped by intervention from professionals?

2 Which professionals might have something to offer this family?

3 Think about strategies for offering support such as: listening to Kathy talk about her family's situation; providing information about locally available services; helping Kathy and Gary to work out what choices and options they have. What would be most valuable to this family?

4 Are there ways that support might be offered that would prevent the family from accepting help?

5 Following your discussions, write down in your own words the best ways of helping this family.

CP6

In the real world

I am Lin, and I'm a childminder. I have worked with many different parents, some of whom have major problems to deal with. I used to think that some of them were their own worst enemies and that they just needed to get a grip on their lives. I can remember thinking things like S should leave her violent partner, or B and R should smoke less and spend what little money they have on meeting their families' needs. There was N who was a teenage mother and I started off thinking that she would have a better future if her child was adopted and she completed her education.

I've come to realise that judging parents like this isn't fair – it's their life, not mine, and I don't know all the details. And it doesn't help if you allow your negative opinions to spill over into your communications with parents. If they feel they are being criticised or seen as a 'bad parent', they won't trust you or feel they can confide in you. If you want to support the family, you have to stay neutral and show that you respect them as individuals, doing the best they can.

Check your knowledge

1 What are the main responsibilities of a key person?
2 How can you ensure that you pronounce and spell the names of family members properly?
3 What does 'confidentiality' mean?
4 Under what circumstances should information be shared with other professionals without parents' permission?
5 What are meant by 'attachment' and 'bonding'?
6 What is meant by 'multiple attachments'?
7 What are 'stranger anxiety' and 'separation anxiety'?
8 Name four different parenting styles.
9 What does 'non-judgemental' mean?
10 Describe three ways that children benefit when practitioners and parents work in partnership.

CACHE Extended Assessment

Theme: Working in partnership

Grading criterion

B2 Analyse ways the provision of equality, diversity and inclusive practice can be ensured in relation to the chosen theme.

1   Think about showing respect for the various forms that a family might take. How might you respond if a colleague:
    * condemned a gay couple living in a civil partnership who had adopted a very young disabled girl, saying it would ruin the child's future and it was irresponsible of social services to place her with them
    * observed a little boy being very aggressive and commented, 'What can you expect when his mother is a single parent?'
    * muttered when the uncle of a child who lived in a large extended family collected him, 'It's someone different every time. Poor little mite must be completely bewildered.'?

2   Search for information about naming systems, such as:
    * what is indicated by Singh or Kaur in the names in the traditions of Sikhism
    * the placing of family and personal names in Chinese tradition
    * the significance of the day of the week a child is born in some West African cultures.

3   Describe ways that a practitioner can interact with parents to show respect for families who are different from their own, and show that all families are welcome in their setting.

This is an example of how you might approach one criterion of your Extended Assessment. You must successfully complete all the criteria at each grade to achieve that grade. You will achieve the highest grade for which you have successfully completed all the criteria. For example, to achieve a B grade you will need to meet the requirements of the B1, B2 and B3 criteria, as well as C1, C2, C3 and D1 and D2.

When trying to understand the requirements for your Extended Assessment, it is always a good idea to talk to your tutors. Fellow learners and workplace colleagues are also useful sources of information.

Further references

The following are sources of useful information on the topic of working with the families of children and young people.

Booklets/leaflets

Griffin, S. (2008) *Inclusion, Equality and Diversity in Working with Children*, Oxford: Heinemann

Lindon, J. (2009) *Positive Relationships: Parents as Partners*, Salisbury: Practical Pre-school Books

Ward, U. (2009) *Working with Parents in Early Years Settings*, Exeter: Learning Matters Ltd

Whalley, M. and the Pen Green Centre Team (1997) *Working with Parents*, London: Hodder Education

Useful websites

To obtain a secure link to the websites below, visit www.pearsonhotlinks.co.uk and search for this book by using its title or ISBN. Click on the section for CP6.

The Sutton Trust

The Joseph Rowntree Foundation

University of Oxford's Health Economic Research Centre for research on family income

Home-Start, which supports vulnerable parents through a home visiting scheme

Working as part of more than one team

CP7

Working with children involves working with other adults, both with colleagues in your workplace and with other professionals who contribute to supporting the needs of children and families. Team working can be very enjoyable and satisfying. There are challenges involved, but when you understand the benefits to you and your colleagues – and to the children and families you work with – you will be able to commit yourself to meeting them.

Learning outcomes

By the end of this unit you will:

1 Understand the value of team working

2 Understand the rationale for working as part of more than one team when working with children and/or young people

3 Understand the reasons for multi-agency working among organisations that are involved with children and/or young people

4 Understand the benefits of cross-functional working to an organisation when working with children and/or young people

5 Know how teams and organisations contribute to integrated working.

In practice

When Maddy started work in the early years sector, she had expected to be working with colleagues in a nursery or children's centre who had undergone similar training to her own. She was surprised to find herself working with a much wider range of professionals, and at first she felt shy and lacking in confidence in communicating with them.

By the end of this unit you will appreciate the benefits for children and families when professionals work together in a coordinated way, and be motivated to overcome any difficulties you find in team working.

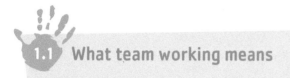

1 Understand the value of team working

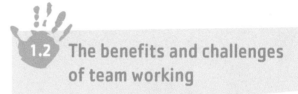

1.1 What team working means

Working with children and young people involves team working.

Key term

Team working – working with other people towards shared aims or goals.

You may find yourself team working with other people who work in the same setting as you, or those whose work base is outside the setting.

1.2 The benefits and challenges of team working

Team working requires each member of the team to play their part, according to their individual expertise derived from their professional qualifications and experience. When you work with other people and you play your part in the overall work of the team, you are likely to find that:

- you are able to make a contribution to achieving outcomes that you could not manage on your own
- you feel pride in what is achieved through the combined efforts of the team, which makes your work more satisfying
- you learn from observing how other people in the team work
- your self-esteem and self-confidence are boosted by the recognition and respect you get from other team members for your efforts and contributions.

Wider team

Immediate colleagues

Social worker

Coordinator of local childminding network

SENCO

Admin staff

Bushra

Manager

Deputy

Catering staff

Speech and language therapist

Other childcare workers

Qualified teacher

Health visitor

Teacher from local primary school

Figure 7.1: *In her role in the children's centre, Bushra works with many other people.*

However, to participate professionally in team working, each person must deal with the challenges of:

- being committed to working towards the shared goals of the team
- contributing actively and positively
- respecting and supporting other members of the team.

Goals

It is essential that you understand the overall purpose of any team you participate in. A setting may have a 'mission statement' and it will certainly have policies and procedures. Practitioners should take advantage of any opportunity to contribute to the development of a team's goals or aims, and to policy.

Find out

At your work placement setting, find out if there is a 'mission statement' which expresses the overall aims. What do this and the setting's policies tell you about what the setting wants to achieve for children and families? In what ways were the practitioners in the setting involved in developing the aims and policies?

Without an understanding of shared aims, it can be difficult to contribute to team working; you may feel at a loss about how to respond to unexpected circumstances or you may misunderstand what other members of the team are trying to achieve.

Contributing

You must be willing to make positive efforts to be an active member of the team. A team of which you are a member cannot be effective if you sit back and do not play your part.

So what does this mean?

To contribute actively and positively to a team, you should be prepared to:

- share your knowledge, ideas and information with other members of the team
- contribute actively to discussion, planning and solving problems
- be open to new ideas and other people's suggestions
- take responsibility for aspects of work where you have the appropriate knowledge and skills
- be reliable, completing work when and how you agreed to do it
- be prepared to be flexible and adapt to changing circumstances
- maintain the confidentiality of what you hear in discussion at meetings, so others feel they can trust you with information about children and families.

Respecting and supporting

Working in a team always requires a degree of give and take, and you should show your colleagues that you respect and value them, and also help them in their work.

So what does this mean?

To be a good member of a team, you should:

- listen to and show an interest in the views of other team members
- offer practical support to other team members
- thank others for their help and congratulate them on their success
- not criticise colleagues behind their back.

If you find yourself in disagreement with another member of the team, approach the difference of opinion in a positive, non-confrontational way. Make sure you keep your own emotions and moods under professional control. Try using phrases like:

- 'I just see things a different way …'
- 'I understand what you say, but I see another side to this …'
- 'What you say is true, but on the other hand …'

1.3 The value of team working when working with children or young people

Team working is productive in many spheres of work, but it is especially valuable in work with children and families. When each member of a team is contributing their knowledge, skills and understanding, the wide and sometimes complex needs of children and families are more likely to be identified accurately and met effectively. A variety of expertise is brought into play to ensure that the appropriate help and support is made available. Families will not experience gaps in provision which would leave them with unmet needs.

Assessment activity 1.1, 1.2, 1.3

1. Make a list of teams in which you have worked in the past. This might include taking part in a school play or show, playing in a sports team, playing in a musical group or working with others to organise an event.
2. What part did you play in the team? How did this relate to the part other people played? What do we mean by 'working in a team'?
3. Make a list of the benefits of team working, especially in work with children and families.
4. Write a description of the challenges you might encounter in being part of a team.

2 Understand the rationale for working as part of more than one team when working with children and/or young people

Why is working as part of a team so valuable?

2.1 Reasons why more than one team, external to the organisation, would be working together

The reality of children's lives is that they have contact with professionals from several different organisations or agencies. This means that teams must sometimes work with other teams from a different setting or workplace.

CP7

Case study: different needs – different teams

Chloe is 3 years old. She spends two days a week at home with her mother and three days with a childminder. She goes to pre-school two half-days a week – her mother takes her one day and her childminder takes her the other. Chloe has cerebral palsy; she sees a physiotherapist and a speech and language therapist regularly.

Angel is 10 months old. Her mother has a drug addiction problem and her father is in prison. The health visitor has been monitoring her growth and development. Recently, concerns about her welfare have become grave and the family court has made an interim care order, placing her in the care of the local authority. She is currently living with foster carers but sees her mother several times a week at contact sessions supervised by social workers. The magistrates have to make a decision about whether it will be safe to return her to the care of her mother or whether she should be adopted. Her interests are represented in court by a children's guardian appointed by Cafcass (Children and Family Court Advisory and Support Service).

Tyrone is 6 years old. He attends a local primary school and goes to an after-school club until his parents get back from work. His asthma makes him susceptible to infections so he sees his GP and the practice nurse quite often.

1 Which teams are involved with each of these children?
2 Why might members of these various teams need to communicate with one another from time to time?
3 What might be the consequences for the children concerned if these teams did not work together?

2.2 Reasons why more than one team, internal to the organisation, would be working together

Similarly, in larger and more complex settings where more than one team works within the same location, teams need to work together to ensure children's well-being.

Case study: teams working together

In the Greenways Park Children's Centre:

- early years practitioners care for children in the day care nursery and run activities at stay-and-play sessions with children who drop in with their parents
- a small catering team provides meals and snacks
- there is a unit providing support to refugee families
- courses are run for parents – in learning English, basic IT skills, preparation for returning to work and various craft skills
- visiting physiotherapists and speech and language therapists hold sessions for specific children
- midwives and health visitors run antenatal and postnatal groups.

1 Why might members of these various teams need to communicate with one another from time to time?
2 What might be the consequences for children and their families if these teams did not work together?

Assessment activity 2.1, 2.2

Work with another learner in your group. Together, make a list of reasons why practitioners from different teams concerned with early years provision and children and families' social care need to work together.

175

3 Understand the reasons for multi-agency working among organisations that are involved with children and/or young people

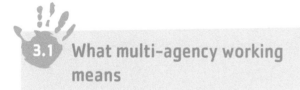

3.1 What multi-agency working means

A child and their family might receive services from a range of agencies such as:

- education provision – school, **education welfare department, educational psychologist**
- childcare provision – nursery, childminder, after-school club
- health services – GP, health visitor, dentist, **physiotherapist, speech and language therapist, paediatrician**, hospital-based medical staff (in **orthopaedic, ENT, ophthalmology, dermatology** or other departments)
- children's social services – social worker, foster carer, Cafcass

- community-based organisations – parent and toddler club, holiday play schemes
- voluntary organisations – pre-school, support organisations for families with disabled children
- housing authorities.

Since the beginning of this century, we have seen a growth in **multi-agency working**. This is a form of team working where each member of the team is an organisation, rather than an individual person.

Key term

Multi-agency working – refers to a range of different services, agencies or teams of professionals working in a coordinated way to provide services for children and young people and their families.

Figure 7.2: *Children and families receive services from many agencies.*

Multi-agency working is difficult to achieve successfully because each service has its separate philosophies, assumptions, terminology, professional standards, budgets and priorities. There are many hurdles to be overcome before we see consistently effective multi-agency working.

Key terms

Education welfare department – local authority department with legal responsibilities including promoting regular school attendance and preventing truancy.

Educational psychologist – assesses and helps children who have learning difficulties and special educational needs.

Physiotherapist – helps people with physical problems caused by impairment, ill health, injury or ageing to become more mobile.

Speech and language therapist – helps people overcome speech and communication difficulties.

Paediatrician – medical professional specialising in the health and development of children.

Orthopaedic department – hospital department concerned with the treatment of impairment and injury of bones and muscles.

ENT department – hospital department concerned with the treatment of disorders of the ear, nose and throat.

Ophthalmology department – hospital department concerned with the treatment of impairments and diseases of the eye.

Dermatology department – hospital department concerned with the treatment of diseases of the skin.

Cafcass (Children and Family Court Advisory and Support Service) – employs specialist social workers to act as children's guardians and represent the interests of children in family court proceedings.

Holistic – an approach that takes the whole person into account, not just one or a few aspects of their health and well-being.

3.2 The benefits of multi-agency working

A particular child and family may use the services of several agencies, but each agency is centred around one aspect of services for children and families. There is a risk that each agency focuses on meeting a limited range of the child and family's needs, in isolation from their other needs and requirements. Children and families do not experience their life in a compartmentalised way, but as one, undivided experience. The main benefit and aim of multi-agency working is to meet the needs and requirements of the family in a **holistic** and coordinated way.

Multi-agency working can make it more likely that children and families are offered the right services at the right time, consistently and in the right sequence. If an organisation can expand their understanding of a child beyond the specialist service their agency offers, they are more likely to have an overall picture of the whole child. It is also more likely that the family will be able to make use of mainstream services which may be more accessible in their own community, rather than relying on a variety of specialist services which are centralised and harder to get to.

Multi-agency working is especially important to families of disabled children who want their child to be seen as a child, not a medical case.

Find out

The introduction of the Early Support programme has been a great step forward for parents of disabled children. Use the Internet to find out how Early Support helps families and makes multi-agency working more possible.

CP7

Besides these advantages for children and families, there are benefits for organisations, settings and practitioners. When information is shared, each professional who encounters the child does not have to start from scratch in assessing the child's development and progress. They can benefit from the knowledge of professionals in other agencies and build on work done so far with the child and family – this saves time. Parents' frustration levels are reduced and that is more likely to lead to a positive and constructive relationship between the family and the agency. Real progress can be made and effective support provided, and this is more satisfying for the practitioners involved. Overlap, where two agencies offer similar support, or gaps where no agency is offering help, can be avoided, and better use is made of the limited resources of settings and agencies.

Case study: sharing information

Liam, who is 4 years old, has a variety of physical impairments and learning difficulties. His parents regularly attend appointments with various agencies. They have to travel 15 miles to the hospital, a difficult journey by public transport, where they have appointments on separate occasions in the paediatric department, the eye department and the orthopaedic department. They have also been to assessments by an educational psychologist and an occupational therapist at local clinics, as well as regular visits to the speech and language therapist and physiotherapist.

Each of these agencies keeps separate records. Every time Liam and his parents attend an appointment, they find themselves having to tell each professional all the details of Liam's impairments, the treatment and therapy he has received so far, and what each of the other agencies is currently offering him and the advice they have given.

They find this exhausting, frustrating and depressing as they recount Liam's problems over and again.

1 How could the departments at the hospital help Liam and his parents?

2 What difference might it make if the various agencies shared information about assessments, treatment and therapy with one another?

Assessment activity 3.1, 3.2

1 Imagine you have to explain to a new practitioner what is meant by 'multi-agency working'. Write down what you will say.

2 Discuss with other members of your group the ways in which each of the following will benefit from multi-agency working:
- Liam
- his family
- the settings he attends
- the professionals who work with him.

3 Following your discussion, write in your own words how you think each would benefit.

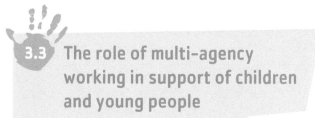

3.3 The role of multi-agency working in support of children and young people

For multi-agency working to be effective, several challenges have to be tackled including:
- sharing information
- understanding and respecting one another's roles
- using common language or terminology.

Sharing information

Sharing information is a key element in the role of multi-agency working. In recent years, there have been a number of high-profile failures to protect a child from abuse which have resulted in a child's death. In each of these cases, several professionals such as social workers, health visitors and GPs, early years practitioners, teachers and the police have been aware of the child and have identified some causes for concern. However, because each kept the information within their own organisation and did not share it with other agencies, no one had an overall picture of the child's life and the true extent of the seriousness of the case was not realised until the child had experienced great harm.

Sadly, there has been reluctance on the part of some agencies to share information with practitioners in another profession. Sometimes, this arises out of concerns about maintaining confidentiality, but the main reason seems to be the lack of clear channels of communication for passing on information and pooling knowledge. It is when communication is lacking that the child 'falls through the net'. Agencies and professionals in many parts of the country are making strenuous attempts to resolve this situation, but so far effective solutions which work consistently to safeguard children from harm have not been found everywhere.

Understanding and respect

The professionals working in each agency may see a child's needs and a family's requirements in a different way because:

- they start from a different knowledge base, relevant to their professional training
- the services and skills they offer are limited to one aspect of the child and family's situation
- they have had different levels of interaction with the child and family so some know them better than others.

Case study: the bigger picture

Liam's family found that:

- the paediatrician carried out formal assessments of Liam's all-round development
- the ophthalmologist diagnosed his visual impairments
- the physiotherapist suggested exercises to improve his mobility
- the practitioners in the nursery he had been attending for two years saw him as a little boy who needed some additional support to be able to play and learn.

1 Which professionals had the broadest understanding of Liam as a person?

2 Why did they have this knowledge?

For multi-agency working to be effective, it is essential that the professionals involved understand one another's roles and responsibilities and develop a clear picture of what other agencies are offering a child and family. Ideally, one agency should be taking the lead and monitoring the family's overall experience of intervention and support. Without such leadership, gaps can arise and some of the family's needs may go unmet.

know the limitations of your own expertise and be ready to consult other professionals when necessary

understand that you may only know one aspect of the child and family, and that they may need others to help meet all their needs and requirements

When contributing to multi-agency working you need to...

be ready to learn new skills from other practitioners

be ready to share information and expertise with other professionals in the interest of children's welfare

value the expertise of other professionals, being courteous and respectful

Figure 7.3: *Requirements of practitioners contributing to multi-agency working*

Language and terminology

One source of communication failure seems to be misunderstandings about the use of language. Each profession has its own terminology and a word or phrase may have subtly but crucially different meanings when used by different professionals. This can get in the way of harmonious team working and result in each agency assessing the child and family in a different way.

When multi-agency working is successful, it becomes possible to undertake joint assessment of the needs and requirements of a child and family, and also joint planning of what support to provide and how to provide it. A tool which can play a part in joint assessment in England is the **Common Assessment Framework (CAF)**.

The CAF provides documents such as an easy-to-use pre-assessment checklist that can be used by practitioners in a variety of agencies – health, education, social care, early years and other provision for children and young people. The aim is to identify children who may need help and support before a crisis point in their life is reached. If attention is paid to their progress and well-being, and difficulties are spotted, appropriate action can be taken.

Key term

Common Assessment Framework (CAF) – an assessment and planning tool used by children's services in England to standardise the assessment and identification of children and young people's additional needs. The CAF promotes the coordination of multiple agencies in deciding how to best meet a child's needs.

Find out

Use the Internet to find out more about the Common Assessment Framework.

Assessment activity 3.3

Seek opportunities to learn from practitioners in your work placement setting about their experiences of multi-agency working. Ask them to tell you about:

- how information is shared with professionals in other agencies and any barriers they have encountered
- any differences they have noticed in the ways professionals in other agencies perceive children and families
- any problems they have found concerning use of terminology
- their experience of the Common Assessment Framework.

It may be possible to make an audio recording of their replies and use the recording to help you write an account of what you have learned from this.

4 Understand the benefits of cross-functional working to an organisation when working with children and/or young people

4.1 What cross-functional working means

4.2 The benefits of working as part of more than one team

Team working may occur where individual members of the team all share the same broad professional background of qualifications and practice (for example, a group of teachers working in a school), or team working can be **cross-functional working**.

A cross-functional team is like a music band in which each person plays a different instrument but they all play the same tune. Each player contributes their specialist expertise but does not need the skill to play the other instruments because the collaboration and coordination of the team is achieved through the tune.

The development of children's centres has seen the growth of cross-functional working, with early years practitioners/childcare workers and teachers in the same work team, sometimes supplemented by health visitors, speech and language therapists and other professionals. Some of these professionals are employed by the children's centre and some are employed by another agency but spend a proportion of their working week as part of the team in the centre.

Practitioners who have the opportunity to work alongside colleagues in a cross-functional team, and/or to work in a multi-disciplinary way with professionals from other agencies, derive the benefits of:

- learning from other professionals by observing them at work and seeing how certain techniques and methods help children and families
- earning the respect of other professionals who observe the skill they use in their work
- having their minds opened to different perspectives and new possibilities
- appreciating the wider aspects of working with children and young people and feeling part of the whole sector, developing a sense of professional pride.

4.3 The benefits to the organisation of cross-functional working

From the point of view of an organisation, cross-functional working among its staff team means the setting can offer integrated provision, meeting a broader range of families' needs and requirements. Children's centres are intended to be 'a one-stop shop' for families so they know where to go when

Key term

Cross-functional working – where a team is made up of individuals who have a variety of expertise but are all working towards shared aims.

they need information, advice or support. This can be achieved through cross-functional working.

Another advantage from an organisational point of view is that it can offer flexible services, deploying staff resources as and when they are needed to provide a particular service. As a child's needs change, so can the balance of the practitioners making up the membership of a team at the relevant time.

Assessment activity 4.1, 4.3

1 Imagine you have to explain to a new practitioner what is meant by 'cross-functional working'. Write down what you will say.

2 Write an account of the way an organisation may benefit from cross-functional working.

Assessment activity 4.2

Work with another learner to draw up a list of the benefits that can be derived from working in more than one team in relation to:

- the child and/or young person
- the carer/parent
- the relevant teams
- the individual team member
- the work setting
- external agencies or organisations.

5 Know how teams and organisations contribute to integrated working

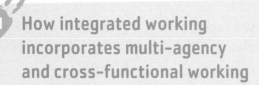

5.1 How integrated working incorporates multi-agency and cross-functional working

For some families, their involvement with various settings, professionals and organisations can become complicated and frustrating. Each may see the family as presenting with a specific 'problem' or need, and address only the aspect of the family's life that falls within the remit of their setting, profession or organisation. But we have seen that the family does not live its life in such a separated way. Each of their needs and requirements is linked to all the others and to their daily existence as a family. What they need is for settings, professionals and organisations to adopt integrated working in order to meet their needs in a 'seamless' way.

Key term

Integrated working – the Children's Workforce Development Council (CWDC) defines integrated working as 'where everyone supporting children and young people work together effectively to put the child at the centre, meet their needs and improve their lives'.

Clearly, multi-agency and cross-functional working have a big part to play in achieving the aim of integrated working. Where organisations and professionals are prepared to take up the challenges of working in teams, putting the child as an individual person at the heart of what they do together, children's needs can be met and their lives can be improved.

The early years of the 21st century saw some encouraging moves towards more integrated working.

- Central government brought policy making and resource decisions together into one department (initially the Department for Children, Families and Schools, now renamed as the Department for Education).
- Local authorities combined education and children's social work services in a single department of children's services.
- Children's centres increased in number and geographical spread. These centres offer a range of separate services in one location such as early education and childcare, health and maternity services, opportunities for adult learning, parent support including outreach/home-visiting services and so on. (Sadly, failure to protect funding for children's centres means that some centres have been closed as part of cuts in public spending.)
- Many schools extended their day so childcare became available beyond the usual school hours on the same premises – an important source of support for working parents.

Many local authorities are now adopting the strategy of the Team Around the Child (TAC).

The Lead Professional brings a variety of professionals from various agencies and settings together to make up the Team Around the Child and to focus on a particular child. Together, the team works out how each can contribute to plans to help support and protect the child and improve their life chances. The membership to the TAC will depend on the nature of the child's needs and can adapt to meet changing needs. In some local authority areas, this approach is being expanded to include the needs of the whole family – the Team Around the Family (TAF).

Key term

Team Around the Child (TAC) – this approach consists of various professionals working together to develop a plan to meet the needs of a child, under the leadership of a Lead Professional.

Find out

Use the Internet to find out more about the Team Around the Child and the Team Around the Family.

Assessment activity 5.1

Imagine you have to explain to a new practitioner what is meant by 'integrated working'. Write down what you will say. Remember to talk about multi-agency and cross-functional working.

In the real world

I'm Will and I work in a children's centre. My daily work brings me into contact with a wide range of professionals, some of them (like me) employed here in the centre. Some of them come here to do pieces of work like assessments of particular children, and some are people who the children see elsewhere (like social workers or medical staff in a hospital or clinic) who seek information from us or make recommendations to us.

There have been times when I have been annoyed or frustrated by the lack of appreciation from workers in other agencies about the nature and importance of what we do with the children when we offer them play and learning experiences. Some don't seem to understand how well we know the parents and how hard we have worked to gain their trust. But I have also been in awe of the skills and knowledge of some professionals who have so much to offer the children and their families. There have been times when I have been confused or left in the dark by some of the terminology they use but as my confidence as a practitioner has grown, I've been more assertive about asking for explanations – people don't always realise they've used a bit of jargon others aren't familiar with.

Overall, I think that working in various teams is helping me develop professionally and is making my job more enjoyable.

Check your knowledge

1 What do we mean by team working?
2 What do we mean by multi-agency working?
3 What is the Early Support programme?
4 What is the Common Assessment Framework?
5 What do we mean by cross-functional working?
6 What do we mean by integrated working?
7 What is the Team Around the Child?

CACHE Extended Assessment

Theme: Working in partnership

Grading criterion

B3 Analyse aspects of your learning from the chosen theme that could improve your future practice.

1   What have you learned so far about working in a team – from reading this chapter and from your own past experience?

2   Think about what it might be like to work with practitioners from different professions. What do you expect to gain from such cross-functional working? What do you foresee being the challenges involved?

3   In what ways will children and families benefit if you become skilled and confident in working in a team with other professionals?

4   Why is integrated working particularly important for children who are at risk of abuse and for disabled children?

This is an example of how you might approach one criterion of your Extended Assessment. You must successfully complete all the criteria at each grade to achieve that grade. You will achieve the highest grade for which you have successfully completed all the criteria. For example, to achieve a B grade you will need to meet the requirements of the B1, B2 and B3 criteria, as well as C1, C2, C3 and D1 and D2.

When trying to understand the requirements for your Extended Assessment, it is always a good idea to talk to your tutors. Fellow learners and workplace colleagues are also useful sources of information.

Further references

The following are sources of useful information on the topic of working as part of more than one team.

Books and articles

Fitzgerald, D. and Kay, J. (2008) *Working Together in Children's Services*, London: Routledge

Gasper, M. (2010) *Multi-agency Working in the Early Years: challenges and opportunities*, London: Sage

Siraj-Blatchford, I., Clarke, K. and Needham, M. (2007) *The Team Around the Child: multi-agency working in the early years*, Stoke-on-Trent: Trentham Books

Useful websites

To obtain a secure link to the website below, visit www.pearsonhotlinks.co.uk and search for this book by using its title or ISBN. Click on the section for CP7.

The Children's Workforce Development Council – this body aims to develop and improve the skills of those who work with children and young people.

Supportive approaches to behaviour management

CP8

Children and young people's behaviour is affected by many different factors. It is important to understand more fully the reasons why children and young people might behave in a certain way in order to know how you might respond to it.

This unit will give you a better understanding of differing models of behaviour management. It will also explore the responsibility of the adult in helping to support childrens and young people's behaviour.

Learning outcomes

By the end of this unit you will:

1 Understand models of behaviour management

2 Understand the detail of a behaviour management model

3 Understand positive support strategies within a behaviour management model

4 Understand why a safe environment for children and/or young people supports positive behaviour.

In practice

Adam qualified last year and has been working at an after-school club for several weeks. Recently he has noticed that the boys in particular have started to try to play fight him and wrestle him to the floor.

At first he was happy to rough play with them but the behaviour has begun to get too aggressive. Last week one of the boys kicked Adam in the stomach and now they have starting calling him names and ignoring him when he tries to discipline them. The children behave well for the other staff. Adam is wondering what to do and whether or not he is cut out for the job after all.

By the end of this unit you will understand different behaviour management models that might help Adam in supporting children to behave well.

1 Understand models of behaviour management

1.1 Exploring models of behaviour

Approaches to behaviour management have changed greatly over time. For example, **corporal punishment** was only banned in English schools in 1986. Until this time children could be hit by their teachers, including the use of canes or other implements.

While teachers are no longer allowed to hit children, and it is against the law for an adult to hit another adult, parents are still able to use physical punishment to manage the behaviour of their children, as long as the punishment is considered 'reasonable'. A punishment such as a smack given by a parent would currently be deemed reasonable even though many people feel that smacking is wrong.

It is not just smacking which divides opinion; differing models of behaviour management do too. Some voices call for tougher punishments for children and young people who behave in an antisocial manner. By contrast, others suggest that we need to understand children and young people better and listen to them if we expect them to behave in appropriate ways. Different behaviour management models give contrasting opinions about how to effectively support children.

Assertive discipline model

Lee Canter (1992) outlines steps to assertive discipline:

1 Understand that adults affect children's behaviour.

2 Adults must display assertive responses.

3 There should be a clear **discipline** plan with rules and consequences.

4 Children should have the discipline plan clearly explained to them.

5 Adults should tell children how to behave properly.

You should recognise when a child is being 'good' and let them know frequently that you approve of their behaviour. He felt that, because children knew they were praised for behaving well, they were more likely to continue to behave in that way. There must also be consequences for not following the rules. In a school environment this could mean losing a privilege such as 'golden time', break time or not being able to attend a school trip.

Canter's model of assertive discipline is straightforward and simple to understand for both children and adults. There is a focus upon praise which helps to raise children's self-esteem and, in turn, if a child is praised and encouraged, they may also respect the adult more.

There is consistency in this model because the rules have been read and understood by both adults and children. Some settings like to draw up a set of 'golden rules' to which the children contribute. Some settings prefer to think in terms of 'rights' rather than rules. Children and adults in the setting both have rights and by understanding these an environment is created where children are in control of their own behaviour.

Key terms

Corporal punishment – physical punishment, such as caning.

Discipline – training someone to obey rules.

Table 8.1: *Rules help protect people's rights.*

Rules	Rights
No shouting	Children and adults have the right to work in a quiet environment.
No hitting or bullying	Children and adults have the right to feel safe and not be threatened or hurt.
No running inside	Children have the right to run in the playground.

Canter's model could be effective in empowering children and making them feel secure. This in turn should lead to children behaving well. However, like all strategies for managing behaviour, it is only effective when used consistently. This approach might work well if parents apply the same approach at home and children and young people do not seek to challenge the rules. However, inconsistent use of praise among parents and staff can lead children and young people to be confused about what the rules really are. Inconsistency of approach can arise if adults do not see a child behaving well and therefore cannot praise them. Adults may also be distracted by children who are not behaving well and are therefore unable to praise the good behaviour of other children.

Young people might be able to understand that we can bend the rules at different times, for example, non-school uniform on special days, but younger children might struggle to understand that behaviour can be acceptable on one day but not on the next.

One criticism of the model is that it is not sensible to praise children constantly just for doing what we expect them to do and that children should not grow up to expect constant praise. Critics feel that the value of praise can be diluted and become less sincere if children are too used to hearing it.

Logical consequences model

Rudolf Dreikurs (1968) author of *Psychology in the classroom*, developed the logical consequences model. He believed that we learn through our environment and the interactions we have with it. He believed that there were three types of logical consequence:

- natural consequence
- arbitrary consequence
- logical consequence.

Natural consequence

Natural consequence happens when there is no adult intervention to moderate the behaviour. Dreikurs's natural consequences model suggests that an adult should not interfere but should allow children to make mistakes and therefore learn their own lessons. For example, Dreikurs's model would say that a child would learn not to touch an oven door if you allowed them to touch it once and they harmed themselves: they would not want to repeat their action.

However, the natural consequence model is not a consistently effective way of supporting behaviour: a child may decide that the action is worth the consequence, even if the behaviour is undesirable. For example, a young person who stays up late at night may feel tired the next day but they might decide that it is worth it in order to stay awake late.

Sometimes it is beneficial that the model is inconsistent because we want children to be able to continue to do things like run around and play, even if they might hurt themselves occasionally.

Arbitrary consequence

This is where the consequence is not immediately linked to the behaviour, for example, if a child hits another child and the punishment or consequence is that they are not allowed to play on the computer. Not playing on the computer is not linked to the unwanted behaviour but it is taking away something the child would enjoy.

This method is only effective if the punishment is given soon after the unwanted behaviour has happened. Young children struggle to make the links between the unwanted behaviour and the punishment.

Logical consequence

A logical consequence is linked to the unwanted behaviour in some way. For example, if a child has pushed into a queue at lunchtime, they can be told to go to the back. The consequence or punishment is directly linked to the action and therefore the child or young person understands the reasons for the punishment.

However, this can be a difficult method to use effectively, especially within a school environment. For example, if a child misbehaves during a PE session, they might be told to sit out. However, this singles the child out and gives them attention. This could make them more likely to want to repeat the behaviour, particularly if the consequence is not significant enough and the attention makes them feel special.

Choice theory model

William Glasser (1998) developed choice theory. He suggested that children are not in control of their own behaviour and adults need to help them to make better choices.

He believed that if children are able to understand that their behaviour affects others, they understand they have a choice in the way that they behave.

He proposed that everyone has five needs, which are set out in **Table 8.2**. When all a child's needs are well met they are less likely to try to meet the needs by choosing behaviours that we see as bad behaviour. For example, a child who does not understand an activity might try to repair their feeling of powerlessness by engaging in attention-seeking behaviour. Choice Theory can be used by a practitioner to understand what frustration a child is experiencing and help them learn new ways of meeting the needs.

Table 8.2: *Glasser's five needs*

Need	Explanation
Survival	Food, shelter and to be kept safe from harm
Belonging and love	Adults should give children attention and create an environment where children can work together
Freedom	Children have the opportunity to make choices for themselves
Fun	Having an interesting, engaging environment and activities
Power	Responsibilities, mutual respect, positive relationships, support, be listened to, accepted, trusted

Love and logic model

Foster W. Cline and Jim Fay (1990) introduced the idea that there are three types of parents. Although they refer to parents in their work, it is equally useful for child carers and teachers working with children and young people. The three types of parents are shown in **Figure 8.1**.

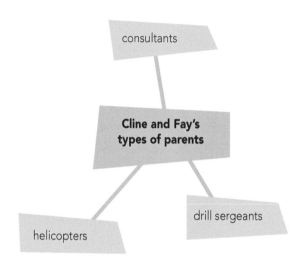

Figure 8.1: *Cline and Fay's parent types*

Helicopters

Helicopter parents hover over their children. They frequently interfere with what their child is doing. This might be controlling their behaviour or their interactions. They make excuses for their children's behaviour and might use guilt to make the child behave.

This style of parenting is now viewed as largely negative and detrimental to the child. It is suggested that these parents are failing to help children to make their own choices and learn things for themselves.

Alternatively, it is argued that this type of parenting might be needed when children are very young as they need to have their interactions and behaviour managed closely in order to keep them safe.

Figure 8.2: *This parent is using guilt to manage the behaviour of their child. What type of parent are they in Cline and Fay's model?*

Drill sergeants

These parents command their children and direct their children's lives. They may tell the child how they should be feeling and what they should be doing, and give them little opportunity to make their own decisions. The parent might have unrealistic expectations and demands. They control their children by threats, punishment and pain (smacking). They might also humiliate the child as a form of punishment.

This style of parenting is dismissed by many people as hugely negative and likely to affect the child's self-esteem and damage their emotional well-being.

Consultants

This type of parent guides and supports their child. They consult with them over important issues and give them the opportunity to make choices. Sometimes the parent helps the child to make good choices through natural consequences. If the adult understands and ignores unwanted behaviour and praises good behaviour, it is believed that the child will learn how to behave well.

This approach to parenting boosts the child's self-worth and self-esteem and it is thought that they become competent decision makers.

This approach is criticised by some for being too liberal. Some people believe that it allows children to manipulate adults and behave in ways that are unacceptable. This behaviour is then often largely ignored and not corrected.

Ginott's model

Haim G. Ginott (1971) believed that adults have a role to play in the way that children and young people behave. Ginott believed that adults need to show children self-control in order for them to understand how to deal with problem situations.

He was mainly considering teachers but the model transfers well into other settings and for parents. The occasions when Ginott felt adults lose control included:

- losing their temper
- calling children names
- behaving rudely
- overreacting
- being cruel
- punishing all children for one child's behaviour
- threatening
- giving long lectures
- making rules without giving the children chance to input.

In contrast to the adult behaviours listed above, Ginott presented the adult who is self-disciplined as someone who:

- does not argue
- invites children to cooperate
- discourages rudeness
- does not criticise
- is helpful.

By considering their own behaviour, Ginott felt that adults could improve children's behaviour.

Some critics believe that this model does not make children take responsibility for their own behaviour.

CP8

If the adult assumes they are responsible for a child's good or bad behaviour, they might fail to make the child take responsibility. This means that the child or young person does not learn what they are doing wrong and why it is unacceptable.

Kounin's model

Jacob Kounin (1970) also suggested that adults' behaviour affected children.

He developed a ten-point concept of how to achieve behaviour change in the classroom. Although his method is concerned with school-aged children, it could be transferred to any group setting.

The ten concepts adults should be aware of

These include:

1 the ripple effect – children react to the way that adults behave

2 'with-it-ness' – being aware of what is going on in the environment

3 momentum – having pace, purpose and structure in the education or play environment – having a suitable beginning and ending

4 smoothness – keeping the session smooth by not having regular interruptions

5 group alerting – making sure that children pay attention and have clear instructions about what is expected of them

6 learner accountability – making sure that children are involved

7 overlapping – keeping activities flowing or overlapping when necessary

8 satiation – when children become too full of learning and then become uninterested, adults need to create an environment and activities that are stimulating and exciting

9 valence and challenge arousal – adults showing enthusiasm and using a range of activities

10 variety and challenge – making activities challenging, stimulating and varied.

Kounin again places emphasis upon the environment and the adult role, believing that children's behaviour will be good if these two elements are right.

One criticism of Kounin's method, like Ginott's, is that there is no mention of children taking responsibility for their own behaviour. Ginott sees the adult as the manager of children's behaviour.

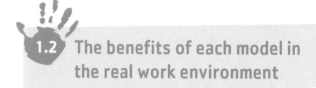

1.2 The benefits of each model in the real work environment

How these models are used in work settings will depend upon the age of the children or young people. It is quite possible that you will need to use a mixture of many models in order to support children's behaviour suitably.

Children and young people at school

Ginott's and Kounin's models are best suited to a school environment because they look to support children as part of a large group. The idea of both models is to maintain a calm and effective learning environment where children feel valued and therefore do not want to behave inappropriately. Both models place a high emphasis upon the adult's role and the importance of being aware of their own actions. A smooth and well-paced lesson does not give the learners an opportunity to misbehave because they are busy and engaged throughout.

Kounin also discusses the importance of knowing when children and young people feel too full of learning and become uninterested. This recognises that children need to rest and unwind. However, this is not largely supported by the hectic curriculum that teachers must deliver, alongside preparing children for regular testing.

Ginott's model considers that an adult has failed if children are not involved in the making of rules. However, many rules are imposed by an authority higher than the teacher and must be obeyed. It is unrealistic to include children in all rule making and as such some rules will be imposed that children must simply follow. This is a reflection of the real world.

The assertive discipline model maintains that children need to be told how to behave properly and a clear discipline plan should be put in place. Schools often use a system of a sliding scale of consequences for unwanted behaviour. Some might have traffic light cards, where an orange card is issued as a warning that behaviour is not acceptable. If the behaviour continues, a red card is issued leading to a more serious consequence such as missing break time or having detention after school.

The benefits of Kounin's model

- Adults create an environment that helps children to behave well.
- Children know what is expected of them because there are clear instructions.
- Activities are well planned and exciting for children.

The benefits of Ginott's model

- The adult or teacher treats children fairly and respectfully.
- Children are empowered to make their own decisions.
- Adults or teachers help children to deal with problems themselves.

The benefits of the assertive discipline model

- Children know exactly what is expected of them.
- Adults are consistent in their responses to unwanted behaviour.
- There are rules that set out how to behave.

Children in early years settings

Glasser's choice theory might be best applied to younger children. If a child can be a taught at a young age that their behaviour has an impact upon others, and start to develop empathy, they might be less likely to behave in a way that causes upset or distress to others. This can be built into personal, social and emotional development sessions at nurseries and pre-schools, for example, during circle time.

Key term

Empathy – the ability to understand and share the feelings of others.

Dreikurs's logical consequences model can be applied with caution when working with young children. Young children need to see the connection between their behaviour and the consequence in order to understand fully what they have done wrong. Older school-aged children are probably able to understand arbitrary consequences providing that there are clear and definite reminders of the consequences. This is often done by means of visual reminders (for example, the red and orange card system described above).

It would be hard to implement fully the Dreikurs's natural consequences in a pre-school setting without a strong risk of the children being harmed.

The benefits of the choice theory model

- Children's emotional development is taken into consideration.
- Children develop empathy for others.
- There is an emphasis upon fun, engaging activities.

The benefits of the logical consequences model

- There is always a consequence for unwanted behaviour.
- The logical consequences model helps children to learn from their behaviour.
- Children learn that they have a choice in the way that they behave.

Adults as role models

All models focus upon the importance of the adult in shaping the behaviour of children. The love and logic model sees the consultant adult as a guide who is capable of boosting children's self-esteem by allowing them to make their own decisions. In an early years environment, children are given greater freedom to exercise their choices. Along with these choices come consequences.

The child soon learns that, if they want to play outside, it is best to put on their coat. Here, the adult models the desired behaviour by wearing their own coat. Following the natural consequences model, the child learns that they will feel cold if they do not wear their coat.

The assertive discipline model stresses that there must be a clear discipline plan in place that the children can understand. In secondary schools, young people might be asked to sign a behaviour contract, agreeing that they will abide by the rules of the school. This is also common in post-compulsory education studies. In signing this they are entering into a contract. If broken there will be immediate sanctions and possible exclusion, in accordance with the school's part of the agreement.

As an adult you must carefully consider your responsibility when working with children and young people. It is important to give children as much responsibility as they can manage, as suggested in the choice theory model. This means that the adult needs to give up some of their responsibility, and that can be quite difficult and potentially frightening. If you allow children and young people to make their own choices, you must have a plan if they turn out to be the wrong choices.

The benefits of the love and logic model

- It considers that it is unacceptable to threaten and humiliate children and young people.
- Consultant adults help to boost children's self-worth.
- Children are supported to make their own decisions.

How is this adult modelling good behaviour?

Case study: Holly's cloud

Holly is 7 years old and is in Rainbow Class. She is lively and chatty and finds it hard not to distract the other children when they are working. She gets quite silly and this can end up with her being told off.

Every Friday the class has golden time where the children can play with special toys and choose what they want to do. Holly has been missing her golden time on a regular basis because of her behaviour. Danielle, Holly's support worker, has noticed that sometimes it is Holly's behaviour on a Monday that means she misses golden time on a Friday. She has usually forgotten by then what she has done wrong and gets quite upset.

Danielle decides to make a poster to help all of the children understand the consequences of their behaviour. The poster has two clouds: one white, one grey. When the children misbehave their name is moved from the white cloud to the grey cloud. They can move backwards and forwards between the clouds if their behaviour improves. If their behaviour does not improve for the whole day, a lightning bolt is added to their name. This means they have missed golden time. Since Danielle introduced this Holly has not missed any of her golden time.

1 Why do you think this method of behaviour management has successfully supported Holly to behave better?

2 Can you think of any potential reasons why this method might not continue to be effective in the future?

1.3 Respecting children and young people's rights

It is everyone's right to be treated fairly and with respect. The Human Rights Act 1998 makes these rights a legal requirement. Although each behaviour management model presents a very different approach to supporting children and young people's behaviour, each fully respects their rights.

The love and logic model presented by Cline and

Fay rejects the helicopter and drill sergeant adults as people who damage children's emotional well-being. This is because they use threats or carry out physical punishment, or humiliate the child or young person. There is no supportive method of managing children or young people's behaviour that causes them physical or emotional harm. This is more likely to result in the child or young person acting in a negative way and is therefore ineffective.

Glasser's choice theory model, where adults listen to and respect children's opinions, focuses on children's and young people's right to free expression. By allowing the child or young person to participate in rule making, mutual respect is created. This leads to children taking more control of their own behaviour. If they make the rules they are less likely to break them.

Each model seeks to create an ordered, calm environment where learning can take place, supported by adults who are aware of how their own behaviour impacts upon that of children.

Ginott stresses the unfairness of punishing all children for one child's behaviour. Punishing children when they have not done anything wrong is not likely to be effective – nor is it upholding their rights. It is more likely to lead to an increase in the children's bad behaviour as they are being punished anyway.

Assessment activity
1.1, 1.2, 1.3

Select two different models of supportive behaviour management described so far.

1 Examine their similarities and differences.

2 Explain how you might put these models into practice in your setting and the benefits of doing so.

3 Describe how in doing this you uphold the rights of the children that you care for.

CP8

2 Understand the detail of a behaviour management model

2.1 Summarising the key points of each model of supportive behaviour management

Table 8.3: *Summary of behaviour management models*

Model	Key points
Assertive discipline Canter and Canter (1992)	Adult determine the rules. The adult asserts their authority by calmly insisting that the child or young person conforms to expectations. Encourages negative and positive consequences for behaviour.
Logical consequences Dreikurs (1968)	Unwanted behaviour is motivated by emotional needs such as wanting attention or exercising power. Children need to understand their motivation for actions. Children should be given choices, e.g. if you do x then y will happen, so they can choose how they behave.
Choice theory Glasser (1998)	The basis is mutual respect without adults controlling behaviour. Children will learn to self-regulate their own behaviour. There should be class rules.
Love and logic Cline and Fay (1990)	Children and young people's self-concept is the prime consideration. Allows children and young people some control. Physical or emotional punishment is not acceptable.
Ginott's model Ginott (1971)	Kindness and respect from adults supports children and young people's behaviour. Improper praise is not helpful. Good communication is needed.
Kounin's model Kounin (1970)	Children and young people need to be controlled by adults. Adult needs to be aware of their own actions. Children and young people need to know what is expected of them.

Reflect

Examine all of the supportive behaviour management summaries listed in **Table 8.3**.
- Can you identify if any of these approaches are used in your setting?
- How effective do you think they are in reality?

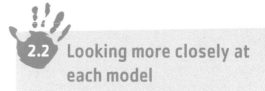

2.2 Looking more closely at each model

When exploring each model in detail, it is helpful to start by looking at the role of the adult and the role of the children. When analysing a particular model you might like to write a list of questions to answer. This will help you to understand fully the detail of the model you have decided to look at.

Your questions might look something like the ones below.

- *How is the adult viewed in this model?*

Each model takes a different view of the adult. For example, the love and logic model sees the adult as a consultant while the assertive model sees the adult as a figure of authority.

- *What is said about the adult's behaviour?*

Some models present the adult's own behaviour as the key to children's good or bad behaviour, while others place less emphasis upon what the adult does.

- *Do adults hold the power?*

The struggle for power is often responsible for unwanted behaviour. In young children this might take the form of a tantrum. In young people it may be manifested in the desire to break the rules, for example, not wearing full school uniform.

Some models mention power and allowing children to have some of the responsibility for rule making. Others place the adult firmly in charge of rule making and discipline.

- *What are the expectations of children in this model?*

Some models expect children to comply and dutifully follow rules while others expect children to be active and involved in rule making.

- *How are children viewed?*

Some models view children as capable of decision making and responsible for their own actions. In another model, children need to be told what to do and are viewed as not fully in control of their emotions.

- *How important are the activities that children engage in?*

What children are doing will make a difference to the way they behave. When children are enjoying their learning and play, their behaviour will be different from when they are bored and not engaged.

If the model discusses activities provided for children it will outline the importance of these.

- *How are praise and reward discussed?*

Some models feel that constant praise is essential in order to build children's confidence and self-esteem while others feel that too much praise fails to be of any value.

Your analysis might conclude with the positives and negatives of the model. This could include how effective you feel it would be in the workplace and the impact it might have upon children.

2.3 Roles in managing behaviour

Everyone has a role in supporting children to play well, including themselves. The most important influencers who shape children's behaviour are the people with whom they have the most contact: teachers, child carers, parents and carers and multi-agency workers.

The supportive behaviour models we have explored in this unit view each individual's role differently. In some models, adults take responsibility for the way children behave by imposing rules and being aware of their own actions. In other models, children are viewed as **collaborators** in decision and rule making.

Key term

Collaborators – people who work jointly on an activity.

Children and young people

Children have a role to play in managing their own behaviour. Even from a very young age, children are capable of making choices about the way that they behave. This capability is affected at different times in their lives by various things. The inability to control emotions fully as a toddler will impact upon a child's later behaviour. In young people, changing hormone levels might affect behaviour and make it more unpredictable. The role of the child or young person is to follow agreed rules, be respectful of those providing them with care or education and to allow themselves to be in the best position to behave well. Drinking alcohol, taking drugs, having unsettled sleep patterns and living an unhealthy lifestyle will make children less able to control their own behaviour.

Find out

Examine your placement setting's behaviour management policy. Is there mention of the role of children and young people in managing their own behaviour?

Table 8.4: *How each model views the role of children and young people*

Model	Role of children and young people
Assertive discipline	• To obey the rules set by the adult • To conform to the adult's expectations
Logical consequences	• To learn to understand their emotions and motives for behaving in an unwanted manner • To make choices about the way they behave
Choice theory	• To show respect to adults • To follow class rules
Love and logic model	• To work collaboratively with adults • To develop rules and problem solve
Ginott's model	• To learn to be responsible • To be accepting of adults and show them respect
Kounin's model	• To know what is expected of them • To follow rules set by adults • To remain engaged

Staff

The adults who provide care and education for children and young people have a responsibility to behave in a way that promotes and encourages good behaviour. A teacher who shouts at children to be quiet is sending a mixed message about what is acceptable behaviour.

Staff working with children and young people must be consistent in their approach so that children feel secure in knowing what the rules are.

Table 8.5: *How each model informs the role of staff*

Model	Role of staff
Assertive discipline	• Set firm rules and make them available for children. • Keep consistent routines. • Be assertive in dealing with unwanted behaviour. • Remain calm.
Logical consequences	• In allowing natural consequences, do not comment or criticise. • Allow for choices in behaviour by explaining clear consequences for unwanted behaviour.
Choice theory	• Show children mutual respect. • Have clear class rules. • Do not seek to control children.
Love and logic model	• Do not use threats or physical punishment. • Allow children to take some of the control.
Ginott's model	• Show children kindness and respect. • Maintain good communication. • Give praise only when it is warranted.
Kounin's model	• Control children's behaviour. • Be alert and aware of what is going on around them. • Explain to children what is expected of them.

Parents and carers

The most important influence upon the way a child or young person behaves is their parent or carer. The expectations for behaviour at home will be the standard by which the child or young person behaves outside the home.

Parents and carers who work in a supportive manner with teachers and child carers will give consistent messages to children about what is acceptable and what is not.

Table 8.6: *How each model informs the role of parents*

Model	Role of parent
Assertive discipline	• Maintain a calm approach to discipline at home. • Be supportive of the rules imposed at school or in the early years setting to help the child to understand their importance.
Logical consequences	• Allow children to explore natural consequences in a safe, measured and caring environment so that they will understand that they have a choice of how to behave.
Choice theory	• Be respectful of those providing care or education for the child or young person to encourage mutual respect.
Love and logic model	• Allow children the freedom to explore interactions and experiences without interference. • Do not make excessive demands, use threats or physical punishment. • Support the child to make their own decisions.
Ginott's model	• Do not over praise children; give praise when it is warranted. • Be respectful of a child's feelings and show them kindness.
Kounin's model	• Help children to understand rules and be supportive of them so that they might find it easier to follow them.

What's happening now?

The introduction of family and children's centres saw targeted support being delivered within the communities where children live. This support involves programmes and courses for parents to help them to be the best parents they can be. This in turn helps to improve the lives of children and young people. As the lives of children and young people improve, the communities where they live also improve because they are less likely to engage in antisocial or criminal behaviour.

Family and children's centres have played an important role in supporting parents and carers. However, some people have criticised their approach by suggesting that the families who need the most support choose not to attend the centres.

Below are two examples of projects that might be run in children's centres to help parents manage their children's behaviour in a supportive manner.

• Family Links Nurturing Programme: this programme is designed to help both adults and children. It encourages each to explore how to manage their feelings and behaviour and improve their relationships inside and outside of the school or early years settings. It encourages families to improve their emotional health and well-being.

• ABC Boys Development Project: this course is designed to help parents to think about how they care for boys. It explains the differences in boys' development (as opposed to that of girls) and how behaviour management should be different in response.

Multi-agency workers

It is quite possible that there might be other professionals working with the child or young person in order to make sure that their needs are suitably met. These multi-agency workers also play a part in making sure that children and young people are supported to behave in a way that is acceptable and meets expectations or follows imposed rules.

The role of the multi-agency worker in each model

Table 8.7: *How each model informs the role of multi-agency workers*

Model	Role of multi-agency worker
Assertive discipline	• Be aware of what the rules are and the reasons for these. • Support the child to understand the possible consequences of not following certain rules.
Logical consequences	• Create opportunities for children to be able to experience natural consequences in a safe environment. • Make any arbitrary or logical consequences clear and understandable.
Choice theory	• Encourage mutual respect by demonstrating acceptance, even if not able to give approval.
Love and logic model	• Empower children and young people to understand that humiliation and physical punishment are unacceptable. • Consult and include children and young people upon matters that concern them.
Ginott's model	• Demonstrate kindness and praise purposefully.
Kounin's model	• Help children and young people to understand the impact of not following rules and the possible consequences for themselves and others.

Assessment activity
2.1, 2.2, 2.3

Choose a behaviour management model that you believe is effective. Write a work placement policy for new members of staff. Your policy should be divided into the following sections:
• an explanation of the principles that underpin your chosen model
• a brief analysis of your chosen model
• the roles of children/young people, staff, parents/carers and multi-agency workers in relation to your chosen model.

3 Understand positive support strategies within a behaviour management model

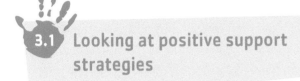

3.1 Looking at positive support strategies

Children and young people need positive support to help them make good choices about the way they behave. The adult has a responsibility to make sure that the strategies they use help them to do this.

In this section you will look at:

- building the child or young person's self-esteem
- acknowledging positive behaviour
- handling conflict calmly
- teaching by example
- ensuring genuine care.

Building self-esteem

Children and young people first develop a concept of themselves and then an 'ideal' concept of themselves. They then use this 'ideal' to judge themselves – who they want to be versus who they believe themselves to be.

Other people play a role in helping the child to create this self-concept. A parent who tells their child they are beautiful and loved will build their child's self-esteem and help to create a positive self-concept. The child is likely to feel valued and secure. A parent or teacher who makes a child feel as though they fall short of their expectations by calling them naughty or making them feel unwanted will damage the child's self-esteem.

Children who are told that they are naughty will develop poor self-regard. Their behaviour might then become more undesirable because they now think of themselves as being naughty and therefore worth less.

By building children's self-esteem you can help to create a positive environment and this is more likely to promote positive behaviour.

Reinforcing a child or young person's achievements and strengths will encourage perseverance and help them to develop a 'bounce back' attitude.

An environment that is both warm and welcoming will allow the child to develop trusting relationships with the adults who are caring for and educating them. Within these trusting relationships children are challenged and able to push themselves to reach their full potential.

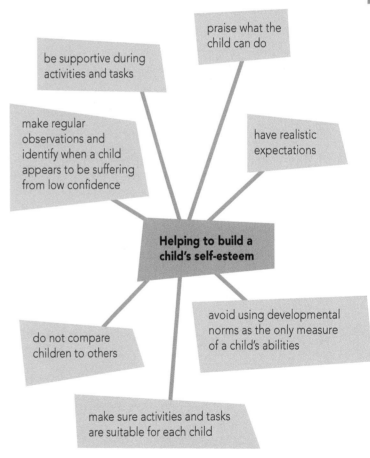

Figure 8.3: *Ways to help build a child's self-esteem*

Acknowledging positive behaviour

Praise is important in supporting children and young people to behave well. Body language can also help to convey praise to younger children such as smiling, giving the thumbs-up and signing 'high five'.

When children get older it is important to make sure that praise is valid and purposeful, otherwise it has no value. Acknowledging desired behaviour is important to children and young people.

In some circumstances there is reward for positive behaviour, for example, a sticker might be given to young children. This is a display of acknowledgement that the child has done well and is often used when a child has completed a school task or visited the dentist or hospital. Young people might be encouraged to gain a sense of social awareness by collecting class points as a reward, or individually collecting merits to obtain a prize at the end.

This concept of behaving in a certain way in order to be rewarded is called 'secondary reinforcement' and is described by behaviourist Burrhus Frederic Skinner (1904–90). In simple terms, Skinner believed that humans do not want to be punished and like to be rewarded. He believed that if you largely ignore negative behaviour and reward positive behaviour, children will behave well.

There is a fine line between reward and bribery. It is important that children do not behave in an acceptable manner only if they are rewarded. Ensuring that genuine praise is given verbally will help children to feel its value. Where tangible rewards are offered, they should be limited to special occasions or used to encourage a sense of collective responsibility for good behaviour. In some schools or nurseries this is achieved by placing buttons in a jar. When the jar is full, all the children are rewarded with a special activity.

Handling conflict calmly

It is very important that the adult deals with unwanted behaviour in a calm manner. As the behaviour models above demonstrate, children and young people's behaviour is affected by the adults around them.

When adults shout or handle conflict in an inappropriate manner, it does not demonstrate to the child and young person how to deal well with conflict themselves.

During times of conflict with each other or adults, children and young people will often feel frightened and confused. If adults take an aggressive or excessive approach to dealing with conflict, the child or young person will become more frightened and more confused. In turn, this leads to more unwanted behaviour.

Adults should offer reassurance and allow the child or young person time to process the situation in their own mind. It can help to talk through what has happened and how they feel as a result. The child or young person needs to understand their own feelings and emotions in order to be able to learn from the experience and to deal with any future conflicts they face.

Teaching by example

As demonstrated in Kounin's model (1970), children and young people react to adults' actions and behaviour. Adults need to consider their own behaviour and the impact that they might have upon the children and young people around them.

Adults who constantly shout demands (we could view these as Cline and Fay's (1990) drill sergeants) are not likely to create a calm and productive environment. This makes it unlikely that children and young people will to be able to learn and develop to their full potential.

Adults who abuse their power over children by threatening or using physical violence have lost control. These actions damage children's self-esteem and emotional well-being, and are ineffective in helping children to behave well.

Modelling desired behaviour, such as treating children with respect, tolerance and acceptance will help children and young people to know what is expected of them.

Ensuring genuine care

All children and young people are individual and behave in different ways depending on the situations in which they find themselves. You can find out about children's individuality by building a relationship of mutual trust, working with parents and carers, and

allowing children and young people to express their own ideas and opinions. There should be individual expectations for each child. Even when they are the same age, there can be vast differences in stages of development. Children and young people must have their individual needs met in order to be able to behave well. By knowing children's routines and interests, adults can develop a supportive plan for care or education.

Case study: Kieron's behaviour

Kieron attends Flower Pre-school three days a week. At the moment Kieron is living with his grandmother because his mother found it hard to look after him. Although he is only 3 years old, Kieron has had a lot of upheaval in his life. He has moved house several times, has spent a short period of time in foster care and has attended three different nurseries before attending Flower Pre-school.

Kieron's behaviour is erratic. He can behave very well at times or can lash out and be a danger to himself and others.

He has a very supportive key person at the pre-school who always talks calmly, shows him lots of affection and praises him when he behaves well.

The pre-school has started to notice small improvements in the length of time it takes Kieron to calm down and yesterday he apologised for behaving badly and asked his key person for a cuddle.

1 Why do you think Kieron is experiencing difficulty with his behaviour?
2 What supportive methods of behaviour management are the pre-school using?

3.2 The importance of expectations for behaviour

It is important to have clear expectations of children and young people, consistent with their development capacity.

A sound knowledge of children and young people's expected pattern of development enables practitioners to be realistic in what children can and cannot do.

There are three principles that are important in managing children and young people's behaviour.

- Children show unwanted behaviour when their needs are not met.
- Some behaviour is linked to children's development.
- Strong and supportive relationships with children are essential.

It is important that children and young people remain challenged and stimulated to avoid boredom. When children and young people are bored they might begin to act in ways that adults consider unacceptable (see **Table 8.8**).

Table 8.8: *Signs that children and young people are bored*

Babies	Toddlers	Children	Young people
Crying	Throwing things	Fidgeting	Not remaining on task, being uncooperative
Grizzling	Being destructive	Wandering	Fiddling, sighing, resting head on table
Turning face away	Crying	Rolling around the floor	Antisocial behaviour, destructive behaviour
	Tantrums	Slouching	
		Shouting	

CP8

Children and young people need and want adult attention. This increases during times of change in their lives. It is important to acknowledge and respond to underlying feelings that might cause unwanted behaviour, while maintaining consistent rules. In times of change children and young people need stability and consistency. If among other changes the rules start to change as well, it can add to feelings of confusion and distress.

There are influences that affect children and young people's ability to act in an expected manner.

- Everyone needs to have adequate sleep in order to feel relaxed and refreshed. Young children find a school day tiring and will struggle to maintain attention. Young people going through puberty require enough rest and sleep to support their bodies while they are undergoing the radical changes that are taking place.
- There are similarities between hunger and tiredness. Babies cannot tolerate being hungry and will cry and be distressed until their hunger is satisfied. Although older children are able to wait for their hunger to be satisfied, they still might find it difficult to concentrate.

Expectations for behaviour should be consistent with children and young people's development.

- Toddlers are still learning about how to interact socially and so snatching, pushing and not wanting to share are to be expected.
- Young children do not have the capacity to explain how they are feeling verbally and so use physical behaviours to express their emotions.

- Young people might have the physical capacity to express themselves verbally, unlike young children, but emotionally this is not always possible.
- Hormonal changes in puberty can cause young people to act in ways that they cannot control, such as mood swings, lashing out in anger and being argumentative.

Rules and routines help children and young people to feel secure. Frequent changes can lead to children and young people feeling confused and anxious. Children also need the adults who care for them and educate them to show them positive regard at all times, even when their behaviour does not meet expectations.

Assessment activity 3.1, 3.2

1 Develop a poster for the workplace environment to give information about the importance of the following strategies:
   - building children and young people's self-esteem
   - acknowledging positive behaviour
   - handling conflict calmly
   - teaching by example
   - ensuring genuine care.

2 Plan a professional conversation with a new member of staff to explain the importance of having clear expectations for children and young people which are consistent with their development capacity.

4 Understand why a safe environment for children and/or young people supports positive behaviour

4.1 How safe environments support behaviour

Strong relationships allow children to gain positive attention from adults. Children who are involved in decisions about their environment feel valued and respected and will display less unwanted behaviour.

Setting realistic expectations and following children's individual interests will make children feel secure and confident. A safe environment will help practitioners to manage unwanted behaviour effectively and also help children to manage their own behaviour.

There might be a variety of reasons why children do not feel safe within their environment:

- Activities are too difficult or too easy and do not offer sufficient challenge.
- Children and young people are unable to express themselves and their opinions are not valued.
- Adults have not fostered secure relationships and so children feel unable to say if they feel unhappy or uncomfortable about things.
- Resources are not well maintained or fit for purpose.

- There are no consistent rules, or the rules frequently change.
- Adults have unrealistic expectations.

Children and young people need to feel a sense of belonging within the environment. They should feel included and part of the setting so that they can be confident in expressing themselves. This is particularly important when they are unhappy or unsettled.

When thinking about the environment it is important to consider everything within it, from the resources to the noise level, the staff and the access to outside spaces. All of these impact upon children and young people's behaviour.

Assessment activity 4.1

Review your workplace environment and produce a review explaining the importance of providing a safe environment for children and young people in relation to behaviour management.

CP8

In the real world

I always found Shanika's behaviour very difficult. She would kick and bite other children at the holiday play scheme. After a while I started to really dislike her. I noticed that the other children didn't seem to like her much either as she often played alone.

Although I didn't mean to, if ever there was a disagreement I would automatically shout out Shanika's name because I thought she was involved. The other children started to call her 'naughty Shanika' and her behaviour just got worse and worse.

Then a new practitioner started at the holiday play scheme. His name was Richard and Shanika instantly liked him. Her behaviour really started to improve.

Richard told me about different models of behaviour management. I realised that I had been contributing to Shanika's behaviour. With Richard's help I started to notice all the good things that Shanika did and made sure that I praised her and made her feel part of the group. She is so much happier now and so am I. I have stopped shouting all the time and started to think about my impact upon all of the children.

Check your knowledge

1 Which behaviour management model discusses the helicopter, drill sergeant and consultant style of adult?

2 What is the term used to describe the process in which children learn not to do something by discovering the outcome themselves?

3 What did Glasser's (1998) choice theory model say were children's five basic needs?

4 Outline the behaviour shown by adults who have 'lost control' according to Ginott's (1971) model.

5 Identify the role of the child or young person in Kounin's (1970) model.

6 Suggest three ways that an adult can help to build children and young people's self-esteem.

7 How might children and young people feel when involved in conflict?

8 Describe how children and young people might demonstrate boredom at each stage of their life.

9 Being hungry affects children's and young people's ability to concentrate. What else is essential to help children concentrate?

10 Describe one factor that might make children feel unsafe in their environment.

CP8

CACHE Extended Assessment

Theme: Children and young people's development

Grading criterion

B1 Discuss the relevance of a recognised theory or philosophical approach in contributing to the chosen theme.

When looking at your extended project, you might begin by examining the way that the models of supportive behaviour management differ from each other. You might like then to explore contrasting ideas and explain how they differ from each other.

Remember to think about how each model views the child.

When thinking about the approaches of each model, you could explain how they affect children and young people's development by introducing the concept of the effects of low self-esteem. You could examine how differing models support the development of children's self-esteem. Ginott stressed how important it is for adults to not lose control. He explains loss of control as overreacting, being cruel and threatening. At this point you could draw in to the discussion Cline and Fay's drill sergeant.

You could complete your discussion by explaining how important it is to nurture children and young people's self-esteem and how this supports their overall development, play and learning. You could then give examples of models that you believe would support children and young people to develop high self-esteem and the reasons why.

This is an example of how you might approach one criterion of your Extended Assessment. You must successfully complete all the criteria at each grade to achieve that grade. You will achieve the highest grade for which you have successfully completed all the criteria. For example, to achieve a B grade you will need to meet the requirements of the B1, B2 and B3 criteria, as well as C1, C2, C3 and D1 and D2.

When trying to understand the requirements for your Extended Assessment, it is always a good idea to talk to your tutors. Fellow learners and workplace colleagues are also useful sources of information.

Further references

The following are sources of useful information on the topic of supportive approaches to behaviour management.

Books and articles

Canter, L. and Canter, M. (1992) *Assertive Discipline*, Bristol: Behaviour Management Ltd

Cline, F. W. and Fay, J. (2006) *Parenting with Love and Logic: Teaching Children Responsibility*, 2nd edition, Colorado Springs: NavPress Publishing

Dreikurs, R. (1968) *Psychology in the Classroom: A Manual for Teachers*, 2nd edition, New York: Harper and Row

Ginott, H. (1971) *Teacher and Child*, New York: Macmillan

Glasser, W. (1998) *Choice Theory*, New York: Harper and Row

Jones, F. (1987) *Positive Classroom Discipline*, New York: McGraw-Hill

Kounin, J. S. (1970) *Discipline and Group Management in Classrooms*, New York: Holt, Rinehart and Winston

Osler, A. (2001) *Children's Rights, Responsibilities and Understandings of School Discipline*, Research Papers in Education 15 (1) pp. 49–67, London: Routledge

Useful websites

To obtain a secure link to the websites below, visit www.pearsonhotlinks.co.uk and search for this book by using its title or ISBN. Click on the section for CP8.

Love and Logic – includes information about behaviour management strategies for parents and teachers.

Behaviour Management – information about supportive behaviour management techniques which includes an explanation of emotional intelligence approach.

The Burrhus F. Skinner Foundation – information about his work which includes information about behaviourist theory.

Information about the ABC programme to support boys' development.

Formal recording for use within the real work environment

CP9

There are many different reasons why you might need to record information formally when working with children and young people, for example, for health and safety or safeguarding purposes.

You must have the appropriate skills and knowledge to record information in a format that is suitable for the person who will read it.

This unit will help you to better understand how and why you need to do this, and develop your skills in recording information in the work environment.

Learning outcomes

By the end of this unit you will:

1 Understand the rationale for recording information in a formal format

2 Understand which format should be used relevant to target reader

3 Be able to use formal recording in the real work environment.

In practice

Katy is a key person for a child who has just started at the nursery where she works. (Being a key person means that Katy is the main person in the setting responsible for looking after the child.)

This will be the first time that Katy has monitored a child's learning and achievement.

She already has some information about the child that the parent has passed on. Katy does not know how she will record the child's progress and wonders whether it will be good enough just to keep the child's parents updated by having an informal chat each week.

By the end of this unit you will know why it is important that Katy records information formally and have an idea of how she might do this.

1 Understand the rationale for recording information in a formal format

CP9

1.1 The value of formal recording

Formal recording of information simply means writing it down and keeping a copy.

The nature of the document will dictate the detail, length and how it is presented. When information is recorded in a formal manner it is usually dated so that the reader will know the age of the document. A name and/or signature will give the document ownership so that the reader immediately knows who has written it.

The key reasons why you might need to record information formally are listed below.

- You might be legally obliged to do so, for example, if it is a statutory requirement under the Early Years Foundation Stage.
- You need to share accurate information several times over.
- You want to make sure that the information is clearly understood.
- The information is of high importance.
- The information gives others directions or guidance to follow.
- The information is to be used as part of a legal investigation.

Recording information formally does not always mean that the paperwork needs to be extensive or written in a particular way.

Two benefits of recording in a formal way are clarity and accuracy. When information is not written down in a suitable manner, vital pieces of information can be lost. This might have serious implications for children and young people. If a child needs to have medicine administered during the day, and the amount and time are not properly recorded, the child might be given the wrong dose at the wrong time. This could put their health and well-being at risk.

When information is recorded formally it can be referred to at a later date or used to help to build up a picture of a situation. The context of the information will always remain unchanged, even when the circumstances surrounding it have long since changed. This can help to clarify a situation and help the reader decide what course of action to take.

When information is recorded formally it is more difficult to distort it or alter it and so it will give an accurate account of an incident or set of circumstances. This is especially helpful where there is confusion or a disagreement about what happened. It is important that recording of information is **objective**, i.e. not influenced by personal opinion or feelings, as this might distort the information and make it inaccurate or misleading. There are occasions when information might be recorded **subjectively**, or based on personal opinion. Reports from some health and medical professionals might be subjective, where they are offering their professional opinion based on their knowledge and expertise.

Recording information can also help to keep children safe by building up a picture of potential hazards in the environment or recording injuries that might indicate the child has been the victim of harm.

Key terms

Objective – information not based on or influenced by personal opinion or feelings.

Subjective – information based on or influenced by personal opinion or feelings.

Assessment activity 1.1

Prepare and carry out a discussion with your group to consider the value of recording information formally, including using different formats, both written and numerical. You might like to frame your discussion around the following ideas.

• Why is it beneficial to make formal records?
• What is the value to children or young people, their families and practitioners?
• Are there any disadvantages?
• What are the different benefits of using written and numerical formats?

2 Understand which format should be used relevant to target reader

2.1 Different formats for recording information

The chosen format for recording information will vary depending on who the intended reader is. Information that is to be shared with parents and carers should be written in plain English and should be free from jargon and abbreviations that parents might not recognise. For example, parents might not know what the 'EYFS' is or that 'next steps' relate to children's learning and not learning to walk.

When sharing information with other agencies it is important to ensure that the language used is common to everyone to make sure there are no misunderstandings. Set formats for recording might also be used because this gives a standard that everyone can follow.

Providing information to an outside agency

Agencies need to work together to best meet the needs of children and young people who require extra support at different times in their life. Agencies might also work together to share information to help make transitions less stressful for children and young people.

Key term

Jargon – words or expressions that a particular group of people might use and which other people might find difficult to understand.

Transition – a period of change.

In these circumstances the method of recording needs to be universally understood and agreed by all those involved to prevent confusion or misinterpretation of what is being recorded.

A successful method of sharing information between children's services in England is the Common Assessment Framework (CAF). This document is used for children and young people who have additional needs that are not met by their current service provider. It helps practitioners to identify children's additional needs in the first instance. It also provides a standard format for use by children's service providers to help them to work together to make sure the child's needs are fully met.

Every Child Matters
Change For Children

Common Assessment Framework for children and young people (CAF)

CAF form

Date assessment started*[1]

Notes for use: If you are completing form electronically, text boxes will expand to fit your text
Where check boxes appear, insert an 'X' in those that apply.

Identifying details

Record details of unborn baby, infant, child or young person being assessed. If unborn, state name as 'unborn baby' and mother's name, e.g. unborn baby of Ann Smith.

Given name(s)* | Family name*

*Male ☐ Female ☐ Unknown ☐ | AKA[2]/previous names

Address* | Date of birth or EDD[3]* | Contact tel. no.* | Unique ref. no. | Version no.

Postcode*

Ethnicity*

White		Black or Black British		Asian or Asian British		Mixed/Dual Background		Chinese & Other	
White British	☐	Caribbean	☐	Indian	☐	White & Black Caribbean	☐	Chinese	☐
White Irish	☐	African	☐	Pakistani	☐	White & Black African	☐		
Traveller of Irish Heritage	☐	Any other Black background▲	☐	Bangladeshi	☐	White & Asian	☐	Any other ethnic group▲	☐
Gypsy/Roma	☐			Any other Asian background▲	☐	Any other Mixed background▲	☐	Not given	☐
Any other White background▲	☐								

▲If other, please specify | Immigration status

Child's first language | Parent's first language

Is the child or young person disabled? Yes ☐ No ☐

If 'yes' give details

Details of any special requirements (for child and/or their parent) e.g. signing, interpretation or access needs

[1] It is recommended that practitioners complete all fields marked with an asterisk(*) to obtain basic identifying date when completing the CAF form
[2] 'Also known as'
[3] Expected date of delivery

Figure 9.1: *A Common Assessment Framework form*

© Local Government Association. Available without charge from the Children's Improvement Board via the LGA's Knowledge Hub

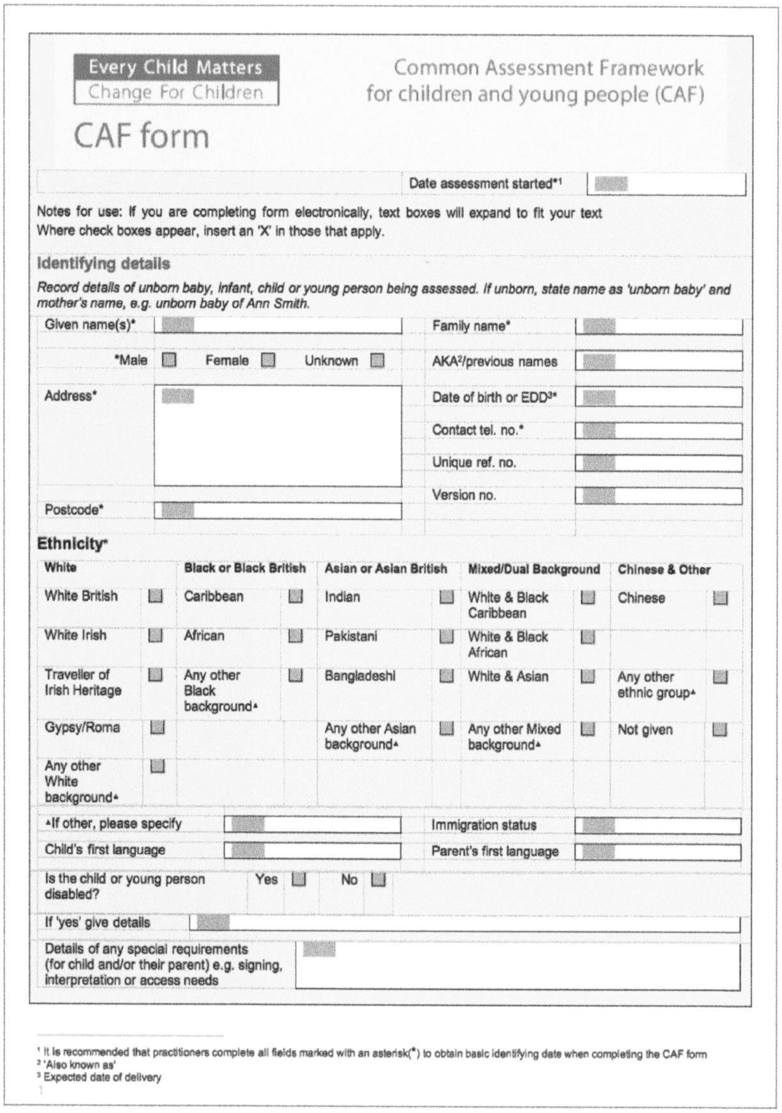

Safeguarding

It is the responsibility of everyone to make sure that children and vulnerable young people are protected from harm. When there is a concern about a child or young person, a designated safeguarding professional might need to share safeguarding/child protection issues with their local safeguarding board. Information like this is incredibly sensitive and so confidentiality will be of utmost importance. The target reader for this information will need to know specific pieces of information in order to be able to take appropriate action. Under these circumstances recording must be done at the time of the concern to make sure that any vital pieces of information are not lost or forgotten. Even if the referral is being made by telephone, it must be confirmed in writing within 48 hours of making the telephone referral.

Special training will help the person responsible for making referrals of this nature to record information accurately. This sort of formal recording must always be treated with urgency, sensitivity and confidentiality by all those involved.

Monitoring progress to support learning and achievement

You will need to monitor the progress of children and young people to make sure that they are reaching their full potential and to identify if any extra support might be needed.

The Foundation Stage Profile became a legal requirement in England in September 2008. This is a method of recording a child's progress and development at the end of the academic year in which they reach 5 years of age. The purpose is to provide parents and teachers with reliable and accurate information about the level of every child as they reach the end of the Early Years Foundation Stage and enter formal education. This helps them to know

what level the child is working at and to plan to meet their individual needs. The document is a standard format and is completed by the professional who is providing the majority of the formal care for the child.

A criticism of the profile when it was introduced was that it was too long and over complicated, while some teachers felt that the sheer volume of information made it difficult to use it effectively.

Every child and young person will have a file containing information about their learning and achievement within their pre-school setting or school. This information is used to ensure that the child or young person is making good progress. If not, additional help might be provided for them. As the child gets older and moves through their schooling, information is shared between teachers and schools before finally being used to decide what exams they should be entered for.

Find out

What methods are used in your placement setting for recording children or young people's learning and achievement?

Discuss with your mentor who these records are shared with and how often.

Internal records in a work environment

In a working environment there will be a lot of information retained for legal, safety and security reasons.

Below is a list of possible records that might be kept in a work environment.

- Registers need to be taken daily to make sure there is a record of who is on site and who is off site or absent. These are a legal requirement because, in the event of a fire, it is essential to know that everyone is accounted for.
- Records of the children's, young people's and staff's personal details, including who to call in the case of an emergency, home address and contact numbers, doctors' details and consent to emergency medical treatment if required.

- A record of accidents suffered by children, young people and staff. These should be signed, dated and kept confidential. Records relating to accidents need to be kept for several years and so will require safe and secure storage.
- Staff should have a regular appraisal of their work. This will help to identify any training needs, monitor progress and help to build an effective staff team.
- Minutes from meetings. It is important that minutes are kept after meetings so that they can be referred back to if required. It also helps people to remember what has been said and what actions, if any, they need to take.
- When working with children and young people it is necessary to keep a list of adults who have had a Criminal Records Bureau (CRB) check. This tells the employer and any other person who might ask that those working with children and young people are considered safe to do so.

These records should be regularly reviewed and updated to confirm that they are still accurate and appropriate for the purpose.

Key term

Appraisal – this is a formal process for assessing someone's work. It helps workers and employers to monitor individual performance and often involves target setting.

Reflect

Imagine that you are going to have an appraisal in your work placement setting.

Write a draft of the things that you might like to discuss at an appraisal. This could include how well you feel you have performed. You should highlight your strengths and weaknesses.

- What qualities do you feel you bring to the staff team?
- If this were your permanent job, what would you like to do to continue your own professional development?

CP9

Health and safety

When maintaining a safe environment it is important to record information for the following reasons:

Figure 9.2: *Health and safety records*

Examples of formats used to record information regarding health and safety include:

- policies and procedures
- risk assessments
- accident forms
- incident forms
- fire drill records
- health plans.

The greatest risk to health and safety is not that an unplanned incident might occur, but that people fail to follow instructions or procedures.

Alerting others

Some recording of information is designed to alert others to safety procedures. Commonly these take the form of posters, charts or leaflets. An example might be where staff are required to lift equipment on a regular basis. It is important that everyone involved in lifting knows how to do so safely to prevent them from being injured. The employer might ask them to read a poster about safe lifting or provide them with a leaflet. The member of staff might then sign to say they have read and understood how to lift equipment safely. They might revisit this information on a regular basis and sign each time to say they have refreshed their knowledge.

Giving instructions and recording events or incidents

There are times when, for safety reasons, everyone must follow directions and do as they are told. When there are a lot of people together a system is needed for managing them quickly if they are at risk. If this was not in place and a situation occurred, panic could spread, resulting in people being harmed.

It is common to have a procedure which everyone must follow in the event of a fire or fire alarm drill. In order to help people do this, there will be a poster displayed identifying the procedure and locating the nearest fire exit. Regular fire drills ensure that everyone is aware of the procedure for evacuating the building. By recording the frequency of the fire drills it will be easy to decide if more practice is required, for example, if there are new people on the premises.

Evacuations are often timed, and if the time taken to evacuate is consistent, the practices appear to be working. If the time fluctuates or is increasing, further information might be needed to help everyone understand the procedure better. Children, in particular, need regular practice to help them remember what to do in the case of an evacuation.

Sharing information

Policies and procedures are in place in all settings to make clear what the setting intends to do, and how they intend to do it. A policy is a statement of intent such as:

At Happy Nursery we will keep children safe.

This is a very big statement and one that needs to be broken down into sections to make it more achievable.

Each of these sections becomes the procedures for explaining how Happy Nursery will go about keeping children safe. An example of a procedure might be:

Procedure for keeping children safe when playing outside

Every morning staff will carry out a risk assessment of the area. Any potential hazards will be removed. Children will be carefully monitored at all times by qualified and knowledgeable staff. Children will be offered adequate shelter from, and dressed suitably for, the weather.

CP9

It is now clearer how children are to be kept safe in the outside area. The procedures would continue to address each area of potential risk or hazard to the children, such as staff recruitment, the environment and outings.

Policies and procedures should be available for parents, carers, new staff, students and volunteers. As there will be a wide range of people reading them, they should be written in a straightforward and easy-to-follow manner. Policies that are hundreds of pages long will not be easily read and understood by those who need to follow them and so they might need to be condensed or summarised. Policies that are kept in locked cupboards or offices are not accessible and are of little value.

Policies and procedures do not just relate to the care of children and young people, they might also relate to the environment. One area of importance is the safe storage of chemicals that might be hazardous to people's health. A cupboard should be provided for this purpose and is usually called a COSHH cupboard.

Medication can also pose a risk to health if not stored and administered correctly. A procedure should be in place for administering medication. Along with the procedure should be a record which might state:

- who administered the medication
- who checked the dosage
- who had the medication
- at what time
- on what day
- what the dosage was.

This helps to reduce the risk of overdose or medication being given to the wrong person.

Identifying risks

Risk assessments are a useful tool in helping to significantly reduce the likelihood of accidents and injury when working with children and young people. A risk assessment can help to alert staff and children to potential dangers and suggest sensible measures which will reduce the risk of that danger causing harm or injury.

CP9

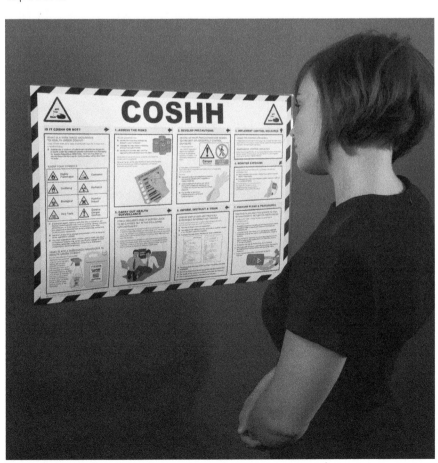

What measures are taken to keep hazardous substances out of reach of children?

Risk assessment form

Hazard	Risk	To who	How to minimise	Review date
The floor mat	The ends present a risk of tripping or falling	All adults and children, especially toddlers who are newly walking	Tape down the edges of the mat	Weekly, to check for loose ends

Figure 9.3: *A risk assessment form*

Risk assessments are often overused because practitioners and settings fear being sued if a child or young person has an accident or injury. In the past this became more likely because of the rise of 'no win, no fee' legal companies. This makes it easier to access the legal system to pursue claims for injuries that might result in a cash payout for the victim.

To prevent this happening, many practitioners and settings tried to take as many risks away as possible, for example, cutting down trees in case a branch falls on a child, or a child falls and is injured while climbing a tree.

In recent years, practice is returning to a more common-sense approach to managing risk; children and young people are being encouraged to develop skills in assessing risks for themselves.

The Early Years Foundation Stage statutory framework (2012) states that all providers must put in place policies for assessing risks to children and that any risk assessments carried out should be reviewed regularly. However, it allows providers to use their own judgement as to whether or not a risk assessment needs to be in writing.

So what does this mean?

- It is important to keep children safe from harm. It is equally important to support children to identify and manage risks for themselves.
- A common-sense approach should be adopted. There is no reason to risk assess the use of pencils because there is little you can do to reduce the risk of a child poking themselves in the eye with a pencil.
- Supportive adults can remind children and young people about potential hazards and use risk assessment where a procedure is needed to make the risk less likely. For example, you could place a sign on a wet floor demonstrating to everyone they might slip if they do not walk carefully.

Written response to enquiries

This is most commonly a request for further information or a complaint. The response to each should be considered carefully. It is courteous to give an immediate acknowledgement to the enquiry and a time frame in which the recipient can expect a full response.

The most suitable response would be in the form of a letter. Key things that a formal letter should contain include:

- the name of the setting (headed notepaper will also include address and telephone number)
- the date of writing
- the name of the person who will receive the letter
- the reason for the letter (this should be outlined in the first line)
- the response should clearly address any questions or points raised
- a statement of intended actions
- the name and signature of the writer.

Some companies will use emails as a written response instead of a letter. **Table 9.1** shows the advantages and disadvantages of letters versus emails.

Case study: Pascal complains

Pascal is the father of a 12-year-old child who attends a youth club at the local village hall. He wrote a letter to the youth club leaders saying that he was unhappy to see two young people smoking outside when he collected his son.

One of the youth club leaders replied by writing on a sticky note, 'kids will be kids' and ending with a smiley face. He left it in Pascal's son's bag.

Pascal is unhappy about the response and is not sure he will allow his son to attend the youth club again.

1 Why do you think Pascal is unhappy with the response?

2 How do you think the youth club leaders should have responded?

Table 9.1: *A comparison of types of written response*

Advantages of a written letter	Disadvantages of a written letter	Advantages of email	Disadvantages of email
Information should be quickly and easily understood Reaches the desired person Efficient Letter can easily be shown to others	The tone of the letter might be misinterpreted Could be delayed or lost in the post Might not be received by the intended person if they have moved house	Instant delivery Is likely to be briefer than a letter Can be accessed 24 hours a day	Reliant upon the Internet working Reliant upon the person checking emails Might be viewed as informal Could be deleted easily in error

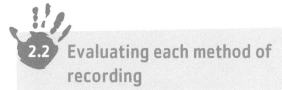

2.2 Evaluating each method of recording

As you have seen, there is a great deal of formal recording involved when working with children and young people. The main reason for this is to support children and young people in making suitable progress in their learning and development, to identify any concerns and to keep children safe from harm.

Below is a summary of each format and the potential failing that might result if it is unsuccessful.

Sharing information with outside agencies

Sharing information is essential in providing consistency for children and young people during transitions and making sure that children's needs and well-being are safeguarded.

However, this is only effective where there is the desire and goodwill to work together. There needs to be mutual respect and acknowledgement of each other's area of skills. For example, a referral needs to be accepted as valid by the person receiving it; therefore they must have confidence in the person who made the referral.

Key term

Referral – this is when a child or young person's case is passed on to a specialist or person in a higher position of responsibility.

Monitoring the progress to support learning and achievement

Gathering information about what children can do, and the next steps in terms of their development or achievement, helps to make sure that children reach their full potential.

However, there might be differences in the quantity and quality of information gathered even within one setting. This information relies upon the judgement of the person recording the information and could easily be misinterpreted.

Maintaining internal records

There are many systems for recording information within a work environment. These are mainly concerned with sharing information and keeping staff, children and young people safe.

These records are effective when they are in place and reviewed regularly. Often as work pressure increases the regularity and consistency of these records tends to decrease. This can mean that they are not always completed fully or updated as they should be.

Providing information about health and safety

It is essential to make sure children and young people are safeguarded. Formal recording helps to ensure that those working with them know their responsibilities and can take action when required to maintain a safe environment.

The most common reason why accidents and injury occur is because of an error of judgement or failing to follow procedures and guidelines fully. After a period of time people might start to take risks because they assume that the risk has diminished. If, for example, a child safely walks downstairs every day for three weeks, a member of staff might not close the stair gate at the top of the stairs. However, the risk of falling has not disappeared and the child is still likely to fall when the gate is left open.

Identifying risk

It is not possible to remove every risk that children and young people face, but assessing risks means that staff and adults working with children can help to reduce the likelihood of injury or accidents occurring.

As we have already seen, there is a danger that well-meaning practitioners and settings try to remove all possible risks from an environment. This means that children and young people are unable to safely assess and manage risks for themselves. If, for example, a young person is not able to use a knife to prepare food during a cookery class at school, they might not be able to use one safely when preparing food themselves at home.

Providing a response to an enquiry

An enquiry from a parent, carer or other service user requires immediate attention and should be treated seriously. It is important that when an enquiry has been made it is responded to in a timely manner.

This needs to be given immediate attention and should begin with an acknowledgement of the initial enquiry. The most likely reason why this does not always resolve the issue is because the response is given without careful consideration and therefore does not answer the question or complaint suitably.

Assessment activity 2.1, 2.2

1 Produce a table to enable you to discuss with colleagues the different formats of recording information you could use to:
   - provide information to an outside agency
   - monitor progress and support learning and achievement
   - maintain internal records within a work environment
   - provide information regarding health and safety
   - identify risk
   - provide a written response to an enquiry.
2 Include an evaluation of each method.

3 Be able to use formal recording in the real work environment

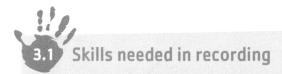

3.1 Skills needed in recording

In order to make sure that formal recording is effective, a range of skills is needed. **Table 9.2** outlines these skills.

Table 9.2: *Skills required when using particular recording formats*

Recording format	Skills needed
Minutes of meeting	• Able to listen and record simultaneously • Able to write quickly using abbreviations when necessary • Familiarity with all those who are present, so need to be good at remembering names
Letter	• Able to communicate key pieces of information in a concise manner • A good level of written English
Risk assessment	• Able to make good judgements about what poses a potential risk and know possible ways to minimise it • Record what you find clearly and in a suitable manner for others to understand
Formal report	• Able to present key information clearly • Know professional abbreviations and key terms, and be able to write in a way that informs others and is objective
Record of learning and achievement	• Have a clear understanding of curriculum frameworks and be able to use and interpret observations • Recording needs to be understood by any reader who is not familiar with the child
Incident and accident reports	• Able to recall information accurately • Knowledge of first aid procedures • Able to write clearly and accurately

CP9

3.2 Analysing recorded formats

It is important that each format for recording is fit for purpose. It needs to give information in a manner that is understandable and suitable. Too much information can be as unhelpful as too little.

Suitability for the target reader

When using recording formats it is important to imagine the target reader (the person who will be reading it) when writing the document. A format designed to be used by other practitioners within the setting can use abbreviations, people's initials and professional terms. However, if the document is designed for parents and carers, it needs to be transparent, straightforward and should not make them feel confused.

When confidentiality needs to be maintained, codes must be used such as 'Child A'. These can be agreed in advance with other agencies to avoid confusion. When writing policies and procedures for a setting, it is important to consider that a new member of staff will be unfamiliar with the environment and so if you say the 'learning and development file' it is unlikely they could find it themselves. However, 'the yellow learning and development file stored in the staff room cupboard' would leave them in no doubt about where to find the file themselves.

Clarity of information

Clarity is not just about writing in a clear and concise manner: it is about writing in a way that gives the information required without excessive jargon.

Information does not need to be long or wordy to get across the message. Bite-sized information giving key facts and pieces of information is probably better understood than 20 pages of information in minute detail. Information should focus on the essential points. This is particularly the case where important directions are given, such as evacuation procedures. People need to know what to do in as few steps as possible – then they are less likely to forget them. Five well-written policies summarised carefully are more likely to be read, understood and followed than 50 pages of policies that are long and overly detailed.

Presentation and accuracy

Records need to be presented in a suitable manner. Body maps are often used to accompany accident records as they can convey information more easily than detailed written accounts of the injury location. The accident record is one document that needs to have accurate details in order to make sure that the information recorded is factual and cannot be misinterpreted. Medication records also need to be accurate in order to make sure that children and young people's health and well-being are not compromised.

Standardised formats are often best to record incidents, accidents and administering of medication because they provide a set area to write in with a clear heading. This leaves little margin for error when completing the document. A pre-written document also means that practitioners can become familiar with where to find information such as dosage of medication, where to sign or what injuries have occurred.

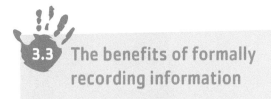

3.3 The benefits of formally recording information

There are many benefits for the work environment of formally recording information. **Figure 9.4** below shows these benefits.

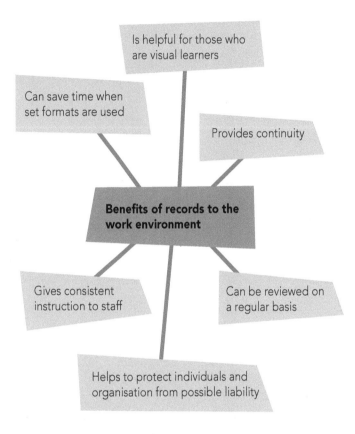

Is helpful for those who are visual learners

Can save time when set formats are used

Provides continuity

Benefits of records to the work environment

Gives consistent instruction to staff

Can be reviewed on a regular basis

Helps to protect individuals and organisation from possible liability

Figure 9.4: *Benefits of formal recording*

Assessment activity 3.1, 3.2, 3.3

1 Gather the following evidence from your workplace setting where you have:
   - recorded minutes of a meeting
   - written a letter
   - conducted a risk assessment
   - made a formal report
   - made a record of a child or young person's learning and achievement
   - reported and recorded an accident or incident.

2 Write an account analysing each recorded format under these headings: suitability for target reader, clarity of information, presentation and accuracy.

3 Then evaluate the benefits for the work environment of formally recording information.

CP9

In the real world

The one thing that really worried me about working with children was the amount of paperwork people said you need to keep.

When I started at my placement they handed me a huge folder full of policies and procedures and I only had half an hour to read them. It made me worry even more.

Then I spoke to my mentor and she said that if I looked on the setting's website there was a summary of the policies for parents to look at. This made it all much easier to understand.

I started to understand what recording needed to be done and because I knew the reasons why we had to do it, it made it easier to follow.

There are still some bits that I don't understand like making a referral and completing the profiles when children leave to start school, but I know how important they are. That is why the people who are responsible for completing them need to have extra training!

Check your knowledge

1 Information that is shared with parents needs to be easily readable. Explain how this can be achieved.

2 Give a brief explanation of the purpose of the Common Assessment Framework (CAF).

3 What information must always be shared with an outside agency by a designated practitioner?

4 When did use of the Early Years Foundation Stage Profile become a legal requirement?

5 Explain why a register needs to be taken daily.

6 Outline the reasons why minutes need to be taken at meetings.

7 Give three pieces of information that should be recorded on an administering medication record.

8 What is the correct course of action when responding to an enquiry?

9 What are the skills needed to record children and young people's learning and achievement?

10 State four benefits of formally recording information.

Further references

The following are sources of useful information on the topic of formal recording for use within the real work environment.

Books and articles

Children's Workforce Development Council (2009) *Early Identification, Assessment of Needs and Intervention. The Common Assessment Framework for Children and Young People*

Department for Education (DfE) (2012) *Statutory Framework for the Early Years Foundation Stage*, DfE Publications

HM Government (2006) *What to do if you are worried a child is being abused – summary*

Useful websites

To obtain a secure link to the websites below, visit www.pearsonhotlinks.co.uk and search for this book by using its title or ISBN. Click on the section for CP9.

Government Education – material for Early Years Foundation Stage and Common Assessment Framework.

Health and Safety Executive – information about conducting risk assessments and outlines requirements under COSHH.

Children's Workforce Development Council – information about the Common Assessment Framework, including a guide for practitioners.

CP9

Research to support practice when working with children and/or young people

CP10

Carrying out regular research relevant to work with children and young people is a very important aspect of practice. Practitioners use research to inform decisions about implementing new ideas or changing practice. Research enables practitioners to check if their work is effective or if there is space for improvement. It is essential for practitioners to have a clear understanding of the research process in order to carry out effective research. In this unit you will learn about the research process and its value when working with children and young people.

Learning outcomes

By the end of this unit you will:

1 Understand research and its value when working with children and/or young people

2 Understand the role of a hypothesis in research

3 Understand methodologies in research

4 Be able to identify a research hypothesis

5 Be able to plan and implement research in relation to working with children and/or young people

6 Be able to present data in relation to the hypothesis

7 Be able to reflect on the research undertaken.

In practice

Your manager has asked you to review how potty training is being supported in the toddler room with an aim of improving communication between the home and the setting during the potty training process.

By the end of this unit you will know how to plan and carry out a small-scale research project taking into account a range of ethical considerations. You will know how to select appropriate methods to help you gather information as well as be able to analyse your data, draw conclusions and identify recommendations for improving practice.

1 Understand research and its value when working with children and/or young people

CP10

Unit CP5 looks at a range of study skills including academic referencing, project planning, sourcing information and research methods. It explores the type of skills required for carrying out a research project. This unit focuses on the process of carrying out research.

In order to work effectively with children and young people it is important to think about your practice. It is not good enough to continue to do things in a certain way just because they have always been done that way. Research enables us to take a close look at what we do in practice and to make informed decisions about implementing new ideas or improving practice. Research is a simple tool that uses many of our everyday skills of observation, discussion, reflection and analysis. Research benefits you, helping you to understand complex issues relating to work with children and young people as well as benefiting the children and your setting.

It is essential that research is purposeful and therefore needs to be both clear and transparent in design. This is achieved by having a clear research focus and careful planning.

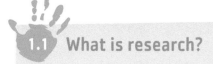

1.1 What is research?

Carrying out research is a vital part of your professional development. Research is a process which allows you to develop a deeper understanding of practice. Through research you can investigate and analyse a situation or issue and make an informed decision about what action to take to improve practice. It will also help you to increase your awareness of how good practice supports positive outcomes for children. Research is not only powerfully informative but also an enjoyable and rewarding part of your professional development.

1.2 Primary and secondary research

Primary research is the data you will gather as part of your study. There are many methods you can use to collect primary data including observations, interviews, surveys or questionnaires.

Secondary research is a summary of existing literature related to your chosen area of research. This could be found in books, magazine articles or on the Internet. The purpose of using secondary research is to set the scene for your study and establish what is already known about your chosen area of research. The advantage of secondary research is that information is easy to find. However, skill is needed to summarise and organise the information. Researchers need to be aware that the disadvantage of secondary research is that information could be out of date and no longer appropriate.

Most research projects start with secondary research as it helps to develop and clarify the research hypothesis or question and the scope of the investigation you are going to carry out. Unit CP5 has further information on primary and secondary research.

Key terms

Primary research – the research carried out by you to either prove or disprove your hypothesis.

Data – the results generated from the findings of your research which you will analyse in order to make any recommendations.

Secondary research – a review of existing research on your selected area of investigation including books, journals, articles and the Internet.

Hypothesis – the question you are setting out to answer or the research statement you aim to prove or disprove.

1.3 The value of research

Research is a vital part of your own professional development. Research enables you to reflect on and evaluate your own practice, informing the choices you make about implementing new ideas, routines or strategies.

Research also enables you to keep up to date with current thinking and new approaches.

Key term

Evaluate – what you think about something – what you judge went well or not so well.

Benefits of research

Research can provide a number of benefits to both you and your practice. These include:

- a deeper understanding of the setting's values and principles
- a deeper understanding of the subject being researched
- a greater ability to apply theory to practice
- enhanced engagement with the children, parents and colleagues
- an increase in your confidence
- an increased awareness of high-quality practice
- an increased ability to be objective.

Keeping a research diary

A research diary will help you to keep a record of your ideas and progress, reflect on the research process and support you in the final stages of writing up your project.

Using a blank notebook, start your research diary. Begin by writing down all the thoughts and ideas you have had already. These may include:

- possible areas to research or topics of particular interest
- what you would like to find out
- possible research questions
- questions for your tutor or workplace supervisor
- possible research data-gathering methods you would like to use
- details of subject-related books, articles or websites.

As you continue along the research process you will add to your thoughts and ideas. The diary is an ongoing part of your project and will help you to reflect on the research undertaken.

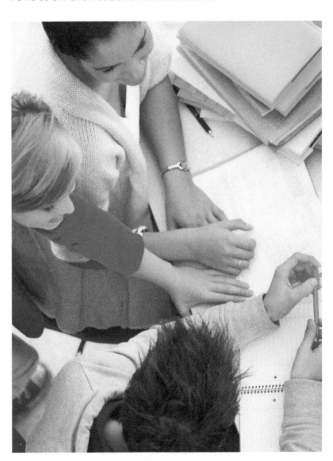

A research diary is a working document that allows you to keep track of your ideas throughout the research process.

2 Understand the role of a hypothesis in research

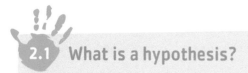

2.1 What is a hypothesis?

A hypothesis is the overall research question or statement which your study aims to answer or test whether it is true or false. The purpose of a hypothesis is to shape and focus your investigation. As well as a hypothesis you may have three or four additional questions which you also set out to answer. These often form part of your interview questions or questionnaires which are used to gather the research data.

Case study: developing a hypothesis

Bina is currently on work placement with 3 to 4 year olds in a day care setting. She has just started planning a research project as part of her course and is focusing on language development. Following a series of observations of the children at snack time she writes the following hypothesis:

'Would the introduction of an adult sitting with the children during snack time provide more opportunities for language development?'

1 Is this something that Bina will be able to prove or disprove?

2 What would be the next stage in developing this hypothesis?

3 How would Bina go about proving or disproving this hypothesis?

How is snack time currently organised?

For what reasons do the children communicate at snack time?

Why is language development so important?

Hypothesis: Would the introduction of an adult sitting with the children during snack time provide more opportunities for language development?

Do the children communicate with adults during snack time?

What opportunities do the children have to develop their language skills already in the setting?

Do the children communicate with each other during snack time?

Figure 10.1: *A hypothesis and the research questions surrounding it*

CP10

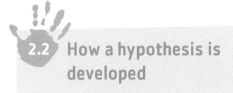

2.2 How a hypothesis is developed

Many research projects start from informal observations of practice, discussions with other learners or professionals in your setting. Or they may arise from something you have read in a newspaper or a professional magazine. For example, you may have noticed patterns in children's behaviour which has led you to investigate schemas or you may have read about enabling environments in a professional magazine and want to investigate this further. By reading more about the subject that you have found inspiring (secondary research) you are able to develop a hypothesis. It is important that your chosen topic is worthwhile as it is more likely to be enjoyable and maintain your interest.

Remember that it can take time to come up with a final hypothesis as it can develop and change as you start reading about your chosen area of research or collecting information for your literature review. Once you have developed a hypothesis, you are able to think about which research methods would best suit your study and produce useful data.

Key term

Schema – a repetitive pattern in a child's behaviour, for example, taking the content of the home corner to another area of the room could be a transporting schema in action; lining cars up could be a trajectory schema.

Find out

Mind maps are a helpful tool in the early stages of research, allowing you to organise your thoughts and ideas in a visual way. They help you to make links between the different subject areas related to your choice of research topic, combining information from different sources as well as summarising the key points.

- Create a mind map of your research topic choice.
- Write your hypothesis or research title in the centre of a large piece of paper. Add details of related subjects to read about, key points raised and any other facts or ideas linked to your hypothesis.
- Try to group related subjects and ideas together.
- Can you make any links between the related subject areas?
- Start reading about your chosen area of research and add any relevant information to your mind map.

Your mind map will be a useful tool throughout your project as you will be able to continue to add information and identify links as you progress.

CP10

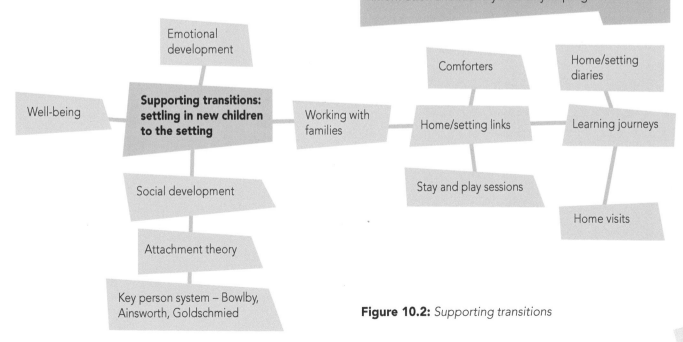

Figure 10.2: *Supporting transitions*

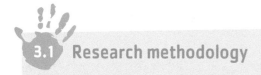

3 Understand methodologies in research

CP10

3.1 Research methodology

Research methodology refers to the approach you take to carrying out your investigation. It includes details of the methods used to collect data as well as any ethical considerations you have taken into account. The methodology section of your final report should be detailed enough for someone else to replicate your study. You would include:

- details of the sample group you are working with, for example, age, number of children and gender
- the context in which your study took place, for example, if the study was conducted inside or outside, how many adults were present, if the children engaged in self-initiated play
- details of your chosen data-gathering methods, the reasons you chose them and any specific ethical considerations you took into account when selecting them
- details of how you piloted any of your research data-gathering methods prior to using them and if any changes were made following the pilot.

It is necessary to provide this amount of detail in your methodology sections in order for the reader of your report to see the depth of your investigation. In early years settings many changes to practice are made due to the outcome of research, therefore it is essential that the methodology shows the research is both sound and reliable.

Key terms

Research methodology – the approach you take to carrying out your investigation including information on the methods you used, the sample group and any ethical considerations.

Ethical considerations – the consideration you have given to making sure your work is moral and respectful of all those participating.

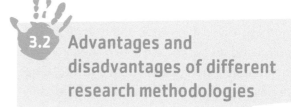

3.2 Advantages and disadvantages of different research methodologies

When you have decided on your hypothesis you can start to think about how you will gather your research data. There are many different methods that you could use to gather data; however, your choice will be influenced by:

- your hypothesis/research questions
- the time you have available to gather information
- those taking part in your investigation (sample group)
- what it is you hope to find out.

The three main data gathering methods used in small-scale research projects are:

- questionnaires
- interviews
- observations.

Questionnaires

Questionnaires are a popular form of data gathering as they give a broad picture of the subject being investigated. However, they do not provide much depth. They are a good way of asking a large number of people the same question but designing an effective questionnaire can be very difficult. To help you design an effective questionnaire you need to think about what you want it to find out and who it is aimed at. You will also need to think about making the layout of your questionnaire attractive and easy to use. Unit CP5 explores the use of questionnaires in more detail.

The following checklist will help you to ensure you design an effective questionnaire.

Questionnaire checklist

- Include a brief introduction to the aim and purpose of the questionnaire.
- Include confirmation that all information will remain confidential and that participants will not be identified.
- Include clear instruction on how to complete the questionnaire.
- Make sure it is attractively presented and easy to use.
- Make sure the questions are in a logical order, with similar questions grouped together.
- Make sure you are consistent in how you are asking people to respond to questions throughout the questionnaire, for example, ticks, numbers, circling words.
- Make sure the questionnaire is not too long. People will be put off completing it if it is too long.
- Make sure it is suitable for the target audience, for example, child friendly if giving to children.
- Stick to single questions; avoid two-part questions as these can be confusing to answer and then difficult to analyse.
- Check the language used is appropriate and avoids jargon and abbreviations.
- Make sure it is clear what respondents should do with completed questionnaire.

Interviews

If you have a small sample group, interviews may be more appropriate than questionnaires as a means of data gathering. Interviews need to be carefully planned in order to gain the information required. They have the advantage of giving the interviewer the opportunity to adapt the questions as they go along, resulting in more information being gathered.

During interviews the interviewee can discuss a particular subject at length and in detail. However, it is very easy for the interviewer to influence responses without knowing they are doing so. To avoid this it is helpful to have a list of clear questions similar to those used in a questionnaire and avoid nodding or smiling too much and saying 'yes', as this can lead the interviewee to answer a question in a particular way.

The following checklist will help you to ensure your interviews are carefully planned.

Interview checklist

- Include a brief introduction to explain the aim and purpose of the interview.
- Confirm that all information will remain confidential and that participants will not be identified.
- Ensure you will be able to stick to the time limit arranged.
- Ensure that questions are suitable for those being interviewed.
- Stick to single questions; avoid two-part questions as these can be confusing to answer and difficult to analyse.
- Check the language used is appropriate and avoids jargon and abbreviations.
- Make sure questions are clear and unambiguous.
- Make sure you give a suitable amount of time for interviewees to answer questions.
- Avoid overuse of nodding, smiling and saying 'yes'.
- Make sure you have a reliable means of recording the interview.

Observations

There is a range of different observational methods that can be used to gather data depending on what you are investigating.

These include:
- narrative
- checklist
- time sampling
- sociogram
- target child
- event sampling
- case study
- participant observation
- non-participant observation.

When deciding which observational method to use, it is helpful to think about what you are trying to find out and how you are going to analyse the data you gather. For example, if you choose to use a checklist to measure how many times a child or adult does something, the information you gather would produce quantitative data.

You will need to consider if you are going to be a non-participant observer or participant observer. A non-participant sits and observes without getting involved whereas a participant observer is involved in the situation being observed. Although potentially distracting to the person being observed, a participant observer can capture a more detailed observation.

It is also important to consider how you are going to record your observations. Written observations are very popular as they are easy to complete but do need to be detailed. Videoing observations and dictaphone recordings of what you see are both popular recording choices as you are able to review the observation many times in order to analyse it.

However, you must remember to gain permission, in writing, from the setting manager as well as anyone you are recording prior to doing so. In the case of children, you must get permission from their parent or carer. You must also inform everyone in the setting when and where you will be recording.

A copy of permission letters should be included in the appendix of your project. Unit CP1 explores the use of observations in greater depth.

The following checklist will help you to ensure you carry out worthwhile observations.

Observation checklist

- Have a clear idea of what you want to observe in relation to your hypothesis.
- Gain permission from those being observed.
- Decide if you want to be a participant or non-participant observer.
- Have a clear idea of how you want to record your observation.
- Consider how effective the observation choice was once completed. If it was unsuitable you will need to choose a different method.

Table 10.1: *Advantages and disadvantages of different research methods*

Method	Advantages	Disadvantages
Questionnaires	<ul><li>Can gather large amount of data</li><li>Allow participants to be anonymous</li><li>Can produce both qualitative and quantitative data</li></ul>	<ul><li>Can take time to analyse and collate</li><li>Can have poor response rates</li><li>Difficult to design an effective questionnaire</li></ul>
Interviews	<ul><li>Provide more depth and detail</li><li>Can probe deeper if needed</li><li>Can adapt approach as going along</li><li>Interviewee can speak at length</li></ul>	<ul><li>Not anonymous</li><li>Time-consuming</li><li>Easy to 'lead' interviewee</li><li>Easy to influence responses</li><li>Require a good rapport between interviewer and interviewee</li><li>Need to be well planned</li></ul>
Observations	<ul><li>Flexible</li><li>Can produce detailed data</li><li>Can take place spontaneously</li><li>Easy to prepare</li></ul>	<ul><li>Difficult to record, cameras can put the children off</li><li>Time-consuming to analyse</li><li>Difficult to remain objective if you know the children well</li></ul>

3.3 Your choice of research methods

Your research hypothesis will influence whether your investigation has a **qualitative** or **quantitative** approach. In order to prove or disprove your hypothesis you may need to investigate colleagues' or parents' ideas, opinions or thoughts about your subject choice or you may need to use a checklist or gather numerical data to support your research questions.

A qualitative research approach usually produces data that is formed of opinions while a quantitative approach produces data that is numerical and can be presented as charts and graphs in your final project. Qualitative data helps to illustrate the numerical data produced by a quantitative research approach.

In many cases research produces both kinds of data. A quantitative approach tends to give a bigger picture of the subject whereas a qualitative approach gives a focused view. Both approaches are useful as they give different perspectives of the chosen subject.

Key terms

Qualitative – findings that result from people's thoughts, ideas and personal opinions.

Quantitative – findings that create numbers and statistics.

Find out

- Make a list of the research subjects you would like to investigate. For each subject formulate a research question or hypothesis.
- Now think about how you are going to answer each question. For each question select two or three data-gathering methods which would reveal the answers to your questions.
- In what way are all of your chosen methods appropriate?
- Is it possible to use your chosen methods in the timescale allowed for your project?

Case study: Alice's research method choice

Alice is keen to do her research project on the outside play area. She has recently read an article about the development of fine manipulative skills and she would like to find out how the development of these skills is supported in the outdoor play area of her nursery work placement. Alice has chosen three data-gathering methods:

- observations of the children during outdoor play
- questionnaires for the parents
- staff interviews.

When Alice starts to design the parent questionnaire she realises that it is not a suitable method for this research subject choice.

1 Why do you think parent questionnaires are unsuitable for this subject choice?
2 Which alternative method would you suggest Alice could use?

CP10

Observations are the most frequently used form of data gathering in early years research. What could the person observing this 4 year old tell about her development?

Assessment activity 1.1, 1.2, 1.3, 2.1, 2.2, 3.1, 3.2, 3.3

Create an information booklet for a level 3 learner who is about to carry out a research project. The booklet needs to include the following information:

- what research is
- the value of research in work with children and young people
- the difference between primary and secondary research
- what a hypothesis is and how it is developed
- what is meant by the term 'research methodology'
- an evaluation of different research methodologies
- an explanation of how the choice of research methodology could be affected by a hypothesis.

So what does this mean?

The research methods you select to collect data will enable you to either prove or disprove your hypothesis. Here are some points to remember when selecting which research methods to use.

- What are you trying to find out?
- How much time do you have to carry out your project?
- What are the ethical considerations for each of your chosen methods?
- Who is taking part in your research?
- Are the methods selected appropriate for the intended user, e.g. child-friendly or jargon-free questionnaires?

4 Be able to identify a research hypothesis

4.1 Producing a hypothesis

Your hypothesis will be founded on your own work-based practice. It will probably have come from initial observations in the workplace setting or from something you have read in a professional magazine or early years book. It is important to discuss your hypothesis as it develops with your workplace supervisor and tutor, as they will be able to advise and guide you. Once you have decided on your final hypothesis it is important that you do not change it. If you do it will have an impact on your chosen data-gathering methods and your secondary research (review of current topic-related literature).

It is important that you keep referring back to your hypothesis when you are conducting your research

and analysing the data as this will help you remain focused. Some learners find it helpful to write down their hypothesis on a separate piece of paper and display it where they do their work. This allows them to remind themselves of what they are trying to find out, which in turn helps them to keep to the subject.

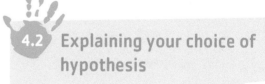

4.2 Explaining your choice of hypothesis

Your choice of research subject and hypothesis needs to be carefully planned so that it is ethical and as a researcher this is your responsibility. Anyone carrying out research needs to consider the ethical issues surrounding their study before they start the investigation.

There are several ethical issues to think about when considering your choice of hypothesis. These include:

- being objective
- confidentiality
- gaining permission from participants
- considering children's rights.

All research must be for the good of the children and setting and have a positive outcome.

Being objective

This is an important part of research. You need to ensure that you only report what you find and do not add your own opinion based on any pre-conceived ideas or bias you might have.

Confidentiality

A key aspect of primary research is the sharing of personal information during interviews or on questionnaires. You will need to ensure that any information given to you during the research process is treated with respect and treated confidentially. Confidentiality means that you will not identify anyone who has taken part in your study. This can be achieved by changing the names of people taking part. The Data Protection Act outlines how data can be collected and stored. It also gives people the right to see any information which is gathered about them.

Gaining permission

Prior to starting your research you must gain permission from the head of the setting. Once you have got the go-ahead for your project you will need to gain informed consent from those taking part. This may be from the children, setting staff or parents. If your research involves interviews with the children you will need to think carefully about how you are going to gain informed consent. You will need to ensure that the children understand what it is you are asking them to be involved in.

Informed consent is an ongoing process. You may find that one day children are happy to take part in your research and the next they do not want to.

However frustrating this might be, the right not to take part needs to be respected. Anyone taking part in your research has the right to withdraw from your project at any time. Therefore it is important to be honest and open about what you are doing.

Children's rights

The United Nations Convention on the Rights of the Child (UNCRC) outlines children's rights, declaring that children have the right to hold an opinion about matters which concern them. It highlights the importance of listening to children. This is also a fundamental principle of the Early Years Foundation Stage, which holds listening to and respecting young children's viewpoints as central to high-quality practice.

Key terms

Ethical – ethics are about conducting your research in a morally correct way. You need to make sure that the research is for the good of the children and the setting and that no harm will come to any of your participants during the research process. You cannot force anyone to take part in your study and you must gain permission from all involved prior to starting your investigation.

Informed consent – participants voluntarily agreeing to take part in your project following detailed discussion of what is involved.

Find out

Look at the United Nations Convention on the Rights of the Child (UNCRC). You can find this by looking at Useful websites on page 247.

Which one of the 54 articles highlights a child's right to have an opinion about matters concerning them and encourages early years researchers to actively involve children in any research that affects them?

Reflect

Think about your hypothesis, research questions and selected data-gathering methods, and consider the following points.

- Are there any sensitive issues that might be raised from your research?
- Could your research have a negative impact on the setting, the children or their families?
- Is there any advantage to the setting from having the research carried out?
- How are you going to ensure that everyone involved is fully aware of your research and what you plan to do with the findings?

Assessment activity 4.1, 4.2

1 Carry out three observations of the area of practice you are especially interested in. In consultation with your workplace supervisor or tutor, develop a hypothesis for research.

2 Create a mind map of the ethical issues and the necessary actions surrounding your chosen hypothesis.

3 Use your mind map as a discussion guide with a small group of fellow learners to explain your choice of hypothesis in relation to working with children and young people.

Case study: Emily's research project

Emily is a second-year early years learner. She is doing work experience in Year 1 of the primary school attended by her younger brother. As part of her course she is required to carry out a small research project in her placement. Emily has a particular interest in social and emotional development and its impact on children's behaviour. She wants to focus her study on one child who sometimes displays aggressive behaviour towards the other children in the class, including on one occasion her brother. Emily has outlined her project to her tutor and placement supervisor saying that she is looking at social interactions between the children. She explains that she is going to use a child study and parental questionnaires as the main methods of data collection.

Emily's placement supervisor asks her to write a brief letter to the parents explaining the research project she is planning and asking them to take part in. However, because Emily is behind with her work, she decides to miss out this stage. In her enthusiasm to catch up, Emily speaks to the class parents in small groups at the end of the day. She asks them their thoughts about behaviour in the classroom and if they think any one child in particular displays aggressive behaviour on a regular basis. She openly discusses the incident involving her brother with one of the groups.

Emily uses her knowledge of how different situations can affect children's behaviour to formulate a questionnaire for the child's parents. The questionnaire includes personal questions about the state of the parents' relationship and employment situation. Emily is surprised when the family complains to the class teacher and she is asked to stop carrying out her project.

1 In what way was Emily's project unethical?

2 In what way was Emily's project not objective?

3 How suitable were the research methods used for this project?

4 What advice would you give Emily about how to resume her project?

5 Be able to plan and implement research in relation to working with children and/or young people

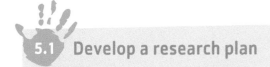

5.1 Develop a research plan

Research projects are longitudinal pieces of work. They involve both primary and secondary research which is time-consuming. Successful research projects need a lot of planning. In order to complete your project on time it is vital that you develop a good research plan. A good plan allows you to set out what you need to do and when. It also allows you, your tutor and work placement supervisor to monitor your progress. Research projects do not always go to plan so it is important to be flexible in your planning. Remember to allow extra time to chase up questionnaires that have not been returned or for the analysis of data. This always takes longer than you think.

Key term

Longitudinal – a piece of work that is carried out over a period of time, for example, six weeks.

Good time management is a vital part of successful research. All research projects have to be carried out within a set time frame and in a particular order. The example of an action plan in **Table 10.2** shows the many aspects of research and when they need to be completed. An action plan can help you to complete your project successfully in the set time frame.

Table 10.2: *Planning and implementing research action plan*

Aspect of research	Date	Comments	Completed
Initial investigation: discussion with work placement supervisor, tutor and fellow students about possible research subjects	January	Discussion with tutor	√
Write a research action plan	January	Show to tutor	√
Read and review what is currently written about your chosen subject (secondary research)	January – February	Share with other students researching similar areas	√
Formulate a suitable hypothesis/research question	January	Tutor to check	√
Gain informed consent from all those involved in the research	February	Write letters to participants	√
Select appropriate methods for data gathering	February		√
Design questionnaires and interviews	March	Pilot with other students	√

(continued)

CP10

Table 10.2: *Planning and implementing research action plan (continued)*

Aspect of research	Date	Comments	Completed
Carry out research	March	Store completed questionnaires securely (confidentiality)	√
Analyse the data gathered	March	Group key points together	√
Present the findings of the research project using a format relevant to target audience	April	Use charts and graphs to show results	√
Reflect on the research process noting what could be done differently next time	April	Conclusion	√
Submit your research project	April	Leave time to proofread	√

Reflect

Using **Table 10.2** to guide you, create your own research action plan with specific targets and realistic dates and use it to monitor your progress.

5.2 Selecting appropriate research methodologies

Once you are happy with your hypothesis you can select the research data-gathering methods most suitable for your investigation. It is very important to make sure that the methods you choose are appropriate as they will affect the quality of your data. In order to generate both valid and reliable data, researchers often select three complementary methods of data gathering which can be used together to give a better understanding of the research subject. This is known as triangulation (see **Figure 10.3**).

Once you have selected the research methods you are going to use to investigate your chosen topic, it is very helpful to carry out a pilot study with someone who will be objective. This involves having a practice run at using your methods. By piloting your research methods you can identify any potential problems, errors or areas you have missed prior to doing it for real. You can then be confident that your methods will be an effective means of data gathering. You could pilot your questionnaires and interview questions with fellow learners. It is important that you write about your findings from piloting your methods, outlining any changes you had to make following the process.

Figure 10.3: *Triangulation*

questionnaires for practitioners, focusing on the children's engagement in activity

gathering data

observations of the children engaged in activity

child interviews focusing on their view of the activity and setting

Key terms

Valid – for data to be valid, it must measure what it set out to measure.

Reliable – data is considered reliable if it can be replicated by someone else using the same methods but at a different time. Piloting your research methods can help to ensure reliability.

Triangulation – the practice of combining three different research data-gathering methods to gain a detailed and genuine picture of what is happening.

Pilot – a practice run to check for errors or any areas that have been missed.

Case study: piloting research methods

Joe has planned to use a questionnaire to investigate the different ways in which parents would like to be involved in the setting. He has discussed the content of the questionnaire with his tutor and work placement supervisor. They are both happy with the questionnaire's structure and content, although they are both concerned that it is too long.

As part of the piloting process Joe decides to give the questionnaire out to a selection of parents at the setting without shortening it. One of the parents asks if Joe could go through the questions with her on a one-to-one basis. Joe agrees to do this but when he analyses the findings from all of the returned questionnaires he notices that the one he assisted with contains answers that he gave as an example during the meeting with the parent. He also finds that many of the questionnaires have not been completed and that there are a number of queries over the use of early years terminology and abbreviations.

1 Do you think the findings from the questionnaires were valid?

2 In what way was this pilot helpful to Joe's actual research?

3 What advice would you give Joe in order to ensure his questionnaires generate both reliable and valid data when used in the actual research?

5.3 Rationale for chosen research methodology

The research methods selected to gather your data are central to your investigation. It is vital that they are carefully chosen to ensure they gather the data necessary to prove or disprove your hypothesis. However, the practicalities of different methods also need to be taken into account. Your chosen methods will be influenced by the time limits of your project as well as the resources available to you and your personal preference. Your chosen research methods will also be influenced by what is considered appropriate for your sample group. You need to identify who you are researching as well as why. In your case your sample group is most likely to be one of convenience as it will be the children, families and practitioners of your workplace setting. It is important to identify your research methods and justify your choices as these have an impact on the overall research findings.

Key term

Sample group – refers to the setting, children and adults that are in the study.

5.4 Implement chosen research methodology

Carrying out research for the first time can be a daunting experience. The following list of tips should help ensure your research goes smoothly.

Good practice checklist

1 Good communication skills are a vital part of research. You will need to be able to write clear, concise letters, negotiate times with your supervisor and feed back to your tutor, as well as conduct interviews in a professional manner. You will need to be able to communicate appropriately with children, their families and practitioners.

2 It is not possible to predict if things are going to go smoothly or not – the children you want to observe may be away or practitioners may be unavailable – but if you are flexible in your approach and adapt your research plan where necessary you will be able to overcome any setbacks.

3 In order to produce high-quality research findings you must remain objective when carrying out your investigation.

4 Questionnaires can be time-consuming and have a poor response rate. Providing envelopes and a deadline can help to overcome this.

5 Practitioners are very busy. Arrange interview times that suit those taking part and stick to the time limit arranged. It is worth remembering that in settings the children will come first so if there is an emergency or incident that requires the interviewee's attention, your interview will need to be rearranged.

6 Before carrying out any observations, have a clear idea about what you want to find out as well as how you are going to conduct the observation (participant or non-participant), what method you are going to use and how you are going to record it.

7 Keep your work placement supervisor and tutor updated on your progress.

5.5 Gather and record research data

Gathering your primary research data is an exciting part of your project. It is the practical side of the process which many students find most enjoyable. As you begin to gather your data you will need to resist the temptation to start drawing conclusions as these will not be a genuine reflection of your findings and in research you must avoid making assumptions.

How you record the data you gather will be up to you. However, it will be dependent on the data-gathering method, the resources available to you and your personal preference.

Data recording methods may include:

- checklists
- notes
- diagrams
- photos
- video recording
- voice recording.

It is important that all secondary research material (your summary of existing literature related to your chosen area of research) is referenced correctly. Referencing is essential as it allows the reader of your work to check the literature used in your project. Unit CP5 has further guidance on referencing.

Assessment activity 5.1, 5.2, 5.3, 5.4, 5.5

Develop a plan for your own piece of research.

1 Create a timeline of the research process which includes details of planning the research project, implementing the project and gathering and recording research data.

2 Your timeline should include any advice and tips you have discovered through your own research experience or any reading carried out so far.

3 Share your timeline with fellow learners and add any advice and tips from each other's timelines that you think will be helpful during the research process.

4 Choose and implement appropriate research methodologies in relation to your chosen hypothesis.

5 Produce a rationale for your choice of research methodology.

6 Gather and record your research data.

6 Be able to present data in relation to the hypothesis

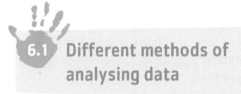

6.1 Different methods of analysing data

Once you have gathered all your research data you are in a position to start analysing it. There are two main ways of organising your data. A tally chart can be used to organise any quantitative data, while colour coding can be used for qualitative data as a means of grouping key themes together. Both methods will give you a visual interpretation of your findings which you can match to your literature review findings, and eventually draw conclusions. They will also give you an idea of how to present your findings in your final project. As qualitative data deals with frequency and quantity you will be able to present it in tables, charts or graphs. Qualitative data represents people's thoughts and opinions and therefore will need to be integrated into the discussion section of your final report to support your argument.

Figures **10.4** and **10.5** show what data looks like before it is analysed and then when the same data is presented as a pie chart.

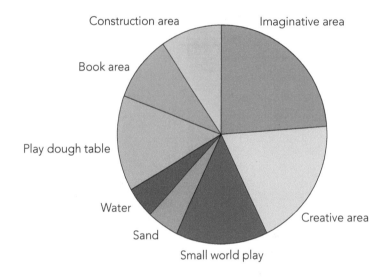

Figure 10.5: *Pie chart created from raw data*

Area	Number of children choosing that area
Imaginative area	‖‖‖
Creative area	‖‖‖
Small world play	‖‖‖
Sand	‖
Water	‖
Play dough table	‖‖‖
Book area	‖‖
Construction area	‖‖

Figure 10.4: *Tally chart of raw data*

Key term

Tally chart – tally marks are used to count or keep score.

241

CP10

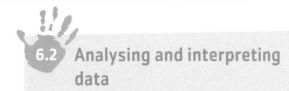

6.2 Analysing and interpreting data

You will need to establish what your research says about your chosen subject. In order to do this you need to ask yourself, 'How does the data prove or disprove my hypotheses?' This is the starting point for analysing your data. It is the 'how' aspect of this question that you need to establish. Once you have done this you will also need to consider if and how your research data supports the literature you reviewed as part of the secondary research process. This is the analysis aspect of your investigation. You should be able to make some clear links between your research findings and what is already said about your research subject. This will form the basis of the discussion aspect of your final report. Unit CP5 has further guidance on analysing data.

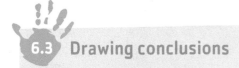

6.3 Drawing conclusions

A sound knowledge of your research subject, through the secondary research process, will enable you to identify the key points raised by the data gathered. Two key questions at this point of the process are:

1 What is the data telling me?

2 How does it support my hypothesis?

It is the answers to both of these questions that will form the basis of your discussion. You do not have to use all the data you have gathered to support your argument in your discussion section. Select the key piece you want to use but make sure you include a range of data so that you can give alternative perspectives in your discussion.

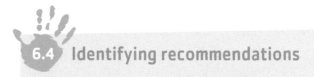

6.4 Identifying recommendations

Research with children is often used as a means of deciding whether or not to make a change to practice. It is therefore vital that any changes are based on genuine, valid and reliable research. It is at this point that you, as the researcher, must acknowledge whether recommendations can be made based on your investigation. If your investigation produces reliable evidence for practice to be changed, and if this is evident in the detailed writing up of your final report, then you are in a position to make recommendations. If, on the other hand, your investigation does not prove or disprove your hypothesis, you must conclude that there is insufficient evidence to propose a change to practice. At this stage it is important that you remember the ethical considerations outlined in 4.2 on pages 234–235: that all research must be for the good of the children and setting and have a positive outcome.

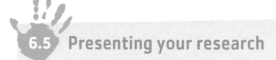

6.5 Presenting your research

Table 10.3 outlines the usual format and content of a research project – the assessment criteria for CP10: Research to support practice when working with children and/or young people has been identified in the right-hand column so that you can see which section of your projects meets which criteria.

Table 10.3: *Research project format*

Section/chapter	Content	Assessment criteria
Acknowledgements	It is good practice to thank all those who have taken part in your project or supported you through the process. This would include the children, families and staff at the setting, your workplace supervisor and tutor as well as friends and family.	
Abstract	A brief summary of your research project to include the aim of your investigation, the methods used and an outline of the main findings. The abstract is usually the last part of your project to be written.	
Introduction	Introduce the subject area you are investigating and the rationale for your choice. Identify the research aims and the hypothesis and any other research questions you aim to answer.	1.1 1.2 1.3 2.1 2.2 5.3
Literature review	A summary of existing literature related to your chosen area of research. This could be found in books, magazine articles or on the Internet. It sets the scene for your study and establishes what is already known about your chosen area of research.	6.2 6.3
Method	A description of how you carried out the research in enough detail for someone else to replicate your study. You would include details of your chosen methods of data gathering, details of the sample group and the context in which your study was carried out as well as any ethical considerations.	3.1 3.2 3.3 4.1 4.2 5.2 6.1
Results	A description of the data gathered. This could include charts, tables and graphs if appropriate. You do not have to write the summary in the same order as the data was gathered. Try to avoid the temptation to analyse your findings here.	6.2
Discussion	An analysis of your research findings making links to your literature review. Group key themes together and put forward both sides of the argument if possible.	6.3
Conclusion and recommendations	A summary of the key points raised by your research referring back to your hypothesis and research aims. Identify what the results may mean for practice. It is important to acknowledge that this is a small-scale research project, therefore it is possible that further investigation would be required before a change to practice is recommended. If your findings are inconclusive then you need to acknowledge this too. By this stage you will have a good idea how you would do things differently next time. Summarise how you might improve your project and the methods used in relation to the hypothesis. If appropriate, make recommendations for practice; however, you need to remember you cannot make recommendations beyond the context of your own study.	6.4 7.1 7.2 7.3 7.4
Reference list	An alphabetical list of the books, articles, journals and websites referred to in your work.	
Appendix items	A research action plan Copies of permission letters Copy of questionnaire Copy of interview questions	5.1

CP10

Find out

Carry out an Internet search for one or two research projects related to work with children or young people.

- Read the projects to get a feel for how research projects are written.
- Try to identify the key aspects of research that have been explored in this chapter.

Assessment activity 6.1, 6.2, 6.3, 6.4, 6.5

Present the data from your research project.

- Evaluate different methods of analysing data.
- Analyse and interpret the data from your own research.
- Draw conclusions on the data in relation to the identified hypothesis.
- Make recommendations as a result of your research.
- Present your findings in a relevant format for your target audience.

7 Be able to reflect on the research undertaken

7.1 Strengths and weaknesses of the research methodologies

The process of reflection is a very important part of practice and can be applied to research as well as every aspect of working with children and young people. Reflection is necessary for deeper thinking and further learning. Reflection is the way we become better at something, therefore it is important to be as honest as possible during the process.

There are four main parts to the reflection process:

- reflection
- planning
- implementation
- evaluation.

Reflection is not a one-off event but an ongoing process.

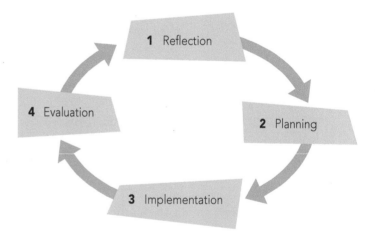

Figure 10.6: *The reflective cycle*

When reflecting on a research project it is helpful to consider both what went well and what you would do differently another time. This should be done throughout the research process as it is easier to reflect on each stage as you go along, making notes in your research diary.

Consider the research methods you selected and ask the following questions:

1 Did all the data-gathering methods used gather the depth of data they were designed to?

2 Did the data gathered answer the research hypothesis?

3 Was the data gathered both valid and reliable?

4 Were the data-gathering methods piloted in order to identify any weaknesses?

These questions will help you identify the strengths and weaknesses of your research methods and enable you to make recommendations for future projects.

7.2 Improving the research process

The reflection aspect of research enables you to identify what could be improved next time. This is an important part of the research process as it enables you to improve and develop your research skills for future projects.

The following reflection activity will help you to identify aspects of your own research that could be improved.

Reflect

Think of your experience completing a small-scale research project.

What advice would you give a learner working with children about to start a research project?

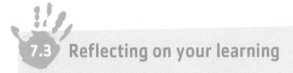

7.3 Reflecting on your learning

Reflecting on your own learning during the research process enables you to identify your developing skills and any that need further improvement. Your research diary will support you to reflect on your own learning during the research process and to identify your skills. Unit CP5 has further guidance on study skills.

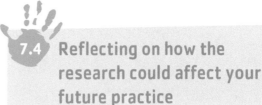

7.4 Reflecting on how the research could affect your future practice

Research is a vital part of professional practice. It is through research that you are able to develop your skills of observation as well as your analytical thinking. Research is a vital means of informing future practice and justifying change.

Reflect

- Read your research diary and highlight areas that you feel show your developing skills as a practitioner and researcher.
- Identify the skills you have used during the research process.
- Which aspects of your practice are these skills particularly beneficial to?
- How will you use and develop these skills in the future?
- What do you think might be the impact on your own practice?

Assessment activity 7.1, 7.2, 7.3, 7.4

Prepare a ten-minute electronic presentation which outlines your research project experience. Refer to your research diary to help you with this task.

Remember to:

- discuss the strengths and weaknesses in your research methodologies
- discuss the ways your research could be improved in relation to your chosen hypothesis
- reflect on your own learning during the research process
- reflect on how your research could affect your own future practice
- prepare to answer questions from the group about your research project.

CP10

In the real world

My name is Beth. I completed the Level 3 Extended Diploma six months ago. I really enjoyed the course and now work with 2 and 3 years olds in a day care setting.

The manager has asked me to think about ways we can improve communication between the setting and parents during potty training. At first I wasn't sure how I was going to do this but then thought it would be an opportunity to put into practice the research skills I learned at college. I started off by chatting with the team about what already happens in the setting and reading about social and emotional development as well as potty training strategies. I had a meeting with my manager to talk through my ideas and soon found I had a research project on my hands. I was really excited about having the opportunity to influence our practice for the better.

I am now in the final stages of writing up my project and am planning a staff development session to share my findings. We will be introducing 'potty diaries' shortly to support communication between our setting and the home while children are potty training. Potty training is an important part of development and it is good to know we are supporting young children in the best way possible.

I feel really pleased that I have been able to do this project. It has improved my confidence and organisational skills as well as developed my professional relationship with the families of the children I work with. I am already thinking of my next research project and can't wait to get started.

Check your knowledge

1 Why is research an important part of working with children and young people?

2 Which everyday skills are used during the research process?

3 Explain the difference between quantitative and qualitative data.

4 Which research data-gathering methods are more likely to produce quantitative data and which would provide qualitative data?

5 What is the purpose of carrying out a literature review as part of the research process?

6 How can you ensure you remain objective when carrying out observations as part of your research?

7 What is meant by the term 'informed consent' and how would you go about obtaining it from those participating in your study?

8 Explain triangulation, including an example in your answer.

CP10

CACHE Extended Assessment

Theme: Professional principles underpinning practice in work with children and young people

Grading criterion

B3 Analyse aspects of your learning from the chosen theme that could improve future practice.

Your CACHE assessor will expect to see that you understand that research with children and young people is a very important part of practice. You will need to demonstrate in your written answer that you have identified and examined your own learning as a result of carrying out a research project – for example, developing your time management and organisational skills, communication and interpersonal skill as well as ensuring your project is carried out in an ethical way and what this entailed. You will also need to identify how the experience of carrying out a research project may impact on your future practice.

This is an example of how you might approach one criterion of your Extended Assessment. You must successfully complete all the criteria at each grade to achieve that grade. You will achieve the highest grade for which you have successfully completed all the criteria. For example, to achieve a B grade you will need to meet the requirements of the B1, B2 and B3 criteria, as well as C1, C2, C3 and D1 and D2.

When trying to understand the requirements for your Extended Assessment, it is always a good idea to talk to your tutors. Fellow learners and workplace colleagues are also useful sources of information.

Further references

The following are sources of useful information on the topic supporting practice when working with children and young people.

Books and journals

Cullan, S. and Reed, M. (2011) *Work-based Research in Early Years*, London: Sage

EYE magazine

Hucker, K. (2001) *Research Methods in Health, Care and Early Years*, Oxford: Heinemann

McMillan, K. and Weyers, J. (2010) *How to Write Dissertations and Project Reports*, Harlow: Pearson

Nursery World magazine

Roberts-Holmes, G. (2011) *Doing Your Early Years Research Project*, London: Sage

Useful websites

To obtain a secure link to the websites below, visit www.pearsonhotlinks.co.uk and search for this book by using its title or ISBN. Click on the section for CP10.

The website of the National Children's Bureau

The website of the Joseph Rowntree Foundation, dedicated to social policy research and development

The website of the Children's Society

The United Nations Convention on the Rights of the Child (UNCRC) on the UNICEF website.

Support children and/ or young people's development of art, drama and music

CP11

Children will have many opportunities to explore art, drama and music through play and thereby enhance their creative development and learning. This unit looks at ways in which practitioners can support childrens and young people's development, and provide appropriate activities and resources to promote creativity.

Learning outcomes

By the end of this unit you will:

1 Understand art, drama and music development when working with children and/or young people

2 Understand learning needs of individual children and/or young people when supporting the development of art, drama and music

3 Be able to plan and implement art, drama and music activities for children and/or young people

4 Be able to reflect on own practice.

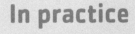

In practice

A pre-school setting has been given a large assortment of recyclable materials. The supervisor has asked the team to come up with ideas about how these can be used to develop children's creativity and enhance the art area. She has also asked everyone to consider how these activities link to the Early Years Foundation Stage learning goals.

By the end of this unit you will be able to plan and provide activities that are suitable for developing children's creativity and show how they link to the early years framework.

1 Understand art, drama and music development when working with children and/or young people

In order to support and plan for children to develop their art, drama and music development, you must understand what this is and the types of opportunities and experiences that fall into this category. Earlier, in Unit CP1, you will have seen how development is holistic and how learning and development never fall into just one category. This unit will help you to identify everyday activities that display elements of art, drama and music and will also help you to consider the wide range of opportunities that exist.

Key term

Holistic – an approach that takes the whole person into account, not just one or a few aspects of their health and well-being.

1.1 Current educational frameworks

Each country within the UK has devised and implemented its own curriculum/framework to support the development and learning of children in the early years. In this section we will take a brief look at the frameworks used in England, Scotland, Ireland and Wales for art, drama and music. For further guidance on the framework used in your country, useful websites are listed at the end of the unit.

England – Early Years Foundation Stage (EYFS)

In England, settings must follow the Early Years Foundation Stage (EYFS), which encompasses learning and development from birth to the end of a child's first year at school (reception year). This is then followed by the four key stages of the National Curriculum. The frameworks of the EYFS have identified criteria which all settings should help children to work towards and achieve. The EYFS was first introduced in 2008 and revised in 2012.

Expressive arts and design

The revised EYFS now identifies seven areas of learning and development. These are divided into three prime areas and four specific areas of learning and development. Expressive arts and design sits within the four specific areas of learning.

Table 11.1: *EYFS specific area of learning – expressive arts and design*

Exploring and using media and materials	Children sing songs, make music and dance, and experiment with ways of changing them. They safely use and explore a variety of materials, tools and techniques, experimenting with colour, design, texture, form and function.
Being imaginative	Children use what they have learned about media and materials in original ways, thinking about uses and purposes. They represent their own ideas, thoughts and feelings through design, technology, art, music, dance, role play and stories.

Scotland – Curriculum for Excellence

The Curriculum for Excellence has been introduced in Scotland to raise the standards of education and to focus on the individual needs of each child. The curriculum spans ages 3 to 18 years and follows on from the national pre-birth to 3 guidance. The entry level of the curriculum covers the same age range as the Foundation Stage used in England. Curriculum for excellence focuses on eight key subject areas and the expressive arts is one of these.

Table 11.2: *Key subject area of expressive arts in Scotland's Curriculum for Excellence*

Art and design	Children have opportunities to be creative and to experience inspiration and enjoyment. They explore a wide range of two- and three-dimensional media and technologies through practical activities, and create, express and communicate ideas.
Drama	Through drama, children have rich opportunities to be creative and to explore real and imaginary situations.
Music	Through music, children will explore sounds and musical concepts, and use their imagination and skills to create their own musical ideas.

The National Curriculum in Wales

The Foundation Phase is the approach in Wales to learning for children from 3 to 7 years of age. It combines Early Years Education (for 3 to 5 year olds) and Key Stage 1 (5 to 7 year olds) of the National Curriculum.

The curriculum in Wales identifies seven areas of learning. Creative development is the area of learning within which you will find art, drama and music.

Table 11.3: *Creative development – Foundation Phase, Wales*

Art, craft and design	Children should have the opportunity to explore and use a variety of materials, make choices when choosing materials and express their feelings and ideas creatively.
Music	Children should have the opportunity to explore and make sound to create their own musical ideas, enjoy singing and using instruments to recognise and describe sounds.
Creative movement	Children should have the opportunity to explore and express their moods and feelings through a variety of movements, and develop their responses to music, pictures, words and ideas.

The National Curriculum in Northern Ireland

The curriculum identifies a foundation stage for children in the early years and defines seven areas of learning, one of which is the arts.

Table 11.4: *The arts in the National Curriculum, Northern Ireland*

Art and design	Children observe and respond to things they have seen and done, investigate colour, lines, shape, texture and patterns, use a variety of materials and develop their own ideas using different materials.
Music	Children learn to use instruments, sing, perform and work creatively with sound.
Drama	Children learn to develop their own creativity through imaginative play, use drama to express themselves freely and to extend their learning.

Find out

Obtain a copy of the EYFS or the equivalent framework for your home country. Look at the creative development aspect. It will really help you further on in this unit.

1.2 Supporting art, drama and music skills

Effective support of activities and experiences will reinforce and extend children's understanding and learning. The role of the adult is crucial in the support process: your ability to recognise what level of support you give during activities can make a difference to the success of the learning opportunity.

The role the adult plays is interchangeable throughout and will very much depend on the needs of the child and the activity they are involved in.

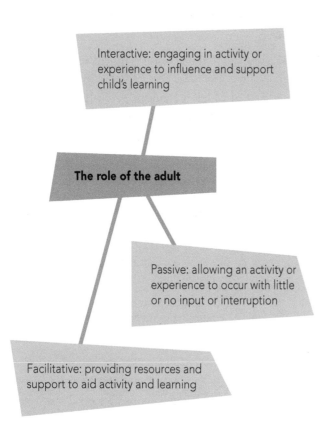

Interactive: engaging in activity or experience to influence and support child's learning

The role of the adult

Passive: allowing an activity or experience to occur with little or no input or interruption

Facilitative: providing resources and support to aid activity and learning

Figure 11.1: *The role of the adult*

Tables 11.5, **11.6** and **11.7** provide you with examples of the roles you can adopt in supporting art, drama and music.

Table 11.5: *Practitioner's role in supporting art*

	Art: Lewis is in the reception class. He is sitting at the junk box modelling table surrounded by a variety of cartons and tubes. He has decided he is going to make a dragon.
Passive	Let Lewis have control of the activity with little intervention – you may be just supervising to ensure his safety.
Facilitative	You may be responding to Lewis's request to help him make his dragon's head stick on! As there is no sticky tape on the table you go to the office to get him some.
Interactive	You sit at the table with Lewis throughout the activity and talk with him about what he is going to make and how he thinks he can do it.

Table 11.6: *Practitioner's role in supporting drama*

	Drama: the children are going to put together a dance to perform at parents' assembly about their learning.
Passive	You allow the children to listen to the music and interpret it in any way they choose without offering ideas or direction.
Facilitative	You provide the children with props and direction to help their dance come to life.
Interactive	You join in the dance with the children and encourage them to express themselves in a variety of ways. You may participate in discussion about what will and will not work in the assembly.

Table 11.7: *Practitioner's role in supporting music*

	Music: during group time the children, aged 3 to 4, ask to sing their favourite songs.
Passive	You invite them to sing their favourite songs then just sit back and listen.
Facilitative	You talk to the children about whose turn it is to choose a song and help them along the way when they forget the words!
Interactive	You sing along with the children, encouraging everyone's involvement, and introduce actions to liven up the session.

So what does this mean?

To support children effectively it is important to:

- know what level of assistance children require
- show that you find the activities interesting and engaging
- question what children say and do to reinforce and extend learning
- praise and encourage children's efforts and achievements
- ensure what you plan is appropriate and achievable
- make activities and experiences come alive with props and resources.

Reflect

Think about the last time you were working with children. Perhaps you were supervising an art activity or involved in a music session. What role did you play during this activity? Can you think of what else you could have done to improve the learning experience of the children?

1.3 Benefits of developing art, drama and music skills

In addition to the sheer enjoyment of art, drama and music activities there are many benefits for young children that not only help in the development of creativity and expression but also many other aspects and areas of their learning. These areas are:

- **imagination:** forming new ideas that can be real or fantasy
- **cognitive skills:** developing a growing understanding of the concepts they have been exposed to
- **problem solving:** helping them to consider how they can overcome an obstacle, for example, finding the best way to stick feathers to a box
- **uniqueness:** helping to identify them as an individual, perhaps through the way they choose to create a collage
- **fine motor skills:** using tools in art, developing use of scissors, playing musical instruments
- **language:** using words and conversation to describe what they see, hear, smell and touch
- **social skills:** joining in conversation and activity with others, participating in roles
- **focusing:** building skills of concentration as they take time to complete a painting or play their part in a drama piece
- **listening:** following instructions or even using their listening skills to recognise or distinguish a piece of music.

From the few examples given you can see the many benefits of creative activities for children's holistic development. Children gain so much from their engagement in art, drama and music that extends way beyond the boundaries of the creative aspect of the curriculum.

Table 11.8 shows how creative activities and play can aid children's play and learning across the prime and specific areas of the EYFS.

In what ways could this activity benefit the child?

Table 11.8: *Creativity across other areas of learning in the EYFS*

Prime areas of learning	Personal, social and emotional development	Through art, music and drama activities children are able to develop a positive sense of themselves as they indulge in free expression. Dancing to a piece of music, creating a collage or taking part in role play allow children to explore who they are and express this.
	Physical development	Through dance children can learn to coordinate and move their body to develop their gross motor skills. Creative activities allow them to explore materials and textures through their senses including touch and enable children to manage and use tools such as scissors and pencils to develop their fine motor skills.
	Communication and language	All activities provide children with the opportunity to speak and to listen. Singing songs and rhymes develops language skills and introduces children to new words. During imaginative play children will often communicate their thoughts and ideas to others, giving a narrative about what they are doing and what will happen next.
Specific areas of learning	Literacy	Mark making and using different tools to create paintings and drawing can help to develop hand/eye coordination which is essential for children's writing. A language-rich environment exposes children to the written meaning of words; labels for art areas and equipment help with early reading. Sharing books with songs, rhymes and stories in them will also develop the children's interest in reading materials.
	Mathematics	Children learn to make connections in their play; any art activity will help children with problem-solving skills which aid mathematical understanding. Children learn about materials and their properties. They can also learn about weight, shape and mass and explore 2D and 3D shapes.
	Understanding the world	Children gain a greater understanding of the world around them through their play. For example, they find out about how things work through the use of technology in dance and drama. Role play can help them understand and play out real-life experiences.

Case study: imaginary play

The manager of the pre-school has noticed that there are a lot of equipment and toys available for children's physical play in the garden but there is little provision for children to get involved in imaginary play. Having watched the children at play, Preeti has noticed they like playing out the story of Goldilocks and the three bears, which has been part of their learning and story time this week. Preeti discusses this with the manager and agrees it would be a good idea to set up the three bears' cottage in the garden. The children help by finding the equipment around the nursery for the cottage, including the right number and size of bears. Now that the playhouse at the bottom of the garden has been transformed into the house of the three bears, it is ready for action.

1 Why do you think the children were eager to be involved in setting up the cottage?

2 How can this activity help children to be imaginative?

3 What is the role of the adult during imaginary play?

4 What other specific and prime areas of learning might you identify in this activity?

Reflect

Think about an art, music or drama session you have recently supported in your setting. What was the learning intention identified for this activity? What other areas of learning do you think this activity also covered? What evidence do you have to show this?

Assessment activity
1.1, 1.2, 1.3

1 Produce a chart summarising children's learning in art, drama and music using your understanding of the curriculum or framework in your country.

2 Make a list of the ways you support children during activities. Next to each one, explain in detail how this support takes place.

3 In pairs or small groups, conduct a questioning session to help you analyse the benefits of developing art, drama and music skills for children. Share and discuss your findings with the class.

2 Understand learning needs of individual children and/or young people when supporting the development of art, drama and music

Children learn in many different ways. Before we can consider the way in which we plan and implement learning experiences, we must first establish how children best receive and interpret information to develop their own understanding and thinking.

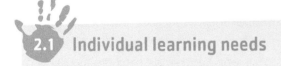

2.1 Individual learning needs

The EYFS recognises the uniqueness of each child and encourages practitioners to encompass this within the planning and delivery of art, drama and music activities. Children learn and develop at different rates. With this in mind it is important that you do not adopt a 'one size fits all' approach when planning children's learning as they all have individual learning needs.

How well you know the children in your care will be crucial in helping to identify their individual learning needs and understand their strengths and capabilities. A sound understanding of the sequences and stages of child development is also extremely important.

Learning styles

Just like adults children learn in different ways. You may be familiar with the following learning styles:

- **visual learners** learn best by seeing things such as handouts, diagrams or photographs
- **auditory learners** learn best through listening and prefer lectures or discussion
- **kinaesthetic learners** learn best through experiences and prefer to learn through games, puzzles and hands-on activities.

Just as learning does not occur in isolation, nor does any one learning style. Adults and children alike may have a predominant learning style that suits them best but we all learn using all our available senses, i.e. we respond to what we see, hear and do. The tables below look at three different learning styles: visual, auditory and kinaesthetic. They also give examples of the types of art, drama and music activities that would support these learning styles.

Table 11.9: *Understanding visual learners*

Visual learners gain valuable knowledge about their environment through their eyes. They gather information and learn through visually stimulating materials being presented to them. They learn from pictures and other visual resources.	
Art	Would find it easier to make something from paper craft if they have pictures showing clearly each stage of the process
Drama	Will be able to engage in puppet play having watched and followed the actions of others
Music	Can imitate the actions of others in music and movement and recall nursery rhymes and songs from picture cues

Table 11.10: *Understanding auditory learners*

Auditory learners gather information to aid their learning by listening and can draw on discussions and conversations with others. Auditory learners are able to develop their own creative ideas by interpreting what they have heard.	
Art	Can create their own collage by following a set of verbal instructions and talking about what they are going to do and what it will look like, for example, 'I am going to use the blue tissue paper for the duck pond just like you'
Drama	Can develop the use of their imagination by giving and responding to a narrative about how play will unfold; for example, 'I will be the mummy and you will be the baby who is going for a sleep'
Music	Can understand and interpret music through the lyrics and melody that is being listened to. May be able to describe in their own words what they have heard. For example, 'the twinkling sound is like a snowflake'

Table 11.11: *Understanding kinaesthetic learners*

Kinaesthetic learners learn best through hands-on experiences and 'doing' rather than listening or seeing. Children will find out how things work by taking them apart and putting them back together again. They will gain a greater understanding of creativity through hands-on experiences in art activities.	
Art	Are able to construct a model using materials such as clay or Plasticine if they have access to one already made so they can feel it and experience it first hand
Drama	May take part in imaginative play when they have observed others at play and then become engrossed and learn from experiencing it for themselves
Music	Touching and exploring musical instruments to help them gain a greater understanding of what they do and the sounds they make

As well as considering the learning styles of children you should also think about children with a **sensory impairment** and how they can be supported to benefit from art, drama and music activities. Working with colleagues and parents can help you gain a greater insight into children's needs and abilities. By doing this you will be able to plan more effectively to ensure their engagement and enjoyment.

A child's learning style may be affected by other contributing factors such as a specific learning need. To ensure that you know what these needs are you must work collaboratively with colleagues, parents and sometimes outside agencies. **Early intervention** strategies can be the key to success when it is identified that a child needs extra support to enable them to access the curriculum. Intervention can come from a range of sources, from those within the setting itself to support from outside agencies (their specialism and knowledge can help a child with a specific learning need). For a child this has endless benefits: not only are they able to access activities and experiences alongside their peers but, with added support, they are more likely to achieve, bringing an increase in confidence and self-esteem.

Key terms

Sensory impairment – describes a condition where there may be a loss or restriction of a child's vision, hearing or sense of taste, smell or touch.

Early intervention – the process of identifying and addressing the specific needs of a child as soon as possible.

2.2 Benefits of acknowledging learning needs

The EYFS has been successful in helping practitioners to recognise the importance of valuing each child as an individual. It also acknowledges that this stretches beyond their physical needs and incorporates their learning needs too. The key person approach identified within the framework recognises the part that this plays in helping a child to develop a settled relationship. It also helps the practitioner develop relationships with the child and their family so their individual needs can be successfully identified and met.

Effective practitioners are those that spend time identifying their key children's learning needs and planning and providing appropriate art, drama and music activities that meet these needs. When needs are met, the child, the practitioner and the setting benefit.

The child

Firstly, and most importantly, it is the child who benefits greatly from a practitioner's clear identification and acknowledgement of their learning needs.

If art, drama and music activities are planned and implemented with the individual needs of the child at the core, children are more likely to:

- be interested in the activity
- be engaged in what they are doing

- be able to achieve
- be able to make connections and develop their understanding
- be able to enjoy what they are doing
- feel valued and enjoy a sense of belonging.

The practitioner

Every practitioner benefits when they have planned effectively to meet the individual learning needs of children. Benefits include:

- an increased understanding of the individual needs of the children
- the development of better relationships with children when their needs are met
- a greater understanding of how to identify specific and individual needs
- the development of effective strategies to support specific and individual learning needs.

The setting

The setting can also benefit greatly as acknowledging and supporting individual needs demonstrates that the setting:

- works in an inclusive way
- understands that each child is unique
- supports staff to acknowledge and provide for the individual needs of children.

Case study: understanding a learning style

Jessica is 4 years old and has been asked by the nursery teacher if she would like to make a rainforest animal collage for the wall display. Eagerly, Jessica makes her way to the art area where she has access to a variety of materials. But this is a new topic and there is no other artwork for her to look at. Jessica stares blankly at the teacher, not knowing what to do next.

1 Why do you think Jessica did not know what to do?
2 What type of learner do you think Jessica is?
3 What could the teacher have done to address her learning style?

Assessment activity 2.1, 2.2

1 Create a poster which explains the potential individual needs for visual, auditory and kinaesthetic learners in relation to art, drama and music.

2 Produce a handout to share with your group that summarises the benefits of acknowledging individual learning needs in order to identify support.

3 Be able to plan and implement art, drama and music activities for children and/or young people

You should have already studied units CYP 3.2 and EYMP 2 in the Children and Young People's Workforce Diploma framework. If you have, you will already have some knowledge and skills to help you plan and implement activities effectively. Having looked at the EYFS requirements for art, drama and music, and the ways in which you can support children's learning, you can now consider how best to plan activities and experiences.

3.1 Planning activities and experiences

Before moving on to develop a plan, make sure you are equipped with as much information as possible that will help you make your plan achievable in the workplace.

Your growing understanding of children's learning and development will be crucial in deciding exactly what goes into your plan.

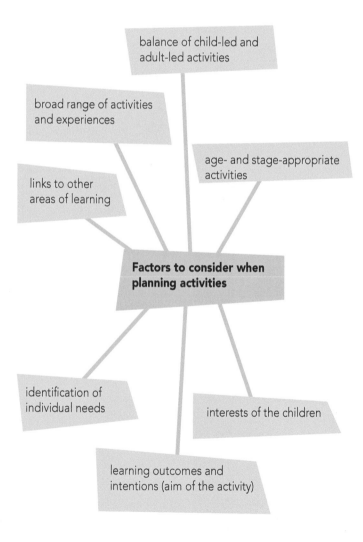

Figure 11.2: *Factors to consider when planning activities*

Case study: successful planning

Martin has been asked by his room supervisor to change the sensory play area to recapture the children's interest. He decides to begin by talking to the children about what they would like.

The children Martin works with are all aged 4 and going to school next term. He sits with a group of children at the sensory tray which is currently filled with coloured rice and pots and scoops for pouring. Martin asks the children what else they could put in the tray. They are full of ideas which they can not wait to share. Martin writes down all of their ideas. At the end of the conversation they have a long list which includes jelly, foam soap, cooked spaghetti, gloop, bubbles, sawdust and cornflakes.

Martin pins the ideas on the wall and explains to the children they will work with each of these materials in turn. Starting with the jelly, Martin develops a plan that involves the children making the jelly before adding it to the sensory tray. Having asked the children what other items they would like to go into the jelly play, Martin and the children add the plastic dinosaurs that they have decided will live in jelly land! The children enjoy exploring dinosaur jelly land for the entire week (with new jelly regularly supplied). They enjoy lots of imaginary play, deciding what is happening in dinosaur jelly land each day.

1 What was Martin's approach to planning?
2 Why was this so successful?
3 Why do you think the children enjoyed this activity so much?

The interests of the children

The case study above demonstrates the benefits of engaging children in planning their own learning. Practitioners take a lot of time and care over gathering evidence to inform their planning – but they often overlook just simply talking to the children about what they want to do. It is important that you ask children this and ensure that they can see that their views, ideas and opinions count by following through and enabling their ideas to be realised.

A broad range of activities and experiences

It is easy to adopt the philosophy of 'If it isn't broken don't fix it'. However, this can create a culture of fixed ideas and approaches to the activities provided in the setting. In turn, practitioners may lack motivation and innovation in their approach to planning. Children will lack exposure to creativity and the scope within this if there is a limited range of activities available. Imagine if you worked in a setting where the creative area consisted of only a paint easel, water tray and sand tray – you would become just as bored as the children.

The following spider diagrams give you some ideas you could consider using. While these provide you with a limited number of examples, your time spent in the workplace should create an anthology of ideas that will stay with you for a very long time. When carrying out activities, make sure you are aware of any allergies children may have to certain foods or substances.

CP11

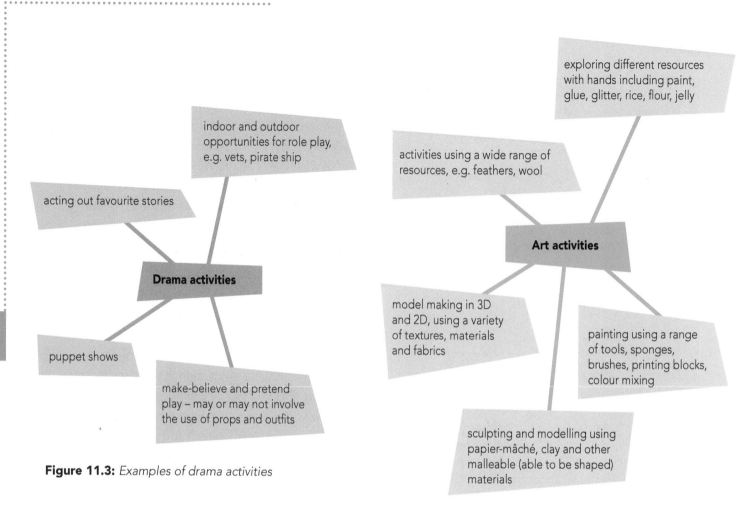

indoor and outdoor opportunities for role play, e.g. vets, pirate ship

acting out favourite stories

Drama activities

puppet shows

make-believe and pretend play – may or may not involve the use of props and outfits

Figure 11.3: *Examples of drama activities*

exploring different resources with hands including paint, glue, glitter, rice, flour, jelly

activities using a wide range of resources, e.g. feathers, wool

Art activities

model making in 3D and 2D, using a variety of textures, materials and fabrics

painting using a range of tools, sponges, brushes, printing blocks, colour mixing

sculpting and modelling using papier-mâché, clay and other malleable (able to be shaped) materials

Figure 11.4: *Examples of art activities*

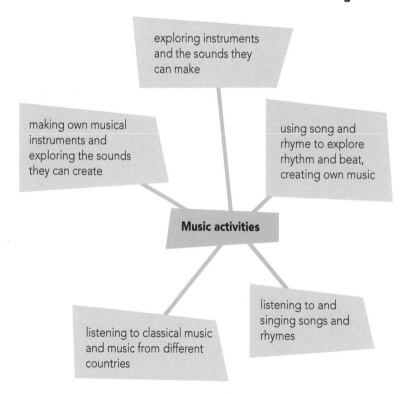

exploring instruments and the sounds they can make

making own musical instruments and exploring the sounds they can create

using song and rhyme to explore rhythm and beat, creating own music

Music activities

listening to classical music and music from different countries

listening to and singing songs and rhymes

Figure 11.5: *Examples of music activities*

Age- and stage-appropriate activities

Some of the ideas identified will be more suitable for some age groups than others. For example, it would be unreasonable to expect a young baby to take part in a 3D model-making activity! Providing activities that are not appropriate for the age and stage of the children you work with has implications for their safety – and it can also lead to them being set up to fail. Any activity provided should be within the realms of possibility while providing the opportunity to extend and challenge children's skills and capabilities. Children are more likely to engage in activities that are suited to their age and stage of development. They are also more likely to see the process through rather than walking away from the activity.

Balance of child-led and adult-led activities

Children are more likely to engage with an activity if it is of some interest to them and when they can exercise some element of control over what they do. It is therefore very important that you consider why you have chosen the activity or experience you intend to implement. If you have picked an idea from the air with little thought about how interesting it will be for the children, the likelihood is that it will not engage them.

However, while it is important to use the children's interests as the basis of the planning cycle, there will also be a need for adult-initiated activities. This is particularly relevant when you have a specified learning intention that would benefit from adult initiation, and when planning activities and experiences that require higher levels of supervision.

Identification of individual needs

Individual needs can refer to both the learning style and the specific learning needs or disabilities of a child. It is important that an inclusive approach is adopted in the planning process and that differentiation strategies are employed to ensure the involvement of all. When considering the individual needs of the children in your care, you must also consider the role of the adult in ensuring differentiation strategies are used.

Learning outcomes and intentions

The EYFS practice guidance details the prime and specific areas of learning which the children should be working towards. Settings make clear links between the development matters statements within each area of learning and their planned activities and experiences; this helps them to think about their role during the activity and the level of support that is given to each child. It can also help with future observations and assessments of individual children as their responses to the activities and experiences can be recorded.

Links to other areas of learning

Although specific aims may be identified for activities, the value of learning across more than one area of the EYFS should be highlighted to demonstrate the holistic nature of development. Learning never occurs in isolation and any activity or experience can hold many benefits for young children across all the areas of learning. Your role is to identify where the strongest links can be made and how you ensure these are promoted in the delivery of the experiences you provide for the children.

Case study: the wider benefits of role play

The role play area in Sunny Side Pre-school has been set up this week as a flower shop. The children have spent much time playing the role of the customers and the shop owner. The area is equipped with an abundance of paper flowers the children have made, as well as silk flowers and fresh flowers they bought on a visit to the local florist.

The learning objectives that the staff identified for this activity included encouraging children to engage in imaginative play and role play based on their experiences.

Having observed the children at play throughout the week, they see the value this has had for other areas of learning.

1 Give an example of how this activity may develop children's communication and language.

2 What other aspect of children's learning and development may have been enhanced by this activity?

Find out

Take a look at the planning format used in your setting. Try to identify within it:

- a broad range of activities and experiences
- age- and stage-appropriate activities
- a balance of child-led and adult-led activities
- identification of individual needs
- learning outcomes and intentions (aims of the activity).

Case study: planning an activity

Neil is an assistant in the pre-school room. He has produced the following plan for a creative activity in the setting.

Activity	Making sound shakers with small groups and using these to accompany music
Learning Intention	To explore different sounds of instruments and to move rhythmically
Links to EYFS	To develop their own ideas through selecting and using materials and working on the processes that interest them
Resources needed	Boxes and containers, scissors, glue, string and tape, different dried foods – e.g. lentils, peas, rice for children to choose sounds – materials to decorate shakers from creative area (feathers, glitter, paper, cellophane, sweet wrappers)
Adult role	Ensure supervision of children using tools, encourage conversation and introduce key words about the sounds their shakers make, questions: 'What makes a loud sound?' 'Which item makes a softer sound?' Encourage problem solving: 'How can you make that stick together?'
Differentiation strategies	AB: provide left-handed scissors for activity. EF: Use picture cue cards to help understanding of activity (show him one I have made).

Figure 11.6: *Neil's activity plan*

Discuss with a colleague and point out where you think Neil has:

- a clear aim for his activity
- recognised individual needs
- identified how this relates to other areas of learning.

Assessment activity 3.1

Look at the planning of the setting then discuss with your supervisor and identify an appropriate art, drama and music activity that will fit in with the current planning that you can do.

Make sure you identify:

- what activity you propose to do
- the aim of the activity (what you expect the children to learn)
- how the plan meets the individual needs of children in the setting
- how the activity develops other areas of learning. Give at least one example.

3.2 Implementing art, drama and music activities

In your workplace, practitioners should work collaboratively to provide a broad and balanced framework of activities and experiences to develop children's art, drama and music. Good communication between colleagues will mean that everyone knows what is expected of them and what they should be doing at any given time. If you have been involved in planning specific activities, it may be that you are the adult who will support children during implementation; you will therefore have a good understanding of why the activity has been provided and what you hope the children will learn and achieve from their involvement. However, if the activity has been planned by a colleague, you must ensure that clear dialogue has taken place so that you know what is expected of you during the activity. It is always important to refer to the planning too. The factors to consider for the successful implementation of activities are listed below.

- **Number of children involved:** when planning an activity you must consider the amount of children involved as this will inevitably affect the support and time you can give each child. Also the nature of the activity can often determine if it is best suited to an individual or group of children.
- **Complexity and duration of activity:** the level of support you need or hope to give can be decided by the activity itself. Something intricate such as model making may need a lot of input, resources and support – for example, using equipment such as scissors may need one-to-one support. Activities that are too time-consuming can mean children lose interest in what they are doing.
- **Ratio of adults:** the level of involvement and support you can give children will be determined by the amount of adults you have to support you. Ensuring ratios are adhered to, and communicating with colleagues about your intentions and how you would like to see the children supported, will mean there is less likelihood that you will be distracted from your supporting role.
- **Resource implications:** you can become mesmerised by the wide variety of materials available in resource catalogues, but materials cost and you must choose carefully to ensure you do not overstretch your setting's budget. This is where your ability, skill and innovation come into play. Think of ways in which you can collate a bank of resources so that cost does not become an obstacle to a well-resourced setting.

So what does this mean?

Think of ways in which you can build your resources in the setting.

- Recycle, recycle, recycle! Keep all those washed-out bottles and cartons.
- Are there any parents or carers who work for a supplier and can negotiate a good deal for you?
- Is there a local fabric shop that can provide the setting with remnants of materials?
- Do not be wasteful; encourage children to do the same.
- Recycling centres can provide resources at little cost. Find out if there is one in your area.

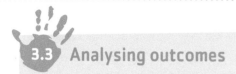

3.3 Analysing outcomes

Analysing outcomes is essential in helping you to evaluate the activities and experiences you have implemented for the children in your care. To do this effectively you will need to consider what was happening in relation to children's learning. Your skills of observation will help you with this – use the information from what you have seen to decide if you have achieved what you set out to do.

Look at your planning sheet and read through the learning intentions you identified for the activity; consider the following questions.

- Why did you choose to do this activity in the first place?
- What did you hope the children would gain from their involvement in this activity?

Then ask:

- Did I achieve my original aim? How do I know this?
- What did the children gain from their involvement in this activity?
- What happened that I did not anticipate happening?

Case study: observing for a purpose

Shona is a learner on placement at a pre-school setting. She has been asked by an early years practitioner to sit at the table where children are involved in a collage activity and make some observations. As she watches the children, who are engrossed in what they are doing, she is unsure about what information she should be recording.

1 What could the early years practitioner have done to ensure Shona recorded some valuable observations?

2 What could Shona have done to help her understand what she should be recording?

Find out

Using the questions identified above, choose a creative activity you have recently undertaken with the children and provide answers. By doing this you are analysing the outcomes of the activity you have provided.

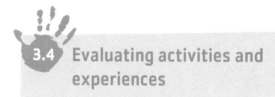

3.4 Evaluating activities and experiences

The evaluation process is crucial in identifying which activities and experiences work in the setting and which ones do not. There is a wide range of factors to consider when evaluating the activities, some of which are evident in the planning process and have been discussed previously. We have also looked at how questioning helps us to analyse the outcomes of activities.

The success of activities can be measured by the children's response and engagement – it will help you to identify future considerations for practice. You would not repeat something that proved to be wholly unsuccessful in practice and failed to capture the imagination and engagement of the children.

Key terms

Analysing – breaking down the outcomes and examining each part.

Evaluation – the process of reviewing what has happened using different perspectives, including those of others.

Case study: when an activity does not work

Carrie planned to make papier-mâché pigs in the toddler room for their display about 'Who's on the farm?'. She planned the activity well and had adequate resources to make the papier-mâché. Carrie invited children to join her at the table and encouraged them to rip strips of paper to paste to balloons. The children lost interest in the activity and Carrie continued to cover the balloons in papier-mâché. The following day, Carrie asked the children if they would like to add another layer of papier-mâché to the now dried balloons. None of the children wanted to revisit the activity and Carrie was left to complete the papier-mâché pigs herself.

1 Why do you think the children lost interest in this activity?

2 How could Carrie adapt this creativity session to engage the children's interests?

By evaluating activities and experiences, you can consider adaptations and changes to make activities a success in the future. Ask yourself a series of questions to help you in the evaluation process.

Questions can include:

- Did the children get involved in the activity?
- How long did they stay at the activity?
- Did any children avoid or refuse to join in the activity?
- Did the children enjoy what they were doing?
- How much support did they need during the activity?
- Did they understand what they were doing?

Reflect

When planning your next art, drama or music activity, make a list of questions that you can answer at the end of the activity to help you in the evaluation process. Look again at the questions on the left – you may wish to use some of these. Can you think of other questions you can ask yourself? Add them to your list.

Find out

How does your work setting evaluate activities and experiences? You may wish to talk this through with your workplace supervisor. Take time to read the evaluations they have written. What key information have you found in these?

Assessment activity 3.2, 3.3, 3.4

Having implemented planned activities for art, drama and music, take time to write:

1 an analysis of the outcome of each activity for children's learning

2 your own evaluation for each activity, showing how it relates to the aim and one other area of learning.

4 Be able to reflect on own practice

Throughout your studies, much time will be given to the process of reflection. Reflecting on practice gives you the opportunity to evaluate the way in which you work and analyse what you have said and done, and helps you to consider future implications for practice. Reflection also gives you valuable information about the effectiveness of activities and experiences you have provided and helps in adapting and improving the provision you offer.

4.1 Reflecting on the planning process

When planning experiences and activities for children it is almost impossible to know beforehand how individuals will respond to them. Children are not textbook cases and will not fit into a box when it comes to pinpointing exactly how they will respond to art, music and drama activities.

Reflecting on the process will help you to identify if it has been a successful tool for the delivery of activities. If it is not, you can reflect on how to adapt it to best meet the needs of the children, staff and setting.

The best plans are works in progress which are added to or altered on a daily basis. This clearly shows that practitioners are moving with the needs of the children and are continually reflecting on practice and seeking better ways of working.

Reflect

Take a look at a plan used recently in your setting. Identify some of the creative activities (art, drama, music) documented on the plan. What adaptations were made to the plan during the week? Why were these adaptations made? What does this tell you about the setting's approach to planning?

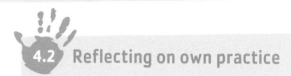

4.2 Reflecting on own practice

Reflecting on your own practice helps you to identify if the activity or planned experience went well, if it needs changing and how you might go about this. Reflection is a learned skill and does not always come naturally; time and experience will help you to become more reflective in your practice. An effective practitioner is one who never ceases to question the effectiveness of what they do and consider improved ways of working and how to achieve them.

Key term

Reflection – giving due thought and consideration to something you have said or done.

evaluate the effectiveness of resources used

identify if the activity was age-appropriate

Reflection will help you to...

consider how you can extend and refine future practice

examine your role in supporting the activity

determine if you achieved what you set out to

Figure 11.7: *The benefits of reflecting on your own practice*

So what does this mean?

To help you reflect on your own practice, consider the following points.

- Make sure you have understood the aim of the activity – this will help you to question what happened.
- Record key information about children's responses and the learning occurring during the activity.
- Be aware of what you are doing and saying throughout.
- Question yourself: How did it go? Did I achieve my aim? How do I know this?

4.3 Drawing conclusions

By drawing conclusions you can think about what happens next. If the activity was an absolute disaster you will already know that you do not want to repeat this experience; you will need to consider what changes you should make to ensure the activity is a success in the future.

If the activity went well, and you achieved your intended aim, you can think about how to extend future practice to benefit children's learning.

Conclusions can be drawn in a number of ways. Many settings:

- choose to record written evaluative information on their weekly plans to help consider future practice
- complete learning journeys or stories for each child in the setting and may record individual next steps to help them plan for the child's learning
- keep their own learning journey with photographs to show evidence of the range and scope of activities they have provided for children and the benefits they have for learning and development.

Drawing conclusions will help you to do the following.

- **Plan for the children's next steps:** the children's responses to activities and your understanding of their stage of development will help you decide what comes next for each child. You can then plan activities to extend their creativity and understanding of art, music and drama using the evidence which shows you where they are at.
- **Identify training needs of staff:** when you are drawing conclusions and evaluating practice, you may be able to recognise your own weaknesses or lack of understanding in a particular area of practice. Sometimes this only comes to light when you have reflected on your own role in supporting children's learning and development. This is an ideal opportunity to target training needs and seek appropriate training to develop your skills and understanding.
- **Examine resources:** conclusions will help you to consider how the environment and the resources within it have impacted on the activities in the setting. Perhaps changes need to be made to the layout of the setting to encourage the participation of all children. Or perhaps an overhaul of the resources will encourage creativity and expression.

Assessment activity
4.1, 4.2, 4.3

Look back at the planning for each of your art, drama and music activities, then write a report that will show:

- how well each activity went and if you achieved your original aim
- what the children learned and enjoyed
- what you did during the activity and how this helped children's learning
- what could be done in the future – what could you change or do differently and why?

In the real world

CP11

I am currently on work placement at my local nursery and I'm enjoying working in the pre-school room. A couple of weeks ago my manager talked to me about the following week's planning which involved activities to celebrate Chinese New Year. Activities included making dragon puppets and dragon dances in a music and movement session. I asked for a copy of the planning so I could take it home and read it over the weekend.

The following week I supported the dragon puppet craft session, ensuring the children had access to a wide variety of resources and materials to create their own dragons. Throughout the activity I sat at the children's level and talked to them about what they were doing with the materials they were using and how to solve problems such as sticking boxes together. The children engaged in the activity until they had completed their puppets. I praised and encouraged the children throughout with comments such as, 'Wow – that looks great! He's a colourful dragon!' With the dragon puppets made, I, my colleagues and the children danced and moved to the dragon music. I encouraged the children to use their whole bodies to move and respond to the rhythm and beat of the music by demonstrating what they could do. Squeals of delight and a room full of moving dragons showed these activities were successful.

My skills were instrumental in these activities being a success because I took the time to read and understand the aims of the activities and how they could be achieved with the support of the adults. I also knew what language to use to engage the children's interest in what they were doing and used questioning to help them through the problem-solving process. Taking time over the weekend to consider how to support the children really helped. Finally the children enjoyed dancing to the music because I got involved in the dance too!

Check your knowledge

1 Where can you find guidance on requirements for supporting children and young people's development of art, drama and music in your home nation?

2 Name the three roles practitioners play in supporting children's art, drama and music.

3 List ways in which you can support children's art, drama and music.

4 What are the benefits of developing art, drama and music?

5 Why is it important to acknowledge the learning needs of children?

6 What factors should you take into account when planning art, drama and music activities?

7 Why is the role of the adult important in the implementation of activities?

8 What does it mean to analyse outcomes?

9 What information do you use to evaluate activities and experiences?

10 Why is the evaluation process important?

Further references

The following are sources of useful information on the topic of supporting children and young people's development of art, drama and music.

Books and articles

Beckerleg, T. (2008) *Fun with Messy Play*, London: Jessica Kingsley Publishers

Drake, J. (2009) *Planning for Children's Play and Learning*, London: David Fulton Publishers

Elkind, D. (2008) *The Power of Play*, Massachusetts: Da Capo Lifelong

Matterson, E. (2010) *This Little Puffin*, London: Penguin

Tassoni, P. (2008) *Practical EYFS Handbook*, Oxford: Heinemann

Tassoni, P. et al. (2010) *Level 3 Diploma Children and Young People's Workforce Candidate Handbook*, Oxford: Heinemann

Wilson, R. (2007) *Nature and Young Children*, London: Routledge

Useful websites

To obtain a secure link to the websites below, visit www.pearsonhotlinks.co.uk and search for this book by using its title or ISBN. Click on the section for CP11.

Education Scotland's website includes details of the Curriculum for Excellence and guidance on the Early Years Framework

The official website for Northern Ireland's National Curriculum

The official website of the Welsh government – a link will take you to education and skills

The official website of England's Department for Education

The official website of the National Literacy Trust

Learning about planning for given frameworks or curricula

CP13

This unit will help you to gain an understanding of planning for children and young people's learning within given frameworks. You will explore why a framework or curricula is required and why it is important to follow it. By exploring a variety of different models, you will gain an understanding of how to support children and young people's learning, and be able to plan suitable activities linked to an identified curriculum or framework.

Learning outcomes

By the end of this unit you will:

1 Understand the rationale for working within given frameworks or curricula

2 Understand a range of models used when planning for children and/or young people's learning

3 Be able to plan to a framework or curriculum.

In practice

Andy is on his work placement at Bunnies Pre-school. One of the requirements of his course is to plan an activity for the children. Andy is worried about this because he is not sure that the pre-school staff do any planning. All the children appear to do whatever interests them and the adults seem to just play with them and take notes.

Andy really likes the pre-school and the children always seem very happy and busy. They all appear to be very skilled in different areas and are developing well.

Each child has a file that staff update daily. Andy wonders if the files might contain the plans for each session.

By the end of this unit you will have a good idea about the type of planning that Andy's pre-school uses and an awareness of the possible model of planning this follows.

1 **Understand the rationale for working within given frameworks or curricula**

1.1 **Identifying different frameworks or curricula**

Young children, children and young people require different curricula or frameworks because they are working at different levels.

The curriculum framework for young children might focus on building essential skills to support the young child's attitude and **disposition to learn**. This will help them to be better learners in the future. Young people spend a long time acquiring the knowledge and skills they will need to equip them for adult life. Therefore, their curriculum will be based around building upon their existing knowledge and supporting them to have the information they need for formal testing, such as GCSEs or A levels.

This unit will focus on the curriculum for England, but it is important to have an awareness of the curriculum in other areas of the UK.

Scotland's Curriculum for Excellence

Children aged 3 to 18 years follow the Curriculum for Excellence in Scotland. It supports children to develop their capacity to become:

- successful learners
- confident individuals
- responsible citizens
- effective communicators.

The curriculum is separated into age levels: early, first, second, third and fourth and senior phase.

There are eight curriculum areas:

- expressive arts
- health and well-being
- languages

- mathematics
- religious and moral education
- sciences
- social studies
- technologies.

Younger children in Scotland are supported by the 'Pre-Birth to Three: Positive Outcomes for Scotland's Children and Families' guidance. This reflects the **ethos** of the Curriculum of Excellence and has four key principles:

- rights of the child
- relationships
- responsive care
- respect.

To find out more about the curriculum for children living in Scotland, look at Useful websites on page 291.

Key terms

Disposition to learn – this is a person's natural inclination or tendency to want to learn new things.

Ethos – the way in which things are run or the culture.

The National Curriculum in Wales

The curriculum covers children aged 3 to 19 years. It comprises the following areas:

- the Foundation Phase for children aged 3 to 7 years
- skills for development
- National Curriculum
- personal and social education
- sex education
- careers and the world of work
- religious education.

CP13

There are seven areas of learning:

- personal and social development, well-being and cultural diversity
- language, literacy and communication skills
- mathematical development
- Welsh language development
- knowledge and understanding of the world
- physical development
- creative development.

To find out more about the Welsh curriculum, look at Useful websites on page 291.

The National Curriculum in Northern Ireland

As with previous curriculums, children at the foundation level follow a slightly different curriculum. Areas of learning in the foundation level are:

- language and literacy
- mathematics and numeracy
- the arts
- the world around us
- personal development and mutual understanding
- physical development and movement.

As children move through the key stages they begin to study religious education, modern languages, environment and society, and science and technology.

Additionally, the curriculum also acknowledges the developing skills and capabilities of children across the curriculum areas. These are:

- communication
- using mathematics
- using ICT.

To find out more about the curriculum in Northern Ireland, look at Useful websites on page 291.

The National Curriculum in England

Young children

In 2008 it became a legal requirement in England for all those registered to provide care for children under the age of 5 years to follow the Early Years Foundation Stage (EYFS). The EYFS (2008) comprised two sections:

- welfare requirements
- learning and development requirements.

Everyone in the UK had to follow the welfare requirements, while the learning requirements applied only in England.

While few would argue with rigid rules about maintaining children's welfare, the learning and development requirements were not well received by all. Some felt that the EYFS was too rigid and would not allow parents to choose to raise their children according to the philosophies that they believed in. Childminders in particular were concerned how they would be able to deliver the requirements of the curriculum as effectively as a nursery or pre-school.

From September 2012 the revised EYFS framework reduced the number of 'benchmarks' or outcomes that children are expected to have mastered by the end of the Foundation Stage. These can be seen in **Table 13.1**.

Table 13.1: *The areas of the EYFS*

The three prime areas	Other areas
<ul><li>Communication and language</li><li>Personal, social and emotional development</li><li>Physical development</li></ul>	<ul><li>Literacy</li><li>Mathematics</li><li>Expressive arts and design</li><li>Understanding the world</li></ul>

Children

After the EYFS, children begin their formal schooling. The National Curriculum was introduced into primary education in 1989. The National Curriculum spans across all ages of compulsory schooling. It is currently under review and new draft programmes of study are likely to be taught in maintained schools from September 2013. Primary-aged children of 5 to 7 years follow the Key Stage 1 curriculum. Children aged 8 to 11 years follow the Key Stage 2 curriculum.

Table 13.2: *The subjects covered in Key Stages 1 and 2*

Core subjects	Foundation subjects
<ul><li>English</li><li>Mathematics</li><li>Science</li></ul>	<ul><li>Art and design</li><li>Design and technology</li><li>Geography</li><li>History</li><li>ICT</li><li>Music</li><li>Physical education</li></ul>

The main source of support for delivery of the primary curriculum is the Primary National Strategy. This includes:

- the primary framework for literacy and mathematics, which gives detailed guidance on planning and delivering these aspects of the primary curriculum
- guidance on promoting particular approaches to the delivery of the primary curriculum such as the free download *Letters and Sounds* which has promoted the use of synthetic phonics to support early reading
- guidance for other subjects, including the arts, ICT, modern foreign languages, music and physical education
- guidance on related whole school issues, including guidance on the 'Social and Emotional Aspects of Learning' (SEAL) and how to develop related skills among pupils.

Young people

Secondary school-aged young people between the ages of 11 and 14 follow the Key Stage 3 curriculum. Young people aged 14+ follow Key Stage 4.

Young people following the Key Stage 3 curriculum broadly study the same subjects as in the primary curriculum with the addition of citizenship and modern foreign languages. In Key Stage 4 learners make some choices about the subjects that they study, choosing from the arts, design and technology, humanities and modern foreign languages. They will also study English, mathematics, science, citizenship, ICT and physical education. Key Stage 3 and 4 schools must also provide teaching of religious education, sex and relationship education, and drugs and career education.

At the end of Key Stage 4 young people sit GCSEs or equivalent examinations.

The main source of support for delivery of the secondary curriculum is the Secondary National Strategy. It has three main categories of support:

- frameworks for English, mathematics, science and ICT

- pedagogic guidance for foundation subjects
- guidance on whole-school subjects such as behaviour, attendance and SEAL.

Key term

Pedagogic – this is the theory of teaching and can be related to different styles and approaches.

Although there are some differences between the organisation, age ranges and subjects covered by the curricula in the differing areas of the UK, the principles that underpin them remain much the same.

All equip children with the knowledge and skills they require to achieve success in learning. There is emphasis upon the role of quality practitioners and teachers delivering the curriculum and the importance of children's rights and individuality.

1.2 Why frameworks or curricula are required

The Education Act 1996 sets out the requirement for a National Curriculum for all children of compulsory school age. The Childcare Act 2006 sets out the requirement for all registered providers of care and education for children under the age of 5 to implement the Early Years Foundation Stage.

All maintained schools must provide a balanced and broad-based curriculum.

The curricula are designed to:

- promote the spiritual, moral, cultural, mental and physical development of children and young people
- prepare children and young people for the opportunities and responsibilities of adult life.

This uniform approach to education means that all children should receive broadly the same foundation of learning. The benefits of this are shown in **Figure 13.1**.

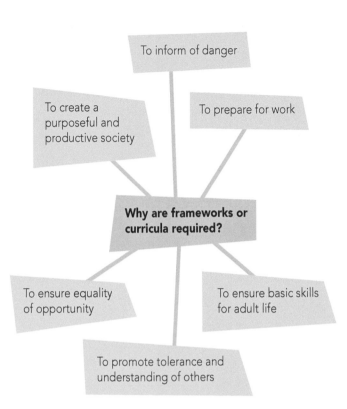

Figure 13.1: *Why frameworks are required*

1.3 The importance of adhering to frameworks and curricula

As you have read above, frameworks and curricula are required to ensure that all children and young people are taught the essential skills and knowledge they need to lead successful, independent adult lives and be responsible members of the society in which they live.

Establishing entitlement

All children and young people are entitled to a good standard of education. This is irrespective of the area where they live, the background they grow up in, whether they live in poverty or affluence and regardless of their gender, ethnicity or culture. Therefore, not following the curriculum in place could disadvantage some children or young people.

Establishing standards

When all children and young people learn broadly the same things, we are able to monitor their progress and make comparisons. Thus, regardless of what school you attend, both you and your teachers will have the same expectations. This information can then be used to monitor how well individual learners, groups or schools are doing. It helps to identify anyone who is not doing so well so that support can be put into place to help improve their opportunities for success. There could be inconsistencies in quality where the curricula or frameworks are not strictly adhered to.

Continuity and coherence

Children and young people make several transitions throughout their education. By adhering to frameworks and curricula, they will be prepared and equipped for each transition when they move between phases or schools or into further education.

Public confidence

It is important that everyone in society has confidence in schools and the results of compulsory education. This leads to parents, children and young people, further education establishments and potential future employers understanding what children and young people are learning or have learned.

Quality in early years

The Early Years Foundation Stage is seen as being particularly effective in making sure that all babies and young children receive the same standard of care. Although there may be differences in the delivery of the curriculum, the quality should be consistent.

Babies and young children might attend very different types of care ranging from a large day care setting to a childminder. Regardless of what type of care they attend, babies and young children will have the same standards of care and learning outcomes. The regulatory body Ofsted ensures that these standards are maintained by conducting inspections of all those who are registered to provide care and education for babies and young children and all school settings.

Find out

What curriculum or framework is followed in your work placement setting?

Discuss with your mentor what resources they use to support the delivery of the curriculum.

Assessment activity
1.1, 1.2, 1.3

Identify the frameworks or curricula which support learning for young children, children and young people.

Discuss why frameworks or curricula are required.

Explain why it is important that you adhere to and work within given frameworks or curricula.

2 Understand a range of models used when planning for children and/or young people's learning

Models can be used to monitor and evaluate how effectively planning is meeting children's individual learning needs. By adopting these approaches it can make it easier to track progress and confirm understanding.

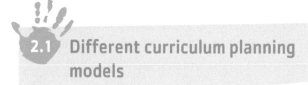

2.1 Different curriculum planning models

Different approaches are used to plan for curriculum activities. These serve a variety of different purposes, for example, to measure achievement, reflect upon effectiveness of the plans and make sure that children and young people are learning.

Bloom's taxonomy

This model was introduced by Benjamin S. Bloom (1913–99). The word 'taxonomy' simply means structure and although he used some fairly complicated words, Bloom's system is quite easy to follow.

Bloom developed his system to make sure that learning objectives could be planned and measured properly. He wanted to make sure that learning was actually taking place and that children and young people were not just recalling facts that had been given to them by their teacher. This is called rote learning – where facts can be recalled but without depth of understanding. For example, many people know that the Battle of Hastings was in 1066, but most do not know much else about the battle. It might be helpful knowledge in a quiz, but it is not much use if you need to answer an exam question about the subject.

Case study: Ayla's alphabet

Ayla is 2 years old and has just started to attend a childminder three days a week while her parents are at work. The childminder asked Ayla's parents about what she likes to do and what she is interested in. Her parents said that she knows all the letters of the alphabet and they want her to be suitably stimulated because she is very intelligent.

The childminder shares an alphabet book with Ayla and notices that she does not seem to recognise the letters or the sounds of letters. Later in the week Ayla starts singing the alphabet when her mother comes to collect her. Ayla's mother says that she also knows all the numbers up to ten because she can count up to ten.

1 Do you think that Ayla knows all the letters of the alphabet?

2 Why do you think that Ayla's parents believe she knows all the letters of the alphabet?

3 What explanation could you give for Ayla's knowledge of numbers and letters?

Bloom identified three domains (categories):
- cognitive domain – relating to thinking, capability and knowledge
- affective domain – relating to attitudes, feelings, emotions and behaviour
- psychomotor domain – relating to manual or physical skills.

Bloom suggested that each domain must be mastered before progressing on to the next.

He suggested that there were levels within each area and that there had to be progression through each level before learning fully took place.

Table 13.3: *A summary of Bloom's domains and levels*

Cognitive	Affective	Psychomotor
• Recalling data	• Awareness	• Copying
• Understanding	• Reacting	• Following instruction
• Applying	• Understanding or acting	• Developing precision
• Analysing	• Organising a personal value system	• Combining skills
• Synthesising (creating)	• Adopting behaviour	• Becoming an expert
• Evaluating		

This appears to be quite a complicated system to use in practice but it can be translated quite easily, as shown in the case study below.

Case study: Stanley's week

Stanley is 4 years old. He likes to watch the television in the morning while eating his breakfast. Each morning he watches a show in which a character sings the days of the week. Stanley starts to be able to sing the days of the week too.

Stanley's mum tells him what day of the week it is and what they do on that day.

Then, Stanley starts to recognise what activity he will do by the day of the week. He will say, 'We go swimming on Monday'.

Stanley will ask what is happening when there is a change to his routine, for example, if he does not go to pre-school because it is a bank holiday.

Stanley begins to know what day follows on from the next. He anticipates what activity he will do, or how many days he must wait for his favourite activities.

Finally, Stanley begins to understand that the days of the week remain unchanged, even when there are special events such as birthdays or Christmas which bring a change to his normal activities. He understands that the days, and not the activities, are the constant.

1 What domain has Stanley mastered?

2 Give an example of a child or young person mastering an activity using the psychomotor domain.

CP13

Affective domain

You can reflect upon the affective domain yourself by thinking about a time when you started a new school or college.

- You became aware of the school rules and expectations because you were told what they were (awareness).
- You followed those rules and expectations because you were told to (reacting).
- You knew the purpose of the rules and the consequences of not following them (understanding and acting).
- You might have reminded others of the rules or questioned whether the rules were fair (organising a personal value system).
- You may have decided that some rules were worth following and some were not (adopting behaviour).
- You might eventually know the rules and expectations so well that you could become a mentor to other students and be able to show them around and explain things for yourself.

Bloom's taxonomy can be applied to children's learning, as shown in **Figure 13.2**. Children and young people start at the bottom and work their way up to the top. This can be used to assess whether real learning is taking place.

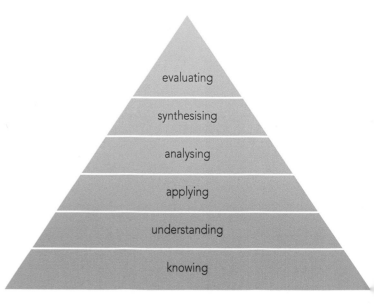

Figure 13.2: *Children and young people's learning (after Bloom*

Kirkpatrick's learning and training evaluation

Donald Kirkpatrick first developed a way of evaluating the effectiveness of training programmes in 1959 and continues to contribute to the development of workplace learning.

He separated this into four levels of measurement:

- reaction of the student – what they thought about the learning that took place
- learning – what they actually learned and how their knowledge has been expanded upon
- behaviour – how they behave and use what they have learned
- results – the effects that the learning has upon them and the wider environment.

Table 13.4: *How Kirkpatrick's model can be put into practice*

Area	Action	Method
Reaction	How the learners feel about what they have learned	A smiley face sheet could be used as an evaluation at the end of the lesson. Some settings use traffic light systems: red means 'I did not understand', orange means 'I think I get it' and green means 'I understand'.
Learning	Increasing of knowledge	This could be a formal test or quiz at the end of an activity. For example, learners must complete a practical test to confirm their knowledge at the end of a first aid course.
Behaviour	Applying the knowledge	This can be identified through observation and monitoring progress. Young people may apply their knowledge during a work placement.
Results	The effect of the knowledge	By gaining GCSEs, you can improve your chances of finding employment or going on to further education. Younger children might use the knowledge to create, such as being able to colour a picture by mixing different paints together to get the colour they need. This gives them a sense of achievement and their independence.

(Kirkpatrick Model courtesy of Kirkpatrick Partners, LLC. www.kirkpatrickpartners.com)

Although this is often applied to training in business establishments, it is a very effective way of measuring how much children and young people are learning and can be adapted to suit even quite young children.

Howard Gardner's multiple intelligence theory

Howard Gardner proposed the theory that there is more than one type of intelligence in his book *Frames of Mind* in 1983.

Table 13.5: *Gardner's intelligences*

Intelligence type	Capability and perception
Linguistic	Words and language
Logical – mathematic	Logic and numbers
Musical	Music, sound and rhythm
Bodily kinaesthetic	Body movement and control
Spatial – visual	Images and space
Interpersonal	Other people's feelings
Intrapersonal	Self-awareness

Gardner also went on to suggest that there might be more intelligences such as:

- naturalistic – the natural environment
- spiritual/existential – religion and ultimate issues
- moral – ethics and humanity.

Gardner explained that these intelligences are preferred ways of learning, behaving or working. They might also be seen as a person's natural strengths. He believed that by developing the areas of strength it would impact upon areas of weakness beneficially and develop learning.

Crucially, Gardner suggested that intelligence cannot be measured on a single scale, for example, with an IQ test. Instead, intelligence is a mixture of abilities.

The 'professional footballer' factor

The popular press has often portrayed professional footballers as not very intelligent people who are unable to express themselves. But their brilliance at football cannot be questioned;

Gardner would therefore suggest that they possess bodily kinaesthetic intelligence. However, this intelligence is not readily recognised by some who feel that, despite their great talent, they must prove themselves academically to be considered intelligent.

Intelligence is often viewed as good and unintelligence is viewed as bad. People who go on to achieve brilliant things can be judged as failures at school because a narrow definition is used to measure their intelligence. Society does not accept that intelligence is something that cannot be easily or accurately measured.

Reflect

- Do the assessment methods for the curriculum or framework used in your work placement recognise children's differing abilities and strengths?
- Are these valued in the same way as linguistic and logical-mathematic strengths?

Fleming's VARK model of learning preferences

The VARK model of learning preferences (Neil Fleming, 2001) is widely used to categorise learners' individual modal preferences. The model identifies four basic preferences for communication about learning:

Visual – visual learners learn best using charts, diagrams and other 'graphic' symbols.

Auditory – auditory learners learn best through listening, questioning and discussion.

Read/write – read/write learners learn best by reading and writing.

Kinaesthetic – kinaesthetic learners learn best through their own experiences and prefer to learn through simulations and hands on activities.

Teachers and tutors can use the VARK questionnaire to help learners to discover their learning preferences.

Table 13.6: *An example of the type of questions that might be asked in a learning style questionnaire*

When you set up a new mobile phone do you...	Read the instructions first	Listen to a friend tell you how it works	Have a go by trying it out
When needing travel directions do you...	Look at a map and follow the directions	Use a sat nav to be told where to go	Follow your instinct
When cooking a meal do you...	Follow a recipe from a cookery book	Ask a friend or relative for ideas and quantities	Add ingredients and taste as you go along
When choosing a holiday do you...	Read through reviews and brochures	Ask opinions of people	Imagine places in your mind where you would like to go
You are a...	**Visual learner**	**Auditory learner**	**Kinaesthetic learner**

Using the questions in **Table 13.6**, think about how you would respond and then highlight the appropriate box. Each section relates to the three different learning styles. Note that, if you compiled a questionnaire like this, it is better not to include the bottom row (so that the recipient is not led by the headings when answering). However, it is included here for your information.

When you have completed all the questions in the questionnaire, it would give you an indication of what your preferred style of learning is. Some people have a mixture of two styles.

The benefit of knowing learning styles

If you can ascertain each child's learning style you can plan activities that will help them to understand and learn in a way that best suits them. A teacher or tutor might plan a range of activities to cover all learning styles if they are aware that children in the class have a mixture of preferred styles. If most of the class are auditory learners the lessons might include lots of discussion rather than handouts and written information.

All young children are kinaesthetic learners and learn best by doing and being active. However, this does not mean that they do not benefit from also having written information, pictures and adults talking to them. This is important because they will develop their preferred style by being exposed to all different types of learning opportunities.

Figure 13.3: *People learn in a variety of ways.*

Differing approaches

It is a legal requirement in England for all those who are registered to provide care for young children to follow the welfare requirements of the Early Years Foundation Stage curriculum. However, some professional organisations can make an application to opt out of the learning and development requirements. This is usually because they follow a particular philosophy or approach.

Steiner Waldorf schools

The first Steiner school opened in 1919 in Stuttgart, for children of workers in a cigarette factory. Today, Steiner schools take children from 3 to 18 years. Steiner Early Childhood settings cater for children aged 3 to 7 years. There is no formal teaching in this age range because it is believed that children are not yet ready for it. This is very different from most schools in England which begin the Key Stage 1 curriculum at the age of 5.

Children do not access computers or television until they are in their early adolescence, as it is incompatible with the Steiner approach and not believed to benefit their development. Therefore, ICT does not form part of their curriculum. It could be argued that, in an increasingly technological age, this could disadvantage children in wider society.

The curriculum in Steiner schools has similarities and differences between mainstream schools. Children study the classics (Latin and Greek), although they will also study modern foreign languages too. They learn about ancient mythology in history and are encouraged to develop their spiritual well-being. Eurythmy is a subject exclusive to Steiner. Like Tai Chi, it is a kind of movement that engages the whole being of a person, not just their physical body.

There are around 20 Steiner schools in the UK. Older children sit GCSEs and A levels as they follow the National Curriculum alongside the Steiner curriculum.

Montessori approach

Maria Montessori opened her first 'Children's House' in Rome in 1907. The Montessori approach sees the adult directing children's learning but the children are actively involved in decision making and are encouraged to be independent by learning practical skills. (It could be viewed as less structured than the Steiner approach.)

The Montessori curriculum covers:

- foundations for learning and development of the whole personality
- skills for learning
- communication skills
- number concepts
- exploration of the wider world
- motor development
- general development.

It is generally viewed that the Montessori approach is compatible with the overarching aims of the Early Years Foundation Stage. Therefore, the two curriculums can sit comfortably together.

So what does this mean?

- An 'approach' is different from a curriculum or framework.
- Many schools which offer a different approach to education still broadly follow a traditional framework or curriculum.

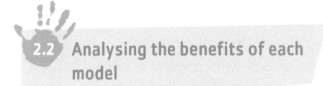

2.2 Analysing the benefits of each model

Each model has individual benefits in its ability to support children's learning. However, each might not be suited to all ages of children or might be difficult to implement in some settings.

Table 13.7 explores the benefits of each model and how it might be effectively used.

Table 13.7: The benefits of each planning model

Model	Benefits	Effective use
Bloom's taxonomy	<ul><li>This is very effective in discovering whether learning has taken place.</li><li>It can be applied to all ages from very young children to adults.</li><li>It can support children and young people to reach their full learning potential.</li></ul>	Bloom's taxonomy can be used in all settings from nurseries to senior schools, because it explores how well children and young people are learning. However, it is better applied to older children because there are too many factors that might influence young children's ability to be judged as achieving in the affective domain, such as tiredness, emotional unsettlement and hunger.

CP13

Table 13.7: *The benefits of each planning model (continued)*

Model	Benefits	Effective use
Kirkpatrick's learning and training evaluation	<ul><li>It places the child or young person's view of what they have learned as most important.</li><li>It helps learners to reflect and improve upon activities for learning.</li><li>It recognises that there are effects upon the environment and the individual so targets or new actions can be set.</li></ul>	The model works well to reflect upon an activity that has happened. As it is important to have feedback from those who are learning, they need to be of an age where they can give that opinion. This model is effective in supporting young people to feel empowered to take some control over their own learning.
Gardner's multiple intelligences theory	<ul><li>It recognises that all children and young people have a talent.</li><li>It can be used to engage and build upon children's and young people's strengths.</li><li>It promotes the idea that the testing of intelligence should use a variety of methods.</li></ul>	The model can be applied to children and young people of all ages. It can be used to empower and raise self-esteem. In a setting where young children are beginning to compare themselves and begin to be streamed into ability groups, it can be very effective in helping children to feel valued and accepted.
Fleming's VARK learning styles	<ul><li>The model helps learners identify their learning preferences</li><li>It allows for varied approaches to giving information and learning.</li><li>It is easy to assess preferred learning styles.</li></ul>	This model is very useful for all children and young people as it helps them to be better learners. This model translates best into schools where children and young people must learn the same thing at the same time, but will have different ways of understanding it.

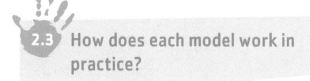

2.3 How does each model work in practice?

Although each model seems to be relatively straightforward in theory, actually putting each model into practice in a real work environment could be quite challenging.

This section will look at how this might be done and what might make it difficult.

Bloom's taxonomy

Bloom's taxonomy categories contain lots of information and children or young people may not follow each step in a uniform way, thus making it difficult to follow.

The pyramid is very helpful in viewing the taxonomy at a glance, but this might mean that the model is not used effectively. However, it reminds practitioners that an ability to recall facts does not demonstrate understanding. This is particularly important when working with young children who are often very adept at repeating things they have heard or been taught. Remember, there is limited value in teaching a child to count up to ten if they do not know what numerals look like because they will not be able to apply their knowledge of counting and numbers.

Examinations rarely ask learners simply to recall facts. They will ask learners to give their opinion, describe, analyse and evaluate to confirm their depth of understanding.

Kirkpatrick's learning and training evaluation

Kirkpatrick's model is simple in its presentation and easy to follow. However, it may be that the results of the learning are not immediately obvious or cannot be seen for some time. This is why there should always be some form of feedback given by the learner. This is the strength of Kirkpatrick's model – because even very young children are able to say whether they have enjoyed and learned something new. (Bloom's taxonomy does not ask for the learner's opinion. Therefore, the extent of what has been learned will not be truly understood.)

Creative methods can be used to gather young children's feedback, for example, by using smiley faces, group discussion or traffic light systems. A drawback of using this method is that the learning has to be complete before evaluation can take place; therefore any issues that arise earlier might not be recognised.

Howard Gardner's multiple intelligences

The wording used in Gardner's intelligence types is not easy to understand but you must be familiar with its meaning in order to be able to use it.

It might be quite difficult to find out the intelligence types of children and young people because there is no means to discover this, for example, through testing. This means that detailed observations must be carried out and this can prove difficult when children get older and follow a rigid curriculum. It is not always possible for children and young people to use their different intelligences to learn about further areas if the nature of the school day does not accommodate it. For example, children might not be able to use music, sound and rhythm during a mathematics lesson because it could be inappropriate and would disturb other children.

So, although adults can become aware of children and young people's individual strengths and areas of intelligence, unless testing and assessment are changed, these are not going to be demonstrated in the overall assessment of children's abilities. For example, there is no GCSE available for interpersonal skills.

Fleming's VARK learning styles

These are easily tested and understood, making them relatively easy to use. Most children and young people will already be aware of how they learn best. The teacher or practitioner has to find ways of supporting these learning styles in the opportunities they provide. However, some will be better at doing this than others. It is time-consuming to think of three different ways of presenting information or learning

and at times it can be difficult to know how to make some elements kinaesthetic. In a more free-flow environment, such as a nursery or pre-school, it is much easier to present learning opportunities in all areas of learning. Many children's toys are already designed to do this.

The role-play area is a good example where children can use all three different learning styles, as shown in **Figure 13.4**.

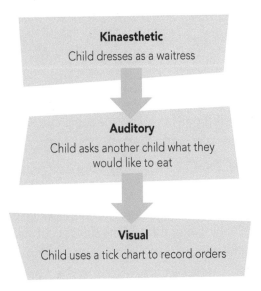

Figure 13.4: *Learning styles in role play*

3 Be able to plan to a framework or curriculum

This section will support you in the development of a plan for an identified framework or curriculum, such as the Early Years Foundation Stage or National Curriculum.

3.1 Developing your plan

There are many different approaches to planning and although all settings will follow the same curriculum or framework relevant to them, the way they implement it will vary.

Thematic approach

Some settings will adopt a thematic approach which involves planning around a theme or concept; this should follow the children's interests or starting knowledge. There are times when this is led by events, for example, a heavy downfall of snow is hard to ignore and so learning might revolve around snow. The majority of settings will acknowledge Christmas as being a time when children are highly excited and interested in events around them and so a proportion of time might be given over to Christmas-style activities.

There needs to be depth to the themes chosen. For example, an interest in knights and castles might lead to 'how we lived in medieval times'. This provides a wealth of learning opportunities in many different subject areas and recognises the holistic nature of development and learning.

Key term

Holistic – an approach that takes the whole person into account, not just one or a few aspects of their health and well-being.

Child-initiated planning

Adults are responsible for planning and organising the environment and resources, but children make decisions about what they want to do, where and with whom. This is the favoured approach for children in the early years. Much of their learning needs to be through discovery and exploration. All young children are naturally inquisitive and curious and will follow their impulse to learn. Activities that are self-directed will teach children far more than anything adults can teach them at this age. You can only truly understand the properties of rain if you are able to go outside and experience the sensation of it on your skin, its taste and the sound as it hits the ground.

This approach requires skilled practitioners because they must lose some of their control over what the children are doing. Because of this it can rarely be adopted in schools where the curriculum is not fluid enough to allow children to follow their own pathways of interest.

Individual education plans (IEPs)

Individual education plans, or IEPs as they are often known, are also sometimes called individual learning plans or individual play plans. They are most commonly used for children who have additional needs. However, they can be beneficial for all children. An IEP usually outlines what a child can already do and suggests ways of supporting them to reach their targets or next steps. IEPs need to be assessed, updated and reviewed to be effective. As children get older they can start to offer their own input into their IEP; this might be shared with the child's family and any other agencies the child works with.

Schemas

Schemas were first identified by Jean Piaget (see Unit CP1 for more detail on Piaget's work). A schema is simply a child's interest or ideas. Children will become engrossed in a schema such as turning wheels, and will find pleasure in recreating this activity over and over again. It is important to plan for children's individual schemas and provide opportunities for them to explore and extend upon these further.

Where to start?

Before planning an activity or experience, or opportunity for learning, it is important to know the children you are planning for. Your plan should start with observation. Watch the children to find out what they like doing, and what their capabilities and interests are.

You might start by exploring a particular subject area. It is important to know what the children already know as you need to build upon their existing knowledge.

Ask yourself:

- What subjects am I interested and knowledgeable in?
- What subjects do the children or young people enjoy most?
- How might my plan support children or young people's learning in this area?

Keeping it relevant to the age range

You might have a fantastic idea about what you would like the children to learn. However, it is important to know the capabilities of the age range you are planning for. If your expectations are too high, the children will become frustrated and confused and this can damage their self-esteem. By contrast, expectations which are too low will mean that the children are not sufficiently challenged, leading to poor behaviour and boredom. Your observations and knowledge of the children will help you to pitch your plans at the right level. It is no use planning an activity or learning opportunity from the Early Years Foundation Stage curriculum if your children are in Key Stage 2.

Ask yourself:

- What curriculum are the children following?
- Do I need to plan for children with additional needs?

- What are the children's capabilities and starting points?

Timescales

How long your plan will last will depend greatly upon the approach you decide to adopt. You may choose an activity that lasts no more than 15 minutes or a theme that spans over a much longer period of time. Some practitioners might approach planning using long-, medium- and short-term plans, as follows.

Table 13.8: *Organising long-, medium- and short-term plans*

Plan type	Learning, activities, outcomes
Long-term (the whole term)	The children will learn about the habitats of animals.
Medium-term (week 1)	During the week the children will learn about the habitats of animals that live in hot countries.
Short-term (daily plan)	The children will look at animals that live in Africa. They will explore how these animals build their homes and the materials available for them.

This approach to planning is most common in formal education. Not all practitioners in early years use this approach. With much more focus upon child-initiated learning, some practitioners feel that when an adult plans in the long, medium and short term they stifle children's ability to lead their own learning and play. In early years, good-quality plans are likely to be more fluid and changeable, directed by children's changing interests. Practitioners are responsive to children's own learning pathways and accompany them on their learning journey, recording their achievement rather than planning it in advance.

Your plan

It is important to consider how you will implement your plan and the practicalities of doing so. For example, turns in a small group activity might need to be brief in order to make sure that all the children have an opportunity to take part. A plan for an individual child might be continued over a longer period of time in order to be able to suitably meet the child's needs.

If you are planning an activity with a young baby, you will need to consider their attention span.

Ask yourself:

- What type of plan will I use?
- How old are the children I am planning for?
- What practicalities do I need to consider, such as using a certain space, equipment or area within the setting?

Expected learning outcomes

You may have an idea of what the children will learn from your plan but you must take care to keep this very fluid. If your outcome is that you want the children to learn about weather in the jungle, will you discount children's knowledge about which animals live in the jungle?

If your expected learning outcomes are too narrow, you might find that very few children achieve what you expect. A broad expectation gives you the ability to see a range of successes. For example:

- 'Children will recognise the colour green and state two animals that are green' is very limiting.
- 'Children will recognise colours and match some animals to the colours they know' gives children more chance of success.

Older children might need to have outcomes that demonstrate their understanding:

- 'Know when World War I started' requires a limited response – young people will know or not.
- 'In what century did World War I start?' gives more scope for estimates.

When thinking about the learning outcomes for your plan, ask yourself:

- What is it that I expect the children to enjoy about the activity or learning opportunity?
- How can I make their interest and enjoyment a learning opportunity?
- How many learning opportunities are realistic?
- How can I assess if these learning opportunities have been met?

Thinking about your resources

It is very important to plan your resources. Be realistic about what you are going to use and whether everything is available.

It could be helpful to have a trial run. A very appealing board game might, in reality, be too difficult or easy and therefore would not be suitable. Knowing this in advance means that you can discount it. If you are planning to provide a craft experience for children, make sure that the resources are fit for purpose: that the glue is strong enough and the cardboard can be cut using the scissors you have provided.

The more creative you are in your choice of resources, the more engaged the children are likely to be.

Make sure that you have all resources available on the day and that there is adequate space and room. Consider yourself as a resource: can you provide the support each child will need? Are the group sizes appropriate and manageable?

Ask yourself:

- Are the resources age-appropriate and fit for purpose?
- Do I need any special requirements to use the resources?
- Can all children access the resources? (Consider any children with special educational needs, disabilities or even less obvious needs such as left-handed children who will need left-handed scissors.)

Using a model of planning

Reflect upon your chosen model before you begin to develop your plan. There might be ways that you can condense very specific ideas into an easy-to-use format – see **Table 13.9** and **Figures 13.5** and **13.6** for ideas.

Table 13.9: *Some ideas for 'at a glance' ways to include models in your planning or delivery of your activity or learning opportunity*

Model	Planning, assessing and using
Bloom's taxonomy	• Colour code the taxonomy triangle and use this to highlight areas of your plans that might encourage each domain. • Use the initial letter of each domain (C, A, P) to highlight areas of your plans that you think might promote each. • Include some activities, questions or tasks that will confirm that children or young people have passed through each domain.
Kirkpatrick's evaluation model	• Make reflection part of the activity or opportunity. • Include a method of assessment, questions or tasks that encourage children or young people to demonstrate their knowledge. • Make snapshot observations during the activity or opportunity to gauge how children are behaving and using their learning.
Gardner's multiple intelligences theory	• Try to incorporate all intelligence type areas in your plan. • If you focus upon one child, find out their intelligence area before you start and use this as the basis for all activities in your plan. • Develop an activity that plays to the children's strengths. • Colour code the intelligence areas and use these to highlight possible opportunities in your plan.
Fleming's VARK learning styles	• Give consideration to each area in your plan. • Allow children to move their learning forward in their chosen learning style, for example, 'draw me a picture of…', 'talk about…' or 'show me…'.

INDIVIDUAL LEARNING PLAN		
Name of child	**Date of birth**	**Group/class**
Interests		
Strengths		
Targets		
How targets will be met		
Who will be involved		
How success will be measured		
Review date		

Figure 13.5: *An individual learning plan*

GROUP LEARNING PLAN	
Group name	**Group age range**

Outline of activity

Expected learning outcomes

How long activity will last

Resources required

Additional support that might be needed

Evaluation

Next steps

Figure 13.6: *A group learning plan*

Assessment activity 3.1

Create a plan to use in your work placement setting that follows a model of planning you have researched. Your plan might relate to an activity, learning opportunity or experience for children or young people.

Your plan should be set out to include:

- the subject area(s) your plan relates to
- the age range of the children you have planned for
- the timescale
- what you expect the children to learn from your activity
- the resources you will use
- any other relevant information relating to your chosen model of planning.

So what does this mean?

- Your plans need to work for you. The information you include can be developed after you have completed the activity; your plan can be a working document.
- Have a really clear outline of what the children will do and how they will do it.
- Know the children you are planning for before you start and build upon their knowledge.

CP13

In the real world

When I started at Raven School I noticed that all the children had their own individual education plans. All the children had very different special needs and I wondered how they were able to learn the same thing at the same time.

I began to get to know the children and noticed that each had their own strengths and talents. Rajia, for example, is really good with numbers and enjoys counting and sorting. Liam loves music and spends his day singing and listening to a tape recorder. He can also clap a rhythm if you show him.

When I started in this unit I didn't realise that there were different models to planning. I became interested in Howard Gardner's multiple intelligences and spoke to my mentor about this. She shared the planning with me. All children have a theme that they follow, but they do this by exploring it through their own interests.

The theme for the autumn term has been 'leaves'. Rajia has explored the different shapes of leaves and sorted them into piles, while Liam has enjoyed the sound of rustling leaves.

Now I understand how planning can meet all children's needs and how using different models of planning can help to make sure that all children are able to access the curriculum.

Check your knowledge

1 In what year did it become a legal requirement for registered providers to follow the Early Years Foundation Stage?

2 Which Key Stage do children aged 5 to 7 years follow?

3 What are the core subjects of the primary curriculum?

4 At the end of which Key Stage do young people sit their GCSEs or equivalent exams?

5 Explain what curricula are designed to do.

6 Give another definition of the word 'taxonomy'.

7 Identify Bloom's three domains.

8 Outline Kirkpatrick's four levels of measurement.

9 What are the additional intelligences Howard Gardner later proposed?

10 Describe how a visual learner might learn best.

Further references

The following are sources of useful information on the topic of learning about planning for given frameworks or curricula.

Books and articles

Bloom, B. (1965) *Taxonomy of Educational Objectives: The Classification of Educational Goals*, New York: Longman

Department for Education and Skills (DfES) (2007) *Letters and Sounds*, DfES Publications

Fleming, N.D. and Mills, C. (1992) 'Not another inventory, rather a catalyst for reflection', *To improve the academy*, Volume 11, pp.137–149

Gardner, H. (2011) *Frames of Mind: Theory of Multiple Intelligences*, New York: Basic Books

Kirkpatrick, D. and Kirkpatrick, J. (2006) *Evaluating Training Programmes: The Four Levels*, San Francisco: Berret-Koehler Publishers

Tassoni, P. and Hucker, K. *Planning Play and the Early Years*, 2nd edition, Oxford: Heinemann

Useful websites

To obtain a secure link to the websites below, visit www.pearsonhotlinks.co.uk and search for this book by using its title or ISBN. Click on the section for CP13.

A government website containing all relevant material for the National Curriculum and Early Years Foundation Stage

The official website of Scotland's website includes details of the Curriculum for Excellence and guidance on the Early Years Framework

The official website for Northern Ireland's National Curriculum

The official website of the Welsh government – a link will take you to education and skills

Pearson Publishing contains a section called ECM in the Foundation Stage and gives samples of planning sheets

Fleming's official site for his VARK model

Supporting numeracy and literacy development in children and/or young people

CP14

The development of numeracy and literacy is often viewed as a set of skills that emerge when a child starts school. However, they develop from birth as babies move from communicating their needs through crying and exploring the world through their senses, to becoming skilful communicators and creative thinkers who learn to question the world around them.

In this unit you will gain a greater understanding of the activities and experiences that help in the development of numeracy and literacy skills from early in a child's life.

Learning outcomes

By the end of this unit you will:

1 Understand numeracy and literacy learning when working with children and/or young people

2 Understand learning needs of individual children and/or young people when supporting the development of numeracy and literacy skills

3 Be able to plan and deliver numeracy and literacy activities for children and/or young people

4 Be able to reflect on own practice.

In practice

Children develop early numeracy and literacy skills best through play. A well-resourced and play-rich setting is essential in developing these skills.

You have been asked by the nursery supervisor to consider how to encourage the children's engagement in mark-making activities both indoors and outdoors using a wide variety of tools and equipment. By the end of this unit you will be able to plan and support appropriate activities using the play environment as a vehicle for delivery.

1 Understand numeracy and literacy learning when working with children and/or young people

If you have no experience in the early years sector, it is easy to assume that the terms numeracy and literacy refer to the processes of reading, writing and maths. Without hands-on experience as a practitioner it can also be difficult to identify the wide range of opportunities that can be used to enhance the numeracy and literacy skills of young children.

To help your understanding of the wider context of numeracy and literacy you can first look to the framework used in your home country. This has been devised to help you to identify ways in which you can support children's learning with realistic expectations and goals that research has proven are suitable for the age and stage of development of the children.

Key terms

Numeracy – the ability to understand and use numbers and mathematical concepts and operations.

Literacy – the ability to understand and apply skills of reading, writing, speaking and listening.

1.1 Current educational frameworks

Each country within the UK has devised and implemented its own curriculum/framework to support the development and learning of children in the early years. In this section we will take a brief look at the frameworks used in England, Scotland, Northern Ireland and Wales for numeracy and literacy. For further guidance on the framework used in your country, useful websites are listed at the end of this unit.

England – Early Years Foundation Stage (EYFS)

In England the framework that settings have to follow is the Early Years Foundation Stage (EYFS) which encompasses learning and development from birth to the end of a child's first year at school (reception year). This is followed by the four key stages of the National Curriculum. The framework has identified criteria which all settings should help children to work towards and achieve. The EYFS was first introduced in 2008 and revised in 2012.

The revised EYFS framework identifies seven areas of learning. These are divided into three prime areas and four specific areas of learning and development.

The prime areas include:
* personal, social and emotional development,
* physical development
* communication and language.

The four specific areas include
* literacy
* maths
* understanding the world
* expressive arts and design.

Table 14.1 summarises what this means for children's numeracy and literacy in the Foundation Stage.

Table 14.1: *Areas of EYFS framework relating to literacy and numeracy*

Area	Coverage	Description
Communication and language (prime area)	• Listening and attention • Understanding • Speaking	The development of children's language and communication skills relies on them being given the opportunity to engage in speaking and listening activities and experiences. This also aids the development of their self-confidence and their ability to express themselves.
Literacy (specific area)	• Reading • Writing	The development of literacy skills involves engaging and encouraging children to read and write. Providing them with a wide variety of early literacy activities will encourage them to read and write themselves.
Maths (specific area)	• Numbers • Shape, space and measure	Mathematical development involves the use of resources to develop children's ability to count, make simple calculations and to describe concepts such as shape, space and measure.

Scotland's Curriculum for Excellence

In Scotland the Curriculum for Excellence has been introduced to raise the standards of education and to focus on the individual needs of each child. The curriculum spans ages 3 to 18 years and follows on from the national pre-birth to 3 guidance. The entry level of the curriculum covers the same age range as the Foundation Stage used in England.

The Curriculum for Excellence focuses on eight key subject areas; numeracy and literacy are identified in the key subject areas of maths and literacy and English.

Table 14.2: *Key areas of the Curriculum for Excellence relating to literacy and numeracy*

Area	Description
Maths	Within the early phase of the curriculum mathematical and numeracy development focuses on three key areas. These are: information handling; money and measure; and shape, position and movement. Experiences and outcomes are identified in the guidance for practitioners.
Literacy and English	Within this area of learning the experiences and outcomes are defined in three key areas: listening and talking; writing; and reading.

In addition to the experiences and outcomes identified in these areas of learning the Curriculum for Excellence in Scotland also identifies the responsibility of all staff to develop and reinforce numeracy and literacy skills across the curriculum in the activities and experiences they provide.

The National Curriculum in Wales

In Wales, the Foundation Phase is the approach to learning for children from 3 to 7 years of age. It combines Early Years Education (for 3 to 5 year olds) and Key Stage 1 (5 to 7 year olds) of the National Curriculum.

The curriculum in Wales identifies seven areas of learning. Numeracy and literacy sit in the curriculum as identified in **Table 14.3**.

Table 14.3: *Areas of the National Curriculum in Wales relating to literacy and numeracy*

Area	Description
Mathematical development	Focuses on developing children's skills to solve mathematical problems and communicate mathematically. Knowledge and understanding are developed in the following areas: handling data; reasoning mathematically; shape, position and movement; number, measures and money.
Language, literacy and communication skills	Focuses on developing children's skills, knowledge and understanding of the following three areas: oracy, reading and writing.

The National Curriculum in Northern Ireland

The curriculum identifies a foundation stage for children in the early years and defines seven areas of learning within this. Numeracy sits within the maths and numeracy aspect of the curriculum and literacy sits within the language and literacy aspect of the foundation stage curriculum.

CP14

CP14

Table 14.4: *Areas of the National Curriculum in Northern Ireland relating to literacy and numeracy*

Area	Description
Mathematics and numeracy	The foundation stage identifies the following areas of learning: number; measures; shape and space; sorting and patterns; relationships.
Language and literacy	The foundation stage identifies the following three areas of learning: talking and listening; reading; writing.

Educational frameworks are under constant review as governments and professionals in the sector discover more about children's learning and how this can be harnessed in practice. It is very important to ensure you are working with current guidance issued by your own country and meet the statutory requirements in the planning and assessment cycle.

When you first come across the education framework used to support and develop children's numeracy and literacy skills it can be quite daunting; there is so much to take in and remember. You would not be expected to know each aspect of the framework from memory but continuous use in the planning, implementation and evaluation of activities and experiences will increase your familiarity and your confidence. Always keep a copy close at hand so you can refer to it regularly.

Find out

Obtain a copy of the EYFS or equivalent framework. Spend time looking through it and reading the two aspects within it that refer to the development of children's numeracy and literacy. Remember that the title of these will vary depending on which framework you are using. Doing so will really help you further on in this unit.

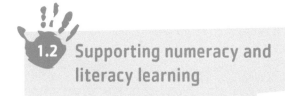

1.2 Supporting numeracy and literacy learning

The role of the practitioner is important in supporting the development of children's numeracy and literacy. It is widely accepted that children learn best through the basis of loving and secure attachments where those around them engage with them and provide stimulating activities and experiences to enhance their learning and development.

Children learn from the moment they are born. In their early years they learn about the world around them through their senses. Literacy skills are developed from the moment a parent talks to their new baby, when a toddler delights in their favourite picture book and when the pre-school child asks for the same bedtime story for weeks on end. Practitioners are supporting children's literacy skills in a wide variety of ways in everyday practice.

Here are just a few examples.

Literacy:
- Communicating with children and encouraging their conversations and communications with others
- Singing songs and rhymes at circle time
- Having a well-resourced book corner which the children can easily access
- Providing a wide range of mark-making activities (patterns in the sand tray, smart boards, finger painting)
- Providing a language-rich environment with signs and symbols to label specific items or resources.
- Using Makaton and pictoral exchange systems
- Computer programs requiring the use of the mouse to develop hand/eye coordination
- Verbal expression in role play, ascertaining who is who and creating narratives of events.

Computers are widely used to support literacy skills in school.

Numeracy:

- Songs and rhymes that involve counting, for example, five currant buns
- Creative experiences such as sand play (adding water to dry sand and questioning what happens when...?)
- Sorting and matching activities
- Role play activities; for example, a greengrocer's would be an ideal activity to introduce children to the concept of counting money and items they want to buy from the shop
- ICT in play including telephones, calculators, clocks and computers
- Puzzles and games that require children to use their problem-solving skills
- Using mathematical language in play
- Using the routines of the setting, for example, engaging the children in pouring the drinks (how many cups?) and offering the fruit at snack time.

From the examples given above it is evident how these activities develop the skills required for literacy and numeracy including:

- the ability to communicate thoughts and ideas
- the ability to recognise the features of text and numbers for their own writing and numerical skills
- the opportunities that develop hand/eye coordination (essential as children learn to put pen to paper)
- the opportunity to delight in numbers beyond their purpose for counting.

Having looked at some of the activities that support children's numeracy and literacy learning we can see that, by providing a wide range of activities and experiences, these skills can be developed. However, it is important to recognise that support does not just come in the form of good-quality resources. Here are some other factors for you to consider in supporting children's numeracy and literacy learning.

- The role of the adult – what you do and how you do it can be the difference between a child being fully engaged in the learning experience or being totally switched off. Play should always be the vehicle for learning and your role in ensuring all the activities and experiences provide play-based learning will determine if the children are engaged in a sustained way.
- The needs of the children – every child is unique and this needs due thought and consideration when supporting their learning. It is essential to know what type of learner a child is so you can offer the appropriate level of support to enable

them to have a rich play and learning experience. Later on in this unit you will find out more about supporting individual needs.

- The complexity of the activity or experience – it is essential you have a clear understanding of where each child is at so you can identify which activities are suitable for their age and stage of development. If you provide experiences and activities way beyond a child's level of understanding, it can lead to failure and ultimately result in a child becoming disengaged in learning.
- The delivery of the activity or experience – the way in which the environment is set up can have an impact on the quality of activities and experiences. It is simply not enough to have a large bank of resources if they are not deployed to best effect. Putting a pot of pens and paper in the graphics area or tipping out some counting objects on a table will not be very inspiring to any child. But if you have armed the graphics area with an abundance of mark-making tools, different-coloured paper, envelopes and an adult, you will capture the interests of the children. Equally if you add to the counting table some electronic resources, perhaps some scales and interesting containers, children will want to experiment and explore.

So what does this mean?

To support children effectively it is important to:

- know what level of assistance children require
- show you find the activities interesting and engaging
- question what children say and do to reinforce and extend learning
- praise and encourage children's efforts and achievements
- ensure what you plan is appropriate and achievable
- make activities and experiences come alive with props and resources.

Case study: making play interesting

Susan is supporting a small group of pre-school children as they play a board game. Each player has a board and a counter. The aim of the game is to be the first to get to the top of their board. Susan encourages each child to roll the dice, move the spaces with little conversation and then asks them to pass the dice on quickly to the next player. Susan calls out the numbers on the dice to speed up the game. The children lose interest and leave the table before the end of the game.

1 Why do you think the children lost interest in the game?

2 What could Susan have done to keep their interest?

3 What opportunities for learning were missed?

Find out

Observe a colleague supporting a numeracy or literacy activity in your setting. Take time to note how they are supporting children's learning during the activity. Are they talking to the children and questioning them about what they are doing? Are they conversing and explaining things to them? What else have you noticed?

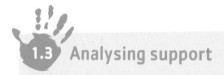

1.3 Analysing support

Understanding the effectiveness of the support you have given children will be shown in how they respond. In turn, this will provide you with the opportunity to consider what was most and least effective on this occasion. Support, as we have already established, comes in a variety of ways – from the role of the adult to the role of the resources provided.

Skills of observation are very important – what we see tells us what works best in any given situation or activity. Hands-on experiences for both the practitioner and the child are the best way to establish the level of support required.

By analysing the support offered to children during activities you can establish the most effective ways of working; it helps you to recognise when you should allow the children to be in control of what is happening and when you may need to step up the level of support.

While some children are confident and able learners, others may experience difficulty which affects their confidence and their ability to join in. In such instances children may need sensitive support and encouragement from an adult who can spend one-to-one time with them to enable them to access learning.

So what does this mean?

There are many ways in which you can analyse the support given to children during numeracy and literacy activities. Here are some for you to consider.

- Discuss what happened with your colleagues.
- Make comparisons between what you anticipated would happen and what actually did happen.
- Ask yourself what worked well and what did not.
- Question the effectiveness of the resources, the activity and the adult.

Find out

Look at the learning intention for a recent activity that you have supported to develop numeracy and/or literacy skills. Now refer to the guidance for communication and language, mathematics and literacy within the EYFS or equivalent framework and see if the effective practice element on the guidance reflects what you were doing. Take time to consider what you could do next time; are there some valuable points for future practice?

Reflect

Take time to reflect on the support you have given during an activity and ask yourself if the children benefited from this. If they did not, what other way might have worked better? This is analysis.

Assessment activity 1.1, 1.2, 1.3

1 Take time to look at the current education curriculum/framework for supporting numeracy and literacy skills that is used by your setting. To show you understand the requirements, make a chart or handout summarising the two areas of learning.

2 Produce a spider diagram that shows the ways in which to support children's numeracy and literacy learning. Be sure to include examples of your own practice.

3 Reflect on the various ways you have supported children's learning and ask yourself what worked well and what could be changed. Write some reflective notes to share with others to show your analysis.

CP14

2 Understand learning needs of individual children and/or young people when supporting the development of numeracy and literacy skills

The EYFS recognises the uniqueness of each child and encourages practitioners to encompass this within the planning and delivery of numeracy and literacy activities. As you will have already discovered (refer to core unit 3.1 Understand child and young person development, Level 3 Diploma for the Children and Young People's Workforce), children learn and develop at different rates.

How well you know the children in your care will be crucial in helping to identify their individual learning needs and understand their strengths and capabilities. A sound understanding of the sequences and stages of child development is also extremely important.

2.1 Individual learning needs

Learning styles

Just like adults, children learn in different ways. Children use all of their available senses to gain a greater understanding of the world around them. Therefore it is important to recognise that, while you may consider a child in your care to have a specific learning style, there will be situations in which they will use one or all of the learning styles identified below. You may be familiar with the learning styles in **Table 14.5**.

Table 14.5: *Learner styles*

Visual learners gain valuable knowledge about their environment through their eyes. They gather information and learn through visually stimulating materials being presented to them such as pictures and other visual resources.	
Numeracy	Children who are visual learners respond to resources such as posters with numbers and symbols and matching number cards.
Literacy	A language-rich environment where text is used to name everyday objects helps this type of learner with letter recognition and formation.
Auditory learners gather information to aid their learning by listening and can draw on discussions and conversations with others. They often have a creative mind as they are able to interpret what they have heard into their own understanding.	
Numeracy	Singing songs and rhymes involving counting will help auditory learners with their understanding of numbers.
Literacy	Speaking and listening activities help children make connections in their learning. They may be able to describe their understanding from the sounds they hear, for example, when playing a sound lotto game.
Kinaesthetic learners learn best through hands-on experiences and doing rather than listening or seeing. They will gain a greater understanding of numeracy and literacy through hands-on experiences in activities.	
Numeracy	Having objects to touch and move and to weigh, count and measure will give children a greater understanding of mathematical concepts.
Literacy	Tracing letters in the sand helps children experience hands-on the way the letters in their name are written.

CP14

Individual learning needs can also refer to a **sensory impairment** or a disability that can affect learning or development. All children, regardless of their individual learning needs, should be able to access the activities and experiences in the setting with appropriate levels of support and where necessary **early intervention** strategies.

Early intervention is important when you have identified a child with particular learning needs – the sooner support can be put in place, the greater the long-term benefits for the child. This is not only crucial for their learning but also for their emotional well-being, confidence and self-esteem. Partnership working to support children's individual needs is important, whether these partnerships are within the setting or beyond. Drawing on the skills and knowledge of other professionals can help in developing practitioners' ability to support the children they care for too.

Key terms

Visual – learn and experience by seeing.

Auditory – learn and experience by hearing.

Kinaesthetic – learn and experience by doing ('hands on').

Sensory impairment – describes a condition where there may be a loss or restriction on a child's vision or hearing, or sense of taste, smell or touch.

Early intervention – the process of identifying and addressing the specific needs of a child as soon as possible.

2.2 The benefits of acknowledging individual learning needs

By acknowledging and providing for children's individual needs you are ensuring that each child in your care will be able to access all the activities and experiences you provide in the setting to develop their numeracy and literacy skills.

Within the overarching principles of the EYFS the benefits of supporting every child are clearly identified in the theme of enabling environments. It is the four guiding principles of the EYFS that every setting should be striving to achieve in the planning and delivery of provision.

Effective practitioners are those that spend time identifying their key children's learning needs and planning and providing appropriate activities that meet them. Planning and providing appropriate activities benefits:

- the child
- the practitioner
- the setting.

Bottles and caps can be used to help children understand mathematical concepts such as size.

The child

Children build firm relationships when they feel safe and secure in a setting; part of this is feeling valued and a sense of belonging. When practitioners take time to identify and acknowledge the individual learning needs of a child, it helps to build their self-belief and give them confidence in their own abilities.

Find out

How does your setting find out about the needs and interests of the children? How is this information used?

The practitioner

The EYFS has brought about many changes and encourages practitioners to become reflective in their practice. Through effective observations and assessments of children, practitioners have increased their understanding of their learning styles and their individual learning needs. By doing so practitioners can identify how children's needs can be met in the setting with different approaches to what they do and also identify when external support and expertise are needed.

The setting

The setting can also benefit greatly: acknowledging and supporting individual needs demonstrates that the setting works in an inclusive way and is committed to meeting the needs of each child to enable them to enjoy and achieve. A setting that recognises the uniqueness of every child is much more likely to thrive in the community as parents seek to find good-quality care and education for their children.

Reflect

Next time you are involved in a numeracy or literacy activity, think about how you adapt your support to the individual needs of the children.

- Do you notice a change in your use of language to aid understanding?
- Have you needed to give a higher level of support to a child to enable them to access learning?

Assessment activity 2.1, 2.2

1 Produce a leaflet for colleagues which explains the potential learning needs of children in relation to numeracy and literacy. Remember to consider auditory, visual and kinaesthetic learners. You may wish to give real examples of practice to explain understanding.

2 Give a presentation to colleagues summarising the benefits of acknowledging the learning needs of individuals to identify support. You may wish to use the leaflet you have already produced as part of your presentation.

3 Be able to plan and deliver numeracy and literacy activities for children and/or young people

Having already studied units CYP 3.2 Promote child and young person development and EYMP 2: Promote learning and development in the early years, in the Children and Young People's Workforce Diploma, you will have some knowledge and skills to help you plan and implement activities effectively. The requirements of the EYFS for numeracy and literacy are clearly detailed in the guidance issued and adhered to by all settings. They provide valuable information for effective practice and the use of appropriate resources. The guidance also helps practitioners to think about the early learning goals, what they are and how they can be achieved. With this guidance in mind we will now look at planning, implementation and evaluation processes for numeracy and literacy learning.

3.1 Planning numeracy and literacy activities

Before starting the planning process it is important to identify and work with the approach used in your work or placement setting. By doing this you will become more familiar with the setting's requirements and you are more likely to enlist the support of colleagues if they are working with a familiar format.

In your workplace practitioners should work collaboratively to provide a broad and balanced framework of activities and experiences to develop children's numeracy and literacy skills. These should not be contained alone in the maths area, or indeed in the book area, but should be readily available in all areas of the environment.

As well as the format and the requirements of the EYFS there are a number of other factors to consider in the planning process.

Figure 14.1: *Factors to consider when planning activities*

A broad range of activities and experiences

In order to move away from the thinking that numeracy and literacy are only about numbers and words, you will need to take a very creative approach in your planning. Many settings have given much thought and consideration to the layout of the environment, both indoors and outdoors, and have adopted a zoning approach to equipping and resourcing it. Instead of using numeracy and literacy as a starting point, it can be very beneficial to turn it around and think how the environment provides for numeracy and literacy learning in a holistic way. By doing this you are more likely to identify a wide range of play-based opportunities to engage children in their own learning.

Look at the zones identified in **Table 14.6** and the examples given to enhance numeracy and literacy skills.

Table 14.6: *Activities which enhance literacy and numeracy*

Zone/area	Numeracy learning	Literacy learning
Role play, e.g. vets	Paying vet bills Counting out dog treats	Mark making when 'writing prescriptions' Taking temperatures, booking appointments, talking and listening to others
Creative	How many boxes to make a tower How many cups of sand to fill the mould	Making patterns in the sand Developing hand/eye coordination through painting
Construction	Building towers of bricks and counting how many Understanding size – bigger than, smaller than	Working together to build a tower. Talking about the tower and how to make it bigger Sharing ideas and experiences
Graphics	Making available resources representing numbers in different ways and for different purposes, e.g. magnetic numbers, tactile number cards, making own number signs	Different materials and tools to mark make Pens, dabbers, chalks and tools (scissors and stencils) to develop hand/eye coordination
Outdoors	Hunting for mini-beasts, recognising similarities and differences, identifying patterns and shapes	Listening to sounds around, the leaves rustling, the wind blowing
Small world	Sorting and classifying animals, e.g. these animals live in a zoo, these animals live on the farm	Adopting roles in play, indulging in two-way conversations as play unfolds
Book corner	Recognising books have a sequence, following page numbers, variety of books exploring different mathematical concepts, e.g. colours, numbers, shapes, textures	Recognising words for labels, naming things, understanding text has meaning, developing early reading concept of left to right
Maths	Lots of resources for counting, matching, sorting, weighing. Providing children with a range of equipment to explore mathematical and numerical concepts, e.g. calculators, timers, weighing scales	Instructions for activities and rules for games help children with early literacy skills
Snack and lunch time	Counting cups, pieces of fruit, how many children, how many plates are needed Estimating volume-pouring drinks	Using words to describe taste and texture. Talking about foods being eaten Communication during social interactions

Age- and stage-appropriate activities

Any activity provided should be within the realms of possibility while providing the opportunity to extend and challenge the children's skills and capabilities. Children are more likely to engage in activities that are suited to their age and stage of development and inevitably will be more likely to see the process through rather than walking away from the activity. Learning is also like building a house, you cannot put a roof on before the walls are built; equally children will not be able to understand the concept of time or money if they have yet to develop their concrete understanding of numbers. In terms of literacy skills children will be unable to write their name until they have developed their hand/eye coordination.

Individual needs

Individual needs can refer to both the learning style and the specific learning needs or disabilities of a child. It is important that an inclusive approach is adopted in the planning process and that differentiation strategies are employed to ensure the involvement of all. When considering the individual needs of the children in your care you may also need to consider the role of the adult. Refer back to what you have read on pages 300–302 about supporting individual needs.

Balance of child-led and adult-led activities

Adult-initiated activities need careful thought and consideration; they should not be tokenistic and should be an extension of what is already happening in the setting. Child-led or child-initiated activities should naturally come from their interests and what they enjoy doing.

If you provide an activity where you sit a child at a table and ask them to practise writing their name, you will find that many children will not want to do this. However, if you put mark-making equipment in the role play area you will find some ready and willing individuals who cannot wait to pick up the clipboards and write other children's names on the waiting list at the doctors. It is both child-led and engaging. Children gain far more enjoyment from mark making when they want to do it or when they see a purpose for it.

Links to other areas of learning

Identifying more than one area of learning in the planning stage of activities and experiences helps practitioners to look at learning and development holistically. Identifying possible learning intentions is not about making a checklist of what you want to see and continuing the activity until you have ticked off everything, it is about thinking of the realms of possibility any one activity or experience may present for the children.

Capturing the interests of the children

Children should be given a purpose for writing and not be expected to write for the sake of it. The same can be said for mathematical development too. Gone are the days when children should be chanting numbers to show they can count from one to ten; in fact we know that this does not teach them the concept of numbers, it only teaches them to memorise in a sequence. Any activity involving words and numbers should be interesting, inspiring and engaging for the children. Knowing their individual interests can be the key to unlocking the potential within an activity.

CP14

Case study: capturing interest

The children at nursery have shown a great interest in the construction work going on across the road from the setting. During outdoor play they spend a lot of time watching the builders and modelling what they are doing in their own play. The nursery teacher talks to the team about developing a construction site at nursery. You have been asked for your input to develop the area and consider how this can aid children's learning.

1 What activities could be used to develop literacy skills?

2 What activities could be used to develop numeracy skills?

3 How can you engage the reluctant participant?

CP14

How might this activity develop these children's numeracy skills?

Learning outcomes and intentions

The EYFS, which details the three prime and four specific areas of learning children are working towards, is something that remains at the forefront of practitioners' minds in the planning process. By identifying what these areas are, you can think about your role in the successful implementation of activities and experiences. When supporting an activity in which you have identified the learning intention to be 'for children to compare properties of objects which are big or small', you will inevitably spend time thinking about the resources to support this and the language and questions you could use to extend a child's understanding during the activity.

Find out

Take a look at the planning format used in your setting. Identify within it:

- a broad range of activities and experiences
- age- and stage-appropriate activities
- a balance of child-led and adult-led activities
- identification of individual needs
- learning outcomes and intentions (aim of the activity).

Assessment activity 3.1

Look at the planning of the setting then discuss with your supervisor and identify an appropriate numeracy and literacy activity that will fit in with the current planning that you can do.

For each activity, make sure you identify:

- what activity you propose to do
- the aim of the activity – what you expect the children to learn
- how the plan meets the individual needs of children in the setting
- how the activity develops one other area of learning.

3.2 Implementing numeracy and literacy activities

Planning can only be realised when you have an organised approach to the implementation. Running in the room minutes before the children arrive will not help in achieving this. Instead you need to pay careful attention to both the indoor and outdoor environments, the resources and activities provided, they way they are set up to stimulate interest and curiosity, and your own eagerness and readiness for the children's arrival.

Having planned and thought about the learning intentions for activities and experiences, you need to think about how these are going to be realised in practice and your role in doing this. Throughout this unit we have looked at the role of the practitioner and this continues to be a crucial element of practice right through to the evaluation process.

Figure 14.2 shows what factors you will need to consider to enable successful implementation of activities.

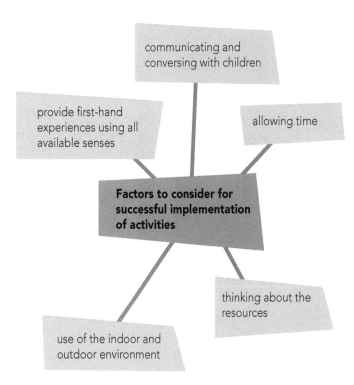

Figure 14.2: *Factors to consider for the successful implementation of activities*

First-hand experiences using all available senses

Numeracy and literacy activities can come alive when children are able to touch, taste, smell, hear and see what they are doing. For example, counting while chopping fruit for a fruit salad or listening to a story accompanied by a puppet can really capture children's interest and help their understanding of early numeracy and literacy.

Find out

Talk to colleagues in your setting about the activities they use for letters and sounds. What first-hand experiences are explored? What senses do the children use to explore these?

Communicating and conversing with children

For the successful implementation of activities, conversation and non-verbal communication are essential in engaging children and keeping their interest in what they are doing. It allows children to share their own thoughts and ideas too; this not only develops their speaking and listening skills but also helps them to make vital connections in their own learning. Conversations should encourage children to ask the adult questions and the adult to ask the children open-ended questions. When doing so it is important to use correct names and terminology so that the children do not become confused by varying descriptions given by practitioners.

Time

You should always consider the amount of time you have allocated for specific activities and experiences to take place. It is important that adult-led activities are not hurried just because you want to get through all the children in one morning. Successful implementation requires time for children to explore ideas and concepts which will help them to make connections and develop their understanding. Children need time to process their thoughts, to question and to draw their own conclusions. Activities that are carried out in a hurried and mechanical way with little time for exploration and questioning have no value for children's numeracy and literacy learning.

Resources

You will already have discovered that a well-resourced play environment helps children learn but this does not mean that settings have to purchase the whole of the educational catalogue to be well resourced. Practitioners should use their imagination when it comes to thinking how resources can be used in a flexible and innovative way. For example, the dried pasta twists that have been used in sensory play to introduce children to texture could be used another day to look at shape or put in the maths area for counting, weighing and measuring. You could even move them to the role play area where children can buy pasta from the shopkeeper and pay for each piece they buy. With lots of thought the scope of resources in activities is endless.

The indoor and outdoor environment

The effective use of the environment is essential in ensuring learning activities have value for children and the transient nature of the environment is important too. While many settings do have zoned

CP14

areas of learning, practitioners should recognise how and when resources can be transported and allow children to do this too.

It is equally important to think about how the outdoor environment can be used to best effect. Most activities that take place indoors can successfully take place outdoors as well. Some children prefer being outside and some may engage particularly well in the outdoor environment where there is more opportunity to explore, run about and let off steam. The natural environment outdoors should be utilised fully to develop children's learning too. Speaking and listening skills can be developed by going on a nature walk around the garden, asking the children what they can see and hear. Opportunities to explore mathematical concepts and numeracy are also in abundance outdoors as they explore space, patterns and sequences in trees, plants, bugs and even the sky.

Case study: the great outdoors

Annie has planned an outdoor activity for the pre-school children. Her learning intention is to help children group objects together according to shape, size or number.

Annie helps the children to put on their coats and wellies and tells them they are going on a bug hunt. Equipped with jam jars, magnifying glasses and scoops they set off for the garden. The children spend a long time lifting up logs and looking at bugs, worms, caterpillars and spiders. Annie talks with them at length about what the different creatures look like, what shape and colour they are and how many legs they have. Annie then provides each child with a piece of paper and pencil so they can draw pictures of the bugs they have found. The children thoroughly enjoyed the activity and could not wait to share their learning with the rest of the group.

1 Why do you think the children enjoyed Annie's activity?

2 What learning occurred during the activity?

3 How could Annie extend the children's learning?

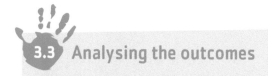

3.3 Analysing the outcomes

Analysing outcomes is essential in helping you to evaluate the activities and experiences you have implemented for the children in your care.

Key term

Analysing – breaking down the outcomes and examining each part.

Analysing any activity takes time and skill and will also require evidence to help you examine what happened and to assess the overall benefits and impacts of the outcome. It is important to keep an open mind when you are doing this as you do not want to cloud your judgement with your own preconceived ideas about how you thought an activity would or should go. Analysing is about what *actually* happened and identifying the effectiveness of the learning activities and experiences that took place.

Analysing the outcomes is one of the cogs within the planning cycle. **Figure 14.3** illustrates this.

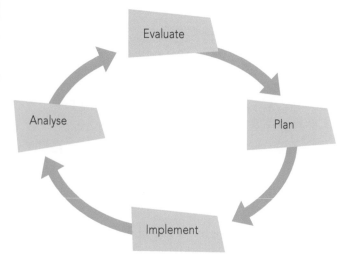

Figure 14.3: *The planning cycle*

Figure 14.3 shows you that the one big question you can ask to help with the process of analysis is, 'Did I achieve what I set out to do? If not, why not?'

To answer this question fully you will need to revisit the planning where you first identified the learning outcomes for the activity you have implemented. Look at what you recorded as a specific aim. You can then ask yourself if this aim was realised in the duration of the activity carried out.

Information for analysis can come from many sources including:

- what you have seen and heard – your observations
- the end result
- input from others.

What you have seen and heard

Your skill of observation really does play a big part in the planning cycle. What you see and hear can provide you with valuable information about the success, appropriateness and benefits of the activities you have planned and implemented. It is not always convenient or appropriate to make written recordings of what is happening as it takes place so you will need to use your memory skills to help you recall valuable information at a later time. Running off to find a pen and piece of paper to record what is happening can be detrimental to what you are doing and may bring a learning opportunity to an abrupt end.

The end result

Seeing the end result can often give you concrete evidence to help you with the process of analysis. If an activity has been designed with a specific purpose, and the children's work is kept to display proudly or use in the setting, then this can give you added information alongside your own observations and reflections. Imagine you have been encouraging children to make shopping lists to visit the supermarket role play in your setting; they may have taken a lot of time and paid a great deal of attention to drawing pictures, symbols and letters to represent the items they want to buy. These lovely lists are the evidence that the children took part in, and enjoyed, this literacy activity.

Input from others

Allowing colleagues to share their perceptions of the outcomes of activities and experiences can really help you examine the effectiveness of what you do. That is not to say they should give criticism about what could have worked better but they should be able to offer constructive thoughts based on what they have seen. Ask them the same questions that you have asked yourself to help analyse the outcome of an activity.

Reflect

Using the questions identified below, choose a numeracy or literacy activity you have recently undertaken with the children and provide answers. By doing this you are analysing the outcomes of the activity you have provided.

- What did you see and hear?
- What was the end result?
- What did others say?

Case study: meeting learning intentions

John has been observing a small group of children in the role play area which is set up as a greengrocer's. He has provided the children with lots of mark making resources and watched as they made signs for the shop, wrote numbers for the prices of the fruit and vegetables, and gave customers shopping lists to write. The children spent a lot of time involved in role play, serving customers, taking payment, and opening and shutting the shop. At the end of play the children shut the shop for snack time. The greengrocer's is littered with the signs the children enjoyed making.

One of the learning intentions for this area was to begin to form recognisable letters.

1 What information might John record to show this learning intention had been met?

2 What other information will inform his analysis?

3 What other learning took place?

3.4 Evaluating activities and experiences

The information you have gathered from the process of analysis will help you with the overall evaluation and to identify what worked well and what did not. Many factors determine the outcome of activities and experiences that you provide for young children's learning as you will have already discovered in this unit.

Key term

Evaluation – the process of reviewing what has happened from different perspectives and drawing conclusions.

The evaluation evidence not only comes from what you have seen and heard but also from what others tell you. As well as using observations of children's responses in the evaluation process, ask them what they enjoyed doing and why. Talk to colleagues too and get their feedback. Share the day's experiences with parents and tell them about the activities their child has been involved in. This gives them a great topic of discussion at home and can often result in feedback from them the very next day.

Evaluating what you have done can help you to seek out and find better ways of working, better use of resources and more appropriate activities. Evaluations can also help you to consider ways to enhance and extend experiences when they have been successful.

So what does this mean?

Next time you support a numeracy or literacy activity, consider some questions you may ask yourself that will help you to evaluate the activity. Look at the examples given below. You may use these or have some ideas of your own.

- What were the children doing?
- Were they engaged in the activity and for how long?
- What was I doing during the activity? Was this useful?
- What learning was taking place? How do I know this?

Find out

Talk to colleagues in your setting and ask them how they evaluate activities and experiences. Compare what they do with evaluations you have carried out. Are there any similarities or differences? What can you learn from this exercise?

Assessment activity 3.1, 3.2, 3.3, 3.4

1 Having planned and implemented a numeracy and a literacy activity for a group of children, produce a report to share with colleagues that analyses the outcomes of each activity in relation to children's learning.

2 Provide information about what went well and what the children learned.

3 Identify if you met your aim.

4 Ensure your report for each activity includes how learning links to one other area of learning.

4 Be able to reflect on own practice

Being able to reflect on your own practice gives you the opportunity to look back over events and happenings and consider how you responded to them. It helps you to look at what you have said and done and provides you with key evidence from which you can draw conclusions. In turn this can impact and benefit what you do in the future. **Reflection** helps to develop not only your practice but also the effectiveness of the provision, activities and experiences you offer.

Key term

Reflection – giving due thought and consideration to something you have said or done.

4.1 Reflecting on the planning process

Reflecting on the process of planning will help you to identify if the plans have been a successful tool for the delivery of activities. If not, you can think about how to adapt them to best meet the needs of the children, staff and setting.

Plans, however, should be approached in a flexible way and all practitioners should be aware of the ever-changing nature of them in response to what is actually happening.

Plans that lack deviation or alteration are not as workable because they do not reflect the ever-changing needs of the children and the environment; in these situations the aims of planned activities are often not achieved.

The process of analysis and evaluation of activities will often happen spontaneously throughout the week. Being able to do this will help you to adapt plans as you go along; if children are not responding to a particular numeracy or literacy activity, it does not have to stay until Friday. Get rid of it or change it! Do something different! Planning should always be a work in progress. When things do not go according to plan, you can be provided with valuable evidence of what to do next or indeed what *not* to do next.

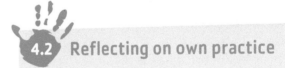

4.2 Reflecting on own practice

Building your skills of reflection takes time and practice; it also requires you to be open minded and ready to accept feedback from others. It is easy enough to ask yourself if you felt an activity was a success and answer the question with a straightforward 'yes', but deeper reflection will help you to dig further into the events that happened and find crucial evidence to justify your answer. By doing this you will often discover the finer details of what you have said and done that will enable you to think about the impact this has had on children's learning and development. This also helps with forward thinking and how you can adapt what you do in the future to achieve the best outcomes in supporting young children.

CP14

4.3 Drawing conclusions

Conclusions can be drawn in a number of ways. Many settings choose to record written evaluative information on their weekly plans to help consider future practice. Many settings complete learning journeys or stories for each child in the setting and may record individual next steps to help them plan for the child's learning.

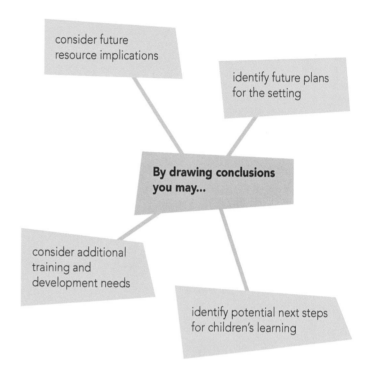

Figure 14.4: *Drawing conclusions*

Identify potential next steps for children's learning

By drawing conclusions from the activities and experiences you have provided for the children, you will be able to think about the next steps in their individual learning. This will not necessarily mean leaping forward and planning for the next learning goal but may include thinking about ways in which you can help develop skills that you have seen emerge – skills that are yet to become established. You can also consider the wide range of opportunities you can present to children to practise the skills they have shown. For example, a child who shows interest in mark making and enjoys drawing circles should be provided with lots of opportunities to draw circles and other shapes and activities to develop their hand/eye coordination. This will help develop early literacy skills without the need to move on to actual letter formation at this stage.

Identify future plans for the setting

While it is important to consider the next steps for individual children, it is equally important to consider the future plans of the setting. The evaluative information you now have to hand may help you think about the direction you want to take with a range of things. This could include future themes and topics, the layout of the environment and best use and deployment of staff.

Consider additional training and development needs

Drawing conclusions will not only benefit what you plan in the future for the children's learning but also help you to plan future learning activities for yourself. By reflecting on your own practice you will be able to identify weaknesses in it or in your knowledge and understanding. By exploring further training and courses you will not only develop your understanding but also your confidence and ability to support learning and play, which can make your work much more enjoyable.

Consider future resource implications

Successfully deployed resources enhance children's learning and development and indeed engage children in activities and experiences. By looking at the effectiveness of these in the evaluation process, you can summarise how you can or should have used them to best effect. You may equally conclude there is a lack of particular resources, for example, ICT equipment to enhance children's learning.

Assessment activity 4.1, 4.2, 4.3

1 Look at the plans for your numeracy and literacy activity (you may also wish to refer to your report) and evaluate the activities you have implemented. With this information, reflect on the planning process.

2 Did the planning reflect what actually happened? If not, why do you think this is?

3 How was your role defined at the planning stage? What did you actually do and how effective do you think you were?

4 What would you do to develop the planning and implementation of numeracy and literacy activities? Think about what changes need to be made, for example, the level of support, resources, layout of environment.

CP14

In the real world

CP14

I'm Ethan and I work at Little Ones Pre-school. During a planning meeting I had a discussion with my room supervisor, Lily, about the lack of interest in the computer. I said that I made sure I put it on every day and that the children could use the drawing game whenever they wanted to but they didn't seem to bother. Lily added that she could see it was always on, and sometimes used by the boys, but she rarely saw any of the girls using the computer.

I took a few moments to reflect before sharing my idea. I suggested we incorporated the computer with other activities the children were doing. At that time we were looking at holidays and places where the children went. I'd noticed that the children had loved the travel agency role-play area. By moving the computer over there they could use it to make pretend bookings. The program on the computer would allow them to save their text and using the keyboard would help with their hand/eye coordination and letter recognition as they typed.

Some of the children had experience of visiting a travel agent and watching the booking agent type in their details. I suggested we could talk about what happens and perhaps take the children to visit a travel agent. This would be really useful for those who hadn't been inside one before. I felt that, if we captured them with this activity, then we could develop their interest in the computer at nursery.

Everyone was really excited by my idea and agreed that this could be the solution we need. Once added to the planning, we carried on with the meeting and discussed the resources and the role of the adult for the activity.

Check your knowledge

1 Where can you find guidance on requirements for supporting children's and young people's development of numeracy and literacy?
2 List three ways in which practitioners support children's numeracy and literacy.
3 Who can help in analysing support given to children?
4 How do kinaesthetic learners best learn?
5 Explain the benefits of acknowledging learning needs.
6 What factors should you take into account when planning numeracy and literacy activities?
7 Why is the role of the adult important in the implementation of activities?
8 What does it mean to analyse outcomes?
9 What information do you use to evaluate activities and experiences?
10 What can the evaluation process tell you?

Further references

The following are sources of useful information on the topic of supporting numeracy and literacy development in children and/or young people.

Books and articles

Beckley, P., Compton, A., Johnston, J. and Marland, H. (2010) *Problem Solving, Reasoning and Numeracy*, London: Continuum

Carruthers, E. and Worthington, M. (2006) *Children's Mathematics: Making Marks, Making Meaning*, London: Sage

Massey, E., Goodman, S. and Featherstone, S. (2007) *The Little Book of Mark Making*, Featherstone Education Ltd

Tassoni, P. (2008) *Practical EYFS Handbook*, Oxford: Heinemann

Tassoni, P. et al. (2010) *Level 3 Diploma Children and Young People's Workforce Candidate Handbook*, Oxford: Heinemann

Whitehead, M. (2010) *Language and Literacy in the Early Years 0–7*, 4th edition, London: Sage

Useful websites

To obtain a secure link to the websites below, visit www.pearsonhotlinks.co.uk and search for this book by using its title or ISBN. Click on the section for CP14.

Education Scotland's website includes details of the Curriculum for Excellence and guidance on the Early Years Framework

The official website for Northern Ireland's National Curriculum

The official website of the Welsh government – a link will take you to education and skills

The official website of England's Department for Education

The official website of the National Literacy Trust

CP14

Observing children and/or young people's play to inform future support

CP15

It is not enough simply to observe what children and young people do and record this. In order to make good use of observations it is important to understand their play so you can plan how to better support their needs in the future.

This unit will help you to consider play theories when you are conducting observations. You should then be able to help children to meet their full potential.

Learning outcomes

By the end of this chapter you will:

1 Understand theories which underpin play for children and/or young people

2 Be able to observe children and/or young people's play

3 Understand how observations of children and/or young people inform future support

4 Be able to reflect on own practice.

In practice

Treetops Pre-school caters for children from 2 to 4½ years of age. Each member of staff conducts daily observations and notes are added to the children's individual files. The staff are collecting lots of information but the children are slow in their progress. The staff are not sure how to use the information they gather for the benefit of the children.

By the end of this unit you will have an understanding of different theories which underpin play for children and how observations can be used to improve the support staff give to children in the future.

1 Understand theories which underpin play for children and/or young people

Play is vital to children and young people's healthy development. It should never be dismissed as unimportant or trivial. Time should be given for children and young people to engross themselves in spontaneous, uninterrupted play. Play is children's 'work' and should be treated as not just important but essential.

One of the most influential current experts in the benefits of play for young children is Tina Bruce. She is an advocate of a free-flow approach to play, where children choose with what and how they play. She has identified 12 features of play and she believes that if more than half of these features are present, the play is of good quality. The 12 features of play are:

1 using first-hand experiences
2 making up rules
3 making props
4 choosing to play
5 rehearsing the future
6 pretending
7 playing alone
8 playing together
9 having a personal agenda
10 being deeply involved
11 trying out recent learning
12 coordinating ideas, feelings and relationships for free-flow play. (Bruce, 2001, p.117)

By referring to Bruce's 12 features of play, practitioners can identify when free-flow play is occurring in order to support it. This in turn ensures that children's play is beneficial to their learning and development.

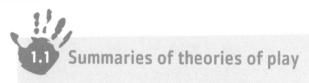

1.1 Summaries of theories of play

Play has a purpose for children and young people. It can help them to work through traumatic events, to rehearse or prepare them for real-life situations, to develop sensory learning, to promote intellectual development and to build social relationships.

Play as therapy

In 1762 Jean-Jacques Rousseau, in his novel *Emile*, discussed how we can learn about and understand children more by watching them play. By the 1930s people were beginning to understand that play served an important function in allowing children to deal with stressful situations and work through their associated feelings. David Levy (1938) introduced the concept of 'release therapy'. Children were encouraged to deal with specific traumas they had experienced by playing with specially provided materials. Levy believed this would allow children to work through their emotions because the play is self-guided and therefore self-healing occurs as part of the process.

Today play therapy is seen as a process in which children can explore their own agenda with the support of well-trained and qualified therapists. Children may decide to explore their past experiences, or current situation. They may not even be conscious of what they are exploring. These experiences will have an effect upon the child and the therapy helps to bring about positive change or personal growth.

Play therapy is child centred and directed. The therapist might not be concerned with what is actually said as play is the child's first language and the best way of expressing themselves.

Case study: expression through play

Edward, aged 4, was travelling in his mother's car when it crashed into a tree. His mother was seriously injured in the accident and Edward suffered a broken leg.

Edward has been playing with the doll's house in the hospital play room. Yesterday he took a figure he calls 'Mummy' and put it inside a toy car. He then pushed the car very hard into the wall and made the figure fall out. Edward then put the figure back into the car and pushed it carefully around the room.

1 What do you think Edward was trying to express through his play?

2 Suggest some other toys that might help Edward work through his feelings.

Virginia Axline (1911–88)

A clinical psychologist specialising in play therapy, Axline developed a code of practice for play therapists. Her code can be summarised in the following way.

- Develop a warm and friendly relationship with the child.
- Accept the child for who they are.
- Establish a relationship that allows the child to express themselves freely.
- Maintain a deep respect for the child's ability to solve their own problems and give them an opportunity to do so.
- Do not direct the child's actions or conversations.
- Do not attempt to hurry the child through the therapy.

In 1947 Axline's work with a 5-year-old child named 'Dibs' cemented the concept that children need to be understood by adults and that play can be a useful way of doing this. Dibs was described by his scientist father and surgeon mother as brain damaged. His behaviour was angry and violent, and he would often bite and scratch other children.

During sessions with Axline, Dibs would paint and read out the labels on the paint pots. He demonstrated that his father discouraged painting (as he felt it served no purpose) by scolding himself as he painted. When playing with a doll's house Dibs would lock the door and close the shutters on the windows. As he spent more sessions with Axline, Dibs began to suggest that he did not want to leave the therapy sessions. He expressed his anger towards his father by using sand and toy soldiers, holding one up and saying 'This is Papa' then punching it to the ground repeatedly. Dibs' mother confided that his birth had been accidental and both she and his father found him difficult. Dibs had several angry outbursts in the play sessions where he expressed his frustration at being locked in his room by his father. Dibs' behaviour began to gradually improve over a period of time. When tested, Dibs had an IQ in the top 1 per cent of the population, disproving his parents' assumption that he had brain damage and demonstrating that his problems were emotional, and likely to be caused by his parents' treatment of him.

The play therapy had helped Dibs to communicate how he was feeling and enabled adults to understand his behaviour.

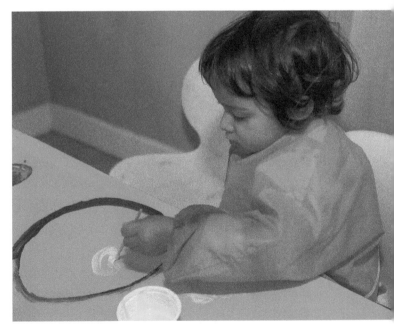

Children are able to use creative activities to express difficult feelings. Why do you think painting is particularly good for this?

CP15

Sigmund Freud (1856–1939)

Freud believed that children play in order to master negative emotions such as anger or anxiety. In 1922 Freud conducted an observational study of an 18-month-old child. While in a cot the child threw all of his toys as far away as he could while making an 'ooooh' sound. The child's mother claimed that this meant 'go away'. He then picked up a wooden reel and threw this over the side of the cot. He pulled it back again by the string and seemed to take great pleasure in watching it reappear. The child repeated this over and over again.

Freud concluded that the reel game was representative of the departure and return of the child's mother. When Freud observed the child again a year later, he continued to play with the reel. This time the child shouted 'Go to war' and threw the reel, then pulled it by the string again to retrieve it. Freud believed that the reel was now representing the child's father. The child believed that he had the power to make his father leave and return whenever he wanted.

This study, Freud concluded, showed that children want to be in control of events. He termed this 'power instinct' and believed that repeating traumatic experiences in dreams and play helped to gain control and understanding of negative events.

Both Axline and Freud interpreted children's play and made decisions based upon what they saw.

Freud's explanation of the reel representing the child's parents is not an obvious link. He also used just one study to form his belief that repeating traumatic experiences helps children to accept them and their associated feelings.

Carl Rogers (1902–87)

Rogers was one of a group of psychologists working just after the Second World War. The group rejected the concept of behaviourism such as that proposed by Burrhus Skinner (see Unit CP1) and the theories of Freud. Instead, the group favoured humanistic psychology (also termed the Third Force).

In the 1950s Rogers established a professional group along with Abraham Maslow (most commonly known for his hierarchy of needs theory) and German psychologist Charlotte Buhler. The group focused on topics such as self-actualisation, health, creativity and individuality. This movement was launched as the American Association for Humanistic Psychology in 1961.

Their approach acknowledged that everyone has their own free will, motives and feelings. Unlike Freud who interpreted what his clients were feeling, Rogers felt that this was too subjective: he believed that the perceptions we have of people alter our ideas about what is happening. Thus if you are aware of a child's circumstances, you are more likely to interpret their behaviour as relating to those circumstances.

On occasions, Freud was dismissive of his clients and felt they were being hysterical. Rogers believed that clients must always be shown unconditional positive regard. This meant that no client would be considered in a negative manner or prejudged. Rogers also felt that therapists should adopt a client-centred approach. This has come to be known as Rogerian Therapy. Rogers felt that therapists needed three qualities including:

* congruence – honesty
* empathy – being able to share someone else's emotions and feelings
* respect – showing unconditional positive regard.

Rogers spent time working in Northern Ireland with Catholics and Protestants and in South Africa with black and white communities. He was nominated for the Nobel Peace Prize for this work.

Play as rehearsal

Children and young people develop emerging abilities and their understanding of the world around them while they are playing. Children use play to practise or rehearse their newly acquired skills and knowledge before putting them into action for real.

Lev Vygotsky (1896–1934)

Vygotsky's work was not translated into English until the second half of the 20th century but it is now highly influential in current approaches to children and young people's learning. Although Vygotsky believed that children were active in their own learning he also stressed the importance of the adult in supporting children to develop their ideas.

Vygotsky discussed the notion of the 'zone of proximal development'. This can be described briefly as what a child can do by themselves and the potential of what they can do when supported by an adult or another older or more skilled child.

Case study: learning with support

Aisha is 2½ years old. On a Tuesday night she goes to her grandparents' house while her parents both work. Aisha spends the evening making cakes with her grandmother. She measures out each ingredient, mixes them together and knows when the cakes are ready because the alarm goes off on the oven.

It would not be possible for Aisha to make cakes by herself, but with her grandmother's help she is able to do each step of cake baking with little support.

Therefore what Aisha can actually do and what she can do when supported by her grandmother are quite different. However, if repeated frequently, Aisha will learn the skills and develop enough knowledge to be able to make cakes by herself.

1 Why do you think Aisha is capable of understanding complicated measurements when her grandmother supports her?

2 Give suggestions why this might be an effective way for Aisha to learn new skills.

Jerome Bruner (b. 1915)

Bruner is a cognitive and developmental psychologist who has been influenced by Vygotsky. Bruner developed a model for the way that children turn experiences into knowledge.

The three stages of the model are:

* enactive mode – children represent and understand using physical actions. They act out their experiences to learn and remember
* iconic – children will use one thing to represent something else or create their own images
* symbolic – children are able to represent and understand the world around them using words

and ideas. They do not need to act out or use an object to represent their experience.

Bruner believed that children and young people have existing knowledge, to which other children or adults add new learning. This is known as scaffolding.

So what does this mean?

We can use an example to understand what Bruner's model means in practice.

Imagine you see three children playing in the garden. They pretend to be hedgehogs by crawling on their hands and knees in the leaves. They have some experience of hedgehogs and are using it to play. This can be viewed as Bruner's enactive mode. The children find some conker shells and push them around saying, 'Let's put our hedgehogs together so they can play'. They then go inside and draw pictures of hedgehogs. The children use their experience of hedgehogs to draw pictures and identify that spiky conker shells look a bit like hedgehogs. This can be seen as Bruner's iconic stage. The children find a book with a picture of hedgehogs on the front and want to talk to a member of staff about hedgehogs. They are using words and other symbols to represent what they know about hedgehogs. This can be considered as Bruner's symbolic stage.

Adults can build on this knowledge by talking to children about where hedgehogs live and the fact that they sleep in the day and come out at night. The children might then incorporate this new knowledge into their play next time

Key term

Scaffolding – the process where adults or other more competent children build upon children's existing knowledge and skills.

Bruner also discussed the concept of a spiral curriculum. Themes or ideas are introduced on a basic level to young children and then revisited throughout schooling with increasing sophistication.

The teaching of sex education is one example of how this might work in practice.

Young children only need to know the basics. It is very common for young children to play at having babies or being pregnant. This might be because they have young siblings and so the experience is familiar to them or they might remember the experience of being the baby themselves. At this stage, any discussion about reproduction would be very simple, using terms that young children would understand.

As children get older it is possible that they might start to pick up sexualised language and behaviour from television or older siblings. At this stage further information would need to be added to help children understand the basic mechanics of reproduction and correct language.

The approach to sex education lessons for young people now helps them to understand the changes that are happening to their bodies and how to protect themselves. Information at this age needs to be detailed and specific.

Reflect

One form of modern-day scaffolding is using the spell check on your computer or predictive text messaging on your mobile phone. You start by trying to write a word and the computer supports you by giving you a number of possible options for that word.

- Is this an effective form of scaffolding knowledge?
- What are the limitations of this type of scaffolding and how does this relate to your practice with children and/or young people?

Play as preparation

Children and young people often use play to help them prepare for future events and stages in their lives. Play can also help them to build the skills required to carry out tasks or activities in future life.

Friedrich Froebel (1782–1852)

A pioneer of his time, Froebel's philosophy on educating young children is still hugely important today. He placed great emphasis upon the importance of play and believed in allowing children the opportunity to play outside as much as possible.

He also disagreed with traditional methods of teaching and felt that children should be given opportunities for free expression. In particular he believed in the importance of symbolic play, in which children use one item to represent another (for example, when young children pick up a banana and use it as though it was a telephone).

Froebel felt that there should be environments where children could undertake practical work and so he designed special resources which he termed 'gifts' to help stimulate children.

John Dewey (1859–1952)

As a philosopher and psychologist, Dewey took a keen interest in schooling and was an influential education reformer. He was also influenced by the work of Froebel.

He believed that children learn best when they are doing things and that education should be based upon real-life experiences. He supported the idea of experimentation and independent thinking in children and viewed them as 'mini scientists'. Dewey recognised children's natural curiosity as being the driving force behind their desire to learn.

He suggested that childhood should be viewed as a stage in its own right, and not a preparation for future life. Dewey said that teachers must know children well, have a good general knowledge and, crucially, they themselves should continue to want to learn.

He felt that theory could be drawn out of practice, and so supported the idea of observing in order to reflect and go on to plan for the future.

Maria Montessori (1870–1952)

Initially Montessori based her work around children with special educational needs. She then focused on supporting children who lived in the poorest parts of Rome. Her approach became so well known and respected that soon Montessori schools began to open in other countries.

There are still many nurseries in England today that follow the Montessori approach while successfully implementing the Early Years Foundation Stage curriculum.

Montessori felt that adults needed to be acute observers of children's play so they could allow them the freedom they require to learn successfully.

Montessori environments were created for children with specially designed furniture and resources. The children were able to select what they wanted to play with and were allowed to do this uninterrupted by adults. The outdoors was also considered to be important and Montessori felt that interaction with and caring for animals helped children to develop an understanding of responsibility.

Children were prepared for adult life by being taught reading and mathematics in a structured way. The experience for children was one of purpose and meaning, and therefore imaginative play was not considered to be of benefit. Children were preparing to be good members of society and little importance was placed upon role play as this was seen as a distraction from reality.

However, moral and spiritual development was regarded as highly important. Montessori felt that children could be easily influenced and so adults needed to interact sensitively with them.

Play as sensory learning

Children use all of their five senses to help them explore and understand the world around them.

Young babies mouth objects in order to feel their properties and texture. Toys designed to stimulate very young children are often designed with this in mind and might include different textures.

Older children will also use all of their senses in order to help them understand. For example, some museums have introduced an artificially created dinosaur smell and recordings of what they imagine dinosaurs might sound like in order to help children understand more about them. These exhibits provide a richer learning experience for children and help them to understand in greater detail.

At what age do you think young children stop mouthing each object they find?

Elinor Goldschmied (1910–2009)

Possibly the most innovative concept of nursery teacher Elinor Goldschmied was the treasure basket. Described in her famous book *People Under Three* (1994), treasure baskets are designed for babies who are not yet mobile. The basket contains a variety of items for the baby to explore involving all of their senses.

lemon · piece of leather · feather · pine cone · shell · large pebble · **Items for treasure baskets** · egg whisk · wooden spoon · wooden peg

Figure 15.1: *Items that might be inside a treasure basket for non-mobile babies*

The foundations of treasure baskets are based upon **heuristic** play. The word 'heuristic' comes from the Greek word meaning 'to discover'. Heuristic play enables children to discover for themselves using natural and/or household objects.

Key points about heuristic play include:

- There is no end product.
- It lasts as long as the child's interest.
- It stimulates all of the child's senses.
- Resources must be safe and non-toxic.
- Resources should be changed as the child's interest in them decreases.

Montessori also felt that children needed to use their senses in order to help them to learn. She created letters made from sandpaper so that children could feel their texture as they ran their fingers over them – this helped them understand how letters were formed.

Margaret McMillan (1860–1931)

In many ways Margaret McMillan was ahead of her time in her approaches to early education. She believed that children learn best through first-hand experiences and that active learning is most beneficial for children and young people. She valued parents and the enduring influence they have upon their children's learning. She was also an advocate of healthy eating and stressed the importance of children eating well-balanced meals in order to be ready and able to learn.

McMillan felt that children should have access to a wide range of materials and should be allowed to explore them freely.

Play as intellectual development

There is no question that children are intellectually stimulated while playing. Play that is planned by adults can be directed to produce desired learning outcomes for children. However, children's spontaneous and self-initiated play often contains far more learning than that planned by adults.

Jean Piaget (1896–1980)

Recognised as one of the most influential figures in understanding children's learning and development, Piaget believed that children should be active in their own learning.

He believed that children go through phases of development where they construct ideas based upon what they have already experienced. This led to the term 'constructivist approach' by which Piaget's ideas became known.

He also used the term '**schema**' meaning children's conclusions or thoughts. **Figure 15.2** shows the processes included in Piaget's schema.

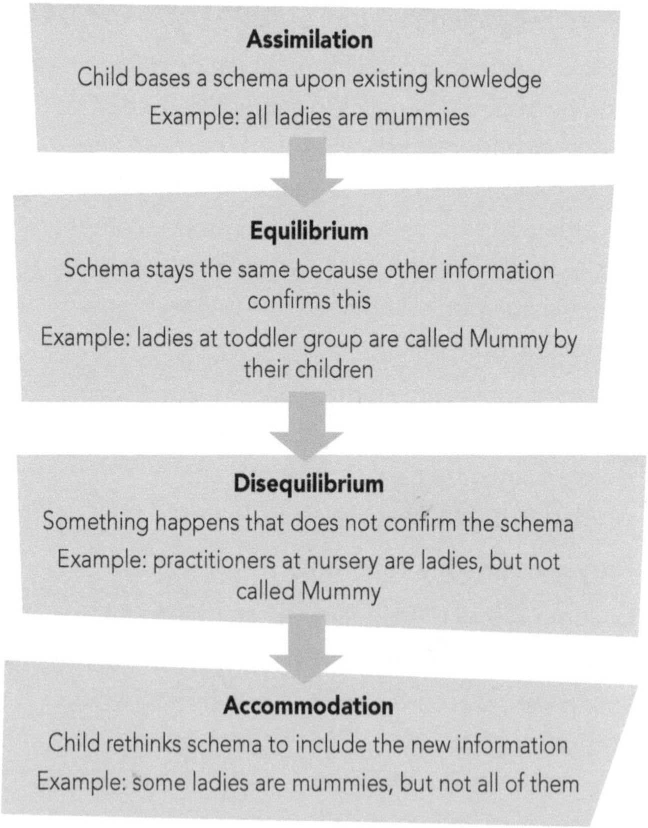

Assimilation
Child bases a schema upon existing knowledge
Example: all ladies are mummies

Equilibrium
Schema stays the same because other information confirms this
Example: ladies at toddler group are called Mummy by their children

Disequilibrium
Something happens that does not confirm the schema
Example: practitioners at nursery are ladies, but not called Mummy

Accommodation
Child rethinks schema to include the new information
Example: some ladies are mummies, but not all of them

Figure 15.2: *Processes from Piaget's schema*

Key terms

Heuristic – used to describe play where children explore objects using their all of their senses. These objects are usually natural or household items.

Schema – in simple terms this means children's thoughts and conclusions.

Children might then incorporate these new ideas into their play. For example, when children role-play with dolls, they might all want to be Mummy. An understanding that there can be other people who care for babies that are not Mummies will help them to develop their ideas further and extend their play.

Piaget also looked at the way children develop and how this affects their intellectual development. He decided that there were four broad stages of development and linked these to anticipated age ranges (for more information about Piaget's stages of development, see Unit CP1).

Although Piaget applied a rigid framework to his theories, he also stressed the importance of children having control over their learning and that children and young people learn best by doing things.

Like Piaget, Vygotsky also believed in the constructivist approach. He believed that children are active in their own learning and placed great importance upon the role of adults and other children in helping children to learn new things.

Apprenticeships are a good example of Vygotsky's belief that, in order to understand something completely, young people need to work with others, thereby scaffolding their knowledge.

Play as social development

Children learn how to interact with others through their play. In group situations children will test out their developing social skills on each other as they play together. In young children this can lead to behaviours that concern adults, such as snatching or aggressive play as children begin to understand what is and is not acceptable when interacting with others.

Mildred Parten (b. 1902)

Through observation of pre-school children Parten identified five separate stages of children's participation in play. Although children may progress in their sociable play according to these stages, there are times when children will choose to play in a particular manner.

1 **Solitary play** – although this is seen as being the first stage of play when children are very young, all children have periods of time when they wish to play by themselves.

2 **Spectator play** – children watch what others are doing but do not want to, or are yet not sure how to, join in. You might see this type of play when young children watch what older children are doing.

3 **Parallel play** – children might be engaging in the same activity at the same time but not interacting with each other. Children might do this when approaching a situation where they do not know the other child or children. By being close to them they might then be invited to join in with them.

4 **Associative play** – two children might be engaging in the same play, such as role-playing being a doctor. The children might use the same resources as each other, but have their own ideas about what they are doing. Conflict is common at this stage: children will want to use the same toys or resources and not want or yet be able to understand how to share.

5 **Cooperative play** – unlike associative play where children have their own agenda, cooperative play involves children negotiating and sharing ideas about how they are going to play. Children can assign themselves roles. Here the children would identify who is the doctor and who is the patient in the role play. Working together, they construct ideas. There might still be conflict when more dominant children try to encourage less dominant children to do things they do not wish to do.

Assessment activity
1.1

You need to have an understanding of the theories which underpin play for children. You should make notes summarising theories in relation to:

- play as a therapy
- play as rehearsal
- play as preparation
- play as sensory learning
- play as intellectual development
- play as social development.

2 Be able to observe children and/or young people's play

2.1 Observing and recording children at play

In order to support children and young people fully, and build trusting relationships with them, it is respectful to seek their permission before conducting observations. Even very young children will be able to understand what you are doing if you use suitable language. You could say something like 'Do you mind if I watch you play so I can find out more about what you like to do?'

As children and young people's play should be self-directed, it would be intrusive to observe them at close proximity; you must find a distance that feels comfortable and does not disrupt them. This will also produce the best results and will help you to gather the information that you require.

Think carefully about when and where you will observe children or young people. Observing them when they are tired, unhappy or distressed will give you plenty of information, but it might not be the information that you expect. You should be alert to how the child is feeling at the time.

Should you choose these times to observe children, it would be unlikely that you could gain permission beforehand. Therefore, it is respectful to confirm with the child or young person that you can use the observation you have recorded.

Thinking about where opportunities might arise

Play as therapy

As you are not a trained therapist, and it is unlikely you will be present at a therapy session, you might find it difficult to observe children engaging in play

as therapy. There are, however, naturally occurring times when children might work through their feelings and emotions.

During times of transition such as starting school, the birth of a new sibling or moving house, children will often incorporate their feelings about these events in their play.

You may already be aware that a child in the setting is about to go through such a transition. The resources that are available in the setting could help the child or young person to work through how they are feeling.

Activities that might provoke such play include:
- role play, dolls and home corner areas
- drawing and creating
- small world play with people and houses.

Play as rehearsal

Children will often use play to rehearse what they can do in order to master their emerging skills and new-found knowledge.

You can see this when children are starting to develop their writing skills. They will confidently make marks in lines as if they are writing sentences. This is a good demonstration of children understanding the concept of what they need to do, but not yet having the skills to do it. Eventually actual letters will emerge and children will be able to write their own name and simple words, then a few words together and eventually the sentences they have been practising.

Activities that might provoke such play include:
- mark-making area
- role play with clothing, cookery items and real-world equipment
- play dough with knives and scissors.

CP15

Older children might practise using make-up and experimenting with different images as they begin to explore what it will be like when they are older.

Why do you think children like to pretend to be adults?

Play as preparation

Children are aware of, and influenced by, everything that they see and hear. Therefore, children will often play in a way that mirrors their own lives. You might see children and young people preparing themselves for forthcoming events while they play. In younger children this is likely to be very straightforward, for example, by pretending that it is their birthday and enjoying being the centre of attention. They are preparing themselves for their actual birthday.

Young people could be encouraged to role-play events that they have not yet experienced in order to help them prepare for the real thing. For example, they could role-play an interview before engaging in work placement. This will help them to understand that they must act differently in a work environment. If they have never been in this situation before, role play can help them to explore what it might be like, making them better prepared for the reality.

Activities that might provoke such play include:
- ICT activities
- non-fiction books in the book corner
- real-life items such as interest tables
- circle time.

Play as sensory learning

The outdoors is one of the best environments for promoting sensory learning. Children can experience the weather elements, for example, the sensation of cold snow on their face and hearing that their footsteps are now muffled. They can experience how the appearance of the outdoor area changes completely when under a thick layer of snow, or the way snow tastes, or its lack of smell.

Children will also use of all their senses when playing inside. Treasure baskets (see page 323) help young children to play using all of their five senses.

Activities that might provoke such play include:
- water play
- cooking activities
- treasure baskets
- gardening and growing produce.

Play as intellectual development

Play is how children learn; therefore you will see children's learning unfold as you observe them in all areas of your setting. Children construct ideas and are capable of demonstrating high levels of thinking as they engage in small group, individual and adult-directed activities.

Activities that might provoke such play include:
- number games and structured games
- ICT activities and programmable toys
- discovery activities such as magnifying glasses
- science-based activities.

Play as social development

Babies are sociable from birth and as a result you will identify social development in all of your observations. Using Parten's stages of play you can see how the child or young person interacts with others socially and consider whether this is desired. For example, if the child is choosing to play alone, is this because of their age?

Most opportunities for social play will be naturally occurring. Activities that might provoke such play include:
- trains, cars or small world towns placed on the floor
- role-play areas

CP15

- craft activities with shared resources
- dens and tents.

You will find that each observation you undertake will link across the different types of play. A single observation might give you a wealth of information that you will need to examine closely.

So what does this mean?

A holistic approach involves looking at the observations as a whole. There might be a specific aim for each observation but do not discount other information you gather as a result.

This can be used to strengthen or inform the other observations you plan to undertake. For example, if three observations demonstrate that Child A plays alone each time, you might then use this information to inform your observation of play as social development.

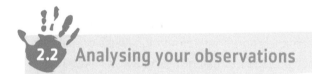

2.2 Analysing your observations

Once you have gathered information in the form of recorded observations, you need to analyse it carefully in order to draw conclusions from it.

Linking to development

You can easily link your observations to development by using your knowledge of developmental milestones. (See Unit CP1 for more information about milestones.)

If you are working with children in the early years age range, you can make good use of the Early Years Foundation Stage framework (or the relevant framework in your country) in order to match stages of development to age ranges. You need to make sure that you know each child you observe as an individual. Children are sensitive to changes and to their own feelings such as being unwell or tired. By knowing them well you will be able to interpret whether the information you have gathered reflects what they are really capable of.

Theories

Table 15.1 lists the key points of each theory relating to the different types of play you have explored. You might find it useful to consider the information you have in relation to these key points – they will help you to gain a better picture of what your observation is telling you.

Table 15.1: *Play theory summaries*

Type of play	Key points
Play as therapy	**Axline** Therapists need to establish good relationships with children. Play therapy helps adults to understand children. **Freud** Children might use one thing or action to represent another. The power instinct – repeating traumatic incidents is beneficial. **Rogers** Children need to be shown unconditional positive regard. A child-centred approach should be adopted. Adults need to show children empathy.
Play as rehearsal	**Vygotsky** Children are active in their own learning. Zone of proximal development – what children can do and what they can do with support. Adults are important in supporting children to extend what they can do. **Bruner** Adults need to build on children's existing knowledge.
Play as preparation	**Froebel** Symbolic play is important – using one item to represent another. Outdoor play should be encouraged. Children should have opportunity for free expression. **Dewey** Children learn best by doing. Children should have the opportunity to experiment. **Montessori** Equipment is specially designed. Childhood is seen as preparation for adult life. The development of morals is considered very important.

Table 15.1: *Play theory summaries (continued)*

Type of play	Key points
Play as sensory learning	**Goldschmied** Heuristic play is key. Natural resources should be provided. **McMillan** First-hand experiences help children to learn best. Healthy diets are important to help children to be able to learn.
Play as intellectual development	**Piaget** Children pass through set stages of development. Children develop schemas that are challenged by experiences. Children learn best by doing.
Play as social development	**Parten** There are five stages of social play: • solitary • spectator • parallel • associative • cooperative.

In order to develop your analysis further you could examine each theory and decide whether your observation results confirm or dismiss it. You might like to offer an alternative opinion or use another theory to compare or contrast your findings.

2.3 The benefits of your observations for children

There is no point in observing children if you do not use the information you gather to enrich their future experiences and to meet their individual needs more closely.

Observations are useful in identifying children's strengths and weaknesses. An area of weakness might lead you to observe the individual again. If you identify a cause for concern you will be able to access additional support to help meet the child's needs. Your observations can be shared with other professionals to help build a clear picture of what is required.

Alternatively, if you identify a strength or particular interest, you can use the information to make sure that the child is suitably stimulated with enriching activities.

Should an observation identify a child who is exploring difficult or uncomfortable feelings through play, you might share the observation with them as a starting point for further discussion. You might also help provide resources that can help the child to work through their feelings and offer additional sympathetic support.

When exploring children's social development, your observations might reveal that a child is finding it difficult to get along with others. You can use this information to plan activities that provide more opportunities for children and young people to work together or interact with each other.

How are practitioners' observations used to inform practice in your setting?

CP15

Assessment activity
2.1, 2.2, 2.3, 3.2

Carry out observations of children or young people in your workplace setting covering the following aspects of play:

- play as therapy
- play as rehearsal
- play as preparation
- play as sensory learning
- play as intellectual development
- play as social development.

Each observation should be analysed in relation to development and theories and give an explanation of how each observation can be used to benefit children or young people. Finally, you should summarise the benefits of using observations to identify support.

3 Understand how observations of children and/or young people inform future support

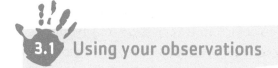

3.1 Using your observations

The information you have gathered from your observations will help you to reflect on your own practice. You can use these reflections to inform how you will meet the needs of the children you are working with.

Use your observations to inform curriculum plans, plan activities with children, assess children and review your resources.

Curriculum planning

Planning a high-quality curriculum framework always begins with observing children.

Observations should be used to discover what the child can do already. (Consider the view of Vygotsky and Bruner that adults need to build upon what children are already capable of.) These observations will help you to build an accurate picture of the child's abilities and emerging skills. As you do this you will also become aware of the child's interests. In turn, you can plan activities and experiences that will be interesting and stimulating for the child.

Consider a young person who is struggling with numeracy lessons. It may be difficult for them to make links between what they are learning and its relevance to them. When young people cannot make these connections they can quickly switch off and fall behind. However, links can be made quite easily. For example, work on percentages could be linked to calculating discounts on clothing and goods when using a student card. The young person will gain the knowledge and skills required by the official curriculum, but in a manner they can easily understand.

You will need to continue to observe children and identify areas for support, then extend the learning to maintain challenge and motivation.

Planning activities

Putting the formal curriculum into practice will mean providing a range of high-quality learning experiences for children.

Now that you have identified what the child can do, and what they are interested in, you need to find ways to extend their learning and offer new challenges. For example, if a child is interested in mini beasts, your challenge is to provide activities that incorporate that subject, while opening up new pathways of learning.

Using observations to inform your planning of activities will help you to consider a range of issues such as:

- Are some activities more interesting to boys than to girls?
- Are children becoming frustrated with some activities?
- Are some types of activities more popular than others? If so, why?

These types of questions might be raised by your observations. By considering each, you should be able to provide activities that meet the required curriculum framework and which also excite and motivate children because they are linked to their interests and are inclusive for all children.

Assessment

Observing children is the best way to assess their capabilities. As children get older they are more formally assessed through tests and examinations.

There is a variety of assessments that practitioners will carry out in order to understand how well children are progressing in their learning and development.

Baseline assessment

This is usually a shared process with parents and carers. It helps practitioners to find out more about the child when they first begin in a setting. Observations will be carried out within the first few days or weeks and might be quite intensive. They should always be based upon information from the parent or carer as they know the child best. Where possible, children should also be encouraged to participate in this assessment by talking about what they like to do.

Formative assessment

This type of assessment is better described as the child's learning journey. Practitioners literally build a picture through repeated observation of what the child can do and where they are heading next. These are commonly called 'snapshots' of what the child is doing or saying. These assessments might be informal but they are vital in drawing conclusions about the child's capabilities, strengths and weaknesses.

Summative assessment

This is likely to be carried out at regular intervals so that the information can be shared with others or new targets can be set.

When children have a special educational need or disability, it is important to reflect upon where the child is in terms of their progress, learning and development. For all children it is also important to draw conclusions about their learning as a whole when they are moving on to another group or setting. This information can then be shared with the new setting and they can continue the learning journey with the child.

An example of this is the assessment carried out when a child reaches the end of the Early Years Foundation Stage (EYFS). This document makes summative and formative assessments of children in the Early Years Foundation Stage.

Resourcing

Resources are not just the items that children play with and use, but the room where they spend their time, the adults who support them and the food that they eat at snack and lunch time.

Observing children and young people will tell you a great deal about the effectiveness of the resources that are available.

Reflect

Look at the mark-making area in your setting. Ask yourself the following questions.

1 Do the mark-making materials such as pens and pencils actually work?
2 Is the paper inviting (or standard A4 plain white)?
3 Are the chairs at a comfortable height for the table?
4 Is it too sparse or too cluttered meaning children cannot easily see what is on offer?

If necessary, address each question and observe the mark-making area again. The improvements you make may change children's interest in the area now.

Your observation might also tell you about staff deployment, who works best in which areas and how you can make better use of individual staff knowledge and skills.

Resources have an effect on the way children behave. An observation might tell you why this is so. If children are over stimulated by one particular resource it may be because that resource is very popular; you might consider making it available more often or at set times when children can unwind again afterwards.

By conducting these types of observations, you can provide the children with fresh activities and opportunities in their learning. It also helps to keep things interesting for the staff – if they are bored by getting out the same activities each day, the children will almost certainly be feeling bored too.

3.2 The benefits of using observations to identify support

Observations can give you a wide range of information about the children and young people you care for. When a practitioner works as a key person (i.e. they have responsibility for looking after and working closely with a specific group of children), they will have a group of children who are

all unique individuals. Each child will have a range of abilities and all of them will be quite different from one another. Although children should not be compared, observations may reveal that children are not progressing as well as is expected for their age. This might be in one or two areas of learning and development or across all areas.

When observations identify that a child is not making good enough progress, support should be offered to help the child reach their full potential. This may mean that the practitioner needs to write up an action plan or seek further support from other agencies and professionals.

There are numerous benefits of using observations to help identify support. **Table 15.2** outlines some of them.

Table 15.2: *Benefits of observations*

Observations can be carried out over a period of time.	A single observation will tell you very little about what the child can do. By conducting observations over a period of time it is possible to see exactly what support is needed and in what areas.
Observations can be shared with others.	Observations are a useful tool to help others understand what support is needed. They can be shared with other professionals who can begin to build up a picture of that child and their individual needs.
They can be used to look at a range of factors.	Observations can be used to look at the child at different times of the day, in different locations and with different people. This builds up a clearer picture of where exactly support is needed.
They are not stressful for the child or young person.	Unlike other forms of evidence gathering or assessment, the child can go about their usual routine without being disrupted or distressed.
The observations can be used to measure success.	When support is in place there needs to be some form of measure as to how effective it is. Observations can accurately do this and then be used to determine what further support is required.

Assessment activity 3.1, 3.2

Explore the effectiveness of using observations to inform:

- curriculum planning
- planning activities
- assessment
- resourcing.

1 Why is observation a useful method of reviewing each of these?

2 Reflect upon why it is beneficial for the child or young person and practitioner to use observation to identify support.

3 What might be the difficulties of using observations as a method of gaining information?

4 Be able to reflect on own practice

It is important to reflect upon your own practice in order to develop professionally. It will help you to recognise areas for development and identify where your training needs are. It will also help you to celebrate your strengths and use them to enhance the quality of care you provide.

4.1 Reflection on planning and carrying out observations

Your observations will tell you a great deal, not just about the children you study, but also about your own skills. It is helpful to reflect upon the experience in order to improve your practice in the future. You could do this by thinking about your planning before your observations took place and the actual implementation. It is important to consider the strengths and weaknesses of your performance.

Planning

The planning stage of your observation is almost as important as when you conduct it. You need to consider carefully who you will focus your observations on – there are likely to be very specific reasons for your choice of child. The reasons for your choice will depend upon how well you know the group. In an unfamiliar group you might select your subjects at random. But where you know the children well, you might choose them because you are already aware of their interests and capabilities or because you have noticed something that you find interesting. This could be the way they play or who they choose to play with.

During your planning you should also gain consent to conduct the observation. You may even decide to ask the children themselves. You will need to consider what you would do if the children do not want to be observed.

The stated aim of your observation might not match the information you eventually gather. In this event, you might need to question whether the aim of the observation was suitable in the first place.

The time and location of your observation should be considered in your plan. Afterwards, think about whether there were any factors outside of your control that played a part in the results of the observation, such as the child feeling unwell or adverse weather conditions.

Implementation

When you reflect on how you carried out your observation, think about the way that the children acted and the way that the observed child behaved on the day. You need to consider whether they behaved as you would have expected or whether their behaviour was not typical for them.

You might like to think about how the children responded to you carrying out the observation and if they were affected by your presence.

Reflect on your chosen method of observation and whether or not it was fit for the purpose you intended. For example, when conducting a narrative observation (see Unit CP1) it is very difficult to watch and record when a child moves around; you might consider whether a different method might have been more effective.

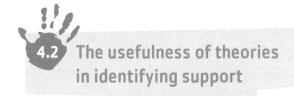

4.2 The usefulness of theories in identifying support

Theoretical approaches help us to understand children and young people better. When you read a theorist's work you can consider your own practice and make connections between the two. The theories you read have been developed over a period of time after extensive research and analysis. However, this does not mean that you have to agree with them. In reality, your observations might directly challenge the theories that you have read about. This is good because the more we learn about children and young people the more we begin to understand them. Society is constantly changing and, as a result, our view of childhood and children, and how best to care for and educate them, also needs to change. The world has changed dramatically since some of the theorists explored in this unit were working – their theories may not be as relevant today as they were when they were written. You might find that these theories provide a basis for your understanding and you can see where they are helpful and positive and where they do not appear relevant.

When you apply each theory to your own observations, think about how they have made you consider where to go next in order to support the children or young people further.

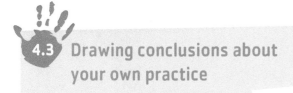

4.3 Drawing conclusions about your own practice

You will have learned a lot about children from your observations. In the process you have probably learned about your own skills and knowledge. It is always important to be reflective so that you can strive to continuously build upon what you do well and take steps to improve any weaknesses.

Think about what you have learned as you progressed through this unit. If you put all of your resources such as class notes and textbooks away, you can think about what you have actually learned. You might like to write this down as bullet points. You are not expected to know exactly what each theorist thought and said but you might be able to remember general ideas. These are likely to be fuller if you have been successful in identifying them in your actual observations. You could highlight any areas you are uncertain of and plan to do some more research or reading.

Next you might like to reflect on how you conducted the observations. You should consider whether you planned enough, whether you were sufficiently organised and how easy you found it to actually carry out your observations.

Finally, now that you have acquired all this new information, consider the implications it will have for your practice. Think about how you will use your new knowledge when planning activities or supporting children at play. You could suggest how your approach has changed and the reasons for this. The conclusions you draw will help you to improve your practice, knowledge and understanding. In turn this will improve outcomes for the children you work with.

Assessment activity 4.1, 4.2, 4.3

Write a reflective account about your experience of conducting observations in your work placement setting.

Your reflection should be broken down under the following headings:

- How you planned and implemented the observations
- How useful the theories are in identifying the support needed for children or young people
- How you will extend and refine your future practice as a result of your experiences and knowledge

CP15

In the real world

I thought that play was unimportant before I started this unit. I had always worried that when the children were playing together it would look as though I wasn't doing anything so I would interrupt and try to get them to learn something. I would ask them what colour the toys were or if they could name the animal in the farm set.

My mentor gently told me that I was disrupting their play and that if I observed children at play I would see what they were learning for themselves.

Now I know about theories of play I understand that children are learning all the time. I use observation to help plan activities that I know will interest the children. It also helps me to identify if the activities I have provided are supporting the children or not.

I also keep track of their development through observations so I know that all children are making good progress.

Check your knowledge

1 Explain the term 'power instinct' as described by Freud.

2 What three qualities did Rogers feel therapists needed?

3 Outline what Vygotsky meant by 'zone of proximal development'.

4 Give an example of symbolic play as described by Froebel.

5 Summarise Piaget's 'concrete operations' stage.

6 What three items might be present in a treasure basket as promoted by Goldschmied?

7 Describe how children might play in Parten's 'associative play'.

8 What should planning high-quality curriculum frameworks begin with?

9 Suggest two benefits of observations to identify support.

10 What is the benefit of drawing conclusions from your own practice?

CACHE Extended Assessment

Theme: Children and young people's play and learning

Grading criterion

B3 Analyse aspects of your learning from the chosen theme that could improve your future practice.

When looking at your extended project, you might like to consider how your understanding of theories of play has contributed to your understanding of children and young people's play and learning.

You could begin by examining what you have learned in this unit. This might now affect the way that you view children's play and you may have increased your skills of observation. You can now use both the knowledge and skills to improve your practice. You should give actual examples of how your practice will be improved. Finally, you might explain the benefit for children and young people of your learning.

This is an example of how you might approach one criterion of your Extended Assessment. You must successfully complete all the criteria at each grade to achieve that grade. You will achieve the highest grade for which you have successfully completed all the criteria. For example, to achieve a B grade you will need to meet the requirements of the B1, B2 and B3 criteria, as well as C1, C2, C3 and D1 and D2.

When trying to understand the requirements for your Extended Assessment, it is always a good idea to talk to your tutors. Fellow learners and workplace colleagues are also useful sources of information.

Further references

The following are sources of useful information on the topic of observing children and/or young people's play to inform future support.

Books and articles

Axline, V.M. (1947) *Dibs in Search of Self*, London: Penguin

Bruce, T. (2001) *Learning Through Play: Babies, Toddlers and the Foundation Years*, London: Hodder & Stoughton

Department for Education (DfE) (2012) *The Early Years Foundation Stage Practice Guidance*, DfE Publications

Goldschmied, E., Jackson, S. and Forbes, R. (1994) *People Under Three, Young Children in Day Care*, 2nd edition, London: Routledge

Jarvis, M. and Chandler, E. (2001) *Angels on Child Psychology*, Cheltenham: Nelson Thornes

Levy, D. (1938). Release therapy in young children. *Psychiatry*, 1, 387–389.

Nutbrown, C., Clough, P. and Selbie, P. (2008) *Early Education: History, Philosophy and Experience*, London: Sage

Pound, L. (2009) *How Children Learn Three: Contemporary Thinking and Theories*, London: Practical Preschool Books

Riddall-Leech, S. (2008) *How to Observe Children*, Oxford: Heinemann

Rousseau, J.J. (1762) *Emile* (2007), Teddington: The Echo Library

Tassoni, P., Beith, K., Bulman, K. and Eldridge, H. (2007) *Cache Level 3 Childcare and Education*, 4th edition, Oxford: Heinemann

Useful websites

To obtain a secure link to the websites below, visit www.pearsonhotlinks.co.uk and search for this book by using its title or ISBN. Click on the section for CP15.

British Association of Play Therapists – information relating to play therapy and associated themes.

The Froebel Institute – information about his work, archives and current practice.

Montessori – discusses Montessori in the modern world and media about the approach.

Managing quality standards when working with children and/or young people

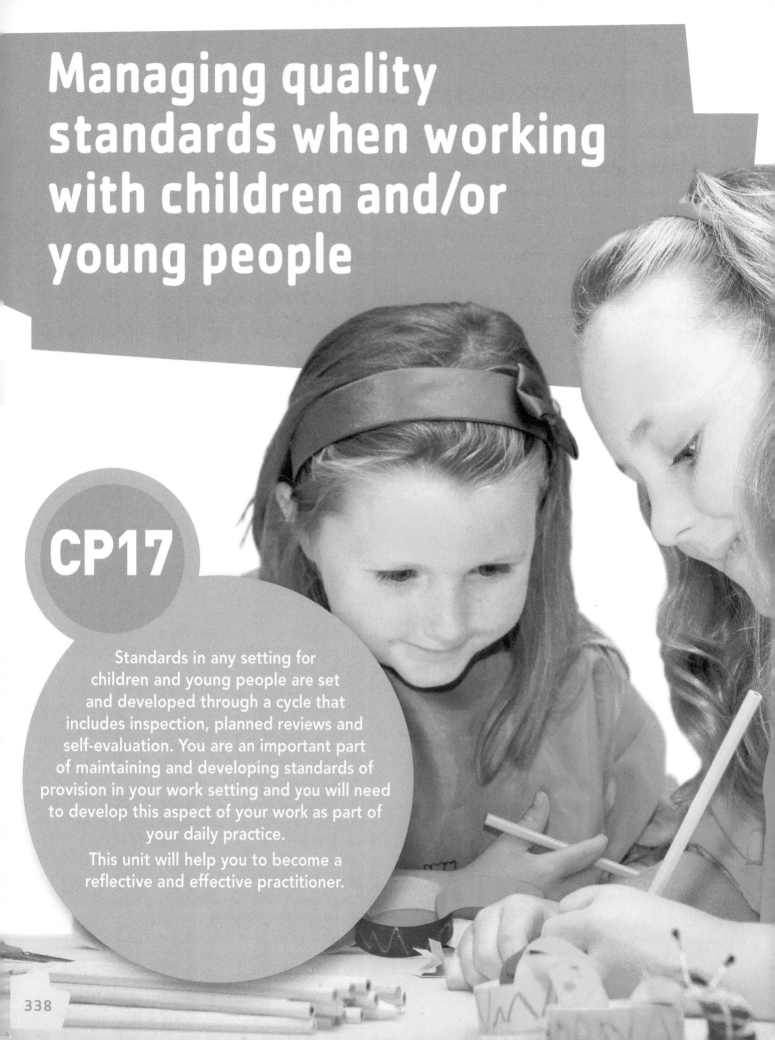

CP17

Standards in any setting for children and young people are set and developed through a cycle that includes inspection, planned reviews and self-evaluation. You are an important part of maintaining and developing standards of provision in your work setting and you will need to develop this aspect of your work as part of your daily practice.

This unit will help you to become a reflective and effective practitioner.

Learning outcomes

By the end of this unit you will:

1 Understand the importance of working to quality standards when working with children and/or young people

2 Understand the purpose of continual review and inspections when working with children and/or young people

3 Understand how to implement a quality standards review

4 Understand the importance of action planning following a quality standards review activity

5 Understand how own role in staff appraisals and continual professional development support maintaining a quality provision for children and/or young people.

CP17

In practice

Jinyi Wong worked in a school in an area where a large section of the community spoke Mandarin. A recent Ofsted report referred to the fact that, at the end of the Foundation Stage, some children were not assessed in their home language of Mandarin and therefore the assessments might not reflect the children's stage of development. There was also discussion after the inspection about starting to audit the setting as part of a quality improvement cycle. The setting used an agreed set of standards and began to review their practice. They also reviewed their assessment process and Jinyi was able to do some assessment in Mandarin as this was her first language.

By the end of this unit you will understand the importance of a planned cycle of continuous review when working with children or young people. You will also discover that you have an important part to play in this cycle and that any setting will only improve for the children and young people as a result. It might even make your work more meaningful and interesting.

Before you read this unit, make sure you have read Unit CP2.

339

1 Understand the importance of working to quality standards when working with children and/or young people

There are many different types of provision for children and young people throughout England, Wales, Scotland and Northern Ireland. Much has been done in the last two decades to set standards for those working with children and young people, from the development of a recognised qualification framework or **statutory framework** to the development of inspections and agreed professional standards. With everyone in the sector striving to meet the same standards, the profile of caring for and educating children and young people is constantly developing and under scrutiny.

Key terms

Audit – a way of evaluating the work environment and expected standards through external and self-evaluation.

Statutory framework – a set of expected guidelines to work towards. This might be in the form of a curriculum or a defined way of working.

1.1 Discuss the statutory frameworks

There are a number of statutory frameworks that set expectations for those working with children. In 2006 the Childcare Act placed a duty on local authorities and their partners to improve outcomes for all young children and reduce inequalities between them. Fulfilling this duty requires a broad and inclusive strategy, part of which should focus on the provision of high-quality early learning and care, following a

range of statutory frameworks. Research has shown that children and young people who experience high-quality provision are well placed to achieve better outcomes in early years and beyond. It is proved that they will also most likely develop more effective social, emotional and cognitive skills that they can use throughout their lives.

Find out

The Childcare Act of 2006 placed a duty on local authorities to improve outcomes for all children. In your study group you could discuss how your local authority does this by using the statutory framework of the Early Years Foundation Stage (EYFS).

If you review **Table 17.1** you can consider some of the statutory frameworks, that are in place to support children and young people in England today. Other home countries use different frameworks, and more information can be found on the websites for Scotland, Wales and Northern Ireland (listed at the end of this unit).

While settings are required to work within expected frameworks, there are internal guidelines that will help you to work towards the quality standards that are expected of you and those working with you in your setting. These are usually defined in the policies and procedures that are explained in more detail in the next section, but will be detailed in handbooks and guidelines for staff, parents and children. See **Figure 17.1** for examples of where these guidelines can be found.

CP17

Table 17.1: *Statutory frameworks*

Framework	Description
The Early Years Foundation Stage Framework (introduced in 2008; revised in 2012)	Practice will meet the required standards by considering the four themes: • Each child is unique • Positive relationships • Learning and development • Enabling environments A profile to be completed for each child before they go to school based on areas of development
Code of Practice for Special Educational Needs	Settings are required to have a SENCO (special educational needs coordinator) who will ensure that children with specific needs are supported according to the framework
Office for Standards in Education, Children's Services and Skills (Ofsted) Inspection Framework	A statutory inspection framework for a range of children and young people's settings. They will expect to see standards of practice and provision as outlined in the relevant inspection framework: • childcare and children's social care • Children and Family Court Advisory Support Service (Cafcass) • schools • colleges • initial teacher training • work-based learning and skills training • adult and community learning • education and training in prisons and other secure establishments • council children's services • services for looked-after children, safeguarding and child protection
English National Curriculum	A framework for learning that is divided into three key stages and has clear expected learning outcomes
Common Assessment Framework (CAF)	A framework that supports vulnerable children and young people and their families

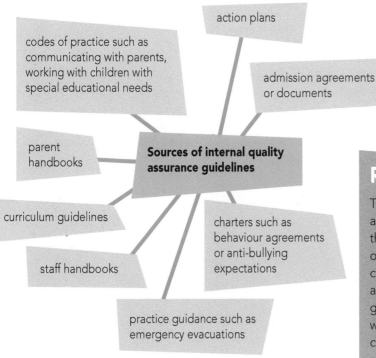

Figure 17.1: *Sources of internal quality assurance guidelines*

Reflect

There is a statutory expectation that there are adult/child ratios which must be adhered to for those working with children from birth to 5 years old. With a learning partner, or in a study group, consider how these standards could be implemented and understood by all adults by creating internal guidelines. You could consider what the guidelines would contain and how they could be effectively communicated to staff.

1.2 The importance of workplace policies and procedures in maintaining quality standards

Unit CP2 describes the important role of policies and procedures in any workplace setting. If you have already read Unit CP2 you will understand that policies that are clearly shared and implemented will ensure that standards are maintained and developed. In order for a policy to help to maintain a set of quality standards, the aim will have to be very clear and the procedures written so that everybody understands how to implement them.

Table 17.2 shows how a range of policies can underpin and maintain quality standards as expected by the EYFS in any early years setting.

Reflect

Read or review the first section of Unit CP2 to help you understand the role of policies within children and young people's settings. This will help you to understand that the policies in any setting relating to children will support the expected standards of any frameworks and are usually based on legislation. It may also further your understanding to look at page 55 of Unit CP2 to learn which legislation underpins policies aimed at maintaining and developing quality provision in your work setting.

Table 17.2: *Policies which maintain EYFS standards*

Policy	Example of how the policy can maintain EYFS standards in the workplace setting
Assessment	Clear policy procedures and guidance to specify how children are given quality developmental assessment checks at 2½ years of age to ensure that any developmental delay is identified and supported as needed
Healthy Eating	Policy procedures to ensure that children under 5 are provided in any setting with nutritionally balanced meals according to government nutrition guidelines
Safeguarding of Children	Clear guidance in the policy procedures for screening all people to ensure they are suitable to work with young children as expected in the EYFS revised framework
Confidentiality	Clearly defined policy procedures to protect the confidentiality of children in the storage of records as required in the EYFS revised framework
Curriculum	To ensure through clear policy procedures that practitioners consider the seven areas of development, which are an important part of planning as recommended in the EYFS revised framework The three prime areas for children under three are: • communication and language • personal, social and emotional development • physical development The three prime areas above and four specific areas for children aged 3 to 5 years are: • literacy • mathematics • expressive arts and design • understanding the world

1.3 How quality standards contribute to achievement of high-quality provision

High-quality provision is achieved by working within quality standards. Working towards these standards is the process of enhancing the experiences of children and their families in any setting. It plays an essential role in ensuring that children will receive the best possible outcomes in their care and education.

The journey that you and your colleagues must make towards higher quality requires:

- teamwork
- commitment
- self-evaluation
- openness to change.

Key terms

Quality standards – when working with children these can be defined as a set of expected outcomes. They are often measured through external inspections such as Ofsted.

Self-evaluation – when preparing for an internal quality review, adults (and sometimes children and young people) who are involved in the setting will be guided in carrying out their own review of aspects of the environment.

So what does this mean?

- As a practitioner in a setting you will be expected to keep everyone informed of any changes to practice and show that you have a commitment to developing your practice accordingly.
- Ensure that you have read the new revised EYFS framework and work with your team to incorporate the revised standards into your daily practice.
- Read more about this framework on the Department for Education website. You can find details of the website in the Useful websites section at the end of this unit on page 366.

The benefits of working towards expected quality standards are that learning can be stimulated through innovation and creativity. Positive change can be made as a result of this in many areas such as improving learning outcomes for each child or raising standards of health and safety.

Learning and developing new skills

The planning and implementation of children's learning should be continually monitored in relation to children's learning outcomes and the standards set by external regulations such as the English National Curriculum and the EYFS. A review of practice in relation to such standards should raise the level of provision and the outcomes for the children involved. This could be as simple as observing how much interaction takes place with children with EAL (English as an additional language) in a reception class and a subsequent plan to ensure more meaningful interaction.

Changing and developing practice

Your practice should always be evolving in your work with children. It is not just the newly qualified who should be open to change but also more experienced practitioners. If you can respond to suggestions for change, however simple, the benefits can be very valuable for children and practitioners. For example, in the last decade, the campaign to give young people a voice has resulted in local and national youth parliaments across the country, giving young people respect as their opinions are listened to at local authority and government level. Young children are encouraged to be given a voice in their own learning through areas such as observation, target setting or student councils. Ofsted will listen to the opinions of children and young people as part of the inspection process.

CP17

Have you seen the value of quality relationships between adults and children in action?

A shared understanding of values and beliefs

Ensure that policies are shared by involving practitioners in the implementation of policies and finding ways to share the values of the workplace setting with everyone, including the children and young people. This could be as simple as displaying the philosophy of the setting alongside photographs of the children enjoying related activities.

Setting goals and targets for improvement

Goals and targets could be agreed as a result of an inspection and could form part of an action plan. To achieve improvement and higher standards such goals and targets need to be shared with everyone. For example, if one goal of a school is to develop communication with parents, it is important to share the goal with the parents and consult with them as to how they think this area could be developed.

Developing interaction with children and young people

Research has proved that quality interaction with children can really raise the level of outcomes for their care and learning, including their behaviour. Considering the results of recognised research such as Every Child a Talker (ECAT) has resulted in raised standards of language and literacy for young children.

Key term

Every Child a Talker (ECAT) – a programme that enables parents and practitioners to support effective language development in young children through a variety of stimulating and relevant experiences.

The main aim of developing quality against expected standards is to develop a culture where practitioners do not feel threatened and are open to change and are reflective in their practice.

So what does this mean?

So that you can feel part of the role of developing and working towards quality standards in any workplace setting you are in, you may need to ask your mentor or manager the following questions

- How will the aims of the setting be shared with me?
- How will I be expected to understand and follow the policies and procedures of the setting?
- How will my performance management or appraisal be related to the work of the setting in developing standards for young children?
- Will I receive CPD (continuing professional development) to help me to develop my practice in areas the setting may be developing?
- How will any action plan be shared with me as a result of an inspection?
- If the setting has set up a quality review process, how can I contribute towards this?
- If I have any ideas to contribute towards developing quality of provision, will there be a chance for me to do this?

The role of the setting is to support practitioners in having the skills to develop expected quality standards through:

- training
- mentoring
- review
- meetings
- understanding the frameworks used
- practical guidance on to how to implement and follow policies and procedures
- sharing any expected quality standards
- involvement in any self-evaluation/quality assurance review
- a system for evaluating any self-evaluation.

This can lead to a sense of pride in the achievements made and standards raised. The role of working towards quality standards may also require external support for practitioners. This could include

- training
- support by advisers
- independent review of provision
- relevant frameworks such as the Common Assessment Framework (CAF) that enable settings to focus on what quality is and how to make the improvements needed.

Key term

Common Assessment Framework (CAF) – an assessment and planning tool used by children's services in England to standardise the assessment and identification of children and young people's additional needs. The CAF promotes the coordination of multiple agencies in deciding how to best meet a child's needs.

Assessment activity 1.1, 1.2, 1.3

Develop an electronic presentation or guide for practitioners. The following areas should be included.

1 Discuss at least two statutory frameworks or internal guidelines that set quality standards for working with children and/or young people.

2 Explain the importance of work place policies and procedures in maintaining quality standards.

3 Analyse the role of working to quality standards in relation to achieving high-quality provision for children and/or young people.

2 Understand the purpose of continual review and inspections when working with children and/or young people

Continual review is an essential part of the maintenance and development of standards of provision in settings for children and young people. Inspections are an important part of the review cycle as they affirm best practice and also indicate where practice needs to be developed.

Key term

Continual review – in any workplace setting this refers to practice and outcomes being evaluated all the time in a variety of ways. Every adult working with children and young people will usually play some part in the continuous review process.

2.1 Quality assurance

In recent years there has been a move to raise the quality of provision for children by giving local authorities the duty to ensure that workplace settings are meeting national standards by participating in quality assurance schemes.

These schemes may be devised by the local authority, be a model from another source or sometimes be written externally.

There are a number of quality assurance schemes that have proved to be successful in the early years sector including:

- 4Children's Aiming Higher
- NCMA (National Child Minding Association) Children Come First

- MCI (Montessori Centre International) Montessori School Accreditation Scheme
- DoE (Department of Education) Investors in Children

Find out

In Unit CP1 you will have seen a reference to ECERS (Early Childhood Environmental Rating Scales). These scales were first devised in the USA and have been developed for use in England. A number of local authorities are using the scales as a model of continuous improvement for the settings in their areas. You can find out more about ECERS in the Useful websites section at the end of this unit on page 366.

Any model of continuous quality improvement that aims to raise standards for children will encourage workplace settings to take responsibility for reviewing their practice against agreed standards and acting upon what they find. Any model should include:

- self-assessment against agreed standards such as the EYFS
- self-appraisal of workplace setting and individual strengths and areas for improvement
- self-produced plans to raise quality of standards
- self-reflection to include celebration of best practice
- self-reflection to identify actions to improve and ways to do this
- self-evaluation of progress made from any action plan.

'Quality assurance' is a phrase that will probably be familiar to you within a variety of contexts. It is an important part of a model of continuous improvement as it reaffirms the best practice of a setting by working towards agreed standards.

If conducted externally, such quality assurance can also give a setting accreditation such as an 'Outstanding' in an Ofsted inspection or the award of a Kitemark (for example, Investors in Children).

Find out

Find out more about Investors in Children by looking at the website in the Useful websites section at the end of this unit on page 366.

Any external quality assurance should:

- be carried out by a relevant professional in the area concerned
- be carried out within an agreed framework
- work to a code of ethics that ensures a fair result
- ensure consistency by using at least two people externally
- ensure the process raises quality effectively in the setting involved.

Any model for quality improvement should consider the outcomes of relevant framework. The following should be part of the model.

- Supporting settings to lead their own development
- Access to training and support in areas identified for development
- Making sure that children, young people and families are consulted on what they want and feel they need
- A way of recognising positive ways in which settings have achieved outcomes for children
- A way of mapping quality improvement standards and outcomes
- Evidence of understanding of frameworks such as ECM and the EYFS
- Guidance and advice for gathering evidence from any self-evaluation
- Guidance for ways of keeping records of children's development and achievements

Case study: an external quality assurance audit

The staff at Green Bow Nursery were taking part in an external quality assurance audit as part of a local authority scheme. It aimed to find out what was going well in their setting and what needed to be developed. The process took five days and the professionals leading the audit held discussions with practitioners, children, parents and other colleagues involved in working with the children at the nursery. The staff were also trained during this time so that they could become involved in the audit on their provision.

The relationships with the children were found to be very positive. However, it was felt, through observation and open discussions with practitioners and parents, that communication with parents could be improved to meet the standards expected by Ofsted. The areas were defined as a result and became part of Green Bow Nursery's improvement plan for the next year with specific times for review.

1 How might this audit have developed the practice of the practitioners at Green Bow Nursery?
2 What could the benefits be of such an audit as part of a model of continuous quality improvement for Green Bow Nursery?
3 What is the difference between an audit and an Ofsted inspection?

Two cycles of quality improvement can be considered in any model. The first would be that of the local authority and the second would be that of the setting once they had received the necessary guidance to implement this confidently.

A model of continuous quality improvement for a local authority should be clear, develop agreed standards, be supportive and encourage open communication.

CP17

CP17

Figure 17.2: *Local authority quality improvement cycle*

A model of continuous quality improvement for an early years or young children's setting should be transparent, and involve and respect the opinions of all the adults and children connected with the setting.

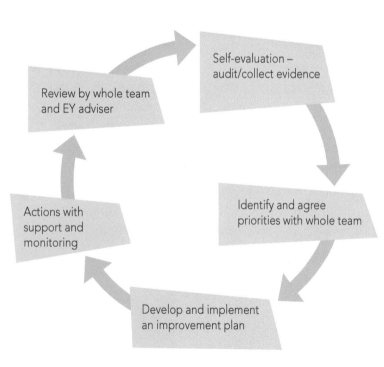

Figure 17.3: *A setting's quality improvement cycle*

So what does this mean?

Carefully review this section about the importance of quality improvement. Then think about the following.

- Have you been involved in a cycle of quality improvement in your setting?
- If so, how were you informed of the areas to be developed and how was your role explained?

Take the opportunity to find out how the workplace setting you are currently in, or have recently attended, has implemented a cycle of quality improvement.

- With a learning partner or your course tutor you could devise an appropriate questionnaire to find out if the practitioners in the workplace know about quality improvement. You should ask permission of the workplace setting manager before you distribute any questionnaire.
- Analyse the results of the questionnaire with a group of fellow learners.

2.2 The importance of inspections

As stated, inspections form an important part of any cycle of quality improvement. An effective self-evaluation process will ensure that the inspection process is likely to be a positive experience and a way of celebrating success. It should also help settings to recognise areas that they may have already identified as an area for improvement and which may be developing.

In Unit CP2 you will have read about the various bodies that inspect settings for children in England, Northern Ireland, Scotland and Wales. To recap, they are:

- England – Ofsted – Office for Standards in Education, Children's Services and Skills
- Northern Ireland – ETI – Education and Training Inspectorate for Northern Ireland
- Scotland – HMIE – HM Inspectorate for Education
- Wales – Estyn – the office of Her Majesty's Inspectorate for Education and Training in Wales.

Any inspection led by Ofsted or another inspectorate will want to see expected standards met in the following areas:

- the workforce
- practice
- content and environment.

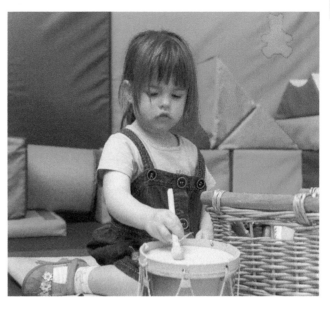

A safe, stimulating environment is a key point of quality for Ofsted.

CP17

Find out

Review Unit CP2 to remind yourself which settings Ofsted is required to inspect in England. To find out more about Northern Ireland, Scotland and Wales, you can read information on the websites listed at the end of this unit.

Key term

Sustained shared thinking – a way of more than one person working together and exploring or solving a problem by using their cognitive skills.

The standards will be followed by the setting in relation to the framework that is being followed. If a setting has developed a quality improvement model then they will be ready for an inspection and see it as a way of affirming standards. Those settings that do not meet the required standards will be clear as to what they have to do next and will be given a time frame before a further inspection.

Table 17.3 shows the key areas of quality that Ofsted inspectors will be inspecting in a setting for children from birth to 5.

Table 17.3: *Key areas of Ofsted (taken from the Early Years Quality Support Improvement Programme (EYQIP) 2008)*

The workforce	• A graduate will be expected to be leading the practice with EYP (Early Years Professional) or relevant status. They will be expected to set the vision and lead the learning culture of the setting • Level 3 with some Level 2 employees with the opportunity to progress to a higher level • A range of CPD opportunities and a chance for staff to progress
Practice	• Clear educational/learning goals • Meeting every child or young person's needs • Sustained shared thinking • Warm, responsive relationships between adults and children • Parent supported in becoming involved in children's learning
The environment	• Meeting ratios as required by the EYFS • A challenging and play-based learning environment as required by the EYFS • A safe and stimulating environment

Ofsted, or any other inspectorate, will not expect any provider to make special preparations for inspection but do expect every provider to be working towards making their provision outstanding. This will ensure that all children have the chance of the best outcomes.

Inspectors want to see that providers take self-evaluation seriously. Settings that do this all the time will know that outstanding provision means continuing to reflect on what works well or not so well. They use their evaluations to strengthen and build on the most effective practice and to remedy any weaknesses they find in areas that are not as good.

The very best providers also seek out good practice across the sector and beyond. They search for ways they may not have thought of to improve what they offer. Providers who do this are ready for inspection.

Ofsted grades

For any Ofsted inspection the quality of provision for the children and young people is reflected in the final grading.

- **Outstanding** – provision that is exceptional and above normal expectations
- **Good** – strong provision in which children and young people are well cared for
- **Satisfactory** – provision that could be better
- **Inadequate category 1** – provision that is weak. Gives cause for concern but is likely to improve without external help or support
- **Category Inadequate 2** – poor provision which needs urgent attention. Gives cause for concern and is unlikely to improve without enforced action from Ofsted and help and support from external agencies

Adult/child ratios

The EYFS has statutory requirements for ratios of adults to children when working with children under 5 years. An inspection helps to ensure that these ratios are maintained as part of providing a safe and more stimulating environment for young children. The ratios that you should expect to see when working in an early years setting are shown below.

- Children aged under 2 years = 1 adult: 3 children
- Children aged 2 to 3 years = 1 adult: 4 children
- Children aged 3 and over = 1 adult: 13 children

2.3 Implementing actions as a result of quality improvement activities or inspections

Once an inspection or audit has taken place it is important to reflect and decide how any recommendations are going to be actioned. This will be the overall responsibility of the governing body/owners or managers of a setting, but every practitioner involved will have some sort of responsibility to ensure the improvements are made. Remember that actions may be arise from:

- an external quality standards review such as a local authority accreditation for being a Healthy Setting
- an internal quality standards review for self-evaluation purposes such as ECERS
- an external inspection such as Ofsted.

Key term

Quality improvement activities or inspection – the actions from these are a way of addressing any issues that might arise.

Case study: quality improvement initiative

Gambledown Primary School was taking part in their local authority's quality improvement initiative, which was a Healthy Early Years Setting Award. As a result they conducted a self-evaluation of their current approach to healthy eating against the expected standards of the award. The award related to the well-being of both children and adults in the setting. The themes included:

- healthy eating
- healthy related exercise
- mental and emotional well-being
- emotional loss and change
- personal safety
- child protection
- staff health and well-being.

As a result of this quality improvement activity the team agreed that they needed to focus on healthy eating in their school, particularly with regard to snack time.

1 List the actions that might be taken to improve the healthy eating snacks at Gambledown Primary School.

2 Who do you think might be involved in implementing the actions and what might they be asked to do?

3 Read the EYFS revised documentation and explain how this Healthy Eating Award supports an aspect of the revised framework.

The best way to implement any actions of a quality improvement activity or inspection is through a carefully planned approach which should be put into a simple action plan that everyone in the setting can understand and follow.

Action plans need to:
- have a clear priority which may be set by the inspectorate, governing body or managers of the setting
- make the success criteria clear so that everyone will know when the action(s) have been achieved
- clarify what needs to be done
- ensure that everyone knows their individual responsibility

- have a timeline so that it is clear when actions should take place
- consider what resources in the form of people, items and money are going to be needed to achieve the actions
- state who is going to monitor the action plan against agreed criteria so that it will be successful.

When the actions have been completed, they must be evaluated to find out what went well and what could have been done better or still needs to be developed. Practitioners need to consider the difference or impact the actions have had upon the setting.

There are a number of people who should be involved in implementing action from a quality improvement activity. The people are shown in **Figure 17.4**.

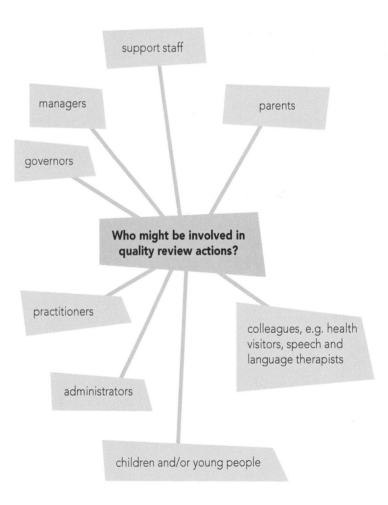

Figure 17.4: *Individuals involved in implementing improvements*

CP17

Below are examples of how to involve the above people in actions from a quality review or inspection.

- Create a questionnaire for parents to find out their views or ideas.
- Identify how individual staff members can address actions in their performance management/appraisals.
- Encourage children to participate in activities such as reviewing an aspect of their environment or making suggestions (they could form a student council).
- Involve practitioners in creating an action plan.
- Give practitioners individual responsibility for part of the action plan.

Assessment activity 2.1, 2.2, 2.3

Choose from one of the following settings:

- a day nursery
- a pre-school group.

1 Research and briefly outline a model of quality assurance for your chosen setting. You will find some models referred to on page 346 of this section. Explain how this model could contribute to raising the outcomes for the children in this early years setting.

2 Find out about the Ofsted inspection framework for early years. Analyse how it could support your chosen setting to:
- develop the learning environment for each child
- improve the practice of those working with children.

3 Summarise the different ways of implementing actions from:
- inspections
- quality improvement activities.

3 Understand how to implement a quality standards review

A quality standards review can take place externally and/or internally. It is a way of ensuring that any statutory frameworks are followed, that the chances for children are equal and that shared standards are maintained and developed.

Any quality standards review will be led by those in charge of the workplace setting but as a member of the team you will have a responsibility to be part of the planning, implementation and actions resulting from any review.

Reflect

Take time to reread the first two sections of this unit to ensure that you understand what a quality review is. Consider the issues below.

- Has any review that you have experienced followed the stages suggested as part of the quality review cycle?
- Who do you think might be involved in a quality review process in an early years setting?
- Consider which aspects of the EYFS framework will be reviewed in an Ofsted inspection.
- Reflect on what you think your role will be in any quality review in a setting you are in or have been in. What sort of support will you need?

3.1 Preparing for an internal quality standards review

Preparation for an internal quality review is a great way to empower all practitioners to take ownership of their practice through self-evaluation. The most effective way to prepare for an internal quality standards review is to ensure that all the adults in the setting are familiar with the standards or expectations of the review. They then need to audit their environment to help support the review. If this review is part of an established cycle, then the practitioners will be developing actions from the last review as part of the process. An internal review could be preparation for an external review such as:

- a quality award
- a quality improvement audit
- an inspection.

A number of areas should be audited as a preparation for any internal review. **Table 17.4** will help you to find out how these areas can form the basis of an effective audit of any environment. You will see that a 'whole setting approach' where everyone is involved in some way is used.

Table 17.4: *The basis of an effective audit*

Area	Action
Workplace documentation To include: - policies and procedures - observation, planning and assessment - guides to the curriculum - information for parents - staff handbook - health and safety procedures - admissions documentation - agendas and minutes of meetings - performance management/appraisal documentation - documentation relating to special educational needs	The person responsible for this initially will be the manager or leader of the setting. To effectively self-evaluate: - working groups could review or develop policies or other documentation - questionnaires could be circulated to parents about the effectiveness of documentation - staff could be asked to evaluate areas such as performance management - health and safety procedures could be measured against requirements such as the EYFS - children's learning and development records could be reviewed.
Resources Could refer to material resources	While the lead in any setting will have an overall view of resources, this is an ideal opportunity to involve practitioners and children in this area through: - an audit of resources - observations of how resources are used and accessibility to children - photographic evidence of resources and children's engagement - engaging in practitioner-led research to gather evidence of effective practice/use of human resources - focus meetings - a plan of resources needed to support any learning activities - displays - planning to show how adults support learning - questionnaires that encourage staff to work together to give answers and review resources and how they are used.

CP17

Table 17.4: *The basis of an effective audit (continued)*

Area	Action
Staffing requirements and skills Refers to ratios of staff required and the staff needed to create a positive environment	The staffing requirements will be the specific responsibility of a lead person but this is a great way to find out what staff think about continuing professional development (CPD) and help them to identify what they need and what they might be able to share with colleagues. • Audit skills through a review of professional records and staff questionnaires. • Review the understanding of ratios against required standards and how they are maintained. • Collect evidence of staff ratios defined for external visits, etc. • Review any policies with relation to staffing. • Review induction documentation. • Review performance management/appraisal documentation.
Partnership working including parents, carers and agency workers	This could be a positive opportunity to gain views from parents and also children and young people. • Key questions should be answered by parents, carers and agency workers in questionnaires. • Carry out a review of policy. • Review communication with external agencies. • Collect evidence of outside agency work with the setting though documentation and discussions with children and young adults.
Inclusive practice Quality improvement should ensure that adults, children and young people involved in the setting follow anti-discriminatory legislation, promote equality of opportunity and positive relationships between children and adults who are different from one another	One of the best ways to review inclusivity is to consult the children, young people or adults you are trying to ensure are included. This can be done through reviewing: • planning • assessment • documentation, such as individual education plans (IEPs) • key questions in questionnaires to parents/practitioners • photographs • displays • any statutory requirements • discussion with children • children's work.
Integrated working Refers to practitioners from a range of professions who may have a close working partnership when supporting individual children. Each setting should be fully networked with a range of services	There will be a designated person to lead on multi-agency working but this is an opportunity to seek views from adults and families involved. This can be done by: • planning • including key questions in questionnaires for other professionals and parents • reviewing documentation • holding discussions • reviewing any related statutory standards.

CP17

Key terms

Performance management/appraisal – a way of evaluating the way a practitioner works through an agreed system of review and target setting.

External agencies – professionals supporting children and young people outside of the setting, for example, social services or speech and language therapists.

Local authorities should provide settings with early years advisers or consultants to help them carry out the work for any internal quality review. They will encourage settings to follow principles such as those outlined by the National Quality Improvement Network including:

• listening to children, young people and parents so you know what they would like

- welcoming all children and young people so that they feel they belong
- promoting your values and principles in all that we do
- all staff working together and sharing their knowledge and experience
- reflecting on your practice and always seeking to improve what you do and how you do it
- working in partnership with all professionals so that you know where to go for support for a child, young person or parent
- making sure childcare is well led and managed
- having training and professional development so that you are skilled and knowledgeable about meeting children and young people's needs
- making sure you have time to monitor your progress
- celebrating successes
- working with the local authority to provide the best-quality experience for children and young people
- making sure you meet more than the minimum Ofsted standards.

Asking the right questions

The questions you ask are important when preparing for an internal quality review because the answers will give you a picture of where the setting is in its development.

Consider a sample of questions below that a key person could be asked to consider in relation to the children's physical development.

- Do you ensure that your key children have the opportunity to move around the room and indoors/outdoors independently?
- Do you use special language to help the child understand concepts such as over, under, around?
- Are your key children encouraged to repeat sensory experiences?
- Do you involve children in preparing food?
- Do you have mealtimes to encourage children to eat and drink independently?

The key person could be asked to grade the answers according to an agreed system and start to contribute to a portfolio of evidence (hard or electronic copy) through photos, observations and assessment. This can be seen as building an overview of practice and celebrating what is being done well. Such a file is sometimes referred to as a Quality Improvement File.

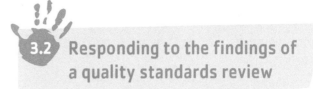

3.2 Responding to the findings of a quality standards review

Responding to a quality standards review is an important part of the quality review cycle. This section looks at actions that should be taken in response to findings of internal reviews (those carried out within the organisation or workplace) and also in response to findings of external reviews (those carried out by an external body).

Within the organisation or workplace

After any audit the following actions should be taken.

- Find out what the next steps are.
- Consider areas of responsibility for the actions, remembering that the more the staff have ownership, the more likely the actions will be to have a positive impact on provision.
- Make a plan to action the findings.
- Ensure that actions match the focus areas of the audit so that the process is clear and smooth and understood by everyone involved.
- Consider the evidence to be collected.
- Consider any professional development needs that may arise from the review.
- Ensure that review opportunities of progress are planned.
- Share the findings of any review, and the plans to address them, with staff and parents.

It is the manager's responsibility to prioritise the actions. If the standards review has been graded, it could be that the most concerning grades are top priority. Evidence can then be collected to show how the areas for action are being improved. Clarification should always be sought if any of the actions are unclear.

Reflect

Think carefully about a workplace setting that you have been in recently.

- Can you think of an area of practice that you felt you wanted to develop when you were there?
- If you had taken part in an internal quality audit, do you think that this area of practice would have been focused on in an action plan?

Remember that good practice is always reflective so it is fine to be aware of what you find difficult.

Carried out by an external body

An external review could be carried out:

- by the local authority as part of a quality improvement programme
- by an awarding body as part of a quality award
- during an inspection such as Ofsted.

The response should:

- relate to the areas of the review concerned
- result in achievable actions in a reasonable timescale
- be shared with as many people as possible in the setting
- consider how any actions could have a positive impact for the children and young people.

In an external audit a setting may be required to carry out certain actions if they are not meeting legislative requirements or the requirements of the audit

A setting may be given a timescale to complete the actions and external consultants or advisers may support professional development by writing and regularly reviewing a focused improvement plan (FIP).

Key term

Focused improvement plan (FIP) – a plan with clear targets and ways to achieve the targets. This is usually shared with everyone in the setting.

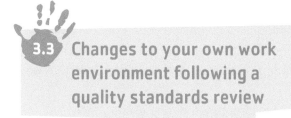

3.3 Changes to your own work environment following a quality standards review

If your setting made changes following a quality standards review then you should expect to see the changes that are summarised in **Figure 17.5**.

achievable, focused improvement plan

identified and agreed improvement priorities

review progress

Areas covered in a standards review

collection of evidence about your focus changes

engaging all staff in the process

plans for any professional development

Figure 17.5: *Common changes following a standards review*

Your setting may be guided by a local authority team, such as the early years and childcare services team, who may request you put together a continuous quality improvement file of supportive evidence.

It is the statutory duty of early years and childcare services to raise the quality of all provisions for the early years.

Some settings may need intensive support to action findings. This may take the form of weekly visits. Other settings will need focused support, for example, if they want help with a specific target. Some settings will just need access to professional training and support.

Assessment activity 3.1, 3.2, 3.3

1 Carefully review this section and then prepare guidance for a setting to explain how they can prepare for an internal quality standards review with regard to the following:
   - workplace documentation
   - resources
   - staffing
   - partnership working to include carers/parents and external agencies
   - inclusive practice
   - integrated practice.

2 Explain how you would respond to the findings of a quality review carried out by:
   - your team as a self-evaluation
   - Ofsted.

3 Describe the ways in which your own workplace setting could make changes following a quality standards review.

4 Understand the importance of action planning following a quality standards review activity

Putting a quality review activity into action in an organised and positive way will benefit the children. However, it is important that change is implemented by involving all the **stakeholders** in the setting so that there is a shared understanding of the aims and focus of any action plan.

4.1 Changes to the work environment

Any changes that are implemented should be clear and:
- focus on the outcomes identified and how any improvements will impact on good-quality practice and enhance individual children's learning experiences
- ensure collaboration with managers and practitioners to identify the needs of the setting
- support the development of practitioners' reflective practice and self-evaluation skills
- use the setting's action/improvement plan as an effective tool for continuous improvement
- clarify the respective roles of practitioners in the setting to support any change
- consider creating an improvement team to monitor and evaluate any changes to be implemented
- specify appropriate levels of support as required
- outline regular monitoring visits from external advisers to the setting to review progress and quality over an agreed period of time.

All changes have to be implemented and made into an action plan. Consulting with key members of any team and gathering a range of viewpoints through discussion, and sometimes questionnaires, will help to ensure that any suggested changes are implemented successfully.

Key term

Stakeholder – someone who has an interest or is involved in the workplace. This could refer to parents, teachers, early years practitioners, governors and multi-agency practitioners.

Case study: responding to feedback

Helper Pre-school is part of a local authority quality improvement scheme. Two early years and childcare consultants paid an external moderation visit to review the pre-school's self-evaluation. They praised the setting for the quality of the relationships observed and identified the need for opportunities for more talking and listening activities.

Liz, the manager, met with her leadership team. They decided to feed back to the whole staff, stressing the positive comments and then seeking ideas to tackle the suggested actions.

It was decided that the standards focused on by the audit should be reviewed with all practitioners, with particular reference to the section on talking and listening. They listed ways that the team could be supported through training to help them develop a more language-rich environment. They also felt that

it would be effective to encourage staff to look at their own talking and listening practice by observing and auditing their own environment. It was then decided that all staff should be given a questionnaire to find out what they understood about talking and listening to children and the support they might need to develop this area.

1 Analyse the way that Liz approached the action relating to talking and listening.

2 Identify and describe any other ways that the practitioners in the setting could be supported in developing the way they talk and listen to the children.

3 How do you think the Helper Pre-school leadership team could monitor the actions and the impact upon the provision of talking and listening activities?

Practitioner research is also a very positive way of involving staff in managing change in a setting. It enables them to find out more about areas of development through a range of practical research that could include:

- visiting other settings
- reading and analysing books, relevant research, articles, journals, etc.
- questionnaires for colleagues or parents
- photographic evidence
- talking to parents
- peer observations
- visiting other settings.

Key terms

Practitioner research – reflective work, often prompted by questioning, carried out by a practitioner in their work setting, with the aim of developing provision.

Peer observation – a way of watching, observing and replicating best practice of colleagues.

Consider **Figure 17.6**, an example of a simple action plan from a day nursery following an internal quality audit.

Focus: Developing the role of the key person with the under 3s						
Action	Implementation	Responsibilities	Time frame	Resources	Evidence of impact	Outcomes
1. Developing settling-in documents for under threes	Training (1 session to introduce and follow-up session to discuss new documentation) Team meeting Visiting Pusey Children's Centre to discuss and view settling in Create and implement documentation	PM (Our LA Early Years Consultant) JF (Under 3s Leader) with under 3s team JF (Under 3s leader) and team	February to May	Pusey training materials Transport Non-contact time for JF	New settling-in plan/ arrangements Settling-in document Reviews from ECC Parents' questionnaire analysis	When documentation is in place Feedback from parents and team A more effective settling-in period Feedback from ECC (Early Years and Childcare Consultant)

Figure 17.6: *Simple action plan following an internal quality audit*

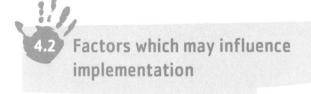

4.2 Factors which may influence implementation

Following a quality review, any factors that may influence potential outcomes of the implementation of actions should be reflected in the action planning.

On your action plan, consider the following factors.

- **Action** – identify a clear focus for the action that is in simple language and understood by all stakeholders.
- **Implementation** or **How?** – consider the ways in which the actions will be implemented and make these very clear on the plan after consultation with colleagues and other relevant stakeholders.
- **Responsibilities** or **Who?** – it is important to ensure that all stakeholders have ownership of their practice and any changes that will develop the quality of provision for children. These people must be identified on the action plan.

- **Time frame** or **How long?** – how long an action will take to be implemented will depend upon a range of factors.
- **Resources** – the resources in any action plan should be identified in terms of what is needed and the people who need to be involved to reach positive outcomes.
- **Evidence of impact to changes in practice** – some settings are encouraged to gather evidence to celebrate the changes they have made in a special file. Such evidence collecting should be considered in an action plan to show how areas have been addressed. This is a great resource to share with parents and to reflect upon as a team.
- **Outcomes/any further action** – the most important factor to consider in any plan is for the people involved to know if an action has been successfully implemented through external visits, reports, internal audits, etc. This can be identified in the last column of the plan.

So what does this mean?

The time frame is a major factor in any action planning. The time given to an action should be specified and negotiated. The range of factors that could be considered when setting a time frame for a focused action may include:

- the level of detail of the area for action
- the activities involved, e.g. a questionnaire may need time to be written, collected and collated
- the time allocation for individual people involved in developing areas as identified
- the ordering time and purchasing of resources
- any financial planning that may have to be sought for or planned for in another financial period.

4.3 Evaluate the process of action planning

The aim of the process should be to create the best possible outcomes for the children concerned. In the process effective implementation will be more likely if practitioners are encouraged to:

- ask themselves challenging questions
- observe themselves in their work
- consult effectively with children and families on their views.

Effective support by the setting should include training and guidance to support practitioners to develop these skills. Practitioners can also be supported to develop ways of conducting peer observations of colleagues through training or by mentors. If an action plan has a focus outcome, and process-related standards and indicators, then practitioners observe and evaluate their practice as it really is.

If it is recognised that making self-assessment judgements is complex and needs evidence, then debate can be encouraged. Practitioners can then decide on, and implement, improvements.

An effective leader of any effective action planning process which results in improved practice will:

- plan training, guidance and resources to support reflective practice
- consult with children and families
- develop peer observation
- promote reflective practice through case studies, diaries, multimedia recordings, discussion with adults and children, and action learning
- develop support networks with settings undertaking quality improvement
- create a culture of sharing issues and learning from each other
- join external networks where providers can share good practice and discuss practice issues.

Reflect

Consider the celebration of the best outcome of any activity that you might have been involved in, in any area of your life.

- How was it celebrated?
- How did it make you, and everyone else involved, feel?
- Why do you think you remember this?
- What impact do you think it had on other areas of your life?

This might help you to remember that celebrating positive commitment or action is vital to the morale of colleagues, parents, children and yourself. It can also act as a reminder that there are many areas to celebrate when addressing any areas of concern in a children's setting.

Assessment activity 4.1, 4.2, 4.3

You are part of a team which has undergone an external audit of your workplace setting. With a learning partner:

- discuss ways in which your team can implement any changes that may be required as part of the audit
- analyse some potential factors which may influence your team's implementation of any actions
- carefully evaluate the action planning process in relation to how the plan can be implemented effectively by your team.

Record your discussion.

5 Understand how own role in staff appraisals and continual professional development support maintaining a quality provision for children and/or young people

Your role in supporting and maintaining quality provision for children is crucial for your development and that of each child. This will encourage you to become a reflective practitioner (as described in Unit CP1), which is essential to your understanding of best practice.

CP17

A reflective practitioner can enable children to enjoy and benefit from their learning.

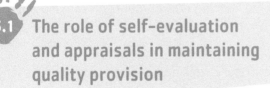

5.1 The role of self-evaluation and appraisals in maintaining quality provision

Self-evaluation is at the heart of being a reflective practitioner and is a skill that you will develop through practice. This process will:

- allow you to set clear standards for all aspects of your provision from staffing, health and safety and the learning environment through to relationships with children, parents, other professionals and the local community
- help you to develop good-quality management and administration systems
- give a clear and shared aim, developing core strengths and focusing on any areas of development within your team, thus enhancing team spirit

- allow you to consult with children and parents, giving you chance to evaluate their opinions and encouraging everyone to feel part of your provision
- demonstrate to parents that you are prepared to reflect and develop to meet the ever-changing needs of their child
- provide and encourage reflective practice
- increase staff participation and develop team building
- identify good practice.

An appraisal is a self-development plan that has very clear and focused targets and is guided by a performance manger over a period of time. It will contain personal targets as well as targets relating to your workplace development or improvement plan. It also allows you time to reflect on your practice and should be a two-way dialogue. Your appraisal should be simple. An appraisal record should be maintained to focus the meeting.

So what does this mean?

An appraisal should have clear targets that can be created by asking simple questions such as 'What do I need to develop'? or 'How can I develop my practice to support the development plan?'

It is a good idea to set appraisal targets which are:

Specific – the goals/targets should be clear and focused

Measurable – the targets/goals can be regularly reviewed to support progress

Achievable – any target or goal can be reached, often by breaking it into smaller steps

Realistic – the target can be reached by the people involved and the resources available

Time-bound – a clear time frame is defined for the goal/target and the steps reach it.

To evaluate your practice regularly in relation to any action plan you can collect a variety of evidence. For instance, when you have organised an activity relating to the action, take time to ask your team for feedback. You could complete a simple learning log in hard or soft copy so that you can refer to it next time you carry out another activity relating to the action plan.

The log can be used as a starting point for discussions in your appraisal. Try to complete it before the meeting is held and consider some simple questions to discuss:

- How did the task relate to the action?
- What did I do well?
- What did not go well?
- What could I change next time?
- What additional training do I need?

If you are given positive and constructive feedback in appraisals, then you will be able to show this constructively in your practice. Praise and encouragement are important.

Even if feedback involves challenging your practice and standards, try to remain positive and be prepared to listen and ask questions; seek training opportunities to help you develop in this area.

Consider the questions you could reflect upon if you were focusing on developing a safe and stimulating setting for the children.

- How do children choose their own resources for their play?
- Does the environment look exciting from a child's eye level?
- How do we involve children in designing and adapting the environments?
- How often are resources checked for safety and quality?
- How confident am I in observing children's use of the learning environment and carrying out changes?

By continually questioning what you do professionally, seeking answers in your daily practice and experiencing more formal self-evaluation or appraisal, you will become an effective resource in implementing and maintaining quality provision for the children you work with.

5.2 The value of continual professional development

Continuing professional development is an important part of your career development and the quality of provision for the children. It makes a difference to your practice and future career, and benefits the children in the setting where you work.

You will have specific development needs that may differ from the needs of more experienced practitioners as you take on new responsibilities.

Priority areas of continuing professional development for you should include:

- ensuring you receive a range of training and the opportunity to take further qualifications
- ensuring you are able to prepare to take on additional responsibilities
- expanding your skills and pedagogy
- developing your behaviour management skills to help you to support the setting.

You should be supported to focus on your training needs which will prepare you to support any development of provision within the setting.

'Research shows that high quality experiences in the early years, including a good home learning environment, have a significant positive impact on children's social, emotional and cognitive development and, therefore, their progress at school and into adult life.

It is vitally important that early years provision is of a consistently high standard, and that providers continually look for ways to improve the quality of the learning, development and care they offer.'

NCMA, 2008

Key term

Pedagogy – refers to a specific strategy or style of education.

Your local authority should have a Workforce Development team which supports the development of each setting and thus contributes towards the quality improvement process.

The team should also be able to provide training in a variety of areas such as:

- child-minding or home-based care
- children's learning and development
- observation and assessment
- supporting young people
- child protection
- paediatric first aid
- leadership and management training.

There are also many opportunities for you to gain further qualifications if you are a graduate while working, for example, Early Years Professional Status (EYPS). This is the graduate-level professional accreditation programme for leading practitioners in the early years sector. The Dame Tickell Review (2011) recommends that this is the approach the government should strive for.

While it is good to provide external training in which all staff can participate, it is not always possible. It is also important for you to feed back your learning to the rest of your team. This will consolidate your learning and enable you to contribute to the development of others. If you are committed to your professional development you can pass your skills and knowledge on to colleagues, as and when appropriate.

Developing this type of learning community is essential to developing practice and can happen without a large financial commitment. Challenge yourself by asking, 'What have I learned today that I didn't know yesterday?' Your motivation, and contribution to the quality provision for the children and young people you are working with, will come from active involvement in professional development.

5.3 Accepting outcomes and taking forward actions

So that every member of a setting can understand any recommendations from a quality review (such as an inspection or audit), they must be encouraged to share the actions required and to accept them as part of their own professional development.

Once the actions have been shared in a focused improvement plan, individuals can evaluate and record their contribution to this through their own appraisal.

Coaching is a key skill to use when appraising staff and encouraging them to identify how to be part of the actions of a focused improvement plan.

Key term

Coaching – a way of supporting colleagues by listening and encouraging them to find their own solutions to problems in a positive and supportive way. Many settings use coaching as part of their whole approach to working with children and young people and colleagues.

Those who are appraising staff and encouraging them to consider how they can contribute to any action plan as a result of a quality review should:

- identify actions that may relate to the individual staff members and provide them with training on relevant effective practice (or encourage them to attend training)
- encourage individuals to innovate and develop their own practice, and to share good practice with colleagues
- support individuals to join relevant organisations and read publications/websites related to their targets
- encourage practitioners to find out about developments in practice which relate to their appraisal targets.

So what does this mean?

It is important to ensure that those supporting the appraisal process are clear about the actions of any quality standards review. They need to be skilled in performance-managing their team through observation and finding ways of encouraging colleagues to move their practice forward in relation to any actions.

Appraisers should be able to:

- relate the appraisal targets of the individual to any workplace action plan
- set clear targets
- encourage the collection of appropriate evidence
- identify and agree any priorities for improvement
- help to create a relevant personal action plan
- review individual progress regularly.

Assessment activity 5.1, 5.2, 5.3

1 Consider how your practice could benefit from self-evaluation and appraisal in relation to maintaining and developing an aspect of quality provision for the children you work with. You could consider one of the following:
   - an aspect of the curriculum such as supporting children's language development
   - behaviour management
   - an aspect of health and safety such as risk assessment.

2 Describe how continuing professional development could support you in your chosen area when working with children.

3 Analyse how you could link outcomes from an Ofsted inspection to your own appraisal. How could you ensure that you were successful in achieving your appraisal targets?

In the real world

My name is Jason and I have just completed my Level 3 training. I am looking forward to starting work in a local children's centre. At the interview the manager and chair of the governing body asked me what I knew about ways of improving quality for young children. They also asked me which standards I thought should be continually reviewed and evaluated. I was able to talk about this and realised that I knew quite a lot! I explained that I had studied the Dame Tickell review of the EYFS. I was aware that these were the standards we should consider when making the learning for the children more challenging, and rewarding for us to support.

I talked about the fact that, in my last practical work placement, they were auditing their environment and I was lucky enough to take part in an audit of the outdoor provision. It was exciting to observe and collect evidence of how the outdoor environment was used. I particularly enjoyed talking to the children about what they would like. I recalled that one of the teachers had started a Forest Schools training course and an outdoor learning consultant came along to give us some training. They seemed to really value quality improvement and I am looking forward to learning more about this when I begin my position working with 3 to 4 year olds in the day care room.

CP17

Check your knowledge

1 Briefly explain what a quality review is.

2 Describe the statutory requirements for the EYFS.

3 Define quality standards when working with children and young people.

4 List five questions which you could ask your manager to help you support quality improvement in a setting.

5 Define the following phrases: a) self-evaluation; b) self-development; c) self-review.

6 What do the initials Ofsted stand for?

7 Explain the term 'time frame'.

8 List the headings that you would expect to find in an action plan following a quality review.

9 Describe what practitioner research is.

10 Briefly explain what continuing professional development is and why it is important in any quality improvement review.

Further references

The following are sources of useful information on the topic of managing quality standards when working with children and/or young people.

Books and articles

National Quality Improvement Network (2008) *Quality Improvement Principles: A Framework for Local Authorities and National Organisations to Improve Quality Outcomes for Children and Young People*, London: National Children's Bureau

Sylva, K., Siraj-Blatchford, I. and Taggart, B. (2010) ECERS-E *The Early Childhood Environment Rating Scale Curricular Extension to ECERS-R*, Stoke-on-Trent: Trentham Books

Tassoni, P. (2010) *Penny Tassoni's Continued Success with the EYFS*, Oxford: Heinemann

Useful websites

To obtain a secure link to the websites below, visit www.pearsonhotlinks.co.uk and search for this book by using its title or ISBN. Click on the section for CP17.

Early Years Foundation Stage Framework

ECERS (Early Childhood Environmental Rating Scales)

The Dame Tickell Review

Early Years Quality Support Improvement Programme (EYQIP) 2008 (ref no) 00669-2008BKT-EN

Office for Standards in Education, Children's Services and Skills

North Somerset Council Website

Glossary

Abbreviations – words or phrases that have been shortened in a piece of writing.

Action research – recording something in action.

Aim – the reason for doing something.

Analyse – to give a detailed examination of something by separating it into components or parts.

Analysing – breaking down the outcomes and examining each part.

Anaphylactic reaction – a serious allergic reaction which is life-threatening.

Appraisal – this is a formal process for assessing someone's work. It helps workers and employers to monitor individual performance and often involves target setting.

Attachment – refers to the emotional tie which develops between a child and another person, usually an adult.

Attachment theory – attachment means an emotional bond between people. The basis of the attachment theory is the way in which caregivers create a secure base for each child to develop.

Attributes – personal qualities.

Audit – a way of evaluating the work environment and expected standards through external and self-evaluation.

Auditory – learn and experience by hearing.

Authentic – meaningful activity relating to real issues.

Bias – an opinion or leaning that is strongly favoured for or against something.

Bonding – the process of the development of these ties.

Cafcass (Children and Family Court Advisory and Support Service) – employs specialist social workers to act as children's guardians and represent the interests of children in family court proceedings.

Cardiovascular – involving the heart and blood vessels.

Cerebral cortex – the part of the brain that is responsible for thinking, perceiving, producing and understanding language. It is divided into areas called lobes which have special functions. They influence intelligence, personality, motor function, organisation and touch.

Coaching – a way of supporting colleagues by listening and encouraging them to find their own solutions to problems in a positive and supportive way. Many settings use coaching as part of their whole approach to working with children and young people and colleagues.

Cognitive development – refers to the development from childhood to adulthood of the thought processes including memory, decision making and problem solving.

Collaborators – people who work jointly on an activity.

Common Assessment Framework (CAF) – an assessment and planning tool used by children's services in England to standardise the assessment and identification of children and young people's additional needs. The CAF promotes the coordination of multiple agencies in deciding how to best meet a child's needs.

Confidentiality – not sharing personal information about a family without parents' permission, except where it is in the interests of the child to pass information to the appropriate professional.

Contents page – a list of sections or chapters that you will find inside the book.

Continual review – in any workplace setting this refers to practice and outcomes being evaluated all the time in a variety of ways. Every adult working with children and young people will usually play some part in the continuous review process.

Corporal punishment – physical punishment, such as caning.

Cross-functional working – where a team is made up of individuals who have a variety of expertise but are all working towards shared aims.

Cultural work – education about celebrating differences within communities.

Data – the results generated from the findings of your research which you will analyse in order to make any recommendations.

Dermatology department – hospital department concerned with the treatment of diseases of the skin.

Describe – to give a detailed description of something.

Discipline – training someone to obey rules.

Disposition to learn – this is a person's natural inclination or tendency to want to learn new things.

Disseminate – to share information widely.

Distributive leadership – a cooperative way of leading.

Duty of care – practitioners must take reasonable care so that a child or young person is not harmed either through their actions or omissions.

Early intervention – the process of identifying and addressing the specific needs of a child as soon as possible.

Early Years Foundation Stage (EYFS) profile – a way of building a record of assessment outcomes throughout the reception year for 4 to 5 year olds, to support the making of final judgements.

Education welfare department – local authority department with legal responsibilities including promoting regular school attendance and preventing truancy.

Educational psychologist – assesses and helps children who have learning difficulties and special educational needs.

Egocentric – a child or adult who focuses on their own interests and opinions rather than considering those of others is considered to be egocentric.

ELMS – effective leadership and management in the early years.

Emotional intelligence – a child or adult's ability to manage a variety of social situations. They can exercise self-control over their impulses and emotions, and show an awareness of others' feelings and emotions.

Empathy – the ability to understand and share the feelings of others.

ENT department – hospital department concerned with the treatment of disorders of the ear, nose and throat.

Ethical – conduct which follows moral principles. Ethics are about conducting your research in a morally correct way. You need to make sure that the research is for the good of the children and the setting and that no harm will come to any of your participants during the research process. You cannot force anyone to take part in your study and you must gain permission from all involved prior to starting your investigation.

Ethical considerations – the consideration you have given to making sure your work is moral and respectful of all those participating.

Ethos – the way in which things are run or the culture of a setting.

Evaluate – what you think about something – what you judge went well or not so well.

Evaluation – the process of reviewing what has happened from different perspectives and drawing conclusions.

Every Child a Talker (**ECAT**) – a programme that enables parents and practitioners to support effective language development in young children through a variety of stimulating and relevant experiences.

Evolutionary psychologist – considers the way humans adapt to their changing physical and social environment taking into account changes to brain structure and cognitive behaviour.

External agencies – professionals supporting children and young people outside of the setting, for example, social services or speech and language therapists.

Fit for purpose – a suitable plan which is likely to achieve what is intended.

Focused improvement plan (**FIP**) – a plan with clear targets and ways to achieve the targets. This is usually shared with everyone in the setting.

Formative assessment – the ongoing recording of children and young people's learning and development.

Free-flow play – takes place in an environment that encourages children to choose and revisit their play. Each child can develop at their own pace, and practise making choices and managing the consequences of choice. This type of play encourages a more flexible and open-ended approach to play.

Gender difference – refers to the differences between boys and girls. There are obvious biological differences but there is some belief that personality and other differences are genetic.

Heuristic – used to describe play where children explore objects using all of their senses. These objects are usually natural or household items.

Holistic – an approach that takes the whole person into account, not just one or a few aspects of their health and well-being.

Hypothesis – the question you are setting out to answer or the research statement you aim to prove or disprove.

Immunisation – the act of protecting someone against infection.

Index – a detailed list of information about the contents of a book together with a reference to the page numbers where you can find each piece of information. It is found at the back.

Informed consent – participants voluntarily agreeing to take part in your project following detailed discussion of what is involved.

Innovation – progress with new ideas.

Integrated working – the Children's Workforce Development Council (CWDC) defines integrated working as 'where everyone supporting children and young people works together effectively to put the child at the centre, meet their needs and improve their lives'.

Jargon – words or expressions that a particular group of people might use and which other people might find difficult to understand.

Key person – the practitioner assigned to each child in a setting to ensure that each child's needs are accurately identified and consistently met. Each key person has special responsibilities for working with a small number of children.

Kinaesthetic – learn and experience by doing ('hands on').

Kinaesthetic learner – a person who learns best by doing something rather than reading about it or being told about it.

Learning community – a place where learning is encouraged for everyone, both staff and service users, visually and practically.

Liberal – willing to respect and accept behaviours, opinions or attitudes that are different from your own.

Lifestyle – the way of living and habits chosen by the child or young person or their family.

Literacy – the ability to understand and apply skills of reading, writing, speaking and listening.

Longitudinal – a piece of work that is carried out over a period of time, for example, six weeks.

Multi-agency approach – a variety of agencies working together as appropriate – for example, speech and language services, social services, etc. to improve outcomes for children and young people.

Multi-agency working – refers to a range of different services, agencies or teams of professionals working in a coordinated way to provide services for children and young people and their families.

Naming systems – ways of constructing a person's name associated with a specific ethnic or religious group.

'Need to know' basis – the professionals to whom information is passed need to have that information to take action to safeguard a child. Other people with no direct role to play in protecting the child should not have access to the information.

Non-judgemental – not thinking or talking about others in ways that judge them or condemn them as wrong because they behave in ways that are based on values, opinions or beliefs that are different from your own.

Non-verbal communication – ways of communicating without words, e.g. crying, body movements and facial expressions.

Numeracy – the ability to understand and use numbers and mathematical concepts and operations.

Object permanence – refers to the fact that objects exist even when they are not seen, heard or touched.

Objective – information not based on or influenced by personal opinion or feelings.

Ofsted – Office for Standards in Education, Children's Services and Skills.

Ophthalmology department – hospital department concerned with the treatment of impairments and diseases of the eye.

Orthopaedic department – hospital department concerned with the treatment of impairment and injury of bones and muscles.

Paediatrician – medical professional specialising in the health and development of children.

Parenting styles – various ways of interacting with children based on differing values about how children should be brought up.

Pedagogic – this is the theory of teaching and can be related to different styles and approaches.

Pedagogical work – encouraging a learning community.

Pedagogy – the principles and methods of teaching and learning. A specific strategy or style of education.

Peer observation – a way of watching, observing and replicating best practice of colleagues.

Performance management/appraisal – a way of evaluating the way a practitioner works through an agreed system of review and target setting.

Physiotherapist – helps people with physical problems caused by impairment, ill health, injury or ageing to become more mobile.

Pilot – a practice run to check for errors or any areas that have been missed.

Plagiarism – this is when you take someone else's work and try to pass it off as being your own.

Policies – principles and guidelines set out by an organisation to meet agreed goals.

Positive reinforcement – a way of motivating a child to behave in a positive way and to help them to make the right decisions about how they behave. Language used is positive and focuses on positive aspects of behaviour rather than negative.

Practitioner research – reflective work, often prompted by questioning, carried out by a practitioner in their work setting, with the aim of developing provision.

Preface – the introduction to the book. It will usually explain the subject covered by the book or the main aims it hopes to achieve.

Primary research – the research carried out by you to either prove or disprove your hypothesis.

Procedures – step-by-step actions that must be followed to meet the agreed goals.

Psychoanalysis – developed by Freud, this is a complex theory about personality and what motivates people to act as they do. It explores unconscious thought process as a way to treat mental illness.

Pustules – blisters filled with fluid.

Qualitative – findings that result from people's thoughts, ideas and personal opinions.

Quality improvement activities or inspection – the actions from these are a way of addressing any issues that might arise.

Quality standards – when working with children these can be defined as a set of expected outcomes. They are often measured through external inspections such as Ofsted.

Quantitative – findings that create numbers and statistics.

Rationale – explains why something is being done.

Referral – this is when a child or young person's case is passed on to a specialist or person in a higher position of responsibility.

Reflection – giving due thought and consideration to something you have said or done. A way in which we review what we have already done in order to improve the way things are done in future.

Reflective dialogue – a group discussion about practice; everyone is actively encouraged to take part.

Reflective practitioner – someone who is prepared to evaluate their work with children, always considering and using their understanding of the theories of child development in practice.

Reliable – data is considered reliable if it can be replicated by someone else using the same methods but at a different time. Piloting your research methods can help to ensure reliability.

Reputable – having a good reputation.

Research methodology – the approach you take to carrying out your investigation including information on the methods you used, the sample group and any ethical considerations.

Sample group – refers to the setting, children and adults that are in the study.

Scaffolding – the process where adults or other more competent peers build upon children's existing knowledge and skills.

Schema – a repetitive pattern in a child's behaviour, for example, taking the content of the home corner to another area of the room could be a transporting schema in action; lining cars up could be a trajectory schema. May also be used to mean a child's thoughts and conclusions.

Secondary research – a review of existing research on your selected area of investigation including books, journals, articles and the Internet.

Self-evaluation – when preparing for an internal quality review, adults (and sometimes children and young people) who are involved in the setting will be guided in carrying out their own review of aspects of the environment.

SENCO – Special Educational Needs Coordinator.

Sensory impairment – describes a condition where there may be a loss or restriction on a child's vision or hearing, or sense of taste, smell or touch.

Separation anxiety – the distress a child shows if the person to whom they are attached is absent or leaves.

Service users – sometimes used to refer to those children and young people who the workplace supports in their care/learning.

Speech and language therapist – helps people overcome speech and communication difficulties.

Stakeholder – someone who has an interest or is involved in the workplace. This could refer to parents, teachers, early years practitioners, governors and multi-agency practitioners.

Statutory framework – a set of expected guidelines to work towards. This might be in the form of a curriculum or a defined way of working.

Stranger anxiety – a child's wariness of people they are not familiar with.

Structure of personality – Freud believed that humans develop their personality in stages and that the areas of personality that develop in each stage play an important part in how children, young people and adults interact with the world.

Sub vocalisation – saying words 'aloud' in your head when reading.

Subjective – information based on or influenced by personal opinion or feelings.

Summative assessment – the way that findings are concluded with contributions from other professionals, parents, colleagues and the child or young person.

Sustained shared thinking – a means whereby the adult extends a child's thinking and understanding of concepts through language. A way of more than one person working together and exploring or solving a problem by using their cognitive skills.

Tally chart – tally marks are used to count or keep score.

Team Around the Child (TAC) – this approach consists of various professionals working together to develop a plan to meet the needs of a child, under the leadership of a Lead Professional.

Team working – working with other people towards shared aims or goals.

Transition – a change from one stage or state to another, for instance, transferring to a new school or dealing with family break-up.

Transitions – important times in a child or young person's life when they move from one key phase to another. Most children will experience these transitions, for example, from home to school. There are also some transitions that are experienced on an individual basis, for example, moving to another area or even to other carers.

Triangulation – the practice of combining three different research data-gathering methods to gain a detailed and genuine picture of what is happening.

Typology – classification of a type.

Unconscious – the thoughts processed that we are not aware of relating to suppressed feelings, personal habits, intuition, complicated phobias and desires.

Valid – information which is well grounded and justified. For data to be valid, it must measure what it set out to measure.

Visual – learn and experience by seeing.

Whistle-blowing policy – highlights how issues regarding child protection can be disclosed in a work setting.

Zone of proximal development (ZPD) – the difference between what a child or young person can do without support and with support followed by a period of independent learning using the skills and knowledge acquired through working with the adult.

Index

accident reports 219, 220
achievement, culture of 114
action planning 351–352,
    357–360
    contributing to 364
    factors to consider 359–360
action research 119
activities 33–34
    see also art; numeracy
Adair, John 112
adult:child ratios 263, 341,
    349, 350
adult, role of 35–37
    positive intervention 36
    sustained shared thinking
        37, 349
advertising and health 83–84
aggression, causes of 15–16
Ainsworth, Mary 19
annotated planning 38
appraisals 213, 354
    self-evaluation 361–362
    SMART targets 362
art, drama and music 248–269
    activities 258–262, 263
    analysis/evaluation 264–265
    benefits for children 253
    role of adult 251–252
assertive discipline model
    188–189, 192–193, 194, 196
    roles 198, 199, 200
assessment of children 38–39,
    331
    assessment policy 60, 342
associative play 325
Athey, Chris 14, 34
attachment theory 13, 19, 41,
    152–154
audit 39, 353–354
    see also quality
auditory learners 32, 255, 256,
    279–280, 283
    and literacy/numeracy 300
autocratic leader/manager 107
Axline, Virginia 319, 328

Bandura, Albert 13, 21, 40
behaviour management 186–207
    policy 52, 60
    positive support 201–204
    realistic expectations
        203–204, 205
    role models 193–194
    safe environment 205
    three principles 203

behaviour management models
    188–195
    analysing models 196–200
    children's roles 197–198
    and multi-agency workers 200
behavioural needs 25–26
behaviourist theories 13
Bloom's taxonomy 276–278, 281,
    282, 287
Bobo doll experiment 13, 21
bonding and attachment 152–153
boredom, signs of 203
Bowlby, John 13, 16, 19, 23,
    41, 152–153
Bruce, Tina 14, 34, 318
Bruner, J. 13, 21, 321–322, 328
bureaucratic leader/manager 107

Cafcass 177, 341
Carter, Lee 188–189
change management 115–116,
    357–359
chickenpox 89, 92
child protection policy 52
    see also safeguarding
child-initiated activities 33
Childcare Act (2006) 55, 274,
    340
Children Act (2004) 55
children's centres 181–182, 184
    and behaviour management 199
choice theory model 190, 193,
    195, 196
    roles 198, 199, 200
coaching 364
cognitive development 13, 20,
    26–27, 40
Common Assessment Framework
    180, 211–12, 341, 345
comparative analysis 134
complaints 216–217, 218, 219
conditioning
    classical 13, 26, 40
    operant 13, 25–26
confidentiality 150–151, 166,
    173, 235, 342
conflict, handling 202
constructivist approach 13, 15,
    324–325
content analysis 134–135
contingency theories 106, 108
continual professional
    development 349, 354, 363
continual review 345–352
cooperative play 325

COSHH Regulations 56, 215
creativity see art
cross-functional working
    181–182
    integrated working 182–183
curriculum planning 270–291
    and observations 330–331
    see also planning
curriculum/frameworks 274–275
    guidelines 340–341
    rationale for 272–276

Dame Tickell Review 363, 365
democratic leader/manager 107
development theories 10–47
    see also theories
Dewey, John 322, 328
diet and nutrition 80–81
disabled children 261, 301
distributive leadership 111
documentation, workplace 353
drama see art
drill sergeants 191
Dunn, Judy 22, 25
duty of care 77, 78

early intervention 167, 256
    and literacy/numeracy 301
Early Years Foundation Stage
    31, 273, 341
    areas of creativity 254
    expressive arts 250
    individual learning needs
        255–257
    numeracy/literacy 294–295
    policies required 56, 342
    Profile 30, 212–213
ELMS model 105
emotional intelligence 16
emotional needs 16–19
enquiries, response to 216–217,
    218
environment 23–24
    and behaviour 205
Equality Acts (2006/2010) 55
Erikson, Erik 18, 29
event sample 23
Every Child Matters (2004) 55
exercise and health 81, 84
expressive arts 250–251

families, working with 146–169
    communication 148–150
    confidentiality 150–151
    intervention 167

practitioners' role 158–160
pressure of life events 163–164
respect for values and preferences 159
sharing information 160
socio-economic factors 165
support in crisis 166–167
types of interaction 148
see also parents
family structures 154–155
feedback 45, 362
Fiedler, F.E. 106
Fleming's VARK learning styles 279–280, 282, 283, 287
focused improvement plan (FIP) 356
food groups 81
food and nutrition 80–81, 84
formative assessment 38–39, 331
frameworks see curriculum
free description 23
free-flow play 27
Freud, Sigmund 13, 16, 17, 29, 320, 328
friendships 22, 25, 37–38
Froebel, Friedrich 322, 328

Gardner, H. 279, 282, 283, 287
gender difference 14, 15–16
Gibbs, G./reflective cycle 44
Ginott, H.M./model 191–192, 193, 195, 196
roles 198, 199, 200
Glasser, William 190, 195
Goldschmied, Elinor 19, 23, 323–324, 329
group learning plan 288

hand-washing 77, 82
hazardous substances see COSHH
health promotion activity 84–88
approaches to 85
evaluating outcome 87–88
planning checklist 86
reflection on role 88
SMART targets 87
health and safety records 214–216, 218, 219
health/ill-health 80–82
diet and nutrition 80–81, 84
emotional/social aspects 82, 84
exercise and health 81
policies/procedures 76–78
rest and sleep 81, 84
role of advertising 83–84
of staff 78
helicopter parents 190

heuristic play 324, 329
holistic approach 14
holistic learners 32
Home-Start 167
Human Rights Acts 55, 195
humanist theory 13, 320
hypothesis, research 226–227
developing 228–229, 234–236
illness 89–92
actions to take 79–80
reporting cases of 92
signs/symptoms 79, 89–91
workplace procedures 92
see also health/ill-health
imaginative play 254, 262
immunisation 93–95
history of 94
schedules 93
implementing a plan 34–38, 39
analysing outcome 38–39
setting up environment 34–35
supporting/facilitating 35–37
inclusive practice 354
individual education plan (IEP) 30, 33, 284
individual learning needs 255–257, 261
individual learning plan (ILP) 32, 33, 287
induction 67
infection 77–78
prevention of 82, 84
information sharing 150–151, 178–179
see also recording
inspections 348–350
integrated working 182–183, 354
Internet research 129, 136
referencing 139, 140
intervention, positive 36
interviews for research 231, 232

jargon 184

key person 19, 60, 149
role 37–38, 154
and transitions 24
Key Stages 1 and 2 31, 273–274
Key Stages 3 and 4 31, 273, 274
kinaesthetic learners 32, 255, 256, 279–280, 283
and literacy/numeracy 300
Kirkpatrick's evaluation model 278–279, 282–283, 287
Kohlberg, L. 16
Kounin, J./model 192, 193, 196
roles 198, 199, 200

laissez-faire leader/manager 107
language development 254
leadership and management 98–123
day in life of manager 109
differences between 103–104
models of 105
motivating staff 112–114
role of leader 101–102
role of manager 102–103
skills 100, 110–114
theories of 106, 108–109
learning 21
Moyles' spiral 28
Piaget on 26–28
role of adult 35–36
stages of 26–27
learning community 117, 118, 363
learning styles 32, 255–256
and literacy/numeracy 300–301
VARK model 279–280, 282, 283, 287
legislation and policies 53–56
life events and families 163–165
lifestyle 84
and advertising 83–84
literacy 296, 300
activities for 304
see also numeracy
local authority 347–348, 363
logical consequences model 189–190, 193, 196
roles 198, 199, 200
love and logic model 190–191, 194, 195, 196
roles 198, 199, 200

McMillan, Margaret 324, 329
management skills 100
see also leadership
Maslow, Abraham 13, 18–19, 23, 29, 40, 320
measles 89, 92
media recording 23
medication policy 57, 215
medication records 220
meningitis 90–91, 92
tumbler test 91
mental health 81, 82
mind maps 229
minutes of meetings 213, 219
MMR vaccine 94
modelling behaviour 36–37, 193–194
monotropism 13, 152

Montessori, Maria 281, 322–323, 324, 328
motivating staff 112–114
Moyles, Janet 28, 105
multi-agency working 38, 176–180, 200, 354
    benefits of 177–178
    information sharing 178–179
    integrated working 182–183
    language and terminology 179–180
    types of services 176–177
multiple attachments 152
multiple intelligences 279, 282, 283, 287
mumps 90, 92
music see art

naming systems 149
National Curriculum 273–274, 341
nature v nurture debate 12, 15
needs
    Glasser's five needs 190
    hierarchy of 13, 18, 40
Northern Ireland 251, 273
    ETI inspections 54, 348
    numeracy and literacy 295–296
note taking 128, 129–130
numeracy and literacy 292–315
    activities 296–298, 306–308, 310
    analysing outcomes 308–309
    current frameworks 294–296
    and environment 298, 307–308
    and individual needs 297–298, 300–302, 305
    planning activities 303–306
    and play 293, 297
    reflecting on practice 311–313
    role of practitioner 296–298

obesity 80, 81
object permanence 27
observation 22–25, 330–332
    and assessment 30
    brief notes 23, 38
    and curriculum planning 330–331
    of environment 23–24
    involving children 31–32
    methods 23, 231–232, 233
    parental 23
    planning stage 333–334
    of play 316–337
    to inform planning 30–31, 38

observational learning 21, 40
Ofsted inspections 53, 54, 72, 275, 348, 349–350
    framework 341
    grades 350
    required policies 68
operant conditioning 13, 25–26
outdoor learning policy 52

parallel play 325
parenting styles 155–157
parents
    and behaviour management 190–191, 199
    feelings/knowledge 158–160
    observations by 23
    see also families
partnership working 354
partnerships with parents 41, 146, 354
    benefits of 162–163
    respect and trust 161–162
Parton, Mildred 325, 329
paternalistic leader/manager 107
Pavlov, Ivan 13, 26, 40
pedagogy 111, 119, 363
peer observation 43
performance management 354, 364
personal development plan 45
personality development 17–18, 29
Piaget, Jean 13, 16, 21, 40
    four stages 26–28, 29
    schema 284, 324–325, 329
pie chart 241
pilot study 238–239
plagiarism 131, 143
planning 33–34
    analysing outcome 38–39
    the environment 32
    flexibility and time 33
    gathering information 30–31
    implementing 34–38
    and individual needs 32
    involving children 34, 37
    stages of 30
    theories underpinning 40–41
planning cycle 308
planning to curriculum /framework 270–291
    child-initiated 284
    factors to consider 285–286
    planning models 276–283, 286–287
    schemas 284–285
    thematic approach 284

play
    as intellectual development 324–325, 327, 329
    and numeracy and literacy 293, 297
    observing 316–337
    as preparation 322–323, 327, 328
    reflecting on practice 333–335
    as rehearsal 320–322, 326–327, 328
    as sensory learning 323–324, 327, 329
    as social development 325, 327–328, 329
    theories 318–325, 328–329, 334
    as therapy 318–320, 326, 328
    twelve features of 34, 318
policies and procedures 48–73, 214–215
    aim and rationale 63–64
    developing a policy 62–65
    differences between 50–1
    exemptions 65
    and EYFS standards 342
    implementation 59, 65, 67–71
    informing practice 56–58
    language level 62–63
    monitoring and reviewing 59, 65–66
    Ofsted requirements 68, 70–71
    promoting 69–70
    purpose of 51–52
    requirements underpinning 53–61
    resources needed 58–59
    and service users 56, 59–60, 69
    and staff 56, 60–61
    and stakeholders 61, 68–69
    structure of 50
positive reinforcement 25–26, 40
power instinct 320, 328
praise 188, 189, 197, 201–202
presenting information 136–142
    evaluating process 143
    formats for 141–142
    letter format 141–142
    methods of 137
    see also project work
primary data 133, 134
procedures see policies
project work 132–136
    academic referencing 139–140
    analysing data 134–135
    data fit for purpose 135, 138

formatting 138
presenting information
136–142
proof reading 139
sourcing information 129,
133–135, 143
spell checking 138–139
stages 132
Protection of Children Act
(1999) 55
protective clothing (PPE) 82
psychoanalytical theory 13, 17
psychosocial development 18
punishment 202

qualitative data 137, 233, 241
quality assurance schemes
346–347
quality improvement model
347–348
action plan 351–352
quality standards 275, 338–366
and EYFS 342
goals and targets 344
guidelines 341
implementing improvements
350–352
inspections 348–350
working towards 343–345
quality standards review
352–356
action planning 357–360, 364
audit 353–354
changes following 356,
357–359
principles 354–355
responding to findings
355–356
quantitative data 135, 136–137,
233, 241
questionnaires 138, 230–231,
232

Race Relations Act (2000) 55,
56
ratios, adult:child see adult
reading: study skills 126–128
recording information 208–223
benefits of 210, 220, 221
evaluating methods 217–218
formats for 211–217
health and safety 214–216,
218, 219
internal records 151, 213,
218
for outside agency 211–12,
217

response to enquiries
216–217, 218
for safeguarding 212
to monitor progress 212–213,
218
referencing in project 129,
139–140
referrals 217
reflective cycle 244
reflective dialogue 118, 119
reflective practice 12, 43, 335
analysis of theories 22–23
BEST practice 120
creative activities 266–267
encouraging 117–120
evaluating theories 43–44
Gibbs' reflective cycle 44
maintaining quality 361–364
numeracy/literacy support
311–313
policy implementation 59
reflecting on research 244
supporting play 333–335
registers 213
relationships, children's
24–25, 37
research 224–247
action plan 237–240
analysing data 241–242
ethical considerations 230,
234–235
good practice checklist 240
methodologies 230–234, 238,
239–240, 245–246
objectivity 235
presentation 242–243
primary and secondary
226–227
qualitative/quantitative
233, 241
recording data 240
referencing theorists 23
reflecting on 244–245
research diary 227, 244
see also observation
resources 331–332, 353
creative activities 263,
266, 267
rest and sleep 81, 84, 204
reward and bribery 202
rights of children 188–189, 195
and research 235
UN Convention on 55
risk assessments 215–216, 218,
219
Rogers, Carl 320, 328
rules and routines 204, 205

safeguarding: information 212
safeguarding policy 60, 342
Safeguarding Vulnerable Groups
Act (2006) 55
scaffolding 13, 21, 321–322,
325
schema 14, 229, 284–285
Scotland 54, 295, 348
Curriculum for Excellence
250–251, 272, 295
secondary data 133, 134
self-appraisal 346
self-assessment 346
self-esteem of children 82, 83,
188, 201–202, 256
self-evaluation 39, 343, 350,
353, 361–362
self-reflection 45, 346
SENCO 149, 341
sensory impairment 256, 257,
301
separation anxiety 13, 153–154
septicaemia 91
sequential learners 32
settling-in 24, 25, 41, 63
sex education lessons 321–322
Skinner, B.F. 13, 25–26, 40,
202
smacking 188
social cognitive theory 21–2
social constructivism 15
social learning theories 13,
21–2, 36
social needs 20–22
social/emotional development 13
socio-economic factors 165
solitary play 325
Special Educational Needs Code
of Practice 341
Special Educational Needs and
Disability Act (2001) 55
SENCO 149, 341
spectator play 325
speed reading 127
spell checking 138–139
spiral curriculum 321
staff
and behaviour management 198
requirements and skills 354
stakeholders 50
and quality review 358
Steiner Waldorf schools 280–281
stranger anxiety 153
study skills 124–145
note taking 128, 129–130
planning your work 132
reading methods 126–128
staying motivated 131

summative assessment 38–39, 331
sustained shared thinking 37, 349
symbolic play 322, 328

target child 23
Team Around the Child (TAC) 183
teams 116, 170
  benefits of 172, 174
  challenges 173
  common purpose 115–120, 173
  conflict 173
  cross-functional 181–183
  encouraging reflection 117–120
  leadership of 111
  more than one team 174–175
  supporting/motivating 112–114, 116–117
  see also multi-agency
thematic analysis 134
theories of
  development/learning 10–47
  informing practice 12–29
  relevance of 42–45
  underpinning work 12, 13
time management 130–131
time sample 23
training and development 114, 267, 363
trait leadership theories 106
transformational leadership 106, 108
transitions 24–25
  settling-in plans 41
treasure baskets 323–324
triangulation 238, 239

values of setting 70, 344
visual learners 32, 255, 256, 279–280, 283
  and literacy/numeracy 300
Vygotsky, Lev 13, 20, 28, 33, 40, 320–321, 325, 328

Wales 54, 251, 272–273, 295
  Estyn inspections 54, 348
Watson, John B. 13
Whalley, M.E. 104, 108
written reports 141

zone of proximal development 13, 20, 33, 40, 321, 328

The author and publisher would like to thank the following individuals and organisations for permission to reproduce photographs:

(Key: b-bottom; c-centre; l-left; r-right; t-top)
Alamy Images: David R. Frazier Photolibrary, Inc. 127, Jennie Hart 15, Inspirestock: 334, Picture partners: 150, 160, 166; Bananastock: Banastock 184; Corbis: Blend Images 67, Tom Grill 74-75; Glow Images: OJO Images. Glow Images: 174; Pearson Education Ltd: Jon Barlow 122, 144, 268, Stuart Cox 215, Ikat Design / Ann Cromack 297, Jules Selmes 36, 52, 98-99, 153, 233, 253, 270-271, 323, 327, 349, Lord and Leverett 20, 42, 120, 224-225, 294, 301, 329, Roddy Paine 361, 7, Studio 8 146-147; Science Photo Library Ltd: DR P. MARAZZI 90t, 90b (mumps); Shutterstock.com: AISPIX by Image Source 365, Yuri Arcurs 227, Aspen Photo 246, Mandy Godbehear 338-339, Hvoyr 336, khwi 168, Robert Kneschke 96, Serhiy Kobyakov 208-209, lightpoet 124-125, Felic Mizioznikov 290, oliveromg 158, 170–171, 216–217, Losevsky Pavel 186–187, Mark Tomicic 72, Suzanne Tucker 206, viii, Eva Vargyasi 316–317, Matka Wariatka 248–249, wavebreakmedia ltd 194, Jaren Jai Wicklund 89, Zurijeta 48–49, vi; Studio 8: 116, 222, 314, 319, 116, 222, 314, 319

All other images © Pearson Education

Every effort has been made to contact copyright holders of material reproduced in this book. Any omissions will be rectified in subsequent printings if notice is given to the publishers.